Cases on Human
Resources Administration

Wendell L. French, 1932-
UNIVERSITY OF WASHINGTON

John E. Dittrich
UNIVERSITY OF KENTUCKY

Robert A. Zawacki
UNIVERSITY OF COLORADO

THE PERSONNEL MANAGEMENT PROCESS
Cases on Human Resources Administration

HOUGHTON MIFFLIN COMPANY   Boston
Dallas   Geneva, Illinois   Hopewell, New Jersey
Palo Alto   London

to Marjorie, Sandy, and Jimmie

PRINTED IN THE U.S.A.

Library of Congress Catalog Card No.: 77-74422

ISBN: 0-395-25531-7

46,419

Contents

Preface

In this book we hope to present to students of modern personnel administration a realistic and thought-provoking array of problems faced by administrators in today's organizations. Administrators are confronted by the traditional issues of recruitment, selection, and promotion, for example; but today they must face them knowing that changes in our federal and state equal employment opportunity laws force them to examine carefully the ways in which they make these decisions. In labor relations, we are now seeing evidence in many cities that public employees are not only organizing themselves to bargain collectively but also confronting municipal administrators with the threat and application of work stoppages as a means of exerting bargaining pressures.

We feel that the use of short incidents and somewhat longer cases in the teaching of personnel management can add a significant dimension to the learning experience by focusing on the applications of personnel concepts and by describing personnel administration problems in a wide range of work settings. We believe that the data gathered in practice and presented in case and incident form offers an excellent medium for an examination of the systemic nature of organizations and, more particularly, the systemic nature of personnel administration functions in those organizations. In our view, the relationships among elements of the personnel management system, such as those between employee selection and employee training and development or between employee appraisal and employee compensation, are difficult to fully capture or describe in text format, but they appear with substantial meaning in the richness and immediacy of real-life situations.

For the student who is not familiar with incidents and cases in the classroom, the incident is a short, easy-to-read description of a situation that typically frames a single issue or points up one particular problem. Cases, on the other hand, are longer, describe a business or organizational setting in more detail, and provide the student with more complexity as well as a broader understanding of the total problems faced by managers responsible for personnel decisions. Frequently, cases pose multiple problems that require attention and point up the interface among subsets of a more comprehensive personnel system. Because of their complexity and length, cases often require an entire class period, and on occasion more than a single period. They can serve as the basis for more detailed analysis and for the preparation of class reports or examinations.

The cases and incidents in this book are arranged in sets of topical material that correspond to the nine parts of Wendell French's book *The Personnel Management Process*, Fourth Edition. These parts are groups of chapters that deal with closely associated functional areas of personnel administration. Part 4 of that text, for example, has chapters entitled "Organizational Objectives and Job Design" (Chapter 9) and "Job Analysis and Description, Performance Standards, and Work Rules and Conditions" (Chapter 10). The corresponding section of this book contains incidents and cases dealing with these topics from which the instructor will choose to structure class discussions.

While the organization of the book is arranged for direct compatibility with *The Personnel Management Process,* the arrangement of incidents and cases in functional area groupings will easily permit its use either as a companion to other texts or as the primary resource material for a personnel course dealing directly with applications and problems.

We have provided a brief guide to the use of incidents and cases for students unfamiliar with the case method. Introductory material at the beginning of each major section is designed primarily to guide readers from section to section and to direct attention to major areas of interest in the case material. For students who wish to examine conceptual material in more detail, we recommend reference to *The Personnel Management Process* text and to the selected readings suggested at the end of each part in this casebook.

We are deeply indebted to contributing colleagues who have taken the time and expended the effort to collect this case information. Their efforts have resulted in a realistic presentation of personnel management that encourages discussion and that presents issues in a thought-provoking manner.

We also wish to express our thanks to Gregory L. Kumpan, Anne S. Reints, Prof. Richard E. Dutton of the University of South Florida, and Prof. John F. DeVogt of Washington & Lee University for their helpful comments on the makeup and content of the manuscript, and to the staff of Houghton Mifflin for their assistance in the entire project.

W. L. F.

J. E. D.

R. A. Z.

About the Authors

WENDELL L. FRENCH is professor of management and organization and associate dean for graduate programs, Graduate School of Business and Administration, University of Washington. He was chairman, Department of Management and Organization, from 1965 to 1968.

Professor French holds a B.A. and an M.A. from the University of Colorado and a Ph.D. from Harvard University. Professor French's fields of interest are organization development, organizational psychology, organizational behavior, personnel management, and laboratory training. He is the author of *The Personnel Management Process* (4th ed., 1978); *Personnel Management and Organization Development* (with Don Hellriegel, 1971); *Organization Development: Behavioral Science Interventions for Organization Improvement* (with Cecil H. Bell, 1973); *Organization Development: Theory, Practice and Research* (with Cecil H. Bell and Robert A. Zawacki, 1978); and has contributed extensively to scholarly journals.

Professor French has served as a consultant to the U.S. Department of Labor; Makah Indian Nation; Electro Scientific Industries, Inc.; Weyerhaeuser Company; the city of Salem, Oregon; Henry Broderick, Inc.; Bureau of Indian Affairs; Anacortes Island Hospital; U.S. Air Force; and many other organizations. During 1968–1969 he was on leave in London, England, doing research and consulting with Imperial Chemical Industries, Ltd. He was director of personnel relations, Mallinckrodt Chemical Works, St. Louis, from 1954 through 1958. He was a member of the Board of Governors of the Academy of Management from 1975 to 1977. He is a member of the NTL Institute for Applied Behavioral Science and is accredited in both organization development and laboratory training by the International Association of Applied Social Scientists. He is a past chairman of the Division of Organization Development of the Academy of Management, past president of the Seattle Chapter of the Pacific Northwest Personnel Management Association, and past vice chairman of the Pacific Northwest Regional Manpower Advisory Committee.

JOHN E. DITTRICH is an assistant professor of business administration at the University of Kentucky in Lexington. Dr. Dittrich currently teaches graduate and undergraduate courses in organizational behavior and business policy. He received his undergraduate education in industrial economics at Purdue University, was granted an M.B.A. at Harvard, and a Ph.D. in administrative theory and organizational behavior from the University of Washington.

A veteran of the U.S. Air Force, Professor Dittrich has also had considerable work experience in the paper industry where he served as regional administrative manager, division personnel manager, and manager of administrative services for the Corrugated Products Division of Westvaco Corporation. In these positions, he was involved extensively in labor contract negotiations, wage and salary administration, and the recruitment and development of managerial employees. He is a member of the American Arbitration Association national panel of labor arbitrators, Academy of Management, and is an active consultant for local and national business and nonprofit organizations.

His research activities have focused most recently on field research into employee perceptions of organizational fairness, a concept based upon equity theory, and on the evaluation of management development efforts. He is the author of the *Instructor's Manual* to *The Personnel Management Process* (3rd and 4th editions) and has contributed extensively to scholarly journals.

ROBERT A. ZAWACKI is associate dean and associate professor of management and organization, College of Business and Administration, University of Colorado, Colorado Springs.

Professor Zawacki received his undergraduate education in business administration at the University of Wyoming and his M.S. from the same institution. His Ph.D. in administrative theory and organizational behavior is from the University of Washington. He is the author of *Organization Development: Managing Change in the Public Sector* (with D. D. Warrick); *Organization Development: Theory, Practice and Research* (with Wendell L. French and Cecil H. Bell, 1972); and has contributed extensively to scholarly journals. He was the co-editor of the 1976 and 1977 *Academy of Management Proceedings*.

Before joining the University of Colorado faculty, Professor Zawacki was on the faculty at the Air Force Academy. At the Academy, he performed a variety of personnel management functions such as personnel officer, cadet professional counselor, director of Academy Research Division, and as an assistant professor of behavioral sciences. He is a member of the International Personnel Management Association, American Society for Personnel Administration, and the Academy of Management. He is an active consultant for local and national business and nonprofit organizations.

About the Contributing Authors

MANOJ TOM BASURAY, Ph.D. (Oklahoma), is assistant professor of management, University of North Dakota. In addition to teaching, he is a consultant in the public sector. He is a member of the Academy of Management and the Southwestern Social Science Association.

RICHARD W. BEATTY, Ph.D. (Washington University), is associate professor of management and organization, University of Colorado. He has served as an organizational consultant in performance evaluation and selection systems, conflict resolution, and organization development. His articles have been published in the leading management and psychology journals and he is the co-author of the book *Experiential Exercises in Personnel Administration*.

PHILIP H. BIRNBAUM, Ph.D. (University of Washington), is an assistant professor of management, Indiana University. He is a consultant to state and federal agencies and numerous private enterprises. He is the author of the book *Management of Interdisciplinary Research Projects in Academic Institutions*.

WALTER A. BOGUMIL, Jr., Ph.D., former assistant dean of the College of Business Administration at Florida Technological University, received his Ph.D. from the University of Georgia. His background includes industrial experience at General Mills, Inc.; the U.S. Army-Tank Automotive Command; and General Motors. He is currently an assistant professor of management, College of Business Administration, Florida Technological University.

LARRY J. BOSSMAN, Jr., Ph.D. (University of Wisconsin–Madison). After graduating from Wisconsin, he was employed on the corporate personnel staff of General Motors Corporation and later joined the faculty of the University of Detroit. In addition to his teaching, he is currently involved in both industrial and hospital consulting where, in the latter, he has worked extensively with the Chicago Hospital Council and several hospitals in the Detroit metropolitan area.

JACK W. BRANDMEIR, Ph.D. (University of Washington), is an associate professor of business administration at the University of Wyoming. He has over thirty years of experience with commerce, industry, and government organizations. He is a member of the Academy of Management and the Mountain-Plains Management Association.

DAVIS W. CARVEY, D.B.A. (Texas Tech University), is an associate professor of management at Pacific Lutheran University. In addition to teaching, he has done a variety of consulting including projects with hospitals, prisons, schools, and private industry. He has done research and published articles concerning psychological/sociological aspects of worker involvement in a work setting.

KENT J. COLLINGS, Ph.D. (University of Washington), is professor and dean of the School of Business, University of Portland. In addition to his teaching, he is an arbitrator, fact-finder, negotiator, and conducts numerous management-development workshops. He is the author of numerous articles and the book *The Second Time Around*.

JAMES C. CONANT, Ph.D., is professor of management, California State University, Fullerton. Prior to teaching, he was staff psychologist for IBM and senior psychologist for General Electric. He is a licensed psychologist in California and New York and a diplomate in clinical psychology, American Board of Examiners in Professional Psychology.

GERALDINE B. ELLERBROCK, Ph.D. (The Ohio State University), is an associate professor of industrial relations, California Polytechnic State University, San Luis Obispo. In addition to teaching, she is a member of the American Arbitration Association Labor Panel (arbitrator), International Personnel Management Association, the Academy of Management, and has functioned as both a management and union consultant.

MARGARET FENN, Ph.D. (University of Washington), is an associate professor in the Graduate School of Business Administration, University of Washington. She is a consultant to manufacturing, religious, banking, government (federal and state), and educational organizations. She has published widely in such leading journals as the *California Management Review, Training and Development Journal,* and *Journal of Contemporary Business.*

C. PATRICK FLEENOR, Ph.D. (University of Washington), is chairman of the Department of Administration, Seattle University. In addition to teaching, he has extensive consulting experience with the federal government, including the Civil Service Commission, the Small Business Administration, and the Veterans' Administration. He is a member of the Academy of Management and has presented research papers at regional meetings.

WILLIAM F. GLUECK, Ph.D., is professor of management at the University of Georgia. A prolific author who has written numerous management and personnel management texts, he is also active in the Academy of Management as a member of the Board of Governors. One of his books, *Personnel: A Diagnostic Approach,* was selected as the outstanding new personnel text for 1974.

AUSTIN GRIMSHAW, D.C.S. (Harvard University). The late Austin Grimshaw was dean of the School of Business Administration, University of Washington, from 1949 to 1964. Prior to becoming dean, he served various academic institutions as research assistant, assistant professor, professor, department head, and functioned in numerous management positions in industry.

JAMES L. HALL, Ph.D. (University of Washington), is an associate professor of management at the University of Santa Clara. His consulting experience includes work in the areas of change, communications, motivation, team-building, and performance appraisal systems. His writings have been published in such journals as the *California Management Review, Human Resource Management, Personnel Journal,* and *Industrial Management.*

GERALD M. HAMPTON, Ph.D. (University of Washington), is an assistant professor of business at Lewis & Clark College. He majored in human resources, marketing, and international business and teaches marketing and international business and policy.

W. D. HEIER, Ph.D. (American University), is a professor of management, Arizona State University. He has extensive experience as a consultant to business organizations of all sizes and to federal and state governmental agencies. He is president, Resources Analysis, Incorporated, and his articles have been published in *Academy of Management Journal, Personnel Magazine, Personnel Journal* and *Training and Development Journal.*

RICHARD C. JOHANSON, Ph.D. (North Texas State University), is a professor of management, University of Arkansas. Prior to his faculty assignment, he was a member of corporate management for over twenty years, operating on an international policy-making level with emphasis in personnel administration, labor relations, and salary administration. He has published widely and is a member of the American Society for Personnel Administrators, American Management Association, and the Academy of Management. He is also listed in *Who's Who in South and Southwest.*

ROBERT W. KNAPP, Ph.D. (University of Michigan), is a professor of business administration at the University of Colorado, Colorado Springs. From 1972–1976 he was associate dean of the College of Business and Administration. His previous experience included two years as assistant professor of business economics, UCLA, and three years as staff economist at the General Motors Corporation. He is the co-author, with J. Daniel Couger, of *System Analysis Techniques.*

THOMAS KUBICEK, Ph.D. (University of Montreal), is an associate professor of management, Concordia University, Montreal, Canada. Before joining the faculty at Concordia University, he was associated for a number of years with several Canadian companies. His last position was corporate comptroller of Inspiration Limited. He is the author of numerous cases and articles and is a member of the Academy of Management.

DAVID KUECHLE, Ph.D., is a professor at the Graduate School of Business Administration, Harvard University, and was formerly on the faculty of the School of Business Administration, The University of Western Ontario. He is the author of the book *The Story of the Savannah* and co-author of the book *The Practice of Industrial Relations.*

HAK-CHONG LEE, Ph.D. (Washington University), is a member of the faculty at the State University of New York at Albany. In addition to numerous articles in academic and professional journals, his publications include the book *Human Resource Administration: Problems of Growth and Change.*

JOEL K. LEIDECKER, Ph.D. (University of Washington), is an associate professor in management at the University of Santa Clara. His consulting experience includes work in the areas of change, communications, motivation, team-building, and performance appraisal systems. His articles have been published in the *California Management Review, Industrial Relations, Personnel Journal,* and *Human Resources Management.*

MICHAEL J. O'CONNELL, Ph.D. (University of Wisconsin–Madison), is deputy director of evaluation, U.S. Air Force Academy. In addition to his primary research position, he has taught management and public administration at the

Air Force Academy, University of Colorado–Colorado Springs, and the University of Northern Colorado. He has published articles in the *Academy of Management Journal, Journal of Applied Psychology*, and *Organizational Behavior and Human Performance*. He was co-editor of the 1976 and 1977 *Academy of Management Proceedings*.

GLENN D. OVERMAN, D.B.A. (Indiana University), is dean, College of Business Administration, Arizona State University. He was U.S. Secretary of the Navy from 1972 through 1975 and is certified for labor arbitration by the American Arbitration Association and Federal Mediation and Conciliation Service. His other leadership roles include president, Western Association of Collegiate Schools of Business (1976–1977); chairman, Faculty Development Committee, American Assembly of Collegiate Schools of Business (1974–1976); and member, Beta Gamma Sigma National Board (1974–1976). He is author of the book *Economic Concepts Everyone Should Know*.

DONALD J. PETERSEN, Ph.D. (Illinois Institute of Technology), is associate professor of management at Loyola University of Chicago. He is a labor arbitrator on the panels of the American Arbitration Association, Federal Mediation and Conciliation Service, and the Public Employee Panels of the state of Iowa. He is also only one of eight arbitrators on the expedited panels of the American Arbitration Association. A co-author of *The Effective Manager's Desk Book*, he has contributed articles on arbitration, industrial relations, and personnel management to the leading labor and personnel management journals.

ALLEN RAPPAPORT, Ph.D. (University of Texas), is an associate professor of business administration at Wichita State University. In addition to teaching, he has been a consultant to both the public and private sectors of our economy and his writings have been published in leading personnel management journals.

HAROLD SHAFFER, Ph.D., is vice president, Retail Electronic Systems, Canada Limited. Previously, he was assistant professor, Faculty of Commerce and Administration, Concordia University, and a director of the School of Retailing, Sir George Williams University. Also, he is the feature writer for a number of Canadian trade publications.

ROBERT A. SUTERMEISTER, M.A. (University of Washington), is professor of management, Graduate School of Business Administration, University of Washington, Seattle. He has extensive consulting experience in public and nonprofit organizations and is a member of labor arbitration panels for the American Arbitration Association and the Federal Mediation and Conciliation Service. In addition to numerous articles, his major publication is *People and Productivity*, 3rd ed.

ROBERT L. TAYLOR, D.B.A. (Indiana University), is associate professor of economics and management, U.S. Air Force Academy. His teaching and research interests are in performance appraisal, organizational communication, and the theory of organizations. He has published and presented over forty papers and his articles have appeared in the *Academy of Management Journal, Business Horizons, Personnel Journal*, and *Industrial Relations*. He is an active consultant and has presented numerous personnel workshops in time management, personnel resource management, and organizational development.

WELDON J. TAYLOR, Ph.D. (New York University), is dean emeritus and professor of organizational behavior, Brigham Young University. His publications have appeared in the *Journal of Marketing, Review of Economics and Business,* and *AACSB Bulletin.* In addition to extensive consulting experience, he is the co-author of *Marketing—An Integrated Analytical Approach,* 3rd ed.

WILLIAM L. TULLAR, Ph.D. (University of Rochester), is an assistant professor of management, University of North Carolina–Greensboro. He has published articles in the areas of selection, social industrial psychology, and computer simulation. He is currently a member of the American Psychological Association and does extensive personnel management consulting in the private sector.

H. WILLIAM VROMAN, Ph.D., is a 1972 graduate of the University of Iowa and has been active in teaching and research work at the University of Georgia and, more recently, at Tennessee Technological University. He is the author of numerous articles, papers, and cases, and is co-author of *Action in Organizations: Cases and Experiences in Organizational Behavior,* a new casebook in organizational behavior.

D. D. (DON) WARRICK, D.B.A. (University of Southern California), is an associate professor of management and organization, University of Colorado–Colorado Springs. Before joining the CU faculty, he held a variety of management positions in business and governmental organizations including directing the Middle Management Development Training Program for Hughes Aircraft. He has authored a number of articles in such leading journals as *Training and Development Journal, Public Personnel Management,* and the *Academy of Management Proceedings.* In addition to extensive consulting experience, he is the co-author of *Organization Development: Managing Change in the Public Sector.*

K. MARK WEAVER, Ph.D. (Louisiana State University), is associate professor of business administration at the University of Alabama. In addition to teaching, he is director of organizational consultants and project director of the Small Business Institute. His research interests are in corporate social responsibility, business ethics, and manpower training programs. His writings have been published in *Personnel Administrator, Human Resource Management,* and *Carroll Business.*

JOHN T. WHOLIHAN, Ph.D. (The American University), is professor of business administration at Bradley University in Peoria, Illinois. Also, he is director of graduate programs in business administration, director of organizational consultants, and project director in the Small Business Institute.

OTHER CONTRIBUTORS

American Arbitration Association

Bruce E. Bondy

Faculty School of Commerce, University of Alberta

James Howell

Henry C. Metcalf

Bruce E. Mullins

Ohio University Press

Ordway Tead

U.S. News & World Report

University of Western Ontario

Introduction to the Case and Incidents Method

The typical personnel manager is often confronted with decisions about personnel programs for which there exist few precedents, few established propositions, and little factual data. Many personnel management texts provide the student and personnel manager with an overview of personnel issues, processes, and systems. However, the reader is still left with the difficult task of relating theoretical concepts to practical situations likely to confront the personnel manager of a complex organization.

To help the reader close the "gap" between theory and an action frame of reference, we have presented a number of cases and actual incidents. All of the cases are based on the reports of actual participants; none are contrived or manipulated to make a specific point. These cases represent the real world. Names and organizations, of course, have been changed in some cases to avoid the possibility of identification. (These cases are not presented as normative models or examples of how-to-do-it. Rather, they are examples of a wide range of personnel problems and issues.)

The cases and incidents have been selected to demonstrate personnel problems in a wide range of environments such as (1) public and private sectors of our economy; (2) both centralized and decentralized organizations; (3) both failures and successes; and (4) small, medium, and large organizations. An analysis of the cases and incidents will reveal the following breakdown:

Geographical location	Percent
Western United States	28
South and Southwest United States	22
Midwest United States	22
Eastern United States	18
Canada	8
Foreign	2
Sector	
Private	73
Public	27
Size	
Large	38
Medium	38
Small	24

THE PROBLEM-SOLVING METHOD

Most leading personnel management texts define the primary role of the personnel manager as decision making. Before managers can make good decisions, however, they must be aware of and follow the logic that leads to problem solving. The major phases of problem solving are:

1. Size up the situation by defining the major and minor problems.

2. Gather relevant data about the major and minor problems. This phase may include the development of a model or theory of the cause of the problem.

3. Analyze the data and the situation.

4. Consider as many alternative solutions as possible.

5. Eliminate from serious consideration those solutions least likely to solve the problem or problems. During this phase you actually compare, test, and evaluate your options.

6. Select the best solution.

7. Implement the solution. In choosing a solution, the problem solver must be prepared to defend the solution and recommend a strategy for implementing it. The optimum solution may be doomed to failure without the proper commitment from the organizational participants who must help implement it.

This book consists of cases and incidents in personnel management. An incident is based on an actual situation, is short in length, and is so precisely stated and to the point that the student can normally point to the major issue. Incidents differ from cases not only in terms of depth of content and the number of complex issues, but also in terms of the phases of problem solving. For example, the critical incidents in this book usually emphasize the first three steps of the problem-solving approach, whereas cases emphasize all phases of the problem-solving approach. The reason that incidents involve only the first three phases is that, without all of the relevant data, students must make too many assumptions, and it becomes very difficult for the class to move towards any reasonable solution.[1]

There are no correct answers to these incidents and cases; rather, each incident or case has numerous solutions, and the learning outcome is enhanced through a good exchange of views by students in the classroom. Thus, we believe that these incidents and cases will support a good analytical base of personnel management theory that is acquired from a leading personnel text and permit "practice" in the classroom. We believe that realistic and workable decisions will follow in the "real world" of personnel management.

[1] John V. Murray and Thomas J. Von der Embse, *Organizational Behavior: Critical Incidents and Analysis* (Columbus, Ohio: Merrill Publishing Co., 1973), p. 10.

Cases on Human
Resources Administration

PART I
A DEFINITION AND HISTORY OF PERSONNEL MANAGEMENT

Personnel management involves the acquisition, development, and utilization of human resources. In these activities, personnel specialists not only assist in the pursuit of organizational objectives but also work to achieve a "fit"—between individuals' capabilities and organization needs—that reduces friction and improves the quality of working life. As human needs and societal standards of human relationships undergo change, the personnel specialist also assists the organization in reflecting these changes in its internal policies and practices.

In very small organizations, general managers perform personnel work as well as other organizational functions. Increases in organization size and an awareness of the benefits of specialization lead to the delegation of functional responsibility and authority.

In the early twentieth century, the enactment of labor legislation and the severity of wartime demand for human resources added complexity to industrial life and tended to emphasize the need for specialists to help general managers by providing key services and advice. Personnel specialists are now found in a ratio of 1 specialist to 100 employees.[1] Indeed, in very large organizations, personnel subfunctions are found in separate departments that in turn contain highly trained specialists concentrating their efforts in even narrower areas of attention.

The current general definition of personnel work remains that of effectively planning, organizing, and controlling—or, more concisely, managing—the acquisition, development, and utilization of human resources in organizations.

[1] Dale Yoder, *Personnel Management and Industrial Relations*, 6th ed. (Englewood Cliffs, N.J.: Prentice-Hall, 1970), p. 17.

1

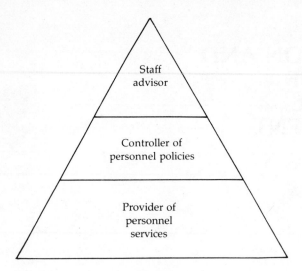

Figure **I-1** Three-part personnel department role pattern

In the complex world of the 1970s, however, behavioral scientists are needed to provide consultative advice, and other specialists serve in the collective-bargaining arena as an interface between organized labor and the employer.

Over the years, the roles of the personnel department have been portrayed as a relatively simple three-part composite figure consisting of (1) a service agent for the organization and its employees, (2) a control agent for management to ensure that management policies and legislative requirements are met, and (3) staff advisors to management at several levels. More recently, a much more complicated role pattern has appeared as more duties have been added and as the degree of emphasis in management philosophy has shifted from the more authoritarian views of the first half of the century to the more humanistic approaches seen today.

In the late 1940s the clear separation of roles and the strong staff role emphasis seen in Figure I-1 were indications of the traditional managerial philosophy of the time. The research of Elton Mayo and others had begun to be reflected in a variety of activities, but the general flavor of organizations and managerial style was essentially traditional and, to a large extent (by today's standards), certainly autocratic.

In the 1950s and 1960s the work of the human relations school was being examined and put to use. In many progressive organizations the department roles became more elaborate. A more professionally trained and more competent managerial population, a general movement away from bureaucracy, and the search by management for new tools to help motivate organization members

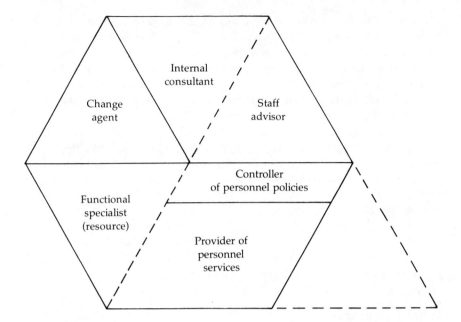

Figure I-2   Modern personnel department roles

were all important elements in making the role pattern more complex. With a shift to management by shared objectives, the staff role became one of a "source of help," and the staff did not simply follow—it initiated action and made its views known. Personnel managers' duties shifted from those of *control* to those of *resource* management, and they became skilled in solving specialized problems. The staff *advisor* emerged as an internal *consultant* on organizational health. *Change agents* emerged to initiate, to stimulate, and to enforce the processes of change in the organization. Figure I-2 is a schematic that describes the evolution of department roles from the simple three-part pattern of Figure I-1 to a more complex arrangement. In some organizations, some of the roles seen in Figure I-2 may not exist or may be seen only at the highest levels. The role pattern for a personnel department in an organization that hasn't moved from a more authoritarian style of management will be seen as similar to the triangle outlined by the dotted line of Figure I-2, the traditional three-part pattern. With a more participative style, the role pattern of the personnel department is likely to include the roles described by the total hexagon. The *control* functions and the explicitly defined staff *advisory* functions will still be needed at some levels in the company for coping with some forms of organizational problems. The balance of roles, however, will have shifted rather decidedly. In retrospect, it seems apparent that roles have been developed to meet the needs of the organization, its members, and society, and the new roles tend to reflect changes in managerial philosophies and styles.

The tentative new roles of *internal consultant* and *change agent* are only now beginning to be seen in some organizations; however, we can feel reasonably sure that the continued emphasis on the behavioral sciences will result in the crystallization of these roles during the next decade. An awareness of the development of these roles and knowledge of their own role patterns for each organization level should help the personnel staff members meet and anticipate the needs of their organizations and their own departments.

In the incidents included in this section, you may wish to consider the departmental role pattern that the organization sees as appropriate for the personnel manager or the personnel department. In the incident labeled "Advice from the First Personnel Text," it is possible to consider the balance of roles seen as important in the 1920s and to compare these roles with the organizational needs of the 1970s and 1980s.

Also, what balance of departmental roles would you recommend to Mr. Fremont in considering the selection of a personnel director? The needs of the president, the management team, and the remainder of the organization's members should all be considered in your deliberations.

SUGGESTED READINGS

Argyris, Chris. "A New Era in Personal Relations." *Dun's Review and Modern Industry* (June 1962): 40–41, 177–178.

Brummet, R.L., W.C. Pyle, and E.B. Flamholtz. "Accounting for Human Resources." *Michigan Business Review*, Vol. 20, No. 2 (March 1968): 20–25.

Fisher, Frank E. "The Personnel Function in Tomorrow's Company." *Personnel* (January-February 1968): 64–71.

Foulkes, Fred K. "The Expanding Role of the Personnel Function." *Harvard Business Review*, Vol. 53 (March-April 1975): 71–84.

French, Wendell L. *The Personnel Management Process*, 4th ed. Boston: Houghton Mifflin, 1978) especially the appendix, "A Chronological History of Personnel Management in the United States."

Gooding, Judson. "The Fraying White Collar." *Fortune*, Vol. 82, No. 6 (December 1970): 78–81, 108–109.

Morris, Richard B., ed. *Bicentennial History of the American Worker*. Washington, D.C.: U.S. Department of Labor, 1976.

Myers, Herbert E. "Personnel Directors Are the New Corporate Heroes." *Fortune*, Vol. 93 (February 1976): 84–88ff.

Singer, Henry A. "The Impact of Human Resources on Business." *Business Horizons*, Vol. 12, No. 2 (April 1969): 53–58.

1

SELECTING A DIRECTOR OF PERSONNEL

ROBERT A. ZAWACKI

XYZ Corporation is a manufacturing firm in Denver, Colorado, that presently employs approximately three hundred employees. The employees do not belong to a union, they are very satisfied with their working conditions, and they perceive their compensation package as equitable when compared to similar jobs in related industries. The corporation has never had a professional personnel director, and each department manager has been responsible for the personnel functions of recruitment, promotion, performance appraisal, and so forth. XYZ Corporation has been very profitable, and the firm has experienced a tremendous increase in sales and number of employees. The president, Larry A. Fremont, anticipates a continuing increase in sales, profitability, and demand for qualified employees. Further, Larry is a strong professional executive who believes in affirmative action programs and is concerned about XYZ's lack of progress in this area. Also, Larry is getting "signals" that a union may try to organize the employees. Because of these anticipated problems and pressures, Larry realizes that he must begin to build a top management team that can help him manage this profitable organization. As part of this team, Larry wants a professional personnel director. He appoints a search committee of five executives and asks you to serve as a consultant to this committee.

At its first meeting, the search committee completed a draft of the job description and the writing of the position announcement. The major points discussed were: minimum requirements, what good personnel experience is, competitiveness, resourcefulness, and the level of experience in business organizations. The committee decided that, to achieve the goals of the committee, the announcement should be as general in nature as possible. The following job announcement was placed in *Personnel Journal, Affirmative Action Register, La Luz, Journal of Black Studies, Denver Post, Rocky Mountain News,* and *Public Personnel Management:*

XYZ Corporation
Director of Personnel/Affirmative Action

The director will be responsible to the President for the activities of the personnel office, which serves all company personnel. Duties include employee relations, staff recruitment, fringe benefits, negotiation with the state department of personnel, training, and affirmative action. A Bachelor's degree is preferred, but persons with unusually strong experience will be considered. Experience must include a demonstrated administrative

5

ability in personnel, a demonstrated high level of interpersonal skills, and a commitment to affirmative action. Salary: $18,000 to $21,000. Send vita by May 6, 1977, to Search Committee, XYZ Corporation, 818 Nome Street, Denver, CO 80437.

The search committee received over three hundred résumés. The five top candidates are:

1. Current Résumé   Randall L. Banks
   Personal Data: Age, 30 years
                     Married, one child
                     Excellent health
   Education: Harvard Graduate School, MBA, 1974
                     Columbia University, BS, 1972
   Experience: 2 years, Assistant to the VP Harvard
                     1 year, Colorado Outward Bound School
   General: A high school achiever
                     Excellent management potential

2. Current Résumé   James E. Andersen
   Personal Data: Age, 41 years
                     Married, 2 children
                     Good health
   Education: University of Minnesota, BS, 1958,
                     major in business administration
                     Numerous management workshops
   Experience: 4 years, Industrial Relations Manager—large western cor-
                     poration
                     2 years, Personnel Director—firm of 100+ people
                     3 years, Manager of Training & Development
                     2 years, Division Personnel Director
                     2 years, Personnel Manager
   General: Grew up in a small town
                     Extensive affirmative action experience
                     Wage and salary consultant
                     Member ASPA

3. Current Résumé   Barbara J. Loosling
   Personal Data: Age, 34 years
                     Married, one child
                     Excellent health
   Education: Colorado College, Bachelor of Arts,
                     major in humanities
   Experience: 7 years, Personnel Manager, May D&F
                     2 years, Elementary Teacher
                     1 year, Substitute Teacher
   General: Weight, 100 pounds
                     Secretary, Heart Association
                     Excellent executive skills

4. Current Résumé   Bryan G. Kumpan
  Personal Data: Age, 31 years
                     Married, 2 children
                     Excellent health
  Education: University of Texas, Bachelor of Education,
                     minor in business education
  Experience: 2 years, Employee Relations Director—for Madison, Wis-
                     consin
                     2 years, Director of Employee Relations—for Iowa City
                     4 years, Social Worker for Detroit's inner-city area, ad-
                     dressing racial problems
                     2 years, Junior High School Teacher
  General: Extensive public-speaking experience
                     Negotiates labor contracts
                     Hard-working, precise, demanding

5. Current Résumé   Kathy J. Jaramillo
  Personal Data: Age, 25 years
                     2 children
                     Excellent health
  Education: 2 semesters, University of Wyoming,
                     no major
  Experience: 1 year, Community Resource Manager—Oakland,
                     California
                     3 years, Legal Aid Society of Model Cities, Unit Affirma-
                     tive Action Compliance Supervisor
                     2 years, Playground Supervisor—city of Denver
  General: Bilingualism (English/Spanish)
                     Instructor in music

QUESTIONS AND REQUIREMENTS

1. You are the personnel consultant to the search committee. What procedures would you recommend the committee follow to increase the reliability and validity of the selection process?

2. Decide what your criteria for evaluation will be and design a personnel form to aid the selection process.

3. Whom would you select for the position of Director of Personnel at XYZ Corporation and why?

2
ADVICE FROM THE FIRST PERSONNEL TEXT: TEAD AND METCALF

The following statement appeared in the preface to the first textbook on personnel management, published in 1920:

> There has been in some organizations an unfortunate tendency to overdevelop some one activity which was of special interest to some executive. But the time is past when hobbies or pet ideas should be allowed to develop at the expense of a rounded human relations policy. The surest index of a personnel executive's grasp of his problem is his ability to keep a sane proportion in the unfolding of his different administrative tasks.

QUESTIONS AND REQUIREMENTS

1. What aspects of personnel management might have been overemphasized in 1920?

2. What aspects do you believe are overemphasized today?

3. As of today, what would be the basic ingredients to a "rounded human relations policy"?

Ordway Tead and Henry C. Metcalf, *Personnel Administration* (New York: McGraw-Hill Book Company, 1920), p. viii. Used with permission of McGraw-Hill Book Company.

PART II
A PROCESS-SYSTEMS MODEL AND MAJOR CONTINGENCIES

Organizations can be viewed as closed or open systems. When managers view organizations as closed systems, they see labor as a factor of production that should be compensated at the lowest rate possible. Managers tend to manipulate employees to increase production. This system has been called "mechanistic," and it is not concerned with the higher-order needs of the employees; rather employees are viewed as "economic workers" who want to avoid pain while striving for money. To protect "economic workers," managers of closed system organizations devise structures that shelter their workers from other sources of influence such as labor unions, government, and other industrial firms. Generally, in recent years, this mechanistic attitude of management has been replaced with an attitude of concern for the employees as human beings, an approach commonly referred to as an open systems or "organic" view.

The organization as an open system is seen as an element of a larger system (environment) of which it is only a part. The organization receives inputs from its environment and utilizes these inputs in the conversion process, which results in organizational outputs to the environment. Figure II-1 displays the basic elements of the organization as an open system.

Thus, the organization is not only dependent upon the environment to provide its human and capital inputs, but it is also dependent upon the environment to accept its outputs (product, service, or waste). This interdependency introduces the importance of feedback to the managers of organizations. *Feedback* is a dynamic information process that helps an organization adapt to its environment and therefore satisfy the needs of society, which aids the survival of the organization.

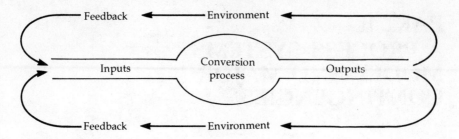

Figure II-1   An open-system organization

For a detailed discussion of the concept of systems see Fremont E. Kast and James E. Rosenzweig, *Contingency Views of Organization and Management* (Chicago: Science Research Associates, Inc., 1973), pp. 37-56.

Personnel management is a dynamic subaspect of the total management process and is an integral part of all divisions of an organization. Thus, progressive personnel management views the organization as an open system that must adapt to changing conditions in a dynamic environment. Within this dynamic environment, personnel management is a general operational process—of managing human resources—that is inherent in all organizations.

The general operational process of managing human resources can be divided into a number of interdependent subprocesses: (1) task specialization, (2) staffing, (3) performance appraisal, (4) training and development, (5) compensation and reward, (6) collective bargaining, (7) organization development, (8) leadership, (9) and justice determination. Whether there is a formally designated personnel department, the point is that these subprocesses of personnel management are inherent in organizations, and they must be done by someone—such as the foreman, the secretary, or the president. Although these subprocesses must be accomplished, this says nothing about the effectiveness of the subprocess. For example, without a personnel department to coordinate the total compensation package, the production manager may hire and compensate employees at a level far above other employees in the organization and even in the local labor market. The production manager is accomplishing the compensation and reward subprocess at the expense of equity within the organization. Thus, there exists a need within organizations to plan, coordinate, and control—*organizationwide*—the personnel management subprocesses that are inherent in all organizations. This objective is normally delegated to the personnel department.

Authority relationships, organizational structures, and types of technology used also affect the subprocesses of personnel management. These three variables are major contingencies that the personnel manager must consider when designing personnel systems. We feel that there is no "one best way" to design personnel systems. Rather, we believe that variables such as authority, structure, and technology are manageable and that the modern personnel manager must be a good diagnostician and must search for an optimal design of personnel systems that fit the situations.

The incidents and cases in Part II emphasize the contingent nature of personnel management in modern organizations. The major contingencies highlighted in the incidents and cases are rapid growth, lack of organization structure, authority and power relationships, technology, motivation patterns, and rapid reductions in staff.

SUGGESTED READINGS

Baker, Frank, ed. *Organizational Systems: General Systems Approaches to Complex Organizations.* Homewood, Ill.: Richard D. Irwin, 1973.

Berthal, Wilmar. "New Challenges Demand that We Change Roles." *The Personnel Administrator,* Vol. 13 (November-December 1968): 33–38.

Coleman, Charles J., and David P. Palmer. "Organizational Applications of Systems Theory." *Business Horizons,* Vol. 16 (December 1973): 77–84.

Couger, Daniel. "Educating Political Managers about the Computer." *California Management Review,* Vol. 11 (Fall 1968): 47–58.

French, Wendell L. *The Personnel Management Process,* 4th ed. Boston: Houghton Mifflin Company, 1978, Chapters 3–5.

———. "Process Vis-à-Vis Systems: Toward a Model of the Enterprise and Administration." *Academy of Management Journal,* Vol. 6 (March 1963): 46–58.

Hollingsworth, A.T., and Jane W. Hass. "Structured Planning in Organizational Development: An Often Neglected Aspect." *Personnel Journal,* Vol. 54 (December 1975): 613–615.

Kast, Fremont E., and James E. Rosenzweig. "General Systems Theory: Applications for Organization and Management." *Academy of Management Journal,* Vol. 15 (December 1972): 447–465.

Lorsch, Jay W., and John J. Morse. *Organizations and Their Members: A Contingency Approach.* New York: Harper & Row, 1974.

Morse, John J., and Jay W. Lorsch. "Beyond Theory Y." *Harvard Business Review,* Vol. 48 (May–June 1970): 61–68.

Scott, William G. "Organization Theory: An Overview and an Appraisal." *Academy of Management Journal,* Vol. 4 (April 1961): 15–20.

Shepard, Jon M. "Specialization, Autonomy, and Job Satisfaction." *Industrial Relations,* Vol. 12 (October 1973): 274–281.

Sokolik, Stanley L. "Reorganize the Personnel Department?" *California Management Review,* Vol. 11 (Fall 1969): 43–52.

3
THE MUSHROOMING COMPANY

WENDELL L. FRENCH

One week ago you were hired as the personnel manager for Pacific Coast Electronics Company. This company has 250 employees at present. It manufactures precision electronic equipment. The company has been working on the development of a new electronic device for the Air Force. The device is now perfected, and the company has been awarded a contract for its production. Over the next 12 months the company expects to expand its employment to about 1200 employees, of which 1000 will be production workers.

Most of the new production workers who will be engaged in assembly operations must be semi-skilled. The other production workers will be skilled technicians engaged in testing operations.

Presently there is no separate personnel department. Hiring has been done by the various line supervisors. What personnel records are kept have been kept by the payroll clerk. All production employees are members of a local electrical workers union. Union negotiations have been handled by the company president. The present contract with the union is due to expire in three months.

QUESTIONS AND REQUIREMENTS

1. What planning do you need to do?

2. What personnel systems need to be designed, and what priority would you give to each?

3. What systematization can be developed in your relationship with the union?

4
E. G. LOMAX COMPANY

AUSTIN GRIMSHAW

The purchasing agent, production manager, production control manager, and plant manager at the Scott branch plant of the E. G. Lomax Company, were all astounded upon coming to work one morning to find waiting on their desks identical copies of a memorandum from the general manager, blistering them for acting without proper authority in jointly making the previous day what they had all regarded at the time as a purely routine decision to drop a vendor, the Castle Stamping Company. The memorandum informed them that the general manager was reversing their decision and that in the future no final actions on such "important policy matters" were to be taken without his specific approval.

The reprimanded executives immediately got together to talk the matter over. None of them had spoken to the general manager since the meeting at which the decision had been made. They concluded, therefore, that the only other man present the day before must have been the one to bring it to the general manager's attention. This man, chief tool engineer at the company's parent plant 200 miles distant, had formerly worked for the Castle Stamping Company. He had been instrumental in having Castle selected as the second source for a new stamping to be used in large quantities at the Scott branch.

Castle had been a source of supply, for some years previously, for other parts used in both Lomax plants. During the early part of this association, while business was generally slack, Castle had been reasonably satisfactory as to delivery and price, although never as reliable as one other stamping source used by Lomax. In the previous years, however, business had been brisk and stampings procurement had become difficult. The attitude of Castle executives remained on the surface as cordial as ever, but deliveries were consistently late, sometimes by as much as six months, and prices were high. Extra charges were billed for short runs made by Castle at Lomax's urgent request in order to keep its lines from shutting down, in spite of the fact that it was Castle's lateness in delivery which caused the emergencies.

Feelings that the amount of business currently being placed was not enough to make Lomax a preferred customer, the latter had offered Castle a share of the business on a new large-volume part. This offer had been enthusiastically received, Castle had made dies at a cost to Lomax of $6,500, and accepted an initial order for 50,000 stampings.

14

The decision to drop Castle and to call in all dies from its plant had been reached the previous day because, in spite of repeated promises, no stampings had been received in the six months since completion of the dies. Also, deliveries on other parts purchased from Castle were most unsatisfactory. The consensus of the meeting, with the exception of one dissenter, the chief tool engineer from the parent plant who happened to be in town and was consulted as a matter of courtesy, was that Castle would never be a trustworthy source of supply and would continue to get the Scott branch into trouble, as long as the supply situation remained tight. The dissenter's point of view was: (1), that the difficulties could be straightened out; (2), that Castle made good parts and could be brought into line on prices; and (3), that the parent plant would be embarrassed by calling in of the dies, since it was currently getting some parts from Castle and might itself be dropped as a customer as a direct result of such hostile action.

The parent-plant chief tool engineer requested that Scott's general manager be called in before the decision was made final. The others present at the meeting refused, saying that the general manager knew all about the troubles with the Castle Stamping Company and on several occasions had indicated that he favored dropping it as a vendor just as soon as this could be done without endangering shipments to Lomax customers.

The production manager said that it was a routine problem with which the general manager should not be bothered, that he customarily left such decisions to the men present at the meeting, that he spent very little time on plant matters, visited the shop only occasionally and concentrated mostly on sales and product engineering problems.

The group also indicated a belief that each of the company's two plants should make its own independent decisions on purchasing. The parent-company plant was free, they said, to keep or drop Castle, as it thought most advisable, regardless of the branch plant's action. Finally, the group argued, the general manager was out of town on a sales trip and the time of his return was indefinite.

The group then discussed what should be done about several dies that had been built for the branch plant's own presses at the parent plant under the supervision of the parent plant chief tool engineer. These dies had been tried out at Scott and had not fitted its presses exactly, according to the production manager. Nor had they incorporated several features of design which the branch plant tool engineer had requested prior to their construction. The meeting broke up in order to permit all interested parties to visit the punch-press department where the dies had been specially set up for retrial and for observation of the disputed points about their operation.

After rehashing the previous day's discussion with the others present, the plant manager, with a copy of the memo in his hand, went in to see the general manager. The general manager, without any preliminaries, immediately said: "I got home hot and tired after a long trip, late last night, and found Tom Norcross [the parent-company chief tool engineer] waiting for me. What do you mean telling Tom that I never get into the shop any more and that I leave all production decisions to the plant executives? Maybe I don't get into the shop during working hours much now, but I often go in there evenings, when I come back to clear my desk, and on weekends. You know very well that I've had trouble more than once with the president because people at the main plant have distorted things we have said and done down here. Try to be more careful what you say to all of them in the future."

Three months later, following a series of completely unsatisfactory further dealings with the Castle Stamping Company, it was dropped as a vendor, at the general manager's express instructions, and all dies were called in.

QUESTIONS AND REQUIREMENTS

1. Give your opinion of the organizational climate at Scott branch plant of the E. G. Lomax Company.

2. How would you measure their organizational climate?

3. Why was the memorandum from the general manager so upsetting to the other managers?

4. What type of leadership style does the general manager display?

5. What additional information do you need to diagnose properly the problems in this case?

6. Imagine that you are the plant manager at the Scott branch plant. What specific actions would you take to improve interpersonal relations with the general manager?

5
THE UNIVERSITY OF OBELISK

TOM BASURAY

The University of Obelisk is one of the two state-supported institutions of higher learning in the south-western state of Obelisk. The University was founded in the last decade of the nineteenth century when Obelisk was a U.S. Territory, and in the past eighty years it has grown from a one building, one curriculum school to an institution of 22,000 students offering undergraduate and graduate degrees in almost all the major academic disciplines. All of the colleges within the University are fully accredited by the appropriate academic associations and are constantly involved in revising, strengthening and updating curricula.

Besides academic endeavors, the University of Obelisk has traditionally maintained a strong profile in the various collegiate athletic programs within the NCAA Big Eight Conference. Because of its nationally ranked football team, as well as its powerful baseball, basketball, and wrestling teams, the University has been very successful in obtaining strong alumni support, financially and otherwise. "The effectiveness of the athletic programs determines the viability of the academic programs at the University of Obelisk" is a common in-house joke among the faculty and staff members at the University.

The main campus of the University is located in the south-central city of Bedford, which is twenty miles south of Garden City, the largest metropolitan area in the state with a population of approximately 600,000. Garden City is also the state capital. The medical college complex of the University is located in Garden City. The University is structured along the traditional academic and non-academic segment lines. In the academic area the Provost is the chief academic officer and reports directly to the President of the University. The non-academic area is divided into seven functional segments each with a vice-president reporting directly to the President (see Figure 1). The College of Medicine has its own Provost and staff departments, and it is administered autonomously under a separate budget.

The present case involves the Residential Programs Office under the Vice-President of the University Community and Research (UCOR) department. The Residential Programs Office was established for the purpose of generating and administering the University policies concerning student life in University housing. The position of the Residential Programs Office in relation to other offices within the division of University Community and Research is indicated in Figure 1.

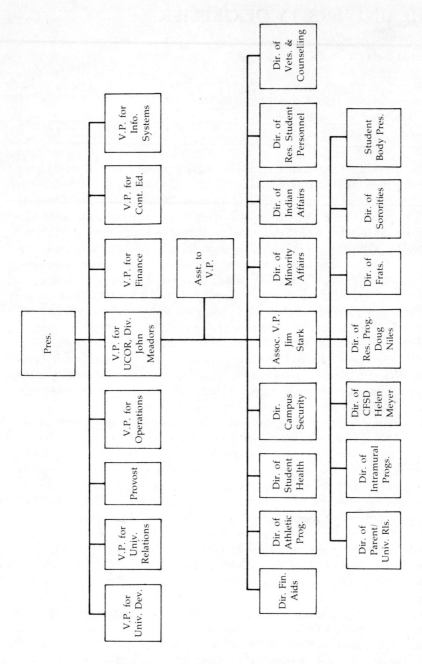

Figure 1   Organization chart for the University Community and Research Division

To understand the role and functions of the Residential Program Office it is necessary to become acquainted with the history of student housing at the University of Obelisk. From the beginning the University has emphasized its residential programs and the policies pertaining thereto. The University maintained extensive campus housing for single and married students. Initially, single students under 21 years of age were required to live in campus housing. However, in the late 1960's, during the period of extensive student unrest sweeping the nation's campuses, opposition to this housing policy was voiced at the University. The intensity of the protests forced the University administrators to look for alternatives. Consequently, in 1971, Mike Berger, the then Director of Residential Programs, successfully proposed a change of the housing policy. Under the newly approved system only the Freshmen students were required to live in the University housing. In the beginning, the new policy generated a heavy outflow of students from campus to off-campus housing. Many of the high-rise dormitories, built a few years previously in anticipation of enrollment expansion, experienced below average occupancy rates. The Housing Office was hard pressed to generate adequate revenues to pay the interest on building-bond issues. Traditionally the housing program had been self-supporting in terms of both current operating expenses and long-term debt amortization expenses. In 1972 the number of single students living in the dormitories dropped from approximately 8,000 to 4,000. To avoid financial loss from such drastic reductions of students, the University Housing Office proposed and received approval for renting 1/3 of the total dormitory space to the United States Postal Institute, a training facility for all U.S. Postal employees that had moved to the campus from Washington, D.C., in 1969. The rental agreement made the housing operations self-supporting. In 1973, due to a shortage of off-campus housing facilities and the inflationary cost-of-living index, many of the students who had moved out of the University housing began to move back. The number of students living in the campus housing facilities rose to 6,000. All available dormitory spaces (not including the ones rented out to the Postal Institute) were filled to capacity. The general feeling among the University administrators was a positive expectation that the trend would continue for some time in the future.

Functionally, the Director of Residential Programs is under the supervision of the Associate Vice-President, UCOR (see Figure 1). The structure of the Residential Programs office is presented in Figure 2. Reporting to the Director are two full-time Assistant Directors and one half-time Graduate Assistant. Five Center Coordinators in charge of several dormitory complexes and 80 Resident Advisors responsible for supervision of dormitories report to the Assistant Directors.

Before 1971 the policies governing student conduct in the University housing were imposed and executed somewhat autocratically. Strict enforcement of the housing policies and punishment for policy violations were carried out. The administrators countered any criticism of housing policies with the argument that housing or any other policies at the University should reflect the values of the state taxpayers. Consequently, the Director of Residential Programs was vested with a substantial amount of authority to promote and execute appropriate policies. However, the actual adjudication of disciplinary cases and subsequent sanctions were meted out by the Judiciary Board composed of faculty, staff and students.

At the professional level, all of the departments reporting to the Vice-President, UCOR, had traditionally been staffed informally with the aid of a highly developed crony system. Such staff members were expected to become members of the informal fraternal system that operated in this area. Promotions within the structure were a function of appropriate connections. The functions of recruitment, selection and promotion were carried out by a few people within the division, though technically the University Personnel Service Department had joint responsibilities. Since the Vice-President, UCOR, John Meadors, spent most of his time in developing good relations with the state legislators and the taxpayers, the day-to-day operations of certain portions of UCOR, including the Residential Programs, were the responsibilities of the Associate Vice-President.

The Associate Vice-President, UCOR, Jim Stark, had joined the University 10 years ago as an administrative assistant to the Director of the Center for Student Development (CFSD). Unlike other professionals within the division who had graduate degrees in Student Personnel, Jim had a Masters degree in English. Another Administrative Assistant, Helen Meyer, joined the division at the same time as Jim. Both were known to each other from their student days at the University. Both belonged to Greek social organizations. Helen had a Masters degree in Student Personnel. At the writing of this case Helen had been promoted to Director, CFSD. The rapid rise of both Jim and Helen can be directly attributed to effective manipulation of their superior's favors. Both were strong believers in the "power-through-connection" principle, and they encouraged the same in their subordinates. All the key staff members reporting to Jim and Helen had been promoted for their loyalties. It was fully understood by all of the staff in this area that substantial politicking was part of the job.

In 1972, the then Director of Residential Programs, Mike Berger, resigned to accept a better position at another university in Pennsylvania. At about the same time, due to declining student residence in University housing, the entire Residential Programs operation was facing critical evaluations. The President appointed an *ad hoc* committee, composed of faculty from the College of Education and students, to study the organization and to make appropriate recommendations. In due course, along with other suggestions, the committee recommended the hiring of a competent professional for the position of Director of Residential Programs.

The critical evaluations of the existing Residential Programs functions forced Jim and Helen onto the defensive. For the first time they found themselves attracting uncomfortable attention of other members of the University. Difficult questions about the overall efficiency of the UCOR and CFSD were being raised.

However, being professionals in the art of survival, they prepared quickly for all contingencies. Jim placed an advertisement for the position of Residential Programs Director in the *Chronicle for Higher Education* (a national tabloid catering to the professionals in this field). This move was instituted to placate the ruffled feelings of all of their critics.

The response to the advertisement was overwhelming, partly due to a depressed job market in the student personnel profession. Jim did not anticipate such a large response. The idea of a true professional working under him made him feel uncertain and apprehensive. Jim and Helen managed to eliminate some outstanding candidates on flimsy grounds during the initial screening of applicants. Others were sent up for review by a selection panel composed of faculty, staff and students. Of these, six candidates were invited to appear for interviews. Three of these were out-of-state applicants, one was an applicant from the other university in the state, and two were from within the UCOR division that had been sponsored by Jim and Helen. Despite all the maneuverings by Jim and Helen to present their candidates in the most favorable light, the selection panel named two of the three out-of-state candidates as most outstanding. The candidate receiving the highest rating was a woman, Gladys Lane, from Indiana. She had a Masters degree in Student Personnel from Indiana University and had extensive professional experience in the field. The second nominee was Norman Price, a Black from Wayne State University at Detroit. The two candidates that Jim and Helen sponsored were ranked fourth and sixth.

Under strong pressure from the selection committee, Jim made an offer to Gladys. However, he did manage to reduce the amount of the offer from what was being paid to Mike Berger, the previous Director. Citing financial difficulties and budgeting restrictions, Jim also managed to reduce the staff help in the Residential Programs Office. Gladys was to have a half-time Administrative Assistant and two secretaries to supervise five Center Coordinators, 80 Resident Advisors and 4,000 students. Jim felt that these negative aspects would discourage Gladys from accepting the offer. To Jim's dismay, Gladys took the job. Gladys could sense the challenge that she was about to face. Her decision to accept the job was based on a desire to prove her abilities against odds by bringing about positive changes within the entire Residential Programs area that, until then, had been run mostly on whims and by fiat. She felt that the extra effort was worth the challenge in terms of personal growth and professional advancement.

In all of these recruitment and selection activities, the involvement of the Personnel Department was minimal. Traditionally the decision and follow-up pertaining to the personnel functions of recruitment, selection, promotion, pay increases or discharges within the UCOR division had been made without any coordination with the Personnel Department. A standard procedure for filling a vacancy had been to decide on a candidate from the subordinate ranks or from a circle of acquaintances and then filing a "Position Vacancy" with the Personnel

Department. The chosen candidate would then be instructed to contact the Personnel Department for the available vacancy. Once the candidate was referred to Jim or Helen for interviews, the Personnel Department would be notified of the choice, and the position would be removed from the list of vacancies.

Gladys worked for two years against tremendous odds to improve the Residential Programs, but it became evident that she was not to receive any support from either Jim or Helen. Any request for policy changes was summarily turned down. While the other universities in the nation were experimenting with new concepts of student behavior and responsibilities in communal living facilities, Jim considered these to be too radical for the University of Obelisk. Since he was the main link between Gladys and other top administrators at the University, Gladys was unable to explore directly the feelings of these officials about some of her proposed changes. Being new to the system, she was not sure of her position at any time. Due to the lack of staff help, she was forced to work 20–25 hours overtime each week without compensation. She was expected to be a professional and to carry out her responsibilities accordingly. Furthermore, certain negative functions that were previously being handled by the CFSD, such as disciplining errant students, were added to her regular duties. Jim and Helen felt that such a move would bring down the brunt of the student wrath on the Director. Finally, after a lot of deliberation, Gladys decided to tender her resignation. It was quickly accepted, and Gladys left the University in August, 1974.

At this point Jim decided to make a bold move. Citing the example of Gladys, he convinced the President and the Vice-President, University Community and Research, about the inappropriateness of hiring someone from out of state as the Director of Residential Programs. He left the impression that such candidates were likely to be too liberal for the University, always a sore point with the top University administrators. He also convinced these officials to not permit other faculty or staff members that were too idealistic to take part in the future screening of professional applicants. This time, consequently, the vacancy in the Residential Programs office was not formally publicized through the usual media. Jim made some informal telephone inquiries about potential candidates from other universities and colleges within the state. Jim and Helen sponsored Doug Niles, a graduate administrative assistant within UCOR, for the position, and in due course Doug was appointed the new Director of Residential Programs.

Before his new appointment, Doug was working as a counselor treating psychologically disoriented students. His record as a counselor was poor. Students with personality and other mental problems who were referred to Doug complained about inadequate help. The Resident Advisors who were responsible for referring troubled students in the dormitories soon started sending them to the University Infirmary where a full time phychiatrist was available. Doug had been in the service for a few years, and part of that time he was in Vietnam working with mentally disturbed soldiers. He came to the University of Obelisk

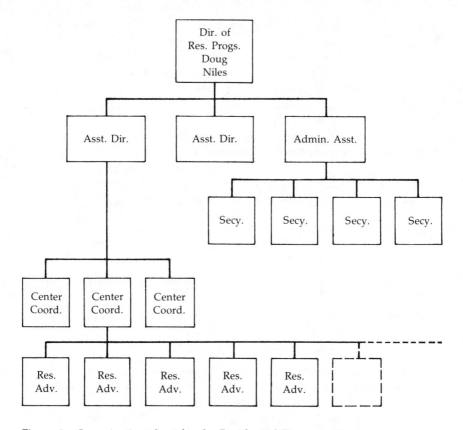

Figure 2   Organization chart for the Residential Programs Dept.

in 1969 to pursue a doctoral program in guidance and counseling. At the time of his appointment as the Director of Residential Programs he was a part-time student finishing up his course work

The five Center Coordinators, each of whom was responsible for the supervision of 16 dormitory complexes, were all professionally trained people. Most of them were in the Ph.D. program in student personnel. A couple of them were ahead of Doug in terms of projected completion date for the terminal degree.

A short time after his promotion Doug demanded and obtained two full-time Assistant Directors in the Residential Programs Office and two part-time secretaries in addition to the staff that he inherited from Gladys. Doug was overheard to comment to his friends that he was not prepared to work 25 hours overtime each week. His main goal was the completion of his educational program in the shortest possible time. Doug's salary was also higher than what Gladys had been getting. Doug resubmitted many of the proposals for change in Residential Programs policies suggested earlier by Gladys. This time they were considered progressive and forward looking. Jim and Helen felt that such policies would help the University attract more students to the University housing. Jim forwarded the proposals to top officials who then approved them.

Subsequent to the introduction of new policies in the University housing, the Center Coordinators and the Resident Advisors were beginning to voice complaints. They were unhappy with the quality of leadership in the Residential Programs Office and the amount of support from Doug in terms of dealing with change. The general feeling among the staff of the Residential Programs Office was one of frustration. They began questioning Doug's decisions and his ability to understand the situation in the housing areas. Moreover, parents of some of the students living in University housing were also becoming unhappy about the new policies. The President and John Meadors, the Vice-President, UCOR, were getting more than the usual number of complaints.

QUESTIONS AND REQUIREMENTS

1. Evaluate the present role of the personnel department at the University of Obelisk.

2. Evaluate the deficiencies of the selection and promotion policies in the division of University Community and Research.

3. What should be done to rectify these deficiencies?

4. Imagine that you are John Meadors, the vice president, UCOR. What specific actions would you take to ensure smoother operations of various personnel functions in the division? How should you deal with Jim Stark?

5. Role play John Meadors and Jim Stark.

6

BIRKENFIELD FURNITURE MANUFACTURING COMPANY

GERALD HAMPTON AND BRUCE MULLINS

Birkenfield Furniture Manufacturing Company, located in the coastal mountains of Washington, is in a unique position. For the first time in years sales are up, and there is a possibility that the company will break even this year. Yet the future of the firm is threatened by an economic turn around. Prosperity, it seems, isn't always what it's cracked up to be.

BACKGROUND

Mr. William McPherson, 52, President and chief stockholder of Birkenfield Furniture, came to Ilwaco, Washington, seven months ago. His background is unrelated to the furniture industry, though his father was a cabinetmaker in New Hampshire. Mr. McPherson attended two years of college at the University of New Hampshire where he studied electrical engineering and mathematics. He dropped out of college in 1942 and joined the Air Corps, and he was stationed in England and North Africa as a flight technician. After he was discharged in 1945, Mr. McPherson moved from New Hampshire to Chicago where he was employed in a large chain retail store. Advancing quickly, McPherson soon became a store manager in Seattle. In 1957, when he was 34 years old, Mr. McPherson purchased a bankrupt plumbing supply company. He was quite successful, and he opened a second store in 1968. Mr. McPherson sold his business in 1974 because he no longer wished to live and work in a congested metropolitan area. For some time he had been looking for a quiet rural area in the Pacific Northwest where he could raise his family in a more natural, relaxed setting.

Ilwaco is a small and quietly conservative town of about 1,500 people. Located on the coast near the mouth of the Columbia River, it is about 150 miles southwest of Seattle. Life in Ilwaco is typical of many small coastal towns. Lumbering and fishing are the major occupations: the work is hard and the rewards are few. The area, though, is unsurpassed for ruggedness and beauty, and the lack of economic growth is sometimes viewed as an asset rather than a liability.

Birkenfield Furniture Manufacturing Company was founded in 1937 by Arvid Johannsen, son of Ilwaco's first mayor. Located in an abandoned salmon

Exhibit **I**   B.F.M.C. partial list of products

Chairs	Factory cost	Factory price
M.W. 0187–74	$10.54	$14.44
M.W. 0630–75	12.68	16.90
M.W. 1015–72	12.97	17.53
M.W. 1103–72	13.58	19.40
M.W. 1204–74	14.78	19.45
M.W. 0617–75	15.98	20.76
B.Z. 0401–75	$ 9.78	$12.07
B.Z. 0919–73	10.37	12.96
B.Z. 1115–74	10.78	13.15
B.Z. 0107–75	12.64	14.70
B.Z. 0804–75	12.64	15.09
Turned components*		
S.R. 1130–74	$ .61	$ .78
S.R. 0414–73	.72	1.04
S.R. 0911–74**	.83	1.10

* Turned components (lathed wooden table legs, bookcase components, etc.) are sold to other furniture manufacturers.
** The code numbers used indicate the customer, month, day, and year of the initial order.

cannery, the company manufactured a narrow line of tables, chairs, and window sashes. The company grew until fire destroyed the old cannery in 1949. Relocated from the waterfront to an abandoned building several blocks away, Birkenfield continued to prosper, or so the company records seemed to indicate. When Mr. McPherson purchased the company he told a business associate, "I find it hard to believe that Birkenfield ever made a dime."

PRODUCT LINES

Birkenfield Furniture is presently manufacturing a limited line of chairs and components for bookshelves, in addition to assorted small items such as cutting boards, macrame beads, wooden toys and chess sets. A more complete description of the product line is given in Exhibit I. The unfinished products are sold primarily to several large furniture manufacturers in the Seattle-Tacoma area. Birkenfield's customers take the assembled but unstained chairs and stain them to match the rest of their product lines. Birkenfield also sells to a chain of discount houses on the West Coast. These discount stores sell the unassembled goods directly to the customer. A more detailed income picture can be seen in Exhibit II. McPherson feels the new sources of revenue will be needed if Birkenfield is to get out of debt and prosper.

Exhibit **II** B.F.M.C. comparative income statements July–Dec. 74;
Jan.–June 75

	July–Dec.	Jan.–June
Revenue:		
Sales	$695,374	$749,605
G.B.H.*	732	449
Net income	$696,106	$750,054
Expenses:		
Cost of goods sold	$327,448	$335,851
Salaries and wages	224,909	235,900
Depreciation	775	1,200
Insurance	8,550	8,593
Utilities	12,400	12,960
Taxes	71,615	72,105
Interest	47,810	50,425
Misc.	4,753	4,915
Net expenses	$698,260	$721,949
Increase to equity	$ (2,154)	$ 28,105

* Sale of woodchips

Exhibit **III** Hourly wage scales, furniture industry

	Ilwaco	Seattle*	Portland*
Ripsaw operator	$3.95	$5.02	$4.93
Gluers	3.90	4.32	4.40
Sanders	3.85	4.58	4.50
Maintenance	3.48	5.07	5.00
Unskilled	2.45	2.95	2.90

* Unionized rates

LABOR FORCE

Birkenfield has several major advantages in the furniture manufacturing industry. Wages in Ilwaco are much lower than in strongly unionized areas such as
Seattle or Portland. The low wages are crucial to Birkenfield because of its lower
productivity and higher wastage. The wood supplies are purchased from
G.B.H. Mills, a local sawmill that has supplied Birkenfield with reasonably
priced raw materials since 1939.

McPherson believes that the labor force at Birkenfield is the company's most
important asset. The typical worker at Birkenfield's is a woman, middle-aged,
loyal and hardworking. Two of the foremen are male, as are the machinists in
the repair shop (see Exhibit IV). Typically, housewives in Ilwaco take outside

jobs to supplement the family income, and they have little inclination toward promotion and advancement within the firm. For many of Mr. McPherson's workers, the income derived from their jobs makes the difference between good times and bad in their families.

PRODUCTION

The two primary disadvantages at Birkenfield are the random production schedules and the age of the building and equipment. The building housing Birkenfield is almost 50 years old, having been constructed in the late 1920's. The two-story wood frame building, typical of that era, houses an assemblage of woodworking equipment, the average age of which is 15 to 20 years. The oldest equipment in the shop still in use is a set of wooden gluing clamps that bear the initials "A.J.," obviously belonging to the founder of the company. The first floor of the building houses the ripsawing, sanding, gluing and lathing departments. The upstairs is given over to storage of raw materials and finished goods inventory. The shipping and receiving dock is behind the main building and is connected to the upstairs storage by an outside freight elevator. The roof of the building was replaced in 1965 after leaking water had damaged finished goods and short-circuited the freight elevator several times. McPherson was amazed at how long and how well the equipment had performed. Much of the credit for the careful maintenance of the machines went to Tom Dimick, the head of the repair shop. McPherson knew that the company would be in a precarious position if something were to happen to Dimick.

A major fault of the present production system is the high percentage of wastage and short production runs. One of the first things McPherson noticed prior to purchasing Birkenfield in February, 1975, was three metal bins overflowing with chipped, cracked or damaged wooden pieces. When McPherson inquired about these bins, he was told that they contained the week's rejects of glued or lathed pieces. These were fed into a wood chipper each week, and the chips were sent by truck back to G.B.H. Mills for reprocessing into various wood products. Birkenfield recovered very little money on these chips in comparison with the original cost of the wood. It was McPherson's contention that most of this wastage was caused by worker or machine error, but a significant portion was caused by excessively warped, knotty or split wood supplied to Birkenfield by G.B.H. Mills. Although Mr. McPherson felt that this situation should be remedied, he felt very reluctant to offend G.B.H. Mills because of the close ties between the two companies through the years. He was also uncertain where he would find an alternative source of wood at a price he could afford in Ilwaco, although one mill up the coast had indicated that they would consider supplying wood to Birkenfield at a cost of 5% more per board foot than what G.B.H. was charging.

The problem of short production runs was, in McPherson's opinion, one of the most significant that Birkenfield faced. As an example, McPherson gives this account:

Two days after I assumed control [of Birkenfield], I received a telephone call from one of the buyers of our biggest customer in Seattle. In short, he made it clear that he desperately needed 50 sets of our dining room chairs, model M.W. 1103-72, *immediately*. When I informed him that we had only 40 sets in stock, he told me in no uncertain terms that that was my problem and that he needed the 50 sets immediately; then he abruptly hung up. I immediately called in John Wright, my head foreman, and told him of the situation. I was obviously still shocked by the man's brashness because John informed me that this kind of thing wasn't new. This particular customer had done it often in the past whenever things got hectic in Seattle. I realized then how much we are at the mercy of the customers; they have us over a barrel! We can't afford to offend any of our customers.

McPherson ordered that all production be halted and shifted to the production of the M.W. 1103-72 order. This caused several other orders to be shunted aside and caused considerable wastage of materials and manpower. As McPherson noted:

In a company that is in our position, it is almost impossible to dictate terms to our customers. There are several other furniture manufacturers in Seattle that would love to handle our clients' business. Something has got to be done about it.

PRESENT OPERATIONS

In an attempt to increase the efficiency of his machines and workers, Mr. McPherson brought to Birkenfield Mr. Allan Lloyd, a production and time-studies man. Lloyd came to Birkenfield very highly recommended, and McPherson felt fortunate to acquire his services. Mr. Lloyd, 31, was a graduate of the MBA program at the University of Southern California and was previously employed as a consultant by a Seattle electronics firm. Having grown up in the Seattle area he was acquainted with Ilwaco, and he anticipated the challenge that Birkenfield offered. His ultimate plan, as McPherson understood, was to gain experience in a small town locale to further his consulting ambitions. His job was to supervise and direct production operations to maximize efficiency and reduce wastage. He reported to Mr. McPherson, and he supervised all line foremen. (See Exhibit IV.)

Mr. McPherson also brought two additional supervisory people: Mrs. Agnes Nelson to keep the books, and Mr. Erik Hanson, McPherson's son-in-law, to help in sales. Hanson had previously been employed at McPherson's Plumbing Company; he now handled, with McPherson, all sales. He was well liked by those who knew him, and Mr. McPherson hoped that one day he would take over the family business. Mrs. Nelson, a widow in her sixties, had previously been the bookkeeper for Mr. McPherson in the plumbing business. She knew exactly how McPherson liked his books kept and was always a cheery face in the office. Birkenfield's previous bookkeeper had left the books in such a sad state that Mrs. Nelson was forced to take home boxes of old records to sort out at

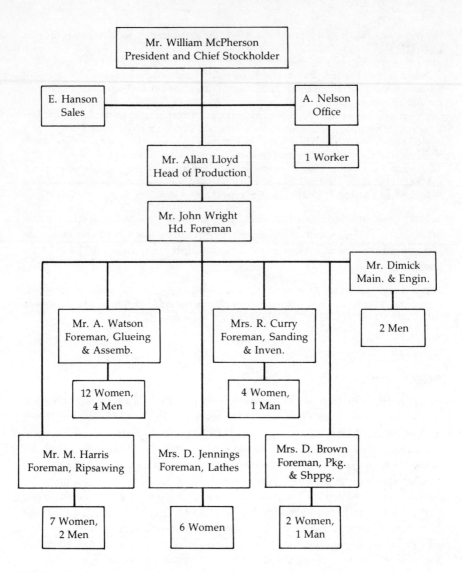

Exhibit **IV** Organizational structure

Total: 53 full-time employees

night. Assisting her was Lynn McPherson, Mr. McPherson's college-age daughter. Together the two of them had spent the summer putting together financial statements that would hopefully aid McPherson in running the company. (See Exhibits II and V.)

On Friday morning, August 15th, Debby Jennings, the lathe department foreman, came rushing into Mr. McPherson's office. She was very upset and appeared to be near tears.

Exhibit **V**   Birkenfield Furniture Company comparative
balance statement 12–31–74; 6–31–75

	12–31–75	6–30–75
Assets:		
Current		
Accts. Rec. Trade	295711	324852
Cash	(1312)	3555
Accts. Rec. G.B.H.	732	751
Prepaid Insurance	1201	1250
Non-Current		
Machinery and Equip.	14807	14738
Land	30000	30000
Building	18100	18100
Accum. Dep.	98105	99305
Inventory Raw Mat.	3987	1787
Inventory Fin. Gs.	14900	12752
Total Assets	476831	507090
Liabilities:		
Current		
Accts. Pay. Trade	38973	40019
Taxes Pay.	171615	173777
Interest Pay.	7770	5214
Non-Current		
Contract Pay. W.F.N.B.**	73700	67497
Total Liabilities	292058	286507
Capital Stock	184773	218377
Retained Earnings	0	2206
Total Stockholders Eq.	184773	220583
Total Equities	476831	507090

** A long-term bank debt secured in 1971

"Mr. McPherson," she started, "You've just got to do something about Mr. Lloyd! Everyone in my department is so upset, they're all about ready to walk out. I'm sorry to come and bother you like this, but you're his boss, maybe you can do something."

McPherson walked out on the floor with Mrs. Jennings. It was true, work had almost stopped in the lathe department; it looked as though the women were about ready to leave. McPherson, still not knowing what had upset the workers, invited the women into his office to talk things over. He surmised that Lloyd had probably said or done something that had irritated the employees.

"It's that damn Lloyd, Mr. McPherson!" one woman started. "He wants us to work overtime again tonight. That's the second time this week! Listen, I've got a husband and four kids to feed and clean up after. You tell me how I can do that if I have to keep working here in the evening. All of us are in the same situation, and there's no way I can keep this job if I have to work overtime every other night."

Mr. McPherson suddenly realized the seriousness of the situation. Birkenfield would go out with the next tide if all the workers walked out on him. McPherson explained to the women that the company was trying to expand sales and that this required building up finished goods inventories, so some overtime was necessary. However, he promised that they wouldn't have to work overtime that night, and he said that he would make sure that they would be informed at least one shift in advance of any future overtime. The women workers seemed satisfied at this and left the office to eat lunch. Taking Mrs. Jennings to one side, Mr. McPherson asked why she hadn't informed him earlier about the labor troubles. In an exasperated voice she said:

"It's that Lloyd again! You told me to report directly to him so that you would have more time to devote to getting the rest of the company straightened out. Lloyd just sits on our complaints and never does anything about them. He's had a couple of good ideas, but he sure doesn't know how to get them across without getting everyone mad at him. A diplomat he's not."

McPherson remembered several instances that seemed to support what the women had told him. Lynn McPherson, Mr. McPherson's daughter who was working at the plant during the summer, had come to her father on several occasions to pass on tips and suggestions offered by workers. The workers seemed to feel more comfortable talking to Lynn rather than to Lloyd or one of the "bosses." This led McPherson to install a suggestion box next to the coffee machine just outside his office. The box, however, yielded fewer results than anticipated. The workers, it appeared, preferred to verbalize ideas rather than commit them to writing.

"I don't really see what they're so upset about," was Lloyd's reply to McPherson's queries. "They can't seem to realize that this business has to grow to get out of the rut it's in, and right now that requires some overtime from everyone. To increase profits we've got to show our customers that we can deliver the goods without delay; maybe then we have a chance. I've been working for six weeks trying to set up standards and improve the production figures, but as close as I've been able to figure it, production has only risen 5%. Most of that came from straightening out the gluing area. Everywhere else I've met nothing but a lot of hostility and resentment. I've never even heard of a worker situation like this before. You'd think these ladies would want the extra money that overtime puts into their paychecks."

McPherson had never considered employee morale low before. Now, however, as he walked from department to department, he saw that the workers weren't as talkative as he recalled they had been some time earlier. He figured that they had all heard of the incident in the lathe department and were in agreement about working overtime. McPherson was curious about why the gluing people had improved while the rest of the plant had apparently declined. McPherson called Alex Watson, foreman of the gluing department, and complimented him on the workers' performance. Watson replied, "Coming from you, Mr. McPherson, that's a real compliment. It's good to feel like someone up front is taking an interest in us out on the floor."

When McPherson prodded him to elaborate on his department's achievements, Watson finally attributed them to a bright girl in his department, Margie Lewis.

"I don't know how she does it, Mr. McPherson, but Margie is just real good with stuff like that. My crew was pretty upset after Lloyd first came through giving orders and telling us all how to do our jobs. But Margie explained them to us, and they seemed more reasonable coming from her than from Lloyd."

Within the next week McPherson almost forgot about the incident of the previous Friday. The women had only worked one day of overtime, and on the surface things seemed to be back to normal. Thursday afternoon, August 21st, McPherson found a telephone message waiting for him from the Washington State Labor Relations Board. When he returned the call he was informed that the board had received a complaint from a group of the workers at Birkenfield. The complaint contained allegations of management harassment, low wages and poor working conditions. The workers had questioned the board about possible actions open to them, including establishing a union shop. McPherson was very disturbed at this revelation, especially since he was generally unaware of such a high level of discontent among his workers. He knew that the company could not afford unionization now; it just did not have the cash to pay higher wages or benefits.

Mr. McPherson realized that the future of Birkenfield was in jeopardy. The decisions that he would have to make now would be among the toughest of his career.

QUESTIONS AND REQUIREMENTS

1. How might McPherson improve the communication problems within Birkenfield? How might he utilize the informal group leaders?

2. What viable choices did McPherson have when the workers confronted him with their problem? Did he choose the best alternative?

3. Are Lloyd's attitude and manner toward the workers evidence of inexperience in managing human resources? Why are the workers upset really? Are they justified?

4. In trying to build up Birkenfield, is McPherson trying to do the impossible? What are his alternatives, and how realistic are they?

5. Why was Margie Lewis able to motivate and influence the gluing workers?

6. Overall, what courses of action would you recommend that McPherson follow? Why?

7

HARMONY LIFE OF HARTFORD

GLENN D. OVERMAN

Harmony Life of Hartford was one of the large insurance companies having more than 8,800,000 policyholders, 350,000 new holders in 1960. New life insurance sold by Harmony Life in 1960, $70 million above 1959 sales, totaled $2,758,000,000, of which individual insurance contributed $1,946,000,000. Premium income on individual insurance, annuities, and health insurance totaled $354 million, of which $13,888,000 was on policies written in 1960.

DATA PROCESSING AT HARMONY LIFE

Since 1953 electronic computers had played an ever-increasing role in the operation of Harmony Life. The nature of the company's business involved the handling of vast amounts of data. The functions which were performed in connection with each policy were divided among sales, underwriting, issuance, billing, collection commission payments, dividend calculations and apportionment, valuation of reserves, claims handling, termination operations (upon maturity, death, and lapse or surrender) and the preparation of general operating reports. Each of these functions included a variety of processing activities which were handled by various types of data-processing equipment.

Functions being performed by the data-processing department of Harmony Life are presented in Exhibit 1. Projects being developed and projects under study are also listed in that exhibit.

ESTABLISHMENT OF THE DATA-PROCESSING DEPARTMENT

Machine equipment had been used by various departments in Harmony Life for many years. The actuarial department (see Exhibit 2 for a partial organization chart) had used various types of machines since 1916. When the accounting department needed equipment in 1942, the actuarial department was reluctant to share its equipment because of anticipated problems in scheduling work from two departments on the same equipment. The accounting department therefore obtained its own equipment. During the next few years a large number of other

Exhibit 1 Data processing in Harmony Life of Hartford in 1961

Activity	Premium notice business[a]			Debit business[b]			Group business[c]		
	Ordinary	Annuity	Personal health	MDO[d]	MPI[e]	Ind.[f]	A&H[g]	Life & DD[h]	Annuity[i]
Sales	D	D	D	D		S	S	S	S
Underwriting	P			S		D			
Issue				P		D			
Premium billing	P	P	P	P	S	S	D	D	S
Premium acctg.	P	P	P	P	S	S	P	P	S
Dividend calculation	P	P		P			P	P	
Valuation	P	P	P	P	P	P	P		
Claims	P	P		S	S	S	P	D	P
Statistics	P	D	D	D			D	D	D

Legend: P—Being Performed; D—Being Developed; S—Under Study.

[a] Policies billed by mail (mostly large-sized policies).
[b] Policies on which premiums were collected at the home of the insured.
[c] Large combination policies covering whole factories or businesses.
[d] Monthly debit ordinary insurance (intermediate-sized policies).
[e] Monthly premium industrial insurance (no longer issued).
[f] Industrial insurance (small-sized policies).
[g] Accident and health coverages.
[h] Life accidental death and dismemberment.
[i] Retirement income coverages.

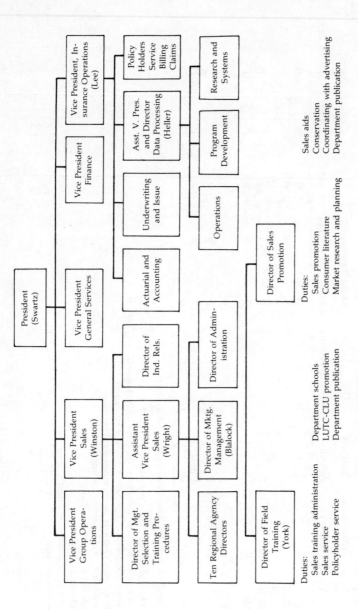

Exhibit 2   Harmony Life of Hartford abbreviated organization chart

Within the past year, some reorganization had taken place in the management of the company, reducing the number of vice presidents reporting directly to the president and combining formerly independent units. A number of the units so combined fell under the direction of the vice president, insurance operations, a new position in the organization.

functional groups obtained either mechanized or electronic data-processing equipment.

By 1958, the large investment in equipment led top management to appoint a committee to study the entire data-processing function. An outside consultant was also employed. Based on the recommendations contained in the two reports, President John Swartz issued an order to begin centralizing responsibility for all data-processing activities into one department and providing for the gradual merger of the existing equipment of all departments.

Mr. O.D. Heller was appointed assistant vice president and director of data processing to administer the new department. Mr. Heller had previously been manager of the data-processing section in the policy department. In this department he had had experience with both major types of data-processing equipment used by Harmony Life, i.e., mechanized punch-card machines and medium- and large-size electronic computers. Mr. Heller had been with the company since 1946. His prior training and experience included a degree in Business Administration and 15 years' experience in systems and procedures work with a large manufacturer of data-processing equipment.

The physical merging of equipment and data-processing activities began in 1949 when two departments were brought under the new centralized control. In 1961, the merger of the data-processing facilities of the remaining departments was completed.

The equipment available to the new department was as follows:

3 large-scale, electronic tube-type computers (plus input and output equipment)	Company owned
5 medium-sized, tube-type computers (plus input and output equipment)	Company owned
80 mechanized data-processing machines (plus auxiliary equipment of key punch, sorters and printers)	Rented

In 1961, a new large solid-state[1] computer (7070) with four auxiliary computers (1401's) were purchased at a cost of more than $1.5 million. Three of the 1401's were to be delivered at a future date. These machines were intended to replace the five medium-sized computers and, in addition, would take over most of the work performed on the mechanized data-processing equipment. It was also planned to use the new equipment to service one functional group (monthly debit ordinary) which previously had not been mechanized.

One medium-sized computer, a 1620, was permitted to remain in the actuarial department for research purposes, although general responsibility for the equipment was retained by the data-processing department. This equipment had considerable processing capacity, but the limited input and output equipment made it more adaptable to scientific or problem-type applications than to

---

[1] This equipment used transistors instead of vacuum tubes and required less servicing and air conditioning.

general business applications. Auxiliary input and output equipment could be purchased, but the irregularly occurring needs of the actuarial department made it difficult to integrate the 1620 with the computers being scheduled for regular business applications, so auxiliary equipment was not a part of the present installation.

PROBLEMS ARISING FROM THE UNIFICATION

The manager of the new data-processing department was not only confronted with the technical problems inherent in the physical merger of data-processing activities but also with the human relations problems which arose from the centralizing of responsibility and equipment outside the functional areas. Managers of these functional areas frequently made requests to the central data-processing department for services which were considered by the manager of the new department to be uneconomical or unsuited for handling by a computer. The manager had frequently rejected such requests and felt that these refusals were resulting in a reputation that the new department was often uncooperative.

Mr. Heller expressed the problem by saying, "How can we control these excessive and uneconomical requests for work on the new computer so that we can live within our budget and still keep good relations with the management of the functional departments which we serve?"

Reasons for this problem, as viewed by Mr. Heller, were:

1. Widespread publicity in the press about the capabilities of computers without explanations of their limitations, costs, and proper role.

2. Lack of rudimentary understanding by functional managers about business uses of computers.

3. Overenthusiastic reports from earlier advisory committees on results which might be expected from the new installation.

4. The presentation of vague service requests that had not been thoroughly analyzed before presentation.

ORGANIZATION AND OPERATION OF THE NEW DEPARTMENT

To carry out his new responsibilities, Mr. Heller organized the new department into three sections: (1) operations; (2) program development; and (3) research and systems. The operations section was the largest of the three and employed about 250 persons. This section was responsible for routine production. Only work that had previously been approved and programmed by the other two sections was handled by operations.

The program development section consisted of 62 persons, chiefly programmers, who did the coding, debugging, and preparing of program tapes for new applications. Only programs approved by the research and systems section were handled by the program development section.

Requests for new computer applications or variations of existing applications were received first by the research and systems section. If the request appeared to the staff of the section to have merit and indicated to them that the person making the request had rather thoroughly thought through his need, the research and systems section made an advisability study. During the study process, requests were often modified in line with suggestions from the research and systems section. This study served as a guide to the department manager in making a decision to approve or reject the request. It also served as a basis for the requesting official to determine if he wished to adopt the new procedure.

An advisability study was sometimes called a "feasibility" study, but the term "advisability" was considered by personnel in the research and systems section as more accurate since a request might be feasible but not advisable because of cost, anticipated change in operation, or other reasons. These studies usually included:

1. Statement of the problem.

2. Description of the present system, including schedules, volumes, personnel requirements, and costs.

3. Findings and recommendations, including the suggested approach and equipment, systems and programming development, time and manpower requirements, estimated computer production time, and costs and suggested conversion schedules.

4. Advantages and limitations of the suggested approach.

5. Net savings or costs.

6. Alternate approaches.

The cost of an advisability study was usually charged to the department making the request. The cost varied greatly according to the nature and complexity of the problem. The written report was often 20 to 25 pages in length.

COSTS OF PROCESSING DATA

The advisability study suggested probable costs of machine time and programming. The actual costs, however, might vary considerably from the estimate, since they were computed at the time of performance. An internal costing group outside the data-processing department allocated costs according to a current rate schedule.

Rate schedules for machine usage were difficult to formalize and publish in advance. The first computer obtained by Harmony Life was rented, and a cost figure of $300 per hour was widely discussed in the company. Later when other computers were purchased, no general rate was quoted, since costs would obviously be affected by many factors, such as rate of depreciation, number of shifts being operated, idle machine time, amount of "set-up" time in relation to running time, etc.

Although the figures were subject to frequent change, the expense analysis and controls unit was currently using the following rates for actual running time on the new solid-state computer:

Number of units	Type of equipment	Rate per hour* (each unit)
1	7070 Central Processor	$110.50
5	729 II Tape Unit	3.50
4	724 IV Tape Unit	4.50
1	1401 Central Processor	18.50
1	1402 Card Reading Punch Unit	2.50
1	1403 High Speed Printer	3.25
2	729 IIA Tape Unit	2.75

* Hourly rates were total costs, including both direct and indirect costs of labor, depreciation of equipment, and general overhead.

All of the equipment listed would be needed simultaneously on most types of computer processing, since input and output data for the Central Processor (7070) was transmitted through the 1401 and its related equipment. The number of tape units required would vary considerably according to the nature of the job. Since the 1401 was also a self-contained computer with a limited memory capacity, some jobs requiring a limited number of variables and limited memory storage could be performed using only the 1401, 1402, 1403, and 729 IIA. Single-problem computations on the 7070 using 20 variables could be processed in approximately 30 seconds.

Before any project could be placed on the computer, a "program" (machine instruction tapes) had to be prepared by the program development section. Costs of programming varied greatly according to the nature of the job. A simple program using a "canned" routine might be prepared for as little as $50. Programs for major applications, such as setting up premium billing on the machine, might require the service of six programmers for two years at a cost of approximately $84,000. Program costs generally ranged from $12,000 to $50,000.

In addition to the cost for running time on the machine and for the initial programming costs, the user was charged for "set-up" time each time the machine was used. This preparation usually included the following steps:

1. Putting on the master instruction tape

2. Clearing the memory drum

3. Reading new instructions into the machine

4. Setting the console instruction buttons

5. Mounting the input and output tapes and possibly other tapes, such as error tapes, factor tapes, etc.

6. Inserting necessary forms in the high-speed printer

These steps usually required five minutes but sometimes ran ten minutes, and they were required whether the anticipated machine running time was five seconds or five hours. Costs for set-up time were calculated at the same rate as running time.

Because of the nature of the machine operation, Mr. Heller was strongly convinced that computers should be devoted to large-volume, continuous-operation types of jobs and that small-volume, infrequent or sporadically occurring jobs could not be economically handled on the large computers because of the set-up costs for short runs.

These sporadically occurring jobs also created scheduling problems since it was difficult to schedule the machine usage in advance if there were no way of knowing whether the job might require three minutes or three hours on a specified day. In order to keep costs down, the new solid-state computer was being carefully scheduled several weeks in advance.

A REQUEST FROM THE SALES DEPARTMENT

In July of 1961, Mr. W.A. York, CLU, training director for the 5,200 agents of Harmony Life, read an article in *National Underwriter* magazine briefly describing a new service being introduced by the sales division of the Mutual Benefit Life Insurance Company, a competitive insurance firm. This service was an individualized proposal setting forth the insurance program that a prospective customer should be carrying. Pertinent facts were obtained from the customer and were fed into the computer which promptly computed a recommended insurance program based on the individual's specific needs.

Insurance programs prepared for the individual prospect were currently in use in the insurance industry. These were of two types. One was a rather simple form which assisted a salesman in comparing a customer's stated insurance needs with his present insurance program and in recommending additional coverage if needed. The form could be completed by the salesman within a few minutes in the presence of the prospect but was based upon the prospect's judgment of his personal insurance needs rather than upon an objective analysis of the facts.

A second type of program planning was done by analysis in the home office. These comprehensive proposals were based upon facts obtained from the prospect by the salesman and included such items as age, income, number and status of dependents, indebtedness, social security status, retirement plan, insurance now in force, veterans benefits, and total assets. These comprehensive proposals required from two to six hours to prepare. All proposals in the past had been manually prepared, and the announcement from Mutual Benefit was the first indication that such a comprehensive personalized proposal might be prepared by an electronic computer.

Mr. York had discouraged the use of comprehensive program planning because of the time required either by salesmen or by the home office, as many computations were necessary with this technique. He felt that salesmen could more profitably spend their time in contacting prospective policyholders and selling them insurance than in spending time doing "paper work." Manual preparation by analysis in the home office was expensive and was generally discouraged. In spite of this discouragement, salesmen occasionally requested the service. Forty proposals of this type had been prepared by Harmony Life during 1960. The average policy value in these cases was $24,453. Of the proposals prepared, one out of every three resulted in a sale, while the average of completed sales without use of the device was one out of every four or five sales presentations. The average annual premium income on the 40 prepared proposals was $1,281, of which the agent received approximately 43% the first year and 9% during each of the following 4 years, plus additional benefits in succeeding years which totaled approximately 3%. Commission rates varied on different types of policies, but the above schedule was representative of typical returns to the salesmen on the premium-notice type of business. This type of business represented 63% of the dollar volume of individual life, annuity, and health sales, and 10% of the total number of policies annually issued by the company.

Mr. York strongly favored the use of the planned program technique if machines could do the detail work at a reasonable cost. Among the benefits which he could see from this new plan were:

1. It would help the salesman to establish a professional counselor-client relationship with the prospect.

2. The prospect who provided the detailed information would be more likely to make a favorable decision.

3. Repeat sales to present policyholders would be easier.

4. The salesmen would not be required to learn any new sales techniques since the principle was already generally understood.

5. The prospect would receive a valuable service by having an answer to the question: How much insurance is enough for me?

The average number of sales annually per agent in 1960 was 56.4. It was Mr. York's opinion that this average was too low and that some technique, such as the proposed program planning, would help increase this average.

Mr. York attempted to obtain information on how the new plan had worked in the competitor's operation. He learned it was used primarily by one general agent who was a large producer, but he could not obtain other details. The competitor reported he believed that the new technique had given his firm a competitive advantage and stated that the new service was being advertised in the *New Yorker* magazine (see Exhibit 3). This information further strengthened Mr. York's conviction that the plan had genuine merit. Because of the availability of the new and superior computer, the 7070, at Harmony Life, he believed it would be possible to provide a more comprehensive sales proposal using a few more variables than that pioneered by the competitor.

Exhibit **3**

Mr. York requested from the data-processing department general estimates of cost for the proposal. He was informed that costs could not be quoted as they were dependent upon the nature of the project and the amount of estimated input and output expected. Mr. York at that time was not able to furnish specific items which should be included in the analysis. He had, however, heard that Mutual Benefit Life used 19 variables in preparing each program. He was also unable to estimate precisely the amount of expected usage as he felt this was dependent upon probable costs and the amount of encouragement given the agents by the home office. He reported that he attempted to determine if the cost might be $5,000 or $500,000, since this would determine whether or not he wished to pursue the matter further. No general estimate could be obtained from the data-processing department. He was informed that the project as presented did not appear to be acceptable for scheduling on the new computer.

In explaining his position concerning cost and usage figures, Mr. York stated:

The home office should provide service to the field agents and to the public. In sales work we can never actually tell whether a specific sales tool will pay out or not. We spend money on a sales brochure, but how can we tell exactly what the return will be? A sales meeting costs money, but we can't measure the direct returns in relation to costs. Indirect sales resulting from the expenditures can't be computed.

Why then must the computer people have definite figures on the usage before accepting a sales idea? I want to be practical about the matter, but I can't be too concerned over internal costs until we've had an opportunity to try out the new procedure to see how it works. Some things must be taken on faith when your judgment tells you it is a good idea. Obviously acquisition cost of new business can't exceed a reasonable figure, but often we can't definitely evaluate this until we try it.

Sales are the lifeblood of our business, and we must move ahead when we are convinced a new idea is a good one.

DATA-PROCESSING DEPARTMENT RESPONSE

When Mr. York made his initial contact, Mr. Heller attempted to determine what would be expected in the form of programming and anticipated output if the new idea were approved. Mr. Heller received the general impression that the project would result in a low-volume, irregularly-occurring operation, so he informed Mr. York that he would be unable to set it up on the new computer. When Mr. York pressed for a general estimate of probable costs, Mr. Heller informed him that such an estimate was impossible without extensive study of the proposal, and this study could not be undertaken unless Mr. York could provide more definite information regarding his proposal. Mr. Heller also informed him that the new computer would soon be heavily scheduled with other types of work which were clearly adapted to the new equipment.

Mr. York inquired if the job might be set up on one of the 650 computers since Mutual Benefit Life had used this type of equipment. Mr. Heller replied that a decision had been made to dispose of these machines to help defray the costs of the new solid-state computer installation. Mr. Heller explained that if one of the 650 computers, valued at $120,000, were retained for Mr. York, the air-conditioning, space, and other costs might bring the total costs to one-half million dollars. These costs would, of course, be charged to the sales department. The possibility of keeping a 650 for the sole purpose of service to the sales department was not acceptable to Mr. York.

In discussing the case, Mr. Heller analyzed it as being typical of the type of request that had to be refused. His analysis was stated as follows:

This is a low-volume job and isn't suited for a large-scale computer. The only low-volume jobs which we should consider are the "by-products" request which can be taken off existing information already in our basic file of stored information. This is not such a request.

Furthermore, we have no way of determining how many emergency or "quickie" requests we are likely to receive if the plan were adopted. Will people be calling in all the time and saying, "I need this bit of information right away," or "I've promised to get this one piece of information out in a hurry?" They forget that the set-up time is the same for one case or a thousand.

This case sounds more like a "gimmick" than a real computer problem.

We don't even know if the other personnel of the sales department support this request. Only the training director has requested it, and we don't know if the sales vice president and the field agents really want this plan. It is true that Mr. York is a good, old-line salesman who knows how to reach men to sell "insurance" instead of "policies," but we don't have any way of knowing if the rest of the sales department will support this idea if we approve his request. Anyway, I doubt Mr. York has really thought through this request. Any computer installation works on a decreasing scale of costs after the set-up has been completed, and he hasn't any information as to whether there might be one case or a thousand cases per week. It sounds like he's acting primarily on a whim based on the report of a sales gimmick at Mutual Benefit.

We have to say "no" to such requests as these because the big computer can be operated only 24 hours a day—not 25 hours—and we can't always be bringing in a new computer for computers are not like punched card equipment where small components can be added at will. It hasn't sunk in on the managers of the other departments that I can't justify asking for another one and one-half million dollar computer just to be of service on every whim they get. We ought to avoid as many of these requests as possible.

It is true that we may nip in the bud some ideas which would save or make money for the company, but we can't "cost them all out" so we are bound to make some mistakes.

We don't have the staff or the time to make detailed advisability studies of every vague idea that comes in to us, and we can't give general estimates of costs without careful study of what is involved. It we did, this would lead to all sorts of trouble. Costs can vary too greatly depending upon what is included in the request. Unless the person has taken time to sit down for a day or two to crystalize what he expects in the form of output, it is usually just a whim, so we say, "No."

In this business can you afford to be a good fellow? If I said, "Yes" to all service requests, I wouldn't ever get our main job done. Costs would go up. Then top management would think I was doing a poor job. I don't mind being called an S.O.B. by lower management as long as top management feels I am doing a good job. After all, this is a selfish world. If by being "uncooperative" we save the company thousands of dollars, then it would seem irresponsible for us to use less than extreme care in scrutinizing requests. People used to come in on Friday afternoon and say, "Put this on the punch-card machines. We want the answers on Monday." We stopped that foolishness. Now they usually have to request service in a written memorandum unless we have real confidence in their sincerity and genuine need.

Our attitude is caused by the way people come to us. It is amazing the requests we get. Historically, machine people have been considered low skilled by others in the company. Now that we have grown up that impression hasn't changed much, yet we no longer can cater to every whim when a great deal of money is involved in programming costs.

Of course, we often provide a real service to a department which has a problem that is suitable for computers, such as mailing a confirmation notice on the anniversary date of a policy which was suggested by our public accounting firm. But the volume in that case was two million. We did a smaller job for payroll recently, and they wrote us a letter of appreciation for our service.

But we take on only those jobs which we feel are worthwhile projects for the company as a whole. Even though the department requesting the service will be charged for it, it is our responsibility to try to keep things off the computer that have no business being on it.

We've given 40-minute talks in the various departments to inform management about the use and misuse of computers. If they know anything about computers, they don't come in with foolish requests, making such statements as, "I want it set up so I can get the information I need in one minute" when it takes much longer than that just to set up the machine. I believe that a general knowledge of computers should be a part of the training of all managers. We have a couple of good examples of men who worked for awhile in this department and are now managers in functional departments. Our relations with these departments are excellent.

MANAGEMENT'S CONSIDERATION

In October of 1961, President John Swartz was presented a formal request from Mr. David Winston, vice president in charge of sales. This request contained a proposal that Harmony Life adopt a sales technique similar to that of Mutual Benefit Life and that the data-processing department be directed to provide the necessary service on the new electronic computer.

The request received by Mr. Swartz had been originated by Mr. York and had been approved by Mr. Blalock, director of marketing management, and Mr.

Wright, assistant vice president for sales. Mr. Winston reported that he had previously discussed the matter with Mr. Lee, vice president of operations, who had rejected the proposal upon the advice of Mr. Heller.

In attempting to arrive at a decision on the request, Mr. Swartz weighed the following possibilities:

1. If the request were approved, this might set a precedent so that other requests of this nature would be directed to him, rather than to the newly-established data-processing department which was technically qualified to make decisions in such matters.

2. The data-processing department might use this approved request from top management as leverage to obtain approval for additional computers.

3. Disapproval of the request might be used by the sales department to shift blame to top management in case sales quotas were not reached in the coming year.

Mr. Swartz was aware that regardless of his decision on the present request, some action was needed to prevent similar cases from arising in the future. Mr. Swartz had pointed out to the board of directors when the new equipment was purchased that the centralization of equipment and responsibility would reduce costs and improve efficiency in data processing. Excessive demands on the new equipment might jeopardize the basic objective of cost reduction, but he was aware that data-processing efficiency required that functional departments have service available when their requests could be economically justified.

QUESTIONS AND REQUIREMENTS

1. Why are the issues of authority, structure, and technology relevant to personnel management?

2. List and discuss some of the human problems at Harmony Life that are consequences of increasing technology.

3. Discuss the relationship and communication between Mr. York and Mr. Heller.

4. Assume that you are President John Swartz, what decision would you make? Discuss the impact of your decision on Mr. York, Mr. Heller, and their subordinates and associates.

8
ECONOMY FASHIONS LIMITED

THOMAS KUBICEK AND HAROLD SHAFFER

When Joe Smart, president of Economy Fashions Limited, engaged the consulting firm of Fleischman and Katz Incorporated to review the organizational and management effectiveness of Economy Fashions Limited, he believed that they would assure him that he was perfectly capable of controlling Economy Fashion which he considered as easy as holding a paper tiger. However, after the first meeting between Fleischman and his chief executives, Smart had the uncomfortable feeling that he was holding a real tiger by the tail. Yet, looking back at his career in Economy Fashions, he had no idea how the tiger evolved and more perplexing what he should do about the beast or more precisely the predicament in which he now found himself.

Economy Fashions Limited were manufacturers of inexpensive men's ready-to-wear and made-to-measure suits, sports wear and young men's clothing with a 1976 sales volume of approximately eight million dollars. The company was founded by Joe's father, Harry, who had come to Canada from England in 1910 and opened an exclusive tailoring shop in Montreal. Harry soon developed a growing clientele as he had been trained by one of London's master tailors and his pleasing personality and English gentlemen's gentleman manner were easy to take by his customers. Soon he enlarged his premises and engaged one, then two, then three assistants.

Because Harry felt that he was working in a limited market he began to make made-to-measure suits for the more exclusive retailers in Montreal. These merchants were so pleased with Harry's tailoring expertise that they asked him to experiment with ready-made suits. Because of his training, he had to sell these suits at higher prices than most manufacturers, but as they contained excellent workmanship and styling, they were eagerly bought by his Montreal accounts. This encouraged him to give up his tailoring shop and go into the manufacturing of made-to-measure and ready-made suits for exclusive retail stores both inside and outside of Montreal.

However, in a few years he realized that the better suit market was limited and he looked for broader areas in which he could expand. He soon realized that mass merchandising was the answer and so he completely altered his production to turn out made-to-measure and ready-to-wear suits that could be sold in the bargain basements of Canada's largest department stores and in low-end men's wear chains. Again he was successful for no matter how inexpensive he made his suits, they still contained a touch of his early training and so they appeared to have more value and style than those of his competitors. In fact, he expanded so rapidly that he was forced to separate his production and rented space for his made-to-measure factory in another building.

In 1934 he saw the coming market for sports wear and decided to manufacture separate trousers, sports jackets and ski wear at a third factory. Again because he gave these garments the unique touch of the master tailor, he was successful even though they were sold to Canadians in the lower income brackets.

Harry's only son, Joe, has always liked the clothing business and even as a young lad he spent all his spare time doing odd jobs around the factories. In this way he learned how to lay out cloth, pack suits, work the pressing machines, etc., and, during his senior high school year, he began to wait on the trade. When he went to college he studied commerce and spent his vacations on the road with the salesmen. In each city that he visited, he talked to as many retailers as he could and from these interviews suggested to his dad a number of ways he thought his father could make Economy Fashion lines more attractive to retailers. Harry listened to his son with a smile but accepted very few of Joe's proposals. However, this never discouraged Joe as he decided that when he was president, he would inaugurate the ideas which he thought would improve Economy Fashions.

When Joe received his B. Comm. he decided that rather than continue college for his master's degree, he would enrol in a designing school in New York and then work for a few years in various men's clothing factories in the States. Then he planned to settle down and make his career in Economy Fashions. Harry was pleased with Joe's interest in Economy Fashions and proud of his academic and business accomplishments, and, after Joe's experiences in New York, Harry offered him a sales territory. Joe accepted and spent the next five years on the road and then moved into his dad's office as vice-president in charge of production and marketing. By this time Harry had begun to think of retiring and so made arrangements for Joe to buy him out. Shortly after the purchase arrangement had been concluded, Harry suffered a heart attack. When he recovered he turned the presidency of Economy Fashions over to Joe and retired to Florida.

It was soon apparent that Joe had inherited his father's tailoring genius and that his academic and practical experiences would make him a much more successful manufacturer than his dad, for the business prospered at a phenomenal rate. As Joe was an avid reader of trade and business papers, he became aware of the potential benefits of developing a specialized factory for young men's clothes and sports wear. After much thought he decided to organize a separate division for this segment of the Canadian population. This entailed renting a fourth factory site but it proved as successful a venture as his made-to-measure, and ready-to-wear and sports wear divisions.

However as Joe passed his middle forties he began to find it increasingly difficult to complete a day's work. He was fairly energetic in the morning but immediately after lunch his strength would ebb and he quickly reached a point

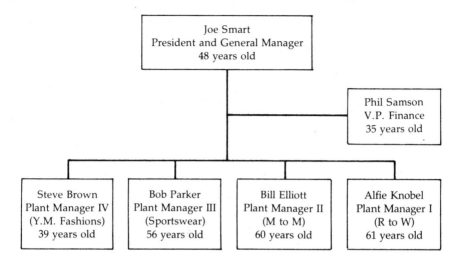

Exhibit 1   Economy Fashions Limited

where he ceased to function as he knew he must if he were to continue to run a successful business. He began to suffer from headaches, indigestion, and insomnia and finally became sufficiently worried about his health to consult his physician. The doctor assured him that his health was good but that he was suffering from too much business pressure. "Try taking things easy," the doctor said, "Go away on a leisurely holiday and when you are rested think about ways to organize your work so that you can take care of the business but still have time to relax and enjoy life."

Joe took the doctor's advice and for the first time in his life went to a small resort village where he knew no-one, and where life was conducted in a leisurely manner. At first Joe had trouble adjusting to the slow pace of the villagers, but eventually he began to accept their leisurely pace and this permitted him to think about Economy Fashions objectively.

To help him examine how the company was operating, he drew up an organizational chart (Exhibit 1). Although this chart gave the impression that Economy Fashions was highly decentralized, Joe knew that he and only he made decisions at all levels. Thus these could be as minor as purchasing another desk for the office or as important as finding the money to finance his operations, finalize style designs, or make changes in manufacturing techniques. He now realized that if he were to take the doctor's advice he would have to make the chart come true by really delegating authority to his executives and then letting them run the company. "I'll be the coach and my executives will be the team," Joe thought. "And in this way we will all work together for the betterment of Economy Fashions."

When he examined the chart more closely, he noticed that he had only one executive at the head office. This was Phil Samson, a smart young C. A. he had hired away from a competitor two years ago because he had heard that Samson was a good systems man and, at the time, Joe felt that systems organization was what he needed most. But although he gave Phil a good salary and the grandiose title of vice president-finance, Joe soon reduced Phil's real function to that of office manager. Before Joe left on his enforced vacation, he had heard rumors that Phil was very unhappy and was looking around for another position.

Joe decided that when he got back, he would elevate Phil to controller as well as vice president-finance and let him look after that end of the business. Moreover, he would hire another bright young man and make him assistant general manager and let him take care of such detailed work as minor analyses, interpretation of data, and so on. This would allow Joe to relax more frequently and still enable him to visit his factories and a certain number of his retail accounts. This was something he had wanted to do for a long time but had never managed because he was either too busy or too tired.

He recalled interviewing a Pierre Laurie who had an M.B.A. from Harvard and some experience in the needle trade. Laurie had claimed that he wanted a bigger challenge than his present position could give him. Joe decided he would hire Laurie when he got back and was pleased with this arrangement because he knew that Samson was about 35 and he thought Laurie was close to 30. Thus he would be a coach to a smart, educated young head-office team which was something he could boast about when he socialized with his competitors.

THE "COACH AND TEAM SYNDROME" CONCEPT

When he looked at the organization chart (the plant manager level), Joe Smart was not happy. All the managers except Steve Brown, who was in his late thirties and whom he hired when he went into young men's fashions were close to or in their sixties and had spent over twenty years with the company. Joe realized that the three older men had always been told what to do by his father and that he had continued with this practice when he took over. Could the four plant managers adjust to a real decentralized structure? Well he had no alternative. For his own good and that of the company he had to break down its functions into natural segments and permit the top executive of each one to run his own show. Joe and his head-office staff would act as advisors—like a head coach and his two assistants.

When Joe returned to his office, he hired young Laurie and within the week called Laurie and Samson into his office for a consultation. This consisted of an outline of his ideas for decentralization which he called his "coach-and-team syndrome" and said he wanted to put it into effect immediately. He was surprised when both young men cautioned a go-slow implementation policy and suggested that he should first test his ideas. Here he was the oldest in the group and he was pushing the youngsters instead of vice versa. Joe felt proud of

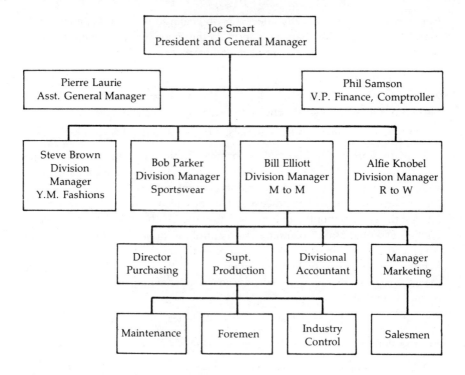

Exhibit 2   Economy Fashions Limited

Note: All divisions have the same internal organizations structures as M to M.

his new-found youth and vigor and dismissed his staff suggestions with "As far as I know, all progress in history is a result of trial and error."

Two weeks after this meeting and without further consultation with his head-office staff or the plant managers, Joe issued a memorandum that introduced his new organizational philosophy. Each plant was to be restructured as a separate division of Economy Fashions and the present managers of each plant would be elevated to the position of product divisional manager. The memo suggested that all executives below divisional manager refer to the revised organizational chart to check on their status (Exhibit 2).

This part of the memorandum concluded with

. . . we are satisfied that an organization on these lines will make the most effective use of the company resources. Furthermore, it will increase our potential to arrive at the best technical solutions aimed at the most valuable markets without incurring the duplication of expense by separate companies.

The memorandum then went on to explain that the divisional managers were to become responsible for all of their factory operations and that these would be judged on the "return-on-capital-employed concept" that had been suggested to Joe by Phil Samson shortly after Samson began to work for Economy Fashions. According to Mr. Samson's formula the following items were to be included in arriving at the amount of capital employed:

1. Fixed plant less depreciation

2. Total divisional volume of sales less the profit margin. (This included a portion of the head office overhead and current depreciation.)

3. Divisional inventories (raw materials, supplies and finished product.)

Each division would become responsible for formulating its own budget which would then become part of the over-all master plan. Divisional budgets were to be prepared by each divisional accountant, who was also responsible for the production of financial and cost statement which were to show two sets of figures: the current month, and the total-to-date. As these reports were considered an essential tool of planning and control, all projections of sales were to cover a period of 15 months. At the end of each quarter, the current budget was to be adjusted to the actual figure and then a new three-months' projection was to be added. The memorandum produced a sample of how the revolving type of budget would look.

	Actual	Budgeted	Tentative
At the beginning of the year	Oct.-Nov.-Dec.	Jan.-Feb.-Mar.	April thru Dec.
End of first quarter	Jan.-Feb.-Mar.	Apr.-May-June	July thru March
End of second quarter	Apr.-May-June	July-Aug.-Sept.	Oct. thru Jan.

As far as expenses were concerned, divisional managers were allowed to spend a thousand dollars without authorization. However, this did not include personal expenses which were to be approved by the corporate controller, nor did it encompass capital expenditures which were considered to be those items whose original costs were a hundred dollars or more and whose life extended over a one-year period. This included office furniture, equipment plant machinery etc.

Joe's memo produced considerable dismay among the newly designated divisional managers and their executives, and a foreboding awareness of the difficulties to come on the part of Laurie and Samson. It did not take long for inter-office memos to move from the divisions to the head office and back again. For example, Steve Brown writes Phil Samson:

Dear Mr. Samson:

It seems clear to me that for the purposes of which we are speaking the investment should be the assets employed by the Division minus the liabilities. To exclude the outstanding payables is in my opinion to deny that this form of financing is of importance to the operation. A rescheduling of our invoice paying only a short time ago served to free a very large sum of money for other purposes and we feel that this phase of the business should not be over-looked. Also it strikes me that monthly comparisons at the head office level would not be worthwhile. This of course is entirely your own affair. But I would suggest that a quarterly review of the divisional performance may be more meaningful.

Steve Brown

Dear Mr. Brown:

Your memo re: the use of the investment base minus the liabilities might have merit when considering the company as a whole. However, for divisional purposes I like to think that all assets used, rather then equity, constitutes the base upon which return is calculated. The rate of return should be determined from the stand point of the user rather than the supplier of capital.

Furthermore, I would like to comment on your discussion with Mr. Joe Smart re: the head office overhead. I would not be disturbed with some bookkeeping inequalities of this nature. I do not think that intention is to equate the different divisions. Since we cannot make the marketing conditions as fairly comparable as possible, I fail to see your concern about such differences of bookkeeping nature. For ultimately each division's performance will be compared against its own target, i.e.: the budget. The success or failure in meeting the target will then be equated and evaluated.

Phil Samson

The divisional managers continued to attack Samson's return-on-capital-employed concept. Mr. Alfie Knobel, manager Ready-To-Wear Division, pointed out that the return-on-capital-employed concept should be replaced by the "return-on-net-worth concept." Mr. Samson rejected this suggestion as impractical and continued to insist that divisional operating reports based on his concept be in his office not later than the seventh day of the following month. He would then review the results of each division with the president and if they indicated a serious departure from the budget, the divisional manager would be called in to explain the cause of the variances.

However, since the divisional managers continued to disagree with Mr. Samson on the return-on-capital-employed concept, divisional reports were often delayed. Jack Jones, the plant accountant in Mr. Knobel's division, strongly objected to Samson's concept and with the connivance of his divisional manager persisted in including certain adjustments in his monthly report which the controller was not ready to accept. This resulted in the correction and revision of several other reports and, thus, all the budgets were delayed. Phil Samson became very annoyed at Jack Jones and complained to the president that Jones was not qualified to do the job. Joe was inclined to believe Phil as for some time now he had had little use for divisional managers and other executives who in his opinion did not use modern management techniques and therefore did not know where they were going. Thus when Joe was on one of his usual plant visits to the ready-to-wear division, he asked Mr. Jones why he came to work at 10:00 a.m. instead of 9:00 a.m. The accountant replied that "My wife was visiting her relatives and unfortunately took the alarm clock with her. Being alone I slept in."

Later on when Mr. Smart asked for the amount of the net divisional contribution for the current month, Jones was somewhat indecisive. Angered by the accountant's apparent incompetency, Mr. Smart suggested that there was not much future for Jones in the company and that he might perhaps be better off if he looked for another position. When Mr. Knobel returned from out-of-town the following day and read Mr. Smart's memo regarding the dismissal of Mr. Jones he became very annoyed and immediately contacted the president. Smart assured Mr. Knobel that he had nothing to worry about as the Personnel

Department had a number of first-class applicants for the position of accountant for the Ready-To-Wear Division and that any of these would do a better job than Jones.

As noted by the above, Mr. Smart was extremely active and now he considered that he was not only head coach but the boss as well. He felt that he had to make every effort to visit each division and give the executives in charge all the help and consultation that his time permitted. Every morning, Joe toured one plant or another and talked to various supervisors and department heads, always stressing the point that he was just one of them; that in his company nobody should be afraid to talk to the boss because "here there was no boss, just one team with the same goal." Whether it was production, quality control, or choosing the right shades of fabrics, Joe was always ready to advise; for as he constantly reminded his team "he had had considerable experience in these lines." His afternoons were spent at the head office except when he would remember the doctor's advice and force himself to stay away from the office and pretend to relax.

Although the reports for the first quarter of 1976 indicated that it would be a good year for all lines of Economy Fashions Limited, both in terms of sales and profits, Mr. Smart felt a vague persistent uneasiness about the company's operations. In particular, he could not understand why Steve Brown had resigned as plant manager of the Young Men's Division and taken a less responsible position with a smaller salary with a competing company. Brown's resignation not only reinforced Joe's feeling that his managers seemed antagonistic to the various proposals that he made but it triggered a decision to engage a firm of management consultants to assess the effectiveness of Economy Fashions' organizational structure. The following is a transcript of the first of several meetings held by Mr. Arthur Fleischman of Fleischman and Katz, Inc. and the Economy Fashions management group that met to review the organizational and management effectiveness of Economy Fashions Limited.

Highlights of the Transcript of a Meeting of the Executive Committee of Economy Fashions Limited held in the Board Room of the company
On July 31st, 1976

PRESENT: Messrs. Smart, Parker, Elliott, Knobel, Samson and Fleischman

SMART: Gentlemen, thanks to your concerted effort we are in the happy position of being a company which, I feel, and the records indicate, is going places. But going places presents problems and I have asked you to attend this meeting so that we can have a frank and open discussion of these problems. I am sure that by now you have all met Mr. Fleischman whom I have retained to study our organization and to advise us on any possible improvements. At this point, I would like to ask Mr. Fleischman to take the Chair and come right to the point, Mr. Fleischman.

FLEISCHMAN: Gentlemen, this is the first of a series of meetings which I would like to utilize for a two-fold purpose: First, I would like to review our investigations of your operations in order to make sure we have a clear picture of how you are managing your company, and the problems you are facing. Second, I would like to start considering some of these issues in terms of their implications for your business. I would like to open this discussion with a question which I feel is indicative of the kind of problems you now face. Why did Steve Brown leave?

PARKER: If I may?

FLEISCHMAN: By all means.

PARKER: Steve and I had a good relationship, and we still meet occasionally. I posed some questions to him and he told me that he quit because of two things. Firstly, he saw no prospects for advancement shortly after Mr. Laurie joined the company, and secondly because he was fed up with heavy responsibilities but no freedom to manage.

SMART: How could he say that? With increasing sales, all our managerial jobs have been getting bigger and bigger, with salaries none of our competitors can match. Furthermore, ever since we decentralized, Steve commanded far more authority and responsibility than he had ever done before. For all practical purposes he was running his own business. If this isn't freedom to manage, I do not know what is. I cannot see what Laurie had to do with Steve.

PARKER: Assistant General Manager is a higher position than that of Division Manager. Steve is extremely ambitious, and with his experience and degree in Business he felt he was well qualified for the Assistant General Manager position. No doubt he saw it as a stepping stone to the position of General Manager.

SMART: General Manager? But Laurie was not hired with that end in mind— and I never even thought of him as part of my executive committee. His main job was to help me with paper work analysis, interpretation of data, and so on. I am sure Steve would not have liked that kind of work or not being on my executive team.

FLEISCHMAN: This seems to me to be a typical case of lack of communication. Normally, the title of Assistant General Manager conveys line relationship. If Mr. Laurie's position is that of a staff employee, don't you think it should be so designated?

KNOBEL: I would like to come back to Bob's remark (points to Parker) regarding the assumption of "heavy responsibilities but no freedom to manage." I believe that the financial set-up we have here is nothing but vaguely defined cost centers, in a centralized company. Yet, our performance, even our competence, is measured with data over which we have little or no control. On one hand, Joe insists on autonomous divisions; on the other he comes to my plant and fires my employees, in my absence, without my knowledge or approval. Would you call this freedom to manage?

SAMSON: If you are referring to Jack Jones, then I would answer. It was I who insisted to Joe, that Jones should be fired. You know very well, Alfie, that he was not qualified to do that particular job. I am sure Joe saved you the embarrassment of having to fire him yourself.

KNOBEL: Phil, was Jones working for you, or was he working for me? If he was working for me, then I was responsible for both his reports and their content. He reported what I told him to report, so any confusion in his reports could be a reflection on the deficiency of your system.

SMART: Don't tell me that you are still sulking over the Jones' case. We have discussed it too often, I don't want to hear about it again.

KNOBEL: Well you asked for a frank discussion. I have mentioned only one of the many causes why people are beginning to be dissatisfied around here. There are others. For instance, I do not believe that my performance can be measured by costs over which I have no control, such as apportioning the head office costs to divisions on the basis of divisional contribution to total sales. Neither do I believe in the formula of performance appraisal through return on capital employed.

ELLIOTT: I'd say Alfie is right. I find that some of my best men are becoming dissatisfied in spite of my trying hard to prevent it. You must realize that as the company gets bigger, its becoming more unwieldy and I believe that unless we stop and consolidate what we are now operating, Economy Fashions may get out of control before we realize it.

SMART: Well, this is exactly why we're here and what I am trying to do. To keep everything under control. With my experience I can assist with various operating problems. At the same time, my mixing with the people promotes an informal atmosphere. I do not want to stifle their initiative by governing them with an iron hand.

ELLIOTT: I don't agree!

SMART: What do you mean?

ELLIOTT: Well, your frequent visits to our plants, whatever the intention, are undermining our authority in the divisions. Instead of discussing operating problems with us, you go directly to our subordinates saying that, in fact, there is no boss in this company. For this reason, if my employees have a problem, they ignore me and wait for your next visit to approach you with it.

SMART: But the trend today is away from the structured organization. The team spirit facilitates a better environment and of course helps to build a better worker morale.

ELLIOTT: Do you feel that it is proper to go around the authority of your divisional managers rather than channeling everything through them? You know, with your attitude you may either encourage talebearing, or the divisional supervisors might acquire the habit of leaning on you as a crutch instead of trying to think for themselves.

SMART: I think that group participation rather than a strict superior versus subordinate relationship is highly stimulating and productive.

FLEISCHMAN: Your intention is a good one Mr. Smart. However, do your regular visits to the plants get the desired results? In my experience I have come across two different practices. One, that the top manager should be concerned solely with strategic functions; the other that both operating and strategic functions are his domain. Both of these seem to be correct. However, their applicability usually varies with the size of the company and the kind of its particular environment.

SAMSON: I have a feeling that we are wasting our time on trivial things, while neglecting bigger issues, such as: better communication, problem of reporting, control, etc.

FLEISCHMAN: I thought you were proud of your budgetary control system?

SAMSON: Well, it is true that we have a better system than a number of our competitors; however, there are still deficiencies in it which need correcting.

FLEISCHMAN: Why do you think your reports are late?

PARKER: I'll answer that! Because the division managers don't believe in them. There is not only a lack of planning but today we are told to do this, and tomorrow to do that. It looks like our only objective is opportunistic exploitation of changing situations regardless of the long-range consequences. Our accountants are overworked because of constant "crash programs" for the head office. I believe that, with a little more planning and organizing all this "extinguishing of business brushfires" could be avoided.

SMART: Our planning must be adaptable to fast movement. You mustn't forget that this is a constantly changing industry. If we miss an opportunity, it will never come back.

SAMSON: And under these circumstances, it takes time to establish smoothly running procedures.

KNOBEL: I agree, but it is not what we do not do here that is worrying us; rather it is what we do and how we are doing it. For instance, there is no doubt that control over expenditures must be maintained. But, I cannot see the practicality of the present limits. Don't you think that all such controls should be built into the divisional budget for which we are responsible, rather than deprive us of the opportunity to buy most of the things we need to operate?

SAMSON: Ours is a pretty common procedure which is followed by the best companies and while theoretically in decentralized operations the budgets should control both the capital and expense expenditures, in practice, some of the best-managed companies are keeping a grip on the purse strings, regardless of the amounts budgeted. Further, our formula of the return on capital employed is a valuable management appraisal tool. Do you know of any better?

FLEISCHMAN: Although this is a good way to check on the over-all company performance, there may be some doubt how equitable it would be for use in divisions like yours. Furthermore, I would call it a method of control rather than an appraisal system.

ELLIOTT: Do I understand you right, Phil, that you are seeking even more control, when I feel that the conflict here results from the fact that the head office controls all purchases, all salaries above common labour, and that most of our designs emanate from the head office? In fact, everything except production seems to be controlled by the head office.

SMART: I never made a secret about it. Our company is centralized for control purposes and decentralized for operating purposes. Under our system many items are budgeted, but must be re-approved by top management at the time actual expenditures are to be made. This procedure could be credited for our excellent cash position.

FLEISCHMAN: Well gentlemen we've made a good start. We have aired several issues. We are all aware of the fact that a lack of tight control over expenditures could run you out of house and home. However, there are other issues equally important we have not touched on yet. For example, how is your organizational structure to be built? Is it at present a typical staff and line organization or is it a functional one? Further, should the functions and the locus of accountability of the plant accountant, the purchasing agent, and the designer be more clearly defined than at present? Maybe we should even determine whether there is any need for job descriptions, or manpower planning, including the retirement age for executives and other personnel. All these areas are serious considerations in a company like yours. I would therefore like you to think about these and other problems which must be solved if we want to formulate a more viable organizational structure for Economy Fashions than it has at present.

Thank you, gentlemen, for coming, and this meeting is now adjourned.

QUESTIONS AND REQUIREMENTS

1. If you were Joe Smart, would you have restructured Economy Fashions? If so, how? If not, why?

2. What is the basic issue facing Joe Smart? Rank order secondary issues.

3. How would you characterize Joe Smart's management style and assumptions about people? Phil Samson's?

4. If you were the personnel manager at Economy Fashions what would you have done to alleviate the tension in the organization?

5. Regarding the firing of Jack Jones, what fallacy(ies) do you see in the statement that Mr. Knobel "had nothing to worry about as the personnel department had a number of first-class applicants for the position?"

6. What problems do you foresee in Economy Fashions's interactions with the consultants?

9
REDUCTION IN FORCE

MARGARET FENN

The Research and Development Division of a large manufacturing company announced that it was reducing its staff by about three percent. The actual reduction would consist of fifty employees from a staff of thirteen hundred and fifty.

Late in November the President of the company sent a letter to all employees informing them of the cutback. The effective dates of the layoffs were to start the first week in January and be completed by the first of April, depending upon the individual circumstances of the employees involved.

By waiting until after the first of the new calendar year to start the layoffs, the company in fact allowed the employees to become eligible for vacations for the new year. The employee would then receive compensation for his vacation time in addition to the Supplemental Unemployment Benefits (S.U.B.) which amounts to one week's pay for each year of service.

It had been rumored through the years that the company had a policy of laying off five percent of its staff each year and subsequently increasing its staff by a like amount. It was argued by those who put stock in the hearsay that the company used this technique to continually upgrade its staff. The company in fact didn't follow the above policy the past few years, although the current reduction in staff was the second in the last three years.

The Research and Development Division was overrunning its budget by about four million dollars on an annual basis. This was given as the principal reason for the staff reduction. The staff reduction would reduce expenditures over a year's time by approximately $700,000.

One particular section within the division was particularly hard hit. Of its twenty-six staff members, thirteen were scheduled to be laid off by the first of February and the balance by the first of April. The reason for the complete elimination of this particular group was that the project it was involved in had been terminated. Many of the members of this group had only been with the company one year. These men were particularly bitter when they were placed on the "available-for-interview" list. Because of the overall budget situation within the R&D Division, being placed on an "available-for-interview" list was tantamount to being placed on a "reduction-in-staff" list.

Many of the employees felt that the timing of the announcement was bad since it was less than a month until Christmas. Other employees felt that the reason as given by the R&D Division for the layoffs was not the real reason. They argued that the parent company had covered the R&D Division budget overruns in past years.

Those employees supporting the company's position that a cutback was required felt that the company announced the layoffs in November so that those affected could have as much notice as possible prior to the actual cutback. Also, they added that the company could have made the layoffs effective prior to the first of the new year, thereby depriving the affected employees of the vacation pay for the subsequent year.

QUESTIONS AND REQUIREMENTS

1. How would you structure and administer the R&D division both to retain some staff and to reduce expenditures?

2. What arguments can be made—pro and con—about the timing and pattern of layoffs?

3. What would you as personnel manager do to soothe the feelings of the terminated employees? How would you reduce insecurity in the remaining staff?

4. What reasons can you give for a large manufacturing company so drastically reducing its R&D division?

PART III
BEHAVIORAL-SCIENCE CONCEPTS AND ASSUMPTIONS

The behavioral sciences are generally regarded as including the disciplines of psychology, sociology, and anthropology. Research in each of these fields has made increasing use of work organizations as focal points for study. The findings of these research studies, therefore, have direct application to personnel and general managers who wish to improve organizational performance in personnel management. While this research has been extremely helpful in each of the six personnel processes, research from all three of the major behavioral science disciplines also has meaning to the organization at large. The concepts of motivation and job satisfaction, for example, draw in large portion from the field of psychology and, to a somewhat less significant extent, from sociology and anthropology. Leadership has also been the object of extensive research work in these fields. Organization climate and even more important the concept of organizational justice relate to a greater extent to organizations and their cultures, subjects addressed by sociologists and anthropologists.

The detailed examination of these topic areas is best done in course work specifically designed to study organizational behavior. For our purposes, however, we can discuss the topics briefly and then point to cases or incidents that illustrate each topic. Motivation is a process that causes persons to behave in specified ways. Models of motivation, such as the Maslow need hierarchy or the Lawler-Porter performance-reward-satisfaction model, are attempts to construct a simple arrangement of elements of a system to explain the motivation of individuals under different conditions. Some authors view job satisfaction as a key element in motivation. Herzberg maintains that some factors, when present to a positive degree, increase satisfaction from work and motivation toward superior effort and performance. Research studies relating job satisfaction to higher levels of performance have not, however, supported this general model. Lawler and Porter, in a more complex model, see job satisfaction as being derived *from* performance and from the rewards associated with the performance. Motivation, in the Lawler-Porter model, is based in large part on individual needs and the expectations that those needs will be met by exerting effort.

Job satisfaction, however, is a useful *objective* for organizations and managers. Indeed, current research and practices are directed at ways in which job satisfaction can be maintained and increased while addressing the issues of high productivity and overall organizational effectiveness.

"The Robert Morton Case" describes a situation involving a history of problems with an employee whom many of us would describe as "not well motivated." As you examine the case, you should determine the factors that seem to produce Robert Morton's behaviors: elements of motivation producing both acceptable and unacceptable acts. Determine what single behavioral science or combination of the three sciences you used as the basis for your analysis.

Effective leadership has been defined as the influencing of individual and group behavior toward the optimal attainment of the organizational enterprises' goals.[1] In turn, a leader is a person who influences others in the direction of the leader's goals. Leadership styles, or forms of leader behavior, have been described in a variety of ways. In one conceptual categorization, leaders have been described as being democratic in their styles at one extreme and autocratic at the other. Another body of leadership behavior research, which originated in the 1950s at Ohio State University, identified initiating structure (a task orientation) and consideration (an interpersonal orientation) as two major dimensions of leader behavior. In this research work, unlike the autocratic/democratic conceptual treatment, a leader can behave in *both* dimensions; that is, he or she can be task *and* interpersonally oriented at the same time. Indeed, research findings tend to demonstrate that the more effective leader emphasizes both dimensions.

Organization climate, a topic that has been given considerable research attention in recent years, is seen as a variable that intervenes between organizational variables such as organization structure or leadership style and the end result variables of productivity and job satisfaction. Four major dimensions seem to be found in many of the organization climate studies:

1. the extent of individual autonomy
2. the extent of structure
3. the reward orientation
4. the extent of consideration, warmth, and support[2]

---

[1] Wendell L. French, *The Personnel Management Process*, 3rd ed. (Boston: Houghton Mifflin, 1974), p. 117.
[2] J.P. Campbell, M.D. Dunnette, E.E. Lawler III, and K.E. Weick, *Managerial Behavior, Performance, and Effectiveness* (New York: McGraw-Hill, 1970), p. 393.

"The Lordstown Plant of General Motors" case describes a well-publicized situation in which a modern high-speed production plant located in a semirural area near Warren, Ohio, encounters worker resistance expressed in terms of extremely high rates of quality defects and grievance levels. In many ways, this case exemplifies problems encountered by management in the highly advanced technology of the 1970s. Readers should keep in mind the factors that form the setting for workers in this case, factors that frame an external environment and those that contribute to the internal climate of the plant.

Organizational justice, the last major topic addressed in this section, relates very closely to organization climate. It refers to the process that allocates rewards and penalties to organization members in some relationship to perceptions of fairness or equity. Distributive justice refers to fairness in the allocation of rewards according to merit. This allocation has been framed in ratio and proportion form by Homans and Adams and is discussed in the research literature on equity theory.

Corrective justice refers to the remedy of injustice or the processes by which individuals can be heard despite actions pending against them. Contract negotiation, managerial reviews, and grievance procedures for both union and nonunion employees all serve to assist in seeing that due process exists for the correction of injustices in the treatment of organizational members.

The incident entitled "I Wasn't the Only One" gives the reader the opportunity to examine the concepts of equity and corrective justice in a situation that might occur in nearly any organization. It is useful to see the extent to which the leadership style of Mr. Minad might have contributed to the total situation.

In all the cases and incidents in this section, several important topics should be considered. First, to what extent has a change in technology (an external factor) caused an internal change in structure, authority relationships, and job requirements? Second, what leadership patterns and organization climates seem evident? Are they appropriate for the technology, the task, and the makeup of members of the organizations? Finally, to what extent did issues of organizational justice appear? In what dimensions?

SUGGESTED READINGS

Adams, J.S. "Toward an Understanding of Inequity." *Journal of Abnormal and Social Psychology,* Vol. 67 (1963): 422–436.

Bennis, Warren. *The Unconscious Conspiracy: Why Leaders Can't Lead.* New York: Amacom, 1976.

Campbell, J.P., M.D. Dunnette, E.E. Lawler III, and K.E. Weick, Jr. *Managerial Behavior, Performance, and Effectiveness.* New York: McGraw-Hill, 1970, 387–410, 412–414.

Carrell, M.R., and J.E. Dittrich. "Employee Perceptions of Fair Treatment." *Personnel Journal* (October 1976): 523–524.

Cass, Eugene L., and Frederick G. Zimmer, eds. *Man and Work in Society*. New York: Van Nostrand Reinhold Company, 1975.

Deci, B.L. *Intrinsic Motivation*. New York: Plenum Press, 1975.

Dittrich, J.E., and M.R. Carrell. "Dimensions of Organizational Fairness as Predictors of Job Satisfaction, Absence, and Turnover." *Academy of Management Proceedings* (1976): 79–83.

Fiedler, F.E. "Engineer the Job to Fit the Manager." *Harvard Business Review*, Vol. 46(1) (September-October 1965): 115–122.

French, W.L. *The Personnel Management Process*, 4th ed. Boston: Houghton Mifflin, 1978, Chapters 6–8.

Gellerman, S.W. *The Management of Human Resources*. Hinsdale, Ill.: The Dryden Press, 1976.

Goodman, P.S., and A. Friedman. "An Examination of Adams' Theory of Inequity." *Administrative Science Quarterly*, Vol. 16 (September 1971): 271–288.

Greene, Charles N. "The Satisfaction-Performance Controversy." *Business Horizons*, Vol. 15, No. 15 (October 1972): 31–41.

Herzberg, F. "One More Time: How Do You Motivate Employees?" *Harvard Business Review*, Vol. 46(1) (January-February 1968): 53–62.

House, R.J., and T.R. Mitchell. "Path Goal Theory of Leadership." *Journal of Contemporary Business* (Autumn 1974): 81–97.

House, R.J., and L.A. Wigdor. "Herzberg's Dual Factor Theory of Job Satisfaction and Motivation: A Review of the Evidence and a Criticism." *Personnel Psychology*, Vol. 20 (Winter 1967): 369–389.

Hunt, J.G., and J.W. Hill. "The New Look in Motivation Theory for Organizational Research." *Human Organization* (Summer 1969).

Jaques, B. *Equitable Payments*. New York: Wiley, 1961.

Kerr, S., and Chester Schriesheim. "Consideration, Initiating Structure and Organizational Criteria—An Update of Korman's 1966 Review." *Personnel Psychology*, Vol. 27, No. 4 (Winter 1974): 555–568.

Lawler, E.E., III. *Motivation in Work Organizations*. Monterey, Calif.: Brooks/Cole, 1973.

————, and J.L. Suttle. "A Causal Correlational Test of the Need Hierarchy Concept." *Organizational Behavior and Human Performance*, Vol. 7 (1972): 265–287.

Litwin, G.H., and R.A. Stringer, Jr. *Motivation and Organizational Climate*. Boston: Div. of Research, Graduate School of Business Administration, Harvard University, 1968.

Roscow, Jerome M. *The Worker and the Job*. Englewood Cliffs, N.J.: Prentice-Hall, 1974.

Roter, Ben. "Personnel Selection, an Update." *Personnel Journal* (January 1976): 23–25, 27.

Rush, H., and W. Wikstrom. "The Reception of Behavioral Science in Industry." *The Conference Board Record* (September 1969): 45–54.

Scanlan, B.K. "Determinates of Job Satisfaction and Productivity." *Personnel Journal* (January 1976): 12–14.

Stogdill, Ralph M. *Handbook of Leadership.* New York: The Free Press, 1974.

Tannenbaum, R., and W.H. Schmidt. "How to Choose a Leadership Pattern." *Harvard Business Review*, Vol. 36 (1958): 95–101.

Vroom, V.H. *Work and Motivation.* New York: Wiley, 1964.

10
THE ROBERT MORTON CASE

RICHARD W. BEATTY

The Crystal City installation was a subsidiary of a major corporation in the defense industry which was kept under tight security. Because of the various federal contracts, the Office of Federal Contract Compliance (OFCC) maintained records on the number of minority employees in the total work force of 3,500. To meet OFCC quotas the company was engaged in programs designed to employ and train the hard-core unemployed as well as special summer programs to aid in the employment of disadvantaged youth. These programs were in addition to the company's regular programs for employees to receive high school equivalency through General Education Development (GED) examinations and college level courses which might help an employee better perform his/her current job or a job to which they might be promoted. In addition to the managerial and technical personnel required to run the plant there were several departments with hourly employees, all represented by one or more unions.

Most of the company's hourly employees entered the company through Plant Services, usually in janitorial jobs and moved upward into higher paying production jobs as their plant seniority increased. The company personnel director reported that the plant had employees with relatively high educational levels because of the stress on education in the surrounding community, the good wages paid, and the prestige of working in the plant. In fact, many of the janitorial jobs are held by persons who the Personnel Department indicated were qualified to hold staff positions with other companies but preferred these jobs because of the pay, prestige, and opportunity for advancement within the Crystal City plant.

One of the plant's employees, Robert Morton, was a twenty-nine year old black who was born and raised in the South. He was intelligent, had finished high school, and therefore the company did not, nor did Morton, feel he qualified for the special program for the hard-core unemployed. He was married, separated from his wife and had no children. Morton lived in a nearby large city requiring about a one-half hour to drive to the plant in good weather (i.e., when there was no snow or ice on the roads, a frequent occurrence in the winters).

Morton was not initially placed in a janitorial position, but was given a job as a night guard in the Plant Protection Department. The personnel department and many long-term janitorial workers thought of the security guard jobs as one of the more prestigious hourly jobs and as one of the better paying jobs in the plant. The guard job required using an automobile to get from place to place to check locks on a specified schedule. The considerable time between checking locks was to be used cruising around the plant looking for unauthorized persons and, as the Chief of the Plant Protection department said, "to provide a tight security image to both insiders and outsiders." It was generally agreed by many plant employees that a lapse in security could have international implications for military defense.

Although Morton had been on the job for almost a year, during the last six months he had begun to report late for work or fail to report to work, use his sick leave, leave work without permission, and frequently was found sleeping in his guard car. Subsequently the night shift captain of the Guard Force gave Morton a verbal warning about his attendance and about his failure to report that he was not coming to work or that he was leaving early. Morton said he understood the seriousness of the problem and especially the need for tight plant security and indicated he would try to improve. Soon he was failing to report for work, late for work, and was leaving early. Again he was given verbal warnings by the night shift captain, the last of which was written and placed in the files of the Plant Protection Department. Morton was then found sleeping in his guard car which was reported to the Chief of Plant Protection who placed a reprimand in Morton's file with the Personnel Department. Morton was informed of this action by a copy of the reprimand placed in his mail box. Morton continued his past attendance patterns which became serious enough that the captain of the night shift decided that at the next incident Morton would be laid off three days without pay. One morning the captain went looking for Morton when he failed to respond to calls over the radio. The captain found Morton's guard car parked in the lot provided for the force. Morton had apparently left work forty-five minutes early. Morton was informed of his layoff by a note in his box when he next reported for work, he said nothing, left, and reported to work three days later. A few weeks later the night captain again could not find Morton, but eventually located him sleeping in his guard car. This incident was reported to the Chief of Plant Protection who initiated discharge procedures which gave Morton two weeks to find another job at the plant before he was terminated from the company.

Morton appealed his termination from the guard force to the company's Equal Employment Opportunity Board, charging that it was a discriminatory action, but the Board found no evidence of discrimination. There had, however, been several incidents of discrimination in the guard force in the past all of which the Board had upheld in favor of the minority persons filing the cases. In fact, seventy percent of the total cases in the plant brought to the Board were found in favor of the minority complainant.

The Chief of Plant Protection then called the Plant Services Manager and discussed the company's poor record of hiring and maintaining minority employees, and the consistent failure to meet minority employment quotas. He then asked the Plant Services Manager to interview Morton, who the chief said should make a good employee because of his intelligence and ability and his 12 months of experience with the company. Morton was interviewed and given a job in janitorial services where he would lose approximately twenty cents per hour, all of his union seniority (in guard services), and the prestige of working in Plant Protection.

On the four-to-twelve shift in Plant Services there were two crews, one in administration and one in production. Each crew had thirteen members composed of a mix of high school graduates aspiring to the better plant jobs, college students planning to leave as soon as they received their degrees or be promoted to managerial positions when they opened, and old-time members of the janitorial staff. Each crew had minority employees, especially chicanos and blacks. The crews were continually in conflict with management over communication problems and lines of authority. For example, Jack Heston, an old-time crew member, described the crews as follows:

> We've always had morale problems. No one ever seems to know what management wants, they always change procedures on us and never tell us, or when they do someone else tells us to do it differently. Nothing ever gets straight around here and everyone in the building thinks he can give orders to the crew.

As Heston indicated, there was often confusion about work assignments and procedures which frequently created tension within the crews, especially when there was a push for the crews to get more done. Such "pushes" usually came after management had held cost-cutting sessions and had taken the manager of Plant Services "over the coals" for more efficiency in the operation of janitorial crews. The crews, however, had developed a way of dealing with this tension as reported by another old-timer, Carl Slater. He said:

> Every time it gets tense around here we know how to keep those bums in line. We make sure we make no mistakes, everyone comes to work on time, and everything is done right. We just don't get any more done. That usually fixes them.

Slater also indicated that there was considerable peer pressure to go along with the "program" and most everyone did.

When Robert Morton first reported to Plant Services he was assigned to the crew in the administration building which had several blacks. After the probationary period of ninety days it was decided that Morton should be moved to the production crew because it had a black supervisor although no black members. This switch was decided upon by the two crew supervisors when the administration building supervisor reported that Morton was again reporting late for work (40% of the time), having unexcused absences, taking his sick leave as soon as it was earned, sitting in the back of the building where he could not be found, sleeping on the job, having a "bad attitude" toward his supervisor and other members of the crew, and being a "poor influence" on other blacks in the administration crew. During the ninety day period he missed twenty-four days of work. He was evaluated every thirty days as is required when an employee is on probation in a new job. These evaluations went into Morton's permanent personnel file and were never discussed with him because as his supervisor said, "he knows what he is doing." Despite this poor performance Morton was not given the "extremely unsatisfactory" necessary to be terminated at the end of the probationary period.

When he reported to the production crew, his behavior changed very little other than he began to take college courses away from the plant which his new supervisor said provided him with some excuses for his lateness. In response to his new supervisor his attitude did not change, but he did appear more willing to listen to what a black supervisor was telling him than he did with his previous white supervisors. He still was frequently found "hiding out" and sleeping on the job.

Several of the members of his crew, both whites and chicanos, described Morton as "arrogant" and they felt he defied them to make comments to show that he was inferior or to differentiate him from other members of the crew. An example of his "arrogance" was mentioned by one white member of Morton's crew who doubled as the late shift cashier in the company cafeteria. One evening Morton entered the cafeteria line with a chicano friend, a guard named Al Lucero. Morton had his "meal chip" with him which is given to employees to provide them a free meal when working overtime. Usually the cashier says nothing if an employee with a "chip" takes an extra piece of pie or two pieces of meat, and only records the cost of the meal. Occasionally someone is questioned for abusing the meal privilege, but very seldom, and only in the case of severe offenses.

As Morton and Lucero went through the line they both took full meals with extra desserts and turned in only one "chip." The cashier felt that Morton was challenging him and "showing off" to his friend by trying to impress him with the benefits of his new job. The cashier said nothing, merely recorded the cost of the meals and then reported the incident to their supervisor. The supervisor discussed the situation with Morton and reported it to the Plant Services Manager. The Services manager told the supervisor to forget the incident because of the past experiences with Morton and because he feared that Morton might file another discrimination case against the plant. Morton, however, did apologize to his fellow crew member who served as the cashier "for the position he had placed him in." And for two weeks Morton was on time for work and his attitude toward the members of his crew seemed to change, but his work habits remained the same.

EPILOGUE

Morton has now been in Plant Services for a year and a half and the same complaints about his lateness, work habits, and attitude remain. He does have two brothers who are successfully employed in the same plant. One was formerly in Plant Services and had good work habits, got along well with his co-workers and was promoted to a production job. Morton's financial needs are apparently being met as he has never borrowed money from the Credit Union or co-workers despite his frequently being docked for lateness or for not reporting to work at all. Another of his co-workers mentioned that all Robert really needed was some personal attention, counseling and for someone to explain what the company expects, what he can get in return, and what supportive services are available to him.

QUESTIONS AND REQUIREMENTS

1. If you were the personnel manager in this organization, how would you handle Robert Morton's case?

2. Brainstorm a list of possible reasons for Robert Morton's behavior.

3. What does your list of reasons for Morton's behavior suggest as ways to motivate and satisfy Robert Morton? What implications does this have for other employees?

11
LORDSTOWN PLANT OF
GENERAL MOTORS

HAK-CHONG LEE

INTRODUCTION

In December 1971, the management of the Lordstown Plant was very much concerned with an unusually high rate of defect Vegas coming off the assembly line. For the previous several weeks, the lot with a capacity of 2,000 cars had been filled with Vegas which were waiting for rework before they could be shipped out to the dealers around the country.

The management was particularly disturbed by the fact that many of the defects were not the kinds of quality deficiency normally expected in an assembly production of automobiles.[1] There was a countless number of Vegas with their windshields broken, upholstery slashed, ignition keys broken, signal levers bent, rear-view mirrors broken, or carburetors clogged with washers. There were cases in which, as the Plant Manager put it, "the whole engine blocks passed by 40 men without any work done on them."

Since then, the incident in the Lordstown Plant has been much publicized in news media, drawing public interest. It has also been frequently discussed in the class room and in the academic circles. While some people viewed the event as "young worker revolt," others reacted to it as a simple "labor problem." Some viewed it as "worker sabotage," and others called it "industrial Woodstock."

This case describes some background and important incidents leading to this much publicized and discussed industrial event.

The General Motors Corporation is the nation's largest manufacturer. The Company is a leading example among many industrial organizations which have achieved organizational growth and success through decentralization. The philosophy of decentralization has been one of the most valued traditions in General Motors from the days of Alfred Sloan in the 1930's through Charles Wilson and Harlow Curtice in the 1950's and up to recent years.

This case was developed for instructional purposes from published sources and interviews with the General Motors Assembly Division officials in Warren, Michigan, and Lordstown, Ohio. The case was read and minor corrections were made by the Public Relations Office of the GMAD. However, the author is solely responsible for the content of the case. The author appreciates the cooperation of General Motors. He also appreciates the suggestions of Professor Anthony Athos of Harvard and Mr. John Grix of General Motors which improved this case.

[1] The normal defect rate requiring rework was fluctuating between 1–2% at the time.

Under decentralized management, each of the company's car divisions, Cadillac, Buick, Oldsmobile, Pontiac and Chevrolet, was given a maximum autonomy in the management of its manufacturing and marketing operations. The assembly operations were no exception, each division managing its own assembly work. The car bodies built by Fisher Body were assembled in various locations under maximum control and coordination between the Fisher Body and each car division.

In the mid-1960's, however, the decentralization in divisional assembly operations was subject to a critical review. At the divisional level, the company was experiencing serious problems of worker absenteeism and increasing cost with declines in quality and productivity. They were reflected in the overall profit margins which were declining from 10% to 7% in the late 1960's. The autonomy in the divided management in body manufacturing and assembly operations, in separate locations in many cases, became questionable under the declining profit situation.

In light of these developments, General Motors began to consolidate in some instances the divided management of body and chassis assembly operations into a single management under the already existing General Motors Assembly Division (GMAD) in order to better coordinate the two operations. The GMAD was given an overall responsibility to integrate the two operations in these instances and see that the numerous parts and components going into car assembly get to the right places in the right amounts at the right times.[2]

THE GENERAL MOTORS ASSEMBLY DIVISION (GMAD)

The GMAD was originally established in the mid 1930's, when the company needed an additional assembly plant to meet the increasing demands for Buick, Oldsmobile, and Pontiac automobiles. The demands for these cars were growing so much beyond the available capacity at the time that the company began, for the first time, to build an assembly plant on the west coast which could turn out all three lines of cars rather than an individual line. As this novel approach became successful, similar plants turning out a multiple line of cars were built in seven other locations in the east, south and midwest. In the 1960's the demand for Chevrolet production also increased, and some Buick-Oldsmobile-Pontiac plants began to assemble Chevrolet products. Accordingly, the name of the division was changed to GMAD in 1965.

In order to improve the quality and productivity, the GMAD increased its control over the operations of body manufacturing and assembly. It reorganized jobs, launched programs to improve efficiency, and reduced the causes of

[2] A typical assembly plant has five major assembly lines—hard trim, soft trim, body, paint, and final—supported by sub-assembly lines which feed to the main lines such components as engines, transmissions, wheels and tires, radiators, gas tanks, front and sheet metal, and scores of other items. The average vehicle on assembly lines has more than 5,500 items with quality checks numbering 5 million in a typical GMAD assembly plant in a 16-hour a day operation.

defects which required repairs and rework. With many positive results attained under the GMAD management, the company extended the single management concept to six more assembly locations in 1968 which had been run by the Fisher Body and Chevrolet Divisions. In 1971, the GM further extended the concept to four additional Chevrolet-Fisher Body assembly facilities, consolidating the separate management under which the body and chassis assembly had been operating. One of these plants was the Lordstown Plant.

The series of consolidation brought to eighteen the number of assembly plants operated by the GMAD. In terms of total production, they were producing about 75% of all cars and 67% of trucks built by the GM. Also in 1971, one of the plants under the GMAD administration began building certain Cadillac models, thus involving GMAD in production of automobiles for each of the GM's five domestic car divisions as well as trucks for both Chevrolet and GMC Truck and Coach Division.

THE LORDSTOWN COMPLEX

The Lordstown complex is located in Trumbull County in Ohio, about 15 miles west of Youngstown and 30 miles east of Akron. It consists of the Vega assembly plant, the van-truck assembly plant, and Fisher Body metal fabricating plant, occupying about 1,000 acres of land. GMAD which operates the Vega and van-truck assembly plants is also located in the Lordstown complex. The three plants are in the heart of the heavy industrial triangle of Youngstown, Akron and Cleveland. With Youngstown as a center of steel production, Akron the home of rubber industries, and Cleveland as a major center for heavy manufacturing, the Lordstown complex commands a good strategic and logistic location for automobile assembly.

The original assembly plant was originally built in 1964–1966 to assemble Impalas. But in 1970 it was converted into Vega assembly with extensive arrangements. The van-truck assembly plant was constructed in 1969, and the Fisher Body metal fabricating plant was further added in 1970 to carry out stamping operations to produce sheet metal components used in Vega and van assemblies. In October 1971, the Chevrolet Vega and van-assembly plants and Fisher Body Vega assembly plants which had been operating under separate management were merged into a single jurisdiction of the GMAD.

WORK FORCE AT THE LORDSTOWN PLANT

There are over 11,400 employees working in the Lordstown Plant (as of 1973). Approximately 6,000 people of whom 5,500 are on hourly payroll work in the Vega assembly plant. About 2,600 workers, 2,100 of them paid hourly, work in van-truck assembly. As members of the United Auto Workers Union, Local 1112, the workers command good wages and benefits. They start out on the line at about $5.00 an hour, get a 10¢ an hour increase within 30 days, and another 10¢ after 90 days. Benefits come to $2.50 an hour.[3] The supplemental unemployment benefits virtually guarantee the worker's wage throughout the year. If the worker is laid off, he gets more than 90% of his wage for 52 weeks. He is also eligible for up to six weeks for holidays, excused absence or bereavement, and up to four weeks vacation.

The work force at the plant is almost entirely made up of local people with 92% coming from the immediate area of a 20-mile radius. Lordstown itself is a small rural town of about 500 residents. A sizable city closest to the plant is Warren, 5 miles away, which together with Youngstown supplies about two-thirds of the work force. The majority of the workers (57.5%) are married, 7.6% are home owners, and 20.2% are buying their homes. Of those who do not own their own homes (72%), over one-half are still living with their parents. The rest live in rented houses or apartments.

The workers in the plant are generally young. Although various news media reported the average worker age as 24 years old, and in some parts of the plant as 22 years, the company records show that the overall average worker age was somewhat above 29 years as of 1971–72. The national average is 42. The work force at Lordstown is the second youngest among GM's 25 assembly plants around the country. The fact that the Lordstown plant is the GM's newest assembly plant may partly explain the relatively young work force.

The educational profile of the Lordstown workers indicates that only 22.2% have less than a high school education. Nearly two-thirds or 62% are high school graduates, and 16% are either college graduates or have attended college. Another 26% have attended trade school. The average education of 13.2 years makes the Lordstown workers among the best educated in GM's assembly plants.

THE VEGA ASSEMBLY LINE

Conceived as a major competitive product against the increasing influx of foreign cars which were being produced at as low as one-fourth the labor rate in this country, the Vega was specifically designed with a maximum production efficiency and economy in mind. From the initial stages of planning, the Vega was designed by a special task team with most sophisticated techniques, using computers in designing the outer skin of the car and making the tapes that form the dies. Computers were also used to match up parts, measure the stack tolerances, measure safety performance under head-on collision, and make all necessary corrections before the first 1971 model car was ever built. The 2300-cubic-centimeter all-aluminum, 4-cylinder engine, was designed to give gas economy comparable to the foreign imports.

The Vega was also designed with the plant and the people in mind. As the

[3] In GM, the average worker on the line earns $12,500 a year with fringe benefits of $3,000.

GM's newest plant, the Vega assembly plant was known as the "super plant" with the most modern and sophisticated designs to maximize efficiency. It featured the newest engineering techniques and a variety of new power tools and automatic devices to eliminate much of the heavy lifting and physical labor. The line gave the workers an easier access to the car body, reducing the amount of bending and crawling in and out, as in other plants around the country. The unitized body in large components like pre-fab housing made the assembly easier and lighter with greater body integrity. Most difficult and tedious tasks were eliminated or simplified, on-line variations of the job were minimized, and the most modern tooling and mechanization was used to the highest possible degree of reliability.

It was also the fastest moving assembly line in the industry. The average time per assembly job was 36 seconds with a maximum of 100 cars rolling off the assembly line per hour for a daily production of 1,600 cars from two shift operations. The time cycle per job in other assembly plants averaged about 55 seconds. Although the high speed of the line did not necessarily imply greater work load or job requirement, it was a part of the GM's attempt to maximize economy in Vega assembly. The fact that the Vega was designed to have 43% fewer parts than a full-size car also helped the high-speed line and economy.

IMPACT OF GMAD AND REORGANIZATION IN THE LORDSTOWN PLANT

As stated previously, the assembly operations at Lordstown had originally been run by Fisher Body and Chevrolet as two plants. There were two organizations, two plant managers, two unions, and two service organizations. The consolidation of the two organizations into a single operating system under the GMAD in October 1971 required a difficult task of reorganization and dealing with the consequences of manpower reduction such as work slowdown, worker discipline, grievances, etc.

As duplicating units such as production, maintenance, inspection, and personnel were consolidated, there was a problem of selecting the personnel to manage the new organization. There were chief inspectors, personnel directors and production superintendents as well as production and service workers to be displaced or reassigned. Unions which had been representing their respective plants also had to go through reorganization. Union elections were held to merge the separate union committees at Fisher Body and Chevrolet in a single-union bargaining committee. This eliminated one full local union shop committee.

At the same time, GMAD launched an effort to improve production efficiency more in line with that in other assembly plants. It included increasing job efficiency through reorganization and better coordination between the body and chassis assembly, and improving controls over product quality and worker absenteeism. This effort coincided with the plant's early operational stage at the time which required adjustments in line balance and work methods. Like other assembly plants, the Vega assembly plant was going through an initial period of diseconomy caused by sub-optimal operations, imbalance in the assembly line, and somewhat redundant work force. According to management, line adjustments and work changes were a normal process in accelerating the assembly operation to the peak performance the plant had been designed for after the initial break-in and startup period.

As for job efficiency, the GMAD initiated changes in those work sequences and work methods which were not well coordinated under the divided managements of body and chassis assembly. For example, previous to the GMAD, Fisher Body had been delivering the car body complete with interior trim to the final assembly line, where often times the workers soiled the front seats as they did further assembly operations. GMAD changed this practice so that the seats were installed as one of the last operations in building the car. Fisher Body also had been delivering the car body with complete panel instrument frame which made it extremely difficult for the assembly workers to reach behind the frame in installing the instrument panels. The GMAD improved the job method so that the box containing the entire instrument panels was installed on the assembly line. Such improvements in job sequences and job methods resulted in savings in time and the number of workers required. Consequently, there were some jobs where the assembly time was cut down and/or the number of workers was reduced.

GMAD also put more strict control over worker absenteeism and the causes for defect work; the reduction in absenteeism was expected to require less relief men, and the improvement in quality and less repair work were to require less repairmen. In implementing these changes, the GMAD instituted a strong policy of dealing with worker slowdowns via strict disciplinary measures including dismissal. It was rumored that the inspectors and foremen passing defective cars would be fired on the spot.

Many workers were laid off as a result of the reorganization and job changes. The union was claiming that as many as 700 workers were laid off. Management, on the other hand, put the layoff figure at 375 to which the union later conceded.[4] Although management claimed that the changes in job sequence and method in some assembly work did not bring a substantial change in the overall speed or pace of the assembly line, the workers perceived the job change as "tightening" the assembly line. The union charged that the GMAD brought a return of an old-fashioned line speedup and a "sweatshop style" of management reminiscent of the 1930's, making the men do more work at the same pay. The workers were blaming the "tightened" assembly line for the drastic increase in quality defects. As one worker commented, "That's the fastest line in the world. We have about 40 seconds to do our job. The company adds one more

---

[4] All of the workers who had been laid off were later reinstated as the plant needed additional workers to perform assembly jobs for optional features to Vega, i.e., vinyl top, etc., which were later introduced. In addition, some workers were put to work at the van-assembly plant.

thing and it can kill us. We can't get the stuff done on time and a car goes by. The company then blames us for sabotage and shoddy work."

The number of worker grievances also increased drastically. Before GMAD took over, there were about 100 grievances in the plant. Since then, grievances increased to 5,000, 1,000 of which were related to the charge that too much work had been added to the job. The worker resentment was particularly great in "towveyor" assembly and seat sub-assembly areas. The "towveyor" is the area where engines and transmissions are assembled. Like seat sub-assembly there is a great concentration of workers working together in close proximity. Also, these jobs are typically for beginning assemblers who tend to make the work crew in these areas younger and better educated.

The workers in the plant were particularly resentful of the company's strict policy in implementing the changes. They stated that the tougher the company became, the more they would stiffen their resistance even though other jobs were scarce in the market. One worker said, "In some of the other plants where the GMAD did the same thing, the workers were older and they took this. But, I've got 25 years ahead of me in this plant." Another worker commented, "I saw a woman running to keep pace with the fast line. I'm not going to run for anybody. There ain't anyone in that plant that is going to tell me to run." One foreman said, "The problem with the workers here is not so much that they don't want to work, but that they just don't want to take orders. They don't believe in any kind of authority."

While the workers were resisting management orders, there were some indications that the first-line supervisors had not been adequately trained to perform satisfactory supervisory roles. The average supervisor at the time had less than 3 years of experience, and 20% of the supervisors had less than 1 year's experience. Typically, they were young, somewhat lacking in knowledge of the provisions of the union contract and other supervisory duties, and less than adequately trained to handle the workers in the threatening and hostile environment which was developing.

Another significant fact was that the strong reactions of the workers were not entirely from the organizational and job changes brought about by the GMAD alone. Management noted that there was a significant amount of worker reactions in the areas where the company hadn't changed anything at all. Management felt that the intense resentment was particularly due to the nature of the work force in Lordstown. The plant was not only made up of young people, but also the work force reflected the characteristics of "tough labor" in steel, coal and rubber industries in the surrounding communities. Many of the workers in fact came from families who made their living working in these industries. Management also noted that the worker resistance had been much greater in the Lordstown Plant than in other plants where similar changes had been made.

A good part of the young workers' resentment also seemed to be related to the unskilled and repetitive nature of the assembly work. One management official admitted that the company was facing a difficult task in getting workers to "take pride" in the product they were assembling. Many of them were benefiting

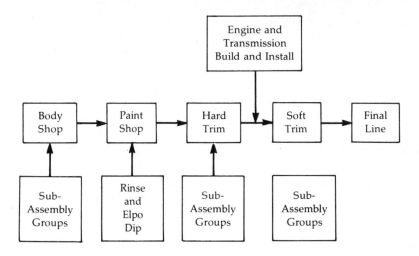

Exhibit 1 Flowchart of major assembly operations

from the company's tuition assistance plan which was supporting their college education in the evening. With this educated background, obviously assembly work was not fulfilling their high work expectations. Also, the job market was tight at the time, and they could neither find any meaningful jobs elsewhere nor, even if found, could they afford to give up the good money and fringe benefits they were earning on their assembly-line jobs. This made them frustrated, according to company officials.

Many industrial engineers were questioning whether the direction of management toward assembly line work could continue. As the jobs became easier, simpler, and repetitive, requiring less physical effort, there were less and less traces of skill and increased monotony. The worker unrest indicated that they not only wanted to go back to the work pace prior to the "speedup" (pre-October pace), but also wanted the company to do something about the boring and meaningless assembly work. One worker commented, "The company has got to do something to change the job so that a guy can take an interest in the job. A guy can't do the same thing 8 hours a day year after year. And it's got to be more than the company just saying to a guy, 'Okay, instead of 6 spots on the weld, you'll do 5 spots.'"

As the worker resentment mounted, the UAW Local 1112 decided in early January 1972 to consider possible authorization for a strike against the Lordstown Plant in a fight against the job changes. In the meantime, the union and management bargaining teams worked hard on worker grievances; they reduced the number of grievances from 5,000 to a few hundred; management even indicated that it would restore some of the eliminated jobs. However, the bargaining failed to produce accord on the issues of seniority rights and shift preference, which were related to wider issues of job changes and layoff.

A vote was held in early February 1972. Nearly 90% of the workers came out to vote which was the heaviest turnout in the history of the Local. With 97% of the votes supporting, the workers went out on strike in early March.

In March 1972, with the strike in effect, the management of the Lordstown Plant was assessing the impact of the GMAD and the resultant strike in the Plant. It was estimated that the work disruption because of the worker resentment and slowdown had already cost the company 12,000 Vegas and 4,000 trucks amounting to $45 million. There had been repeated closedowns of assembly lines since December 1971, because of the worker slowdowns and the cars passing down the line without all necessary operations performed on them. The car lot was full with 2,000 cars waiting for repair work.

There had also been an amazing number of complaints from Chevrolet dealers, 6,000 complaints in November alone, about the quality of the Vegas shipped to them. This was more than the combined complaints from the other assembly plants.

The strike in the Lordstown Plant was expected to affect other plants. The plants at Tonawanda, New York and Buffalo, New York were supplying parts for Vega. Despite the costly impact of the worker resistance and the strike, the management felt that the job changes and cost reductions were essential if the Vega were to return a profit to the company. The plant had to be operating at about 90% capacity to break even. Not only had the plant with highly automated features cost twice as much as estimated, but also the Vega itself ended up weighing 10% more than had been planned.

While the company had to do something to increase the production efficiency in the Lordstown Plant, the management was wondering whether it couldn't have planned and implemented the organizational and job changes differently in view of the costly disruption of the operations and the organizational stress the Plant had been experiencing.

QUESTIONS AND REQUIREMENTS

1. What was the central issue at the Lordstown plant? What were the subsidiary issues?

2. If you were the personnel director at the Lordstown plant, how would you solve this case?

3. How would you go about setting up a mid-level supervisor training program that could deal with the problems in the plant?

4. Using Herzberg's two factor theory, how would you enrich the assembly-line jobs? How would you maintain motivation after the enrichment peaked?

5. In what areas could the union help in solving the plant's personnel problems?

6. What actions would you take as personnel director to keep this situation from recurring?

12
CANADIAN AUTO CORPORATION

THOMAS KUBICEK

When Mr. Frank died suddenly in 1959, his assistant, Mr. Black, was promoted to succeed him as plant manager. Mr. Black had a fifteen-year record of loyal and satisfactory association with the company. During World War Two he had held the position of mechanical engineer; later he had assumed further responsibility as maintenance superintendent and finally, when the war ended, he became Assistant Plant Manager under Mr. Frank. His new boss was a strong-willed, hard-working six-footer who was widely respected throughout the plant. Although Frank had not given Black much opportunity to make important decisions around the plant, Mr. Black enjoyed working for Mr. Frank. In fact everybody believed that the two made an excellent team. While Mr. Black knew how to handle with ease both the analytical and bureaucratic problems in the plant, Mr. Frank who had grown up through the ranks, radiated almost a biological control of his "tribe." This produced a plant community dominated practically with "naked-ape" rule. The backbone of this community was the Protestant Ethic under which performance counted most.

"If I catch you smoking again at the job," said Mr. Black as he witnessed Frank handling a problem in the plant, "I'll punch your nose right in." Yet at another time he would quite gently care for a man who accidently fractured his leg in the Plant.

In this climate the job was usually done to the satisfaction of the Divisional bosses. Black once said to one of the Head Office engineers: "There is not one man in the plant who would ever dare to tell Frank that a thing in the plant could not be done. 'All you need is to want to, and that's what I am paying you for,'" he would say.

To Mr. Black he would often remark: "People get as much power as they can grab. This applies to everybody, to you, to me and to my subordinates."

To his boss, the Divisional Manager, he once said: "Black is a good engineer. He is loyal and a hard worker too. Once he is fully trained, he will make a good

This case was prepared by Professor Thomas Kubicek of Sir George Williams University, Montreal, Quebec, Canada, as a basis for classroom discussion and not to illustrate either effective or ineffective handling of an administrative situation. Some issues integrated into this case were adapted from R.H. Guest, *Organizational Change* (Homewood, Ill.: R.D. Irwin, 1962), by special permission from the publisher.

plant manager. And it seems to me that he is sufficiently 'full of piss and vinegar' to take over my job tomorrow."

Since he was very familiar with the everyday routine, when he became the Plant Manager, Mr. Black continued "as usual." At the beginning he managed quite well. No serious problems arose for some time. However, at the end of the 1960 recession, the automobile industry started "going all out" to meet the demands of the market. Plant "A" and some of its sister plants in the Canadian Auto Corporation were asked to step up the speed of the line and to begin operations on a two-shift basis. Schedules had to be rearranged. New hourly workers together with a number of supervisory staff had to be recruited and trained.

Following these changes, in the judgement of top management, Plant "A" began failing to adjust to the new output demands. In comparison with other plants (where some problems may also have been noted) in Plant "A" costs were too high, and schedules were not being met. It looked like something was obviously wrong.

During 1961 and 1962, the number of contacts between division and plant had been increasing. Divisional staff members representing Accounting, Quality Control, Material Control, Personnel, and other functions were in frequent contact with their subordinate counterparts in the plant, as well as with the Manager himself. Dealers of the product were complaining about poor delivery dates and alleged quality defects.

Faced with the increase in directives from above and cognizant of Plant "A"'s low performance position, Mr. Black, the Plant Manager, seemed forever trying to show his boss, the Vice-President, and Division Manager that he was carrying out orders.

IF WE ONLY HAD A 30-HOUR DAY

It just so happened that Jim Gordon, an M.B.A. student from Toronto, had temporarily joined the staff of the plant manager's office as a summer employee in 1962. It was his intention to draw directly from the experiences of Mr. Black for his dissertation. Joining the organization at the precise moment when it was beginning to experience new production strains, Jim was quite surprised when he accidently overheard Mr. Black complaining to his production manager: "They just don't know in the central office what we have to face. They don't know how to get down to our level. They think everything can be done by schedule, no matter how fantastic. They keep saying to me, 'Why can't you do it? So-and-so in the other plant can.' When I answer that if 40 cars an hour are not enough, give me new machinery, they quickly shift to something else."

"Why don't you insist on new machinery?" interrupted Martineau, the Production Manager.

"Oh, I do, but they always manage to brush me off. I've always been able to roll with the punches, but now I get butterflies in my stomach when I get this kind of pressure on me. If we only had a 30-hour day everything would be just fine. We could do both, live up to our schedule and accommodate the people from the Head office for their changes."

DELEGATION—YES. ABDICATION—NO.

Mr. Black said that he never had quarrels with the need for delegation. But: "To allow people to do their work any way they see fit is not delegation. It's abdication," he was fond of saying. "If something goes wrong am I not the one who still is responsible?"

MR. BLACK'S MEETINGS

With increasing pressure on the production in Plant "A," the number of meetings between the Plant Manager and his Department Heads were gradually increasing. Most of the meetings, however, were not scheduled on a regular basis.

They were called as a direct result of some directive due to an emergency situation in the plant. One Department Head, whom Jim met in the cafeteria, commented on one of the meetings by saying: "We spent half of our time making explanations about why something went wrong and who did it. The other half of our time was spent debating the personal differences of our superiors. All the while each person tried to cover up for his own department while also trying to prove he was carrying out orders as Mr. Black said we should. A further distraction was caused by Mr. Black being called away to the telephone to answer 'important messages.'"

JIM TALKS WITH THE GENERAL SUPERINTENDENT

Every day at about 4:30 in the afternoon, Jim Gordon made his way to the Plant Superintendent's office. Joe Simard was a pleasant man, if somewhat browbeaten after a life given over to the welfare of the plant. It was his idea to give Jim a lift home each day after work. As the two men walked to the parking lot, Jim could see that Joe Simard was worried.

"Problems?" Jim asked politely.

"Oh, the usual," smiled Joe.

Since Jim's job was arranged for him by those "at the top," he found that he had to be careful not to let anyone think he was prying into the discontents of the plant in order to report anyone. Jim found that the men soon accepted him as an interested equal.

They reached the Buick parked in the lot. As Joe carefully drove the car through the plant gates he sighed. Jim looked over and smiled.

"I'm glad that this day is over," said Joe.

"Rough, eh?"

"It's a madhouse. While the Production Manager is pushing to keep up the schedule, the big boss demands something else. Most of the time I manage to talk to Martineau, but I can hardly explain things to Mr. Black. If he is checking on a complaint, that has a priority over everything else. A few months ago Martineau suggested, (and Mr. Black agreed) that I should be mainly concerned with preventive maintenance and manufacturing process development. This would leave the Production Manager free to do the production planning, fabrication and assembly. However, nothing has changed. All three of us, myself, the boss, and the Production Manager still continue checking on snags and ordering people around. No wonder then, when I or my foreman see the Plant Manager coming in, we all run away because we know that it means trouble."

Jim smiled. "Is it that bad?"

"Not always," said Joe, "but, for instance, a few days ago my boss came to me and said, 'Get this done right away', but he never suggested how it was to be done. He never asked me how I thought it should be done. He just stood there and insisted. So in front of him I had to go down and chew out my foreman and then the foreman chewed out the men. That seemed to satisfy my boss and maybe the thing will always get done, but there is a bad feeling all round. Under these conditions my foremen don't make any decisions. They just follow orders and grind their teeth."

"That's quite bad," said Jim.

"Yeah, that's right, and that's the way it is all the way up," continued Joe. "Yesterday I was ordered, this time by the Production Manager, to personally investigate two cases of hourly workers. This should be the foreman's job. Yet he insisted. In one case the missing man's wife had already called up the plant doctor, who had notified the foreman. Can you imagine how the man felt when I called later to find out why he was absent?"

JIM AND A GENERAL FOREMAN

Steve Buzowski was a big man with a rough, back-slapping good-natured humour. One of twenty or so General Foremen, between 38 to 40 years old, he was always in the habit of speaking his mind. Since Steve's general good humour was wearing a bit thin, it wasn't long before he was telling Jim what was wrong with the whole company.

"Mistrust," said Steve.

"Mistrust?" asked Jim.

"Yeah. In other plants, top management usually has a good opinion of the average worker. Not here. This plant works in an 'atmosphere of suspicion and fear.' Everyone thinks the other guy is worse. Naturally, production is low and the bosses think just because we've got rules everything should go by the book."

"Have you talked to the Plant Manager?" asked Jim.

"Listen, the only time I have anything to do with the Plant Manager is when he comes down to chew me out about some mistake somebody else made. We're not business associates, you know, I just work for him."

Steve stabbed a blunt index finger at Jim for emphasis.

"Now don't get me wrong. I'm not afraid of any discipline. If I'm going to be chewed out for something I did, well fine, but I want it done by my own boss."

As Jim was leaving, Steve turned to him and said, "This is no way to run a plant, is it?"

JIM HEARS THE FOREMAN'S VIEW

Jim's involvement in the Plant's affairs seemed to him more and more interesting as the days progressed. "Can't they see what's wrong?" thought Jim, as he went to the cafeteria for his coffee break. After getting a coffee and a doughnut, Jim sat down alone at a table near several foremen. He was just about to bite into the doughnut when a gruff voice bellowed behind him.

"Hey kid, you're smart, ain't you?"

Jim turned to confront a huge dirty face.

"I beg your pardon?" asked Jim, uncertain of the rough man.

"Come here, we wanta talk to you."

Jim joined the men at their table.

"My name's Birkett, kid, Wally Birkett," said the man, smiling at Jim. They shook hands and Wally introduced the other men. Jim smiled and nodded to each man.

"You a spy, kid?" asked Wally.

Seeing the amused expressions on their faces, he said, "Sure, wanta see my black book?"

They all laughed. Jim told them that he was a student.

"What are you studying?" asked Wally.

"Business," answered Jim.

"Business!" exclaimed one man.

"You'll get a lot of 'business' around here," roared Wally, "everybody else's business including your own."

The men laughed.

"Is it that bad here?" asked Jim.

"Bad?" snorted Wally, "Fifteen years I've put in at this plant and I got nothing to show for it. Sure, I get paid, we all get good money, but there's a something money can't buy."

"What?" asked Jim.

"Respect." The men agreed with Wally.

"The foreman is supposed to be the front man of management, ain't he? Well, there just isn't any recognition for the foreman around here. He isn't management or labour. No recognition from the top, no respect from the bottom. You just don't exist. That is except when they think you did something wrong.

Then they are all over you. Top management is just a bunch of hypocrites. The damned Plant Manager keeps stressing the three 'C's, which mean 'Centrally Controlled Cooperation.' It's controlled all right! But there's no cooperation. Everybody wants to cut the other guy's throat!"

Jim learned that the foremen believed that as far as internal communication was concerned, there was an overwhelming number of contacts involved in the issuance of orders by superiors and that this communication took place in response to immediate technical and organizational emergencies.

WHY WAS THE LINE OUT OF BALANCE?

One General Foreman Jim talked to had this to say: "We can't keep to the schedule, and our quality is shot to hell. Some of us know what the trouble is, but does the boss come down and get our opinion? Hell, no. This line is out of balance because they keep bunching the work flow. But they're not interested in flow upstairs, just production. Then of course we have a daily line-up of 60–80 cars in the repair area to have either steering adjusted, or breaks repaired, or other faults fixed."

Jim and the General Foreman happened to be walking through the plant when the General Foreman stopped and pointed to a man in overalls who seemed to be dashing around in confusion.

"Crazy guy—that foreman. Complained to me that he had a man who was too tall for the job—too tall, can you beat that? He wasn't, of course, and I told him so. I told that crazy guy not to go making any moves without consulting me first."

JIM MEETS THE MAN IN THE MIDDLE—THE FOREMAN

One of the foremen Jim had met in the cafeteria with Wally cornered Jim and after checking to see if anyone could hear him, said:

"You doing a report, kid?"

"No, just making notes for my class."

"Yeah, well, in your report you should say something about the General Foremen, see?"

"General Foremen?"

"Yeah. In most companies the foreman and the supervisor cooperate. My General Foreman is strictly business. The only time I see him he bawls me out—in front of my men. That looks bad, you know. He takes my authority away. The men know he's the real boss so they don't listen to me. The foreman just has to take it. And while the men have a union, the foreman doesn't have any place to complain—he's right in the middle."

"Sure. Why, just yesterday, my General Foreman bawled the hell out of me because I didn't want to put a big man in a cramped-up job inside of the car body. It didn't make sense."

"Complain."

"To whom? I get so mad sometimes I could scream. There is always somebody interfering. And the men don't like it at all, so they get even with them if they can.

"For instance, last week as I was standing and talking with John Smith, one of our tool makers for whom I had just lined up a special rework job that was rather pressing, the Superintendent comes rushing in puffing like a steam engine.

" 'Well, sir!' he says to John, not paying any attention to me, 'here is a rush job which I must have for this afternoon. Since this is a special for one of our best customers I do not want any mistakes done.'

"He handed John the Factory Instruction Sheet [usually called the F.I.S.] issued by Engineering at the Divisional Office. It called for manufacturing and assembling one air-conditioning fan unit. John was studying the F.I.S. which indicated various data including the numbers of drawings applicable. Then I noticed a sudden change in his face. His eyes shone brighter. 'It was about ten days ago,' John was thinking, 'that I made a 12-inch fan. Exactly like this one. Yet that one called for collar drawing No. 1565 and why should this be 1563?' John remembered well the number because the girl in the drawing room sent him by error No. 1566 and he had to exchange it since it would not match. 'Could this be something new or different? Perhaps the supervisor might know.' Smith turned towards the supervisor who in the meantime was watching him like a hawk. He started slowly: 'there is something . . . ,' but the supervisor did not give him a chance to finish his sentence. 'I do not want to hear any excuses. I know you are very busy, but this must be done by tonight. And remember, you have your specifications, so follow them to the letter. I'll come by to pick it up myself before you leave tonight.'

"John swallowed his unfinished sentence and answered dryly: 'Aye-Aye, sir.'

"When the supervisor took the finished unit later in the afternoon, he ran off with not so much as a thank you. But he returned the next day and, hell, was he mad. He screamed: 'What the hell did you do? The damned thing does not work. The collar is too short. It has no suction.'

" 'That's funny,' says John with a big dumb grin. . . . 'I followed the F.I.S. exactly as you said. Maybe the Head office people made a mistake?'

"Of course, John knew all the time that the fan would not work. Personally, I don't blame him."

"Is it always like this?" asked Jim.

"Yes, always putting the heat on us: Don't talk back. Do as you are told and rush it. Then, when anything goes wrong, they are yelling their heads off. No sir, this isn't the first time."

After ten weeks at C.A.C. Jim Gordon felt more confused than ever. Without a doubt his present experience conflicted with the three neat categories of supervision he had been taught at University: *Communication, management of*

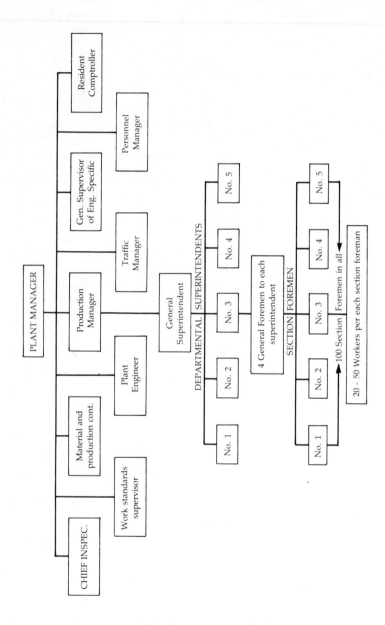

Organization chart of Plant "A" (before and after 1958)

Please note: (1) Staff functions similar to those under the Plant Manager are also at the Divisional Office which is in charge of several plants. (2) Non-production groups constituted about one third of the plant population. (3) Production Manager is in charge of all operations directly related to the assembly of the product. (4) The structure below the Superintendent is identical for both of the two shifts.

work, and *management of people.* No matter how he looked at the situation in Plant "A" the categories didn't seem to apply. He could see no clear contours but only a blurred overall picture. In an effort to distill his impressions of the many people and the operations in which they were involved, and to further avoid making any hasty conclusions, he formulated the following three questions. Once back in the quiet of the University, away from the pandemonium of the plant, he felt that he would be able to answer the questions intelligently and freely, without the possible danger of biased thinking.

QUESTIONS AND REQUIREMENTS

1. Compare the leadership styles of Mr. Frank and Mr. Black.

2. An author once said that some people *act* like executives, and that some people *perform* like executives. This depends to some degree on their managerial role perception. What would you say was Mr. Black's perception of his role as a manager? Was his understanding of his managerial role similar to that which his superiors had in mind for him? If there was a conflict between these two interpretations of what the proper role should be, what were the causes, and what might be the consequences?

3. If Mr. Black were to hire you as a consultant to help him with his difficulties, what fundamental recommendations would you suggest to improve the effectiveness of his division?

13
PRECISION WOODCRAFT, INC.

ALLEN RAPPAPORT

In the Summer of 1974, Ken Bender was considering the recommendations he should make to Mr. Ron Bahn, President of Precision Woodcraft, Inc., after a lengthy examination of the company. Precision Woodcraft is principally a subcontractor of interior items for the major light aviation manufacturers. Although it subcontracts for four companies (hereafter referred to as A, B, C, and D), Company A is by far its largest purchaser and its biggest money maker.

Precision Woodcraft recently began experiencing absenteeism and high employee turnover. Ken thought that the labor problems hindered Precision Woodcraft's ability to deliver quality merchandise on time. Furthermore, Ken believed that the employees of one of Precision Woodcraft's customers would charge the company with what was, in effect, installer-related damage and poor installation workmanship. He noted that the company received complaints and returns from all customers but was not sure about the percentage of total returns to shipments.

HISTORY OF THE COMPANY

In making his examination, Ken had assembled background data on the company and its only local competition. Precision Woodcraft, Inc. had its beginnings in 1953 as a two-man shop producing patterns for woodwork builders. In 1966, the plant was moved to its current location in order to be closer to its principal customers and major shipping thoroughfares. In response to increased demand, the plant size was doubled in 1970 to 13,420 square feet and the work force was expanded to sixty. While the company produces both standardized and custom woodwork items, standardized products account for 80% of about $2.5 million in annual sales revenue. Refreshment centers, bars, toilet bases, flight-deck dividers, and map cases make up the bulk of their products. Precision Woodcraft also maintains a sheet metal shop and a machine shop to produce metal parts and fittings.

Until 1971, Precision Woodcraft did not have any competition in their industry. At that time H.H. Woods was formed. Originally contracting for custom one-time-only jobs, H.H. Woods has increased its market share and eventually obtained all of Precision Woodcraft's profitable flight-deck divider business with

Company A. Recently, H.H. Woods has made incursions into Precision Woodcraft's map case and refreshment center business. In addition, Company A has started to turn to H.H. Woods for other custom work. Precision Woodcraft is approximately ten times as large as H.H. Woods. Ken regarded H.H. Woods as primarily a single-order or prototype shop. He felt that H.H. Woods was not capable of a long production run.

MANAGEMENT RESPONSIBILITIES

In developing the organization chart, Ken found that Mr. Bahn is responsible for purchasing, bidding on contracts, and many corporate planning responsibilities. He selects and promotes all personnel and administers retirement and insurance programs. In keeping with his open-door policy, Mr. Bahn frequently gets requests from production workers for items such as new sawblades. Mr. Bahn works in the plant from time to time and takes an active role in production work.

The assistant manager is responsible for assigning all work and seeing that the scheduling and inventory functions are properly administered. The supervisors are responsible for training their personnel, quality control of their products, attaining their personal daily production quotas, and meeting schedules established by the planner and the assistant manager.

THE PRESIDENT

Mr. Bahn sat in his attractively paneled office and discussed his company. He recalled how he first got into the woodwork business. "You know, I've been in aircraft a long time," he reflected. "I started out at Company B working across the aisle from the pattern makers in the experimental shop. I was really fascinated by pattern making and decided I wanted to be a pattern maker. In order to learn the trade, I found a company that would train me and I worked six months at night learning to be a pattern maker. At the end of six months I transferred across the aisle and became a pattern maker at Company B. I went on to become the supervisor of the experimental pattern shop. Through my contacts in the trade, I received promises of a year's production orders if I would go into the pattern business." Mr. Bahn smiled to himself as he remembered the situation. "I was young and green when I started," he said. "I went into business with a partner. We had just gotten set up when we found out that the orders that we were promised went to the lowest bidder." His face grew solemn again as he discussed the following events. "That's when we knew we were going to have to get out and hustle some business. My partner only stayed with me for a couple of months and the first couple of years were pretty tough."

"My knowledge of weight-saving techniques in aircraft led to developing interior furnishings with a paper honeycomb core and a high-pressure laminate covering combining a natural wood appearance with the strength and lightness

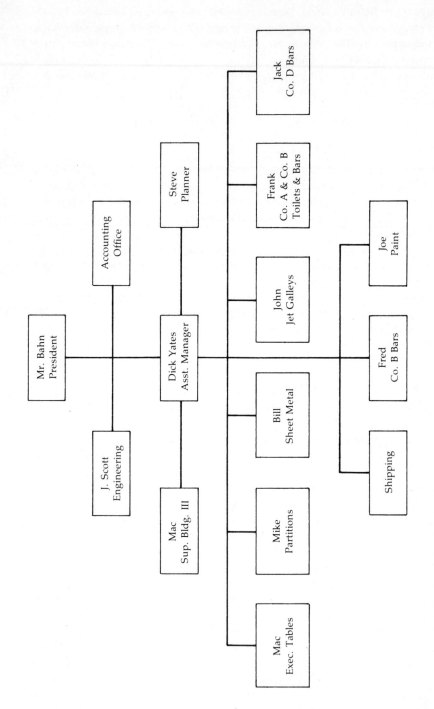

Precision Woodcraft organization chart

required by the aircraft industry. Eventually, I moved out of patterns into more lucrative aircraft interior business." Mr. Bahn showed Ken Bender a lightweight honeycomb core which Ken could stand on. The core would bend but not break and still be intact afterward.

Mr. Bahn leaned back in his office chair again and recalled some of the problems. "For years I ran this place out of my shirt pocket. In 1970, the business had grown so much that I found that I couldn't run everything. In fact, the company was in real trouble. At that time a 'high aircraft official' came in and helped me to organize the company as you see it now. Before that time I didn't have any departments. Everyone worked everything."

"We've had a turnover problem here for the last couple of years," Mr. Bahn admitted. "The aircraft companies pay an average of $3.50 an hour which provides a lot of competition for qualified help, and in the summertime we always have some men leave who want to work outdoors. I keep in close contact with local vocational schools and colleges offering industrial arts training, but it is difficult to recruit qualified help."

"Even though the aircraft companies offer fairly high wages, I don't think wages are the whole answer to the turnover problem. Twelve of my employees made in excess of $12,000 last year. This is a respectable income. The turnover problem results from my inability to find qualified personnel in the first place. If a kid comes in and says he would like to give it a try, I am not interested. I want people who are aiming toward a career in wood craftsmanship. I send applicants to the testing service at the local employment agency, but they never show up to take the tests. I tried to use school grades to predict future performance, but this has not been successful."

THE ASSISTANT MANAGER

The assistant manager is a college graduate with a major in business administration. He has been in his current position for approximately a year and a half although he has worked a total of four years at Precision Woodcraft. He obtained the position of assistant manager shortly after marrying Mr. Bahn's daughter. Dick comments that, "Sure, I know that the employees still resent me. They still go to see Ron (Mr. Bahn) instead of me, but I think the trend is slowly changing." Dick had introduced a number of scheduling and record keeping procedures in the company that met with disfavor on the part of the workers. "Before I took over as assistant manager," Dick continued, "there were no real record keeping and scheduling procedures at Precision Woodcraft. All of the data was kept in Ron's head. The new system has helped to make the company more businesslike." When asked why he thought the employees had resisted the new procedures, Dick stated that, "The employees think of themselves as craftsmen and didn't like to keep records like common production workers."

THE PLANNER

Steve has been the planner at Precision Woodcraft for three years. For the past year and a half, he has been helping the assistant manager. He stated that, "Recent changes initiated by the assistant manager have definitely improved the quality of planning and scheduling." He admitted that there were "still a number of problems in the system but in the future Precision Woodcraft would have a better information system to base decisions on."

THE SUPERVISORS

Frank's job is to supervise the production of refreshment centers for Companies A and B and toilet bases for Company B. He, like the other supervisors, works alongside his subordinates in actual production of the products. "My biggest problems are inadequate time to perform my job, lack of qualified help, tying up machinery, and lack of precision tooling, in that order. I also have production delays due to shortages of purchased parts and parts from subcontractors. I use a Theory Y approach towards workers once they have proved themselves. We have a personality clash between sheet metal, production, and finish departments which contributes to production slowdowns. I often lose workers to groups that are behind but can not get help when I am in a similar situation. I don't know whom I report to and feel that there is a poor flow of communications at Precision Woodcraft."

Mac is the supervisor for executive table fabrication for Companies A, B, C, and D. He is in his forties. He only has a high school education but has taken a management development course and proudly displays a diploma on the wall. He has been with the firm the longest, having joined it in 1956. He is also the only supervisor with a private office. Mac's workers are predominantly women and though he admits to having some difficulties with them, he has been all-in-all pleased with their performance. "I feel that a lack of skilled help is the company's biggest problem. It leads to high material loss and inefficient production. Precision Woodcraft can't get good help because its wages are too low and because it had 50 different wage scales for 50 different people. A shortage of hardware has also been a problem and caused me to be late on production schedules."

Bill is the supervisor of the sheet metal department. He has been with the company four years and had previously worked in a machine shop. "I am an easy-going guy and do not intend to let anyone pressure me. I work at my own pace. I have few supervisory powers even though I am supposed to be supervisor. The assistant manager frequently gives instructions to the sheet metal workers without even informing me." Bill was also concerned with the health hazard brought about by sawdust and scrap all over the floor and sawdust in the air. "Mr. Bahn had promised that he would hire a janitor and fix the air-filtering system but nothing had happened in six months."

John is the supervisor of the group that makes Company B's refreshment centers. At 27 he is the youngest supervisor in the plant. He has a degree in business administration. "I was originally hired as a foreman but the workers wouldn't accept me since I hadn't served my apprenticeship in the shop. Mr. Bahn then put me in my present position where I am now more or less accepted by my workers." Although John acknowledged the existence of the assistant manager, he was unsure of what the assistant manager's responsibilities were. John complained about the amount of turnover the firm was experiencing. "I have tried to train four new men in the past year but really didn't have the time. Low wages are the principal reason for the high turnover. Often fixed (location) equipment is tied up when I need it and the required hand tools are either broken or missing from their storage locations."

THE WORKERS

Henry is a middle-aged man who has spent the better part of his life in the cabinet making profession. For the past eight years, he has worked for Precision Woodcraft. "The new ping-pong table and basketball goal are evidence of the company's concern in bringing employees closer together. I have seen the company's profit picture for the year and am not happy that the company could continue to make more money and not improve wages."

Joe is a young warehouseman in his twenties. He has only worked at Precision Woodcraft for one year. "I like my job and the people I work with, but I am looking for another one. Until two years ago, Precision Woodcraft had a maternity benefit in its insurance policy. Due to the large number of older workers in the company at that time, this coverage was dropped for a slightly lower insurance rate. I want to have children but it would be too much of a financial hardship to do so without insurance." Other workers expressed feelings very similar to Joe's.

Don has only been with Precision Woodcraft a few months since finishing school. Don was a product of a vocational school program. "I am not satisfied with Precision Woodcraft's training program. They use an on-the-job training system. The only problem is that you have to start from scratch. Everyone has his own way of building and keeps it a closely guarded secret. Hell, I was assigned to build a refreshment center the other day and nobody would even give me the saw bill (list of materials) for it." He turned, picked up a blueprint and continued in a sarcastic tone of voice, "They taught me how to read prints in school, but they never taught me how to supply information that wasn't there."

Harry has been with Precision Woodcraft 12 years. "I like Precision Woodcraft and the friendships I have formed here." He didn't have as nice of an opinion of the assistant manager, however. "The assistant manager's only 'claim to fame' was that he had married the boss's daughter. Why, he can't even manage himself, let alone manage this business," he said sarcastically. "I sure hope Ron (Mr. Bahn) finds someone else to take over this business before he retires. There is no way this company can stay together with Dick (the assistant manager) in charge. I am bothered about the retirement program. It is a vested program with contributions made by the employee and employer being invested. I want to see some accounting of what each employee had invested on an annual basis."

Sharon was one of a small but growing contingent of women workers at Precision Woodcraft. Like most of the others, she is a mother with all of the ensuing problems and responsibilities. "The company doesn't really understand my special situation. We do as good a job as the men, perhaps better," she intoned. "Sure, we have to miss a few days with sick kids, but we more than make up for it on the job." She thought for a moment and then continued, "I guess we just don't have very good communications with our bosses. They just don't seem to understand us."

FORMER EMPLOYEES

Jerry had been with Precision Woodcraft five years when he left it to go back to aircraft engineering. "My main reason for leaving was a lack of communication with my boss, although low wages contributed to my decision. I rarely could get any answers or commitments from Mr. Bahn. Once commitments were made I couldn't get Mr. Bahn to stand by them. This left me in a continually embarrassing situation since I dealt with Companies A through D on a daily basis. When the companies complained to Mr. Bahn, I was continually blamed by him for causing the problems."

Harold worked 15 years for Mr. Bahn as cabinet maker and shop foreman. Mr. Bahn still refers to him as his former right-hand man. "I quit Precision Woodcraft because of a broken promise. Mr. Bahn had promised me 25% of the business when I went to work for him. Mr. Bahn kept putting me off as the business continued to prosper. When I put our agreement to the test by demanding my share in writing, Mr. Bahn denied ever offering as much as 25% and told me that he would give me 1% of the business in ten years. This infuriated me, so I took what savings I could scrape up and started H.H. Woods. I am still bitter about my treatment and have hired several people away from my former employer."

Dick is a young man who worked but a couple of months in the finish department before quitting. "The pay is really low, man," Dick explained. "I can get better pay lugging meat at the packing house." Dick also explained his dissatisfaction with his supervisor. "My boss was all right, I guess." He explained with a shrug of his shoulders, "The real problem was that I never knew who I was working for. Mr. Bahn was always snooping around, and when my boss would tell me one thing, it seemed like five minutes later Mr. Bahn would tell me something different. I never knew what to do."

Larry had been a supervisor in the refreshment center department. He had quit after eight years for a variety of reasons. "There were always more jobs than there were people and people were continually being shuffled between departments in order to make up production shortfalls. I was expected to train help but was never given time to do so. In fact, I never really felt like a supervisor at all. I felt more like a lead man, someone who set the example."

THE COMPETITOR

H.H. Woods is a small concern also dealing in the general aviation market as a subcontractor for interior woodwork items. Currently, it has made serious inroads into Precision Woodcraft's sales only in Company A. H.H. Woods has done some custom and prototype work for Companies B and D but prefers not to because of a lower profit margin for these products. This is true even though it is much better suited than Precision Woodcraft to compete in this area. The owner of H.H. Woods has stated that he will compete with Precision Woodcraft along its entire standardized product line thus attacking it at its strength. This strategy, while risky, offers lucrative profits if successful. H.H. Woods also receives help and encouragement from Company A in this endeavor.

COMPANY A PERSONNEL

Mr. Weir has been a purchasing agent for Company A for ten years. During that time he has become intimately acquainted with Precision Woodcraft and its products. "My main problem with Precision Woodcraft is getting deliveries on time," he reflected. "It's like pulling teeth to get commitments and once I get them I have to keep on them daily to get my order on time." When asked about H.H. Woods, he allowed that "I am still cautious about giving them large orders but have been impressed with their reliability and am considering ordering more from them."

John Allen, an interior foreman, is a rough man who doesn't take "no" for an answer. "I have had considerable trouble with Precision Woodcraft getting products that would fit in my aircraft without extensive rework. Precision Woodcraft will take items back quite readily but that transportation and rework causes considerable delay which means both a loss in money to the company and a delay to the customer." According to Allen, H.H. Woods "made a quality product" and he had "been pressing the purchasing agent to shift more business to H.H. Woods."

Five interior installers were interviewed at random. All favored H.H. Woods' products over Precision Woodcraft's products. Three of the five were able to point out examples of poor workmanship or units that deviated from blueprints. In all cases, the installers had negative opinions of Precision Woodcraft's quality of workmanship. When asked which of the two vendors they would recommend to their boss, they overwhelmingly chose H.H. Woods.

Mr. Chris, the styling manager for Company A, is responsible for determining all interior and exterior configurations of aircraft for model year styling changes.

He is also responsible for the maintenance and serviceability of aircraft in the field. He is involved from the design concept stage through the prototype or test model to the production stage. Essentially, his designers engineer the design and prepare the specifications that the woodwork subcontractor must work to. In addition, he has a major role in determining which vendor will get production contracts.

Mr. Chris had "a rather low opinion" of Precision Woodcraft. He bases this opinion on "a number of delays and broken promises on deliveries." Mr. Chris works on a tight schedule and any delays "could mean the loss of a competitive edge. I have actively stimulated H.H. Woods to bid on contract items in order to decrease my dependency on Precision Woodcraft. In fact, if there were any suitable alternate vendors, I would drop Precision Woodcraft in a minute."

Mr. Green has the responsibility of designing aircraft interiors for model year changes and seeing that prototypes are built to specification. He has dealt with Precision Woodcraft for six years and hasn't been the happier for it. Mr. Green cited "a number of situations where I have had to call several times about an order only to be put off for another week." He also related that "several times when the order finally arrived, it would not be made to specification or would be constructed with alternate materials." He felt that "the situation has alleviated some since Precision Woodcraft had hired a new liaison man but was still not satisfactory."

QUESTIONS AND REQUIREMENTS

1. How would you evaluate the president's method of personnel selection?

2. How does Precision Woodcraft's functional arrangement compare with its organizational chart?

3. In what ways is Precision Woodcraft both a healthy and an unhealthy organization?

4. If you were the personnel manager, how would you rank their problems? What solutions would you offer?

14
THE INITIATION OF MAJOR LEGO

MICHAEL J. O'CONNELL

Ten months ago Major Lego became the new supervisor of a small Air Force research office. He was the fourth in a series of military officers, each of whom had held the job approximately two and a half years. Never having supervised Civil Service employees before, Major Lego was unfamiliar with Civil Service personnel regulations and was quite naive about the informal politics involved in the performance appraisal system and subsequent cash awards. He soon learned that there were no norms or formal procedures in the research office after which he could pattern his own performance appraisal decisions.

All four people in the office are women, and they represent a broad range of education and experience. Mrs. Troth, GS-7 Statistical Assistant, is clearly the informal group leader and has been in the job for 14 years. She handles the delegation of tasks within the work group and maintains a spirit of cohesiveness and comraderie. Mrs. Weitz is also a Statistical Assistant, GS-6, and has been in her job for 16 years. Her reputation, along with Mrs. Troth's, is well known throughout the agency since they are both able to perform their duties with little or no supervision. They are well aware of what data is available and how to obtain it, and they often conduct data analyses and prepare statistical reports on their own. The other two ladies in the office are also statistical assistants, GS-5 and 4, and have been in their jobs for 7 and 2 years respectively.

Civil Service regulations require that each employee be given an annual performance review. Several possible ratings or rewards can be given: unsatisfactory, satisfactory, outstanding, a quality salary increase, a one step increase on the pay table, or a sustained superior performance cash award. The last three awards require considerable effort and extensive justification and documentation on the part of the supervisor.

In reviewing the ladies' records, Major Lego found that Mrs. Weitz had received a sustained superior performance award 13 years earlier and an outstanding rating four years ago. Mrs. Troth had received a sustained superior performance award five years earlier and an outstanding rating four years ago. Otherwise these ladies and the two junior ladies in the office had received satisfactory ratings. Apparently the performance appraisal and reward system has not been given very high priority of interest in earlier years.

Lately the agency grapevine revealed to the ladies in the research office that sustained superior performance cash awards and quality step increases were awarded to several women in other offices. Last week Mrs. Troth approached Major Lego to discuss Mrs. Weitz' performance appraisal, which is due in two months. Mrs. Troth felt very strongly that Mrs. Weitz should be recommended for a quality step increase.

Unfamiliar with the agency's policy, Major Lego informally checked with his boss and the deputy of the agency about the possibility of a quality salary increase for Mrs. Weitz. He was informed that the fiscal budget included a set amount to be allocated to cash awards and quality step increases. Each agency on the base was given an annual quota, but it could use its own criteria in allocating these awards to its employees. The agency in which the research office was located had no announced policy or criteria for allocating monetary awards. Such decisions were made by the agency chief, his deputy, and the directors of the six directorates in the agency. The likelihood of an employee receiving a cash award appeared to be a direct function of a first line supervisor "selling" the proposal to his boss, who would then convincingly persuade the agency chief and the other directors.

The agency deputy told Major Lego that the allocations for this year's cash awards had been made some time ago. There was no money left for cash awards, and it would be impossible to get a quality salary increase for Mrs. Weitz this year.

Major Lego had promised to tell Mrs. Troth what he would do for Mrs. Weitz. He is scheduled to meet with Mrs. Troth this afternoon.

QUESTIONS AND REQUIREMENTS

1. How should Major Lego handle the current performance appraisal for Mrs. Weitz? What should he tell Mrs. Troth?

2. What should Major Lego do to insure a quality salary increase in the future for Mrs. Weitz?

3. What could be done to change the casual attitude toward performance appraisal by the military supervisors in the research office?

4. Should the agency change the decision process by which high performing employees are recommended for quality salary increases and sustained performance awards? What procedures would you recommend?

15
ST. LUKE'S HOSPITAL (A)

Two days after she assumed her duties as director of nurses and of the nursing school of St. Luke's Hospital, Jenny Stewart started on the first of her "get acquainted" rounds. As she turned the knob of the door to the operating room, she heard her name called. The supervisor of the Pediatrics Department approached.

"Won't you let me show you around my department?" Miss Robbins asked. "An operation is in progress, and I think they would prefer that you wouldn't go into the operating room now."

"I know there's an operation going on," the director answered. "That's why I'm going in. You see, I want to observe the methods being used."

Miss Robbins looked uncomfortable to Miss Stewart. "I know that's a very natural desire on your part, but I do hope you will put it off until you are better acquainted. *Please* come with me today and see my department."

Miss Stewart thought the nurse's request rather strange; nevertheless, she looked over the Pediatrics Department and did not return to the operating room. The same afternoon Lois Richards, supervisor of nurses in general surgery, appeared in the doorway of the director's office.

"I understand that you intended to call on us in the operating room this morning," she said.

Miss Stewart looked up from her desk and saw a trim, wide-awake looking woman. "Ah, then you're Miss Richards," Miss Stewart said. "Won't you come in. As a matter of fact, I should like to have dropped in on you this morning but I was sidetracked; so I had to postpone my first visit."

Miss Richards remained in the doorway. "Well, I thought I'd better tell you that you will not need to call on us. When any discussion comes up between the operating room and the nursing office, I come here to settle it."

Miss Stewart was surprised by the flatness of Miss Richards' remark, but she said, "I'm glad to hear that. This is certainly the place for any discussions between department heads to take place. But I shall want to visit you to acquaint myself with the technique used in surgery and with the students in your department."

"Well, I suppose you can come if you want to, but our surgeons won't like it very much. You see, we feel that our technique isn't open to question; so we hardly need any advice. *I* see that the students do their work well. You needn't have any worries about work in my department."

Miss Stewart smiled. "I can assure you that I'm not worried about the work or the technique used in your department. I just want to get acquainted."

"All right, come ahead, but remember that I told you it would be better if you didn't," Miss Richards said over her shoulder as she disappeared from the doorway.

Miss Stewart felt bewildered. She could not recall anything in her long experience as a nursing instructor and as a director of nursing schools which would have prepared her for what she believed was an antagonistic attitude on the part of the operating room supervisor.

Jenny Stewart's career included graduation from a large midwestern college, graduation from a school of nursing, ten years as teacher in schools of nursing, and seven years as director of schools of nursing. In addition she had spent one summer at the University of Wisconsin, taking courses in anatomy and bacteriology. Before accepting her first position as director of a nursing school, she had taken a course in nursing school administration at the University of Chicago.

As director of nurses and the nursing school at St. Luke's, Miss Stewart was directly responsible to the board of directors, although the superintendent of the hospital was nominally her superior. She planned to carry her serious problems to the superintendent, however, because she believed that her work would be easier and more pleasant. The superintendent of the hospital was Carleton B. Fischer, ex-city editor of the local *Centreville Press.* He had no training in hospital administration, but Miss Stewart considered him cooperative and intelligent. He was 50 years of age, a college graduate, and had been appointed to his position the previous July.

As director of nurses, Miss Stewart was responsible for the proper care and treatment of all patients in the 250-bed hospital.

Her responsibilities as nursing school director included the education of student nurses, the selection and employment of graduate assistants, and the overseeing of nurse instructors. A Nursing School Committee helped her formulate educational policies and advised her on disciplinary matters concerning student nurses.

The director of nurses, Miss Stewart had learned, was expected to take the advice of the Nursing School Committee on vitally important policies. When the committee was of the opinion that any drastic action needed to be taken in the nursing school, it notified the board of directors of its decision. Miss Stewart was an ex officio member of both the Nursing School Committee and the board of directors.

As she sat in her office contemplating what the operating room supervisor had said, Miss Stewart wondered if she had said anything to make Miss Richards angry. She concluded that she had not.

Three days later Miss Stewart visited the operating room while surgery was

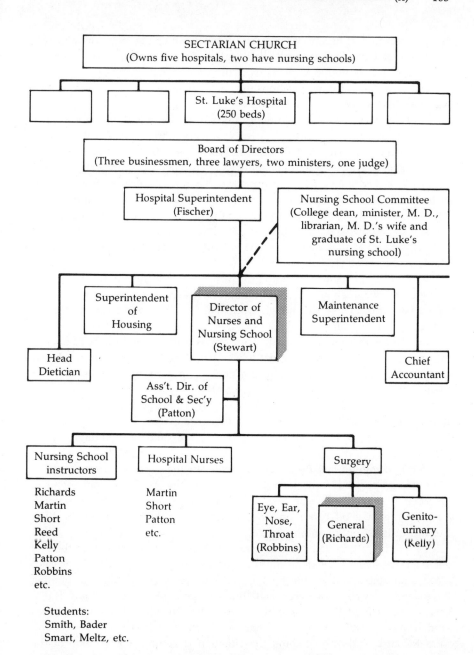

Exhibit I   St. Luke's Hospital organization chart

being performed. She observed carefully the work of the surgeons and was satisfied that what Miss Richards had said about their technique was correct. The surgeons appeared to Miss Stewart not to notice that she was present. She remembered that in former positions the doctors had seemed pleased when she watched them work.

About two weeks later two student nurses from the operating room, Clarice Maltz and June Bader, appeared in Miss Stewart's office. Miss Bader was in tears. Between sobs she blurted out, "Miss Richards kicked me. I used a forceps to take a soiled sponge off the table, but before I reached the sponge rack to hang it up, she kicked me so hard I dropped it. Then she struck my arm with an instrument and screamed in my ear. She said I was a little fool and if I knew anything I would have had the sponge on the rack. When I bent over to pick it up, she kicked me so hard I fell over. Oh, I hurt all over!"

"That's right, Miss Stewart," said Miss Maltz. "I was there when she did it. She kicked her and she hit her."

Miss Stewart, believing that both girls were immature and emotionally upset, thought that imagination and exaggeration must have played a great part in their account of the incident. She thought Miss Maltz's, "That's right, Miss Stewart," rather childish.

She asked both girls to sit down. They talked over the importance of operating room work. She told them that tensions in the operating room developed easily and that the life-and-death responsibility of persons in the room often led them to be irritable at times.

"We understand that," Miss Bader said. "Dr. Tompkins can be very snappy during surgery, but I think he forgets it afterwards."

"We don't like to have our clothing torn by the supervisor, though," Miss Maltz added.

After a 15-minute talk the student nurses left the nursing director's office. Miss Stewart decided to check on the condition of the operating room gowns to ascertain if they would tear easily. Her investigation showed that enough gowns were in good condition. A few which might have torn easily Miss Stewart ordered put to another use.

Miss Martin, a graduate assistant teacher, accosted Miss Stewart in the hall some ten days later. "I hate to confront you with a problem so soon," she said. "You undoubtedly know that for the past four years our directors of nursing have stayed only about one year each. But what you probably don't know is that each one has tried to do something about the way Miss Richards mistreats student nurses. What happens is that the director leaves in a few months and Miss Richards stays on. I think the situation is getting worse. One of the students—Bernice Smith—came to my room last night and showed me bruises on her legs. Miss Richards had kicked her while they were in the operating room. Bernice said that she was going to tell her parents but the other girls talked her out of it. They're afraid to let any outsiders know about the situation for fear that Miss Richards will find out about it and have her "gentleman friend," Dr. Schwartz, make life miserable for them for the rest of their training period. Bernice told me about Virginia Smeck who has scratches from her shoulders to her wrists—the result of Miss Richards' fingernails when something went wrong in the operating room. Bernice asked me not to take her word for it but to see for myself, but I told her that the best thing for me to do, since I knew about all this already, was to tell you about it. You are, after all, the only one whose position gives you the right to do anything about it."

"Yes, you're quite right," Miss Stewart answered.

"I heard that Clarice Maltz and June Bader tried to tell you but that you didn't quite believe them. I realize that you haven't been here long enough to know everything that's going on, so I thought I'd tell you about this myself," said Miss Martin.

"Miss Bader and Miss Maltz did come to see me," Miss Stewart admitted. "But, you see, they were so emotional at the time. . . . Besides, the story they told me just didn't fit into our way of life today—not the American way of life, anyway. I thought that the girls might not understand the intensity of the operating room situation. . . . I still think their story is most unusual to say the least. How about you? Are you convinced that all you've told me is true?"

"You don't live in the nurses' home, Miss Stewart; so you don't know how thin the walls are. For years I've heard that sort of thing discussed. Since Miss Richards hasn't lived in the nurses' home for years, the students discuss her rather freely. I don't know whether or not they realize that anyone else can hear them. You know, your predecessors knew about this situation, but they found themselves in pretty hot water when they inquired into it. I want to tell you how badly I feel about it, though, because I know if you attempt to do anything about it, you will have to leave, too. And you've been here such a short time."

"You can stop worrying about my leaving," said Miss Stewart. "I'm asking you now to tell me anything that you know to be true and are willing to declare to the board of directors."

Miss Martin said, "Oh, I don't want to get mixed up in it at all. But for your own information I'll tell you this: the doctors are back of Miss Richards one hundred percent. They will probably like you in direct proportion to the completeness with which you let Miss Richards alone." She hurried away.

The next day Miss Stewart made it a point to look up Virginia Smeck. The director noticed the scratches. "Why, Miss Smeck, what happened to your arm?" she asked.

"Oh nothing—just a little accident. Excuse me. I've got to hurry to the laundry. Miss Richards sent me for some linen."

Miss Stewart asked Miss Richards to come to her office later that day. The operating room supervisor arrived two hours after the director's request. Miss Richards sat down near Miss Stewart's desk.

"I'm wondering, Miss Richards, if it is difficult here to get students to carry out procedures as taught or if, on the whole, they are quite sincere in their efforts," she began.

"The modern girl is just plain dumb, very careless, and often insubordinate. But don't worry. I don't let them get the best of me."

Said Miss Stewart, "Those are rather harsh words, Miss Richards. What do you mean—insubordinate?"

"Oh, you know very well what it means," Miss Richards replied.

"If there's a question of insubordination, don't you think I should know about it?" asked Miss Stewart.

"I haven't come up against anything yet that I couldn't handle. The students all act the same, but I take care of them."

"But, Miss Richards, if I am to cooperate with you in the handling of students, it seems to me I ought to know a little more about their foibles. What do you mean they all act the same way?"

"Is this kind of talk all you called me down here for?" Miss Richards asked abruptly.

"Something like that," Miss Stewart answered. "You said that you don't let the students get the best of you. Just what do you mean?"

"You take care of the nursing office business and I'll take care of operating room business. See!" Miss Richards replied.

"Are you implying that I should not be interested in what goes on in the operating room?"

"I'm telling you frankly to keep out of what goes on there. Otherwise you'll be sorry. Now I'm busy, and I think I'll go." Miss Richards rose to leave.

Miss Stewart quickly walked to the door and held her hand on the knob. "It's not time for you to go just yet," she said. "I insist upon answers to my questions. As two grown women we should be able to lay our cards on the table and keep levelheaded while we do it."

"Well, just what do you want?" asked the operating room supervisor.

Miss Stewart said, "I'll come directly to the point then. Some very unpleasant stories concerning your treatment of students have been told to me. They are very hard to believe, yet at the present time there is no one but you who can prove whether or not they are true. Did you ever shake, scratch, or kick student nurses in the operating room?"

"Certainly not. I'm warning you to keep out of my business. If you don't, you'll be sorry I can promise you."

Miss Stewart continued, "If I ever attended to my own business, I'm doing it now. I still hope that you can prove that you do not do that sort of thing."

Miss Richards pushed the director aside and left the office.

Other matters of importance came to the attention of Miss Stewart in the next few days, and she did not have time to think about the affair with Miss Richards.

A week later the nursing director asked Miss Richards to step into a room where they could be alone to talk for a few minutes.

Miss Richards answered, "Our schedule has been heavy today, and our cleaning will take all afternoon. I cannot talk to you today."

Although Miss Stewart tried to find opportunity for another interview, she was never able to find the operating supervisor alone. One of her two graduate assistants was invariably nearby. The nursing director asked her secretary, Miss Patton, about the assistants. Miss Patton, who was also assistant director of the nursing school, told Miss Stewart that Miss Short, the first assistant, was the best graduate assistant on the staff in the school of nursing. Miss Reed, the other assistant, Miss Stewart learned, was also an efficient nurse. Both nurses got along well with Miss Richards.

When the nursing director finally found Miss Richards alone, she asked the supervisor to come into her office. Miss Richards replied: "I do not intend to have time to talk to you."

QUESTIONS AND REQUIREMENTS

1. If you were the personnel manager in the hospital, how would you handle Miss Richards? Miss Stewart? The students?

2. How could Miss Stewart more effectively have handled this problem? Could the problem be just a personality conflict?

3. Discuss why the organization's leaders permit Miss Richards to behave in a way that might have negative consequences for the hospital.

16
ST. LUKE'S HOSPITAL (B)

Two days after Miss Richards, the supervisor of nurses in general surgery, had told Miss Stewart that she did not intend to find time to talk with her, Helen Sommers, an alumna of St. Luke's, visited the nursing director at her apartment. In the course of their evening's conversation together, Miss Sommers confirmed what Miss Stewart had learned about Miss Richards.

"I still have some scratch marks on my arm, thanks to Miss Richards," she told Miss Stewart.

The nursing director went to see the superintendent of the hospital the following day. She told him of her concern about the mistreatment of student nurses and waited for his reply.

"I don't doubt that what you say is true, Miss Stewart," he said. "As a matter of fact, I've heard something about this myself from two or three members of the community. I don't mind telling you that the situation has me worried, but frankly I don't know what to do about it. What would you suggest?"

"Well, first of all, I feel directly responsible for all the nurses in the entire Nursing Department. Miss Richards' treatment of student nurses reflects as much on me as it does on the school of nursing. I was thinking that it might be best to take the matter to the Nursing School Committee first. Then . . . well, then perhaps I'll have a better idea of what to do about it."

"I think that would be the thing to do," Mr. Fischer said. "Please keep me posted on what the outcome is. I'm deeply concerned."

Miss Stewart promised to do so and left. That evening she wrote a list of grievances against Miss Richards. In it she included statements made by nursing students, Maltz, Bader, Smith (to Miss Martin), Miss Martin, Miss Sommers, and Superintendent Fischer. Three days later she took the statements, signed by herself, to the bimonthly meeting of the Nursing School Committee which was composed of a retired doctor, a minister, a college dean, a librarian, a graduate of St. Luke's nursing school, and a doctor's wife who was also a registered nurse.

At the meeting Miss Stewart laid before the committee the statements which she had prepared. Although some members of the committee expressed sur-

Reproduced with permission from Ohio University Press.

prise at the disclosure of maltreatment of nursing students by Miss Richards, some committee members, it seemed to Miss Stewart, seemed to know about the state of affairs.

The college dean asked why the situation had not been reported before.

Said Miss Stewart, "I think my short tenure of office and the fact that the last four directors of nursing have occupied the position for a relatively short period of time make the answer to that question rather obvious."

"Something certainly ought to be done if this is true," said the minister, "and from the evidence Miss Stewart has cited, it certainly appears to be true. I think Miss Richards should be made to resign."

The doctor said, "Let's not be hasty in our judgment, ladies and gentlemen. Our surgeons are very proud of their record of no infections. It seems to me that they would be extremely averse to anything which might lead to Miss Richards' resignation and the possibility of incompetent nursing in general surgery."

"Are our nurses of no consequence as young women, sir?" the minister asked.

"Certainly no one wants to see them mistreated," the doctor rejoined, "but it seems to me that we must not lose sight of the fact that Miss Richards has a reputation as an efficient nurse in surgery."

"Or the fact that nurses are not easily hired these days," rejoined the college dean. "It seems to me. . . ."

The nursing school graduate interrupted him. "I wonder if the fact that one of our surgeons, Dr. Schwartz, dates Miss Richards could explain her being allowed to mistreat students without reprimand. I know of certain instances in which nursing students have been mistreated, and I think—in reply to Dean Harmon's question before—that each student has been somewhat hesitant about reporting Miss Richards for fear that certain surgeons might make their lives miserable during the rest of their training."

"But that's foolish," said the doctor.

"Foolish, but possible. I worked in operating rooms, and I've seen that sort of thing; so I know it can happen," she answered.

The doctor's wife finally moved that the Nursing School Committee recommend to the board of directors that the director of nurses be given complete support in any measure to stop physical violence in the operating room. The motion was carried unanimously.

Miss Stewart, as an ex officio member of the board of directors, decided to take the recommendation to the next board meeting, the following Monday, but she first talked to Mr. Fischer. He advised her to consult the board. In the meantime Miss Stewart again attempted to talk to Miss Richards. The operating room supervisor told her that she was far too busy to be bothered with trivialities. Miss Stewart waited another day before she tried to interview Miss Richards again. They met in the hall outside the operating room. Miss Stewart said, "I'd like you to drop into my office this afternoon."

Miss Richards' reply was: "Stop bothering me."

On Monday evening Miss Stewart arrived at the directors' conference room early. She watched the various directors as they entered and made mental notes of what she remembered about them from their previous meetings. She nodded to the Reverend William Blakesly when he entered. (He had been chiefly responsible for informing the board of Miss Stewart's qualifications for the position of supervisor.) He had introduced her to Dr. Stephen R. Rauch, an elderly, retired minister, and James B. Davison, a lawyer, two more members of the board. Miss Stewart knew well the chairman of the board, Judge Selwyn C. Roberts of the State Supreme Court, and Thomas L. Alberts, a businessman, whom she had met because of his daily visits to the hospital to see his daughter who was recovering from an operation. Miss Stewart knew the other members were either lawyers or businessmen who were prominent in the community.

After the usual order of business, Miss Stewart asked for and was granted the floor.

"Gentlemen," she began, "I'm sorry that so soon after our first meeting together I must place a problem before you; nevertheless, a situation has come up with which I am unable to cope, so I've come for some advice. First, I would like to read to you a resolution of recommendation from the Nursing School Committee." She read from a paper: "The Nursing School Committee of St. Luke's Hospital hereby recommends to the board of directors that Miss Jenny Stewart, director of nurses of the hospital, be given complete, unwavering support in any measure to prevent physical violence under the guise of teaching in the operating room."

Miss Stewart awaited comments; when none were forthcoming, she continued:

"I had intended to seek the board's permission to ask Miss Lois Richards, supervisor of nurses in general surgery, to resign her position, but just before I came to this meeting I received her resignation sent through the mail—special delivery. So now you see that Miss Richards has perhaps solved the problem which I am posing for you. Of course, there is one possibility of difficulty: Miss Richards states that her two assistants will leave with her, but I do not accept her statement as final for them."

The members of the board expressed surprise.

"What's this all about?" asked one of the businessmen. "What prompted this resignation?"

In answer Miss Stewart read the report which she had presented to the Nursing School Committee.

"And now you'd like permission to accept Miss Richards' resignation?" Davison, the lawyer, asked.

"That's correct," Miss Stewart answered. "There is no other course open in view of the evidence, is there?" she asked in surprise.

Davison looked at Judge Roberts, who recognized Alberts.

"Now, Miss Stewart, don't you think that you're being a little hasty? I believe we can easily have one of the doctors explain to Miss Richards that she must not continue to mistreat student nurses," said Alberts.

"I'd like to ask you a question, Mr. Alberts," Miss Stewart said. "Do you think that she will listen to a doctor and suddenly mend the ways in which she has been conducting herself for so long? And suppose she decided not to change her attitude, what then?"

The judge answered for Alberts. "It seems to me that we would then know that we had the wrong doctor speak to her. We could easily arrange to have the right man speak to her."

"And in the meantime the students would continue to be kicked and scratched?"

"That is your responsibility," one of the businessmen interjected.

"No, it isn't. For my part I won't be responsible for what goes on in the operating room—I can't be—if Miss Richards is not responsible to me, and right now she's not."

"But, you can't avoid your responsibility to the entire hospital. After all, you haven't yet found a way to influence Miss Richards," said elderly Dr. Rauch. "You wouldn't want to remember that you failed in your job because you were unable to make Miss Richards responsible to you."

"Believe me, Dr. Rauch, I would much rather that Miss Richards and I could have settled this. I had not given up really trying until last Friday. I attempted to see Miss Richards twice to talk the matter out—even after my meeting with the Nursing School Committee, but she rebuffed me on both occasions. As a matter of fact, since I began to show interest in the matter of physical violence in the operating room, it seems to have increased. I have no reason to believe that a truce will be called while we wait for doctors to find time to talk this matter over with her. I want to accept her resignation. Of course, I realize that I must have the sanction of this board before I can."

"Have you talked to Mr. Fischer about this?" Davison asked.

"Yes, I have, and he recommended that I bring the problem before the board."

The judge said, "Miss Stewart, you know that Dr. Tompkins, our leading surgeon, is out of town for a few days. Would you not rather we just hold Miss Richards' resignation until you have a chance to talk this situation over with him?"

"No, I wouldn't. Dr. Tompkins does not share any of the responsibility over student nurses with me," Miss Stewart answered.

"But, Miss Stewart, you must remember that Miss Richards has been with us for four years. During that time we have never had any complaints about her techniques in the operating room," one of the lawyers said.

"And after all, the primary purpose of a school of nursing is to teach students to do accurate work," Alberts added. "The results have been excellent for four years; so Miss Richards must have carried out the responsibility of teaching the students an accurate technique. I would hate to think what might have happened to my daughter while she was in the operating room if the nurses, as well as the surgeons, were not doing competent work. Miss Richards must be teaching them something of a very definite value in the operating room."

"I have to agree with Mr. Alberts," said the Reverend Mr. Blakesley. "Miss Stewart, you certainly realize that the lives of patients who go into the operating room must be safeguarded at all costs."

"And I agree with you that every patient must be safeguarded at all costs," said Miss Stewart. "But it seems to me that the real question is: Is physical violence to nursing students a necessary cost?"

A brief silence ensued, then the judge spoke:

"You must realize, Miss Stewart, that you are not only asking the board to decide whether the hospital can get along without a trusted employee or not but that—well, you see—you are so new in your position. . . . It is hard for the board to decide by such an action as you now ask us to take—that you have already proved yourself, er—equal to the situation which confronts us. I say that with no sense of recrimination. As far as I know, the board is completely satisfied with your work . . . and your interest in the hospital is undoubtedly founded upon a sincere desire to do your job well."

Davison said: "No one has mentioned yet the scarcity of nurses today. It might be some time before we can get a capable successor for Miss Richards. In the meantime, Miss Stewart, can we expect that the lives of patients will be safeguarded in the operating room? There is such a shortage of nurses that it might be dangerous to lose Miss Richards at this time."

"I'd like to remind the board that there are two capable nurses who are Miss Richards' assistants in the operating room: Miss Short and Miss Reed. Although both of them are only graduate assistants, I believe that at least one of them should be capable of taking over the responsibilities of operating room supervisor in general surgery. From what I've seen of Miss Short and from what I've heard of her previous record, it seems to me that we would not be inviting trouble if the board would appoint her to the position of supervisor."

"But you said yourself that Miss Richards promised that the two assistants would leave with her," said one of the lawyers.

"And I added that I didn't accept her statement as final for them. . . . "

"But both those girls are only graduate assistants," said Alberts.

"From the tenor of the conversation which I've been hearing around the table," the judge said, "I would surmise that the board is not yet ready to approve the resignation of Miss Richards. . . . "

"I move that we lay on the table this matter of accepting Miss Richards' resignation," said Alberts.

Davison seconded the motion, and it was carried unanimously.

The judge said, "Suppose, Miss Stewart, that you attempt to interview Miss Richards again between now and the next time the board meets. I'd like you to come into the next meeting and report any progress that you've been able to make toward securing her cooperation in this matter. I think I am expressing the feelings of the entire board when I say that we are assured of your deep-rooted interest in the case, and I also want to assure you that the board is completely in sympathy with your attitude toward the—the conduct—in the operating room.

You can count on the board to cooperate with you in any further decisions that are made."

The meeting was adjourned, and Miss Stewart left. She walked slowly back to her office, repeating to herself: "And now what can I do?"

QUESTIONS AND REQUIREMENTS

1. Would you accept Miss Richards' resignation?

2. What additional facts do you need to make a decision in this case?

3. As the personnel manager, what recommendations would you offer to the Board of Directors? Why?

4. What would you advise Miss Stewart to do?

17
THE PRODUCTION DEPARTMENT

C. PATRICK FLEENOR

KCDE-TV is one of two television stations in Tuttle, a city of 100,000 population with a metropolitan area of 175,000.

KCDE-TV (and radio) had serious morale problems for some time, especially in the television production department. KCDE employed 85 people in six departments: general office; data processing; news; engineering; radio; and television production. The television production group formed the single largest department with about 20 people. The functional areas of the production department are: announcing; directing; switching; camera operating; and video tape operating. See Exhibit 1 for descriptions of these functions.

As in the case with many small to medium-sized stations, KCDE was looked upon as a training ground by many members of both management and staff. This was a reason management occasionally offered for not granting a raise to an employee. It was suggested to the employee that if he wished to remain at KCDE he had better accept his present wage as the maximum for the foreseeable future. He then would find it necessary to move on to a bigger city if he expected to be paid more for the same job. The turnover, especially in the radio and production departments, was high.

Since there was no union representation, each employee negotiated his own salary with management. There was no published salary range, but staff members knew that the approximate ranges in 1970 were as follows:

Announcers	$850–960/month
Directors	850–925
Switchers	775–825
Video Tape Operators	750–825
Cameramen	700–750

The salaries were based on a 48-hour, six-day week. Much conversation among the crew members centered around what they all agreed was a low pay scale. As one of the crew members put it regularly in conversation, "Now where else can you work a six-day week, a night shift, and virtually every holiday for such lousy money?"

Benefits were another sore point. The company made group insurance available, but there was no retirement program. Though it provided paid vacations, the company only paid the vacationing employee for two 40-hour weeks. The two-week paycheck, then, was less than what the employee was accustomed to by sixteen hours of overtime.

Working conditions with regard to physical comfort and safety were adequate and about average for the industry.

Exhibit 1

Announcers are responsible for performing live commercials and programs and for providing audio recordings for locally produced slide, film and video tape commercials. Since the work load is variable, they typically have other duties (e.g., writing commercial copy or reading news for the radio station).

The director is ostensibly the most creative member of the crew. He is responsible for the "on-air" presentation. He either recommends a set for a commercial or program, or he approves an idea presented by some other member of the crew. The director is in charge of all activities during the actual broadcast or recording session.

The switcher, sometimes referred to as the technical director, performs the physical operations at the control board required to put various video sources on the air and to mix the sources at the director's command. He also is responsible for loading slides and film on the various projectors.

The video tape operator loads and "cues" video tapes on the video tape machines for the playback of commercials and programs on the air. He also sets up the machines for the recording of commercials and programs. The video machines are extremely complicated and quite difficult to operate, requiring a practiced touch for trouble-free operation.

The cameramen operate the large studio cameras, moving them on the director's cue and selecting the shots the director asks for. The cameramen do the actual construction of the sets, and they do most of the lighting, sometimes under the direct supervision of the director.

An additional member of the operating crew is an engineer, who is not a member of the production department. He is expected to provide technical advice to the director. His primary responsibility, however, is the maintenance of the expensive and complicated electronic equipment.

It was a common feeling among the crew members that they were being "used" to some extent by management. The men knew that many general office workers for the city's major private employers and the state government were making more money than they, working better hours and shorter weeks. Adding salt to the wound was the feeling that the television job required infinitely more creative ability than the general office worker needed or had. At the same time, most felt that their jobs were intrinsically interesting and far more challenging than office or administrative work.

Great animosity was directed toward the assistant general manager of the station. His previous post was chief manager of the station in which some members of the engineering department tagged him with the nickname "Overkill." This name was inspired by his tendency to overreact to situations. On one occasion he had fired an employee for smoking in the television control room. Though parts of the studio and control areas were posted against smoking, members of the staff looked upon this regulation as trivial. Care was taken to not smoke only when the assistant general manager was in the immediate area.

"Overkill" threatened more than once to have a vital piece of equipment removed " . . . unless you guys take better care of it." The threats were obviously hollow since the station couldn't operate without the equipment. He had been heard to refer to the operating crew and the engineering department, or various members, as "coolies."

The leader of the production department itself was not spared the crew's wrath. Every member of the crew looked upon Gary Brown, the production supervisor, as "a miserable, two-timing s.o.b.," as one of the switchers put it. More than one of the men had had the experience of making a request for a raise only to find, some weeks later, that the production supervisor had "forgotten to take it up," or to be told "this just isn't the right time to ask." It had been observed by everyone in the production staff that Gary often delivered different versions of a story to upper management than he gave to his subordinates. It was generally felt that he always sided with management, especially "Overkill," rather than backing his subordinates.

The general manager of the station, Gordon Frederick, was a retired military officer and an ex-mayor of the city. He was active in political causes and was out of town frequently, leaving the day-to-day operation of the station to the assistant general manager. Most of the staff members looked upon Frederick as being a slightly befuddled autocrat since he conducted regular "inspections" when in the building and indulged a fetish for small detail, such as seeing that the flags were removed from the flagpole in front of the building promptly at sunset. He was responsible for, and for the most part the author of, a booklet of company rules and regulations called the Blue Book. In the Blue Book were voluminous descriptions of each job title within the organization and page upon page of rules pertaining to coffee breaks, use of company telephones, and virtually every other activity within the building.

The Blue Book was treated with varying degrees of contempt by most staff members and with utter contempt by the production department. Those who had been in the military insisted that parts of the Blue Book text were lifted wholesale from military manuals. It was felt that the book's only value was to management, in that some obscure regulation could be used to chastise an employee while other rules were totally ignored. For example, the Blue Book stated that the company had a policy against members of the same family being employed at the studio. However, "Overkill's" son worked as a full time cameraman, one of the directors' wives worked in the office, and the TV Program Director's husband served as a technician.

The Blue Book also contained rules for communication between departments, the management feeling being that the rank and file of one department should not communicate directly with their counterparts in other departments in matters of operations. For example, if a newsman became upset at a cameraman, director, or any other member of the production staff in connection with a newscast, he was to inform the news director, who would then take the matter up with the production supervisor. This rule was totally ignored.

Though the Blue Book delineated a very rigid chain of command, it was fairly common for orders to the production crew to come from "Overkill," the program director, or Brown, the production supervisor. On occasion, in the case of an equipment failure or similar emergency, these orders would conflict, resulting in confusion until the three decided upon a common plan.

Job security was felt to be nonexistent. Many of the workers felt directly threatened by "Overkill" and verbally expressed their fear of his capricious behavior.

Seemingly arbitrary changes of staff upset some of the men. In early spring of 1970, one of the directors was moved to the position of video tape operator. Though his salary was left at its old level, this move involved a real loss of prestige. No explanation was given to members of the crew. A cameraman was promoted directly to the position of director, by-passing several switchers. Again there was no explanation.

Sabotage, in the name of "games," became quite common among the operating crew. It was not too unusual for a film projector to be mis-threaded, causing the film to be torn to ribbons when the projector was started and resulting in program down-time. Program sets would occasionally topple over during a video taping session, or microphones would refuse to work. One favorite trick was the tripping of master circuit breakers for the control room areas. Another was pounding on the wall of an area where an announcer was on the air. One of the more ingenious acts involved the wiring of a prop telephone on the TV news set. The phone was then rung during a newscast, causing the newsman to "break up." Though members of management never appeared to suspect sabotage, its occurrence was by no means rare.

Also in the spring of 1970, Ron E., an announcer, came to work for KCDE radio. The television and radio control areas were adjacent to one another, and some of the announcers worked both radio and television. There was a great deal of social contact between employees of both sides.

At the end of his first pay period, Ron became tremendously upset. His check totalled about $50 less for the two week period than he expected. According to Ron, the radio station manager had hired him at $900 a month, but his first check was paid at the rate of $800 a month. Ron promptly complained to his supervisor, and the matter was taken to the general manager. He informed Ron that the radio station manager did not have the authority to hire an announcer at such a salary as Ron had been promised. There was no offer to compromise on the salary. Frederick offered to pay Ron's moving expenses back to the city Ron had left just weeks before. Ron's answer was, "And what the hell am I supposed to do for a job if I do return?" Feeling that he had no choice, Ron accepted the lower salary.

In May, about a month after the salary episode, Ron began questioning other employees about the possibility of unionizing the station. His idea was met with great enthusiasm by the members of the production department. More than one of them indicated that though they did not like unions, they liked the management of KCDE even less. The few holdouts expressed fear for their jobs, but no one expressed any pro-management thoughts.

Several meetings were held with union representatives, and the union formally notified Mr. Frederick of their intention to organize the production department. This action was met with disbelief on Frederick's part, followed soon by a meeting to stress to employees that "the door is always open, and you know we're interested in your problems." Union "horror" stories soon followed, accompanied by a frigid atmosphere and veiled threats by both sides. Rumor generation reached very high levels.

In early August, Ron E. was fired for "inattention to duties." He filed an unfair labor practices suit against the station management with the National Labor Relations Board. The filing of the suit served to freeze the unionization proceedings until the suit was resolved.

In the meantime, Frederick, Brown and "Overkill" turned to a well known management consulting firm for help in analyzing the organizational and personnel problems.

QUESTIONS AND REQUIREMENTS

1. What kinds of individual and group defensive behaviors occurred in this case?

2. Using Herzberg's framework, which hygiene factors are present? Which motivators?

3. What expected results of autocratic leadership are present in this case?

4. What elements of distributive justice and corrective justice are lacking? What elements are present?

18
I WASN'T THE ONLY ONE

JACK W. BRANDMEIR

Sally had been secretary to Mr. Minad for almost six years. Her position was more administrative than secretarial, although she did type Mr. Minad's letters and did take the minutes for meetings of a Divisional Policy Board. Sally's work was administrative in the sense that Mr. Minad was a laissez-faire manager who provided little direction to his department managers or staff. Thus Sally looked after many routine matters, coordinated intra-departmental items, maintained liaison with other divisions and processed all personnel paper work for Mr. Minad's division without consulting him. Mr. Minad traveled extensively and relied upon his organization to keep things going. Sally had over twenty years of progressive and varied experience in business before going to work for Mr. Minad and had been very highly recommended by executives in the region where she had previously lived.

Mr. Minad has been promoting a new building for his division. The President had made remarks to the effect that he would not approve the proposal when it reached his desk. Although Mr. Minad knew this, he was contacting architectural firms who might submit preliminary building concepts and eventually bid to do a full design. Mr. Minad believed that a well prepared proposal, supported by sound architectural and locational analytical data, would convince the President and other headquarters executives.

Mr. Minad then organized a trip to another region of the country to confer with an architectural firm. A member of the Divisional Policy Board and a junior executive to the Manager of one of the departments of Mr. Minad's division would accompany him. It was standard practice in the company for the President to approve all travel requests. A prior president had approved these automatically, and some thought that his office used a signature stamp in the request form space

Approved   Disapproved
V.R. Gehen, President _____

So far the new President, Mr. M. I. Leeper, had not disapproved travel requests. Copies of the travel requests for the three-man trip came back from the President's office, and Sally promptly filed them. Mr. Minad and the others made the trip and submitted Travel Expense Reimbursement forms. These went from the divisional accountant to the company headquarters Comptroller for payment and were refused. The Comptroller's office produced the original Travel Requests which bore the signature of M. I. Leeper under Disapproved. Mr. Minad was angry at this development. He and his co-travelers had to meet several hundred dollars of travel costs out of their own pockets.

Sally received a severe letter of reprimand from Mr. Minad for not notifying him of the disapproval before he took the trip. Sally complained to her co-workers, "Our accountant signs those requests after the President to show that we have the funds in the budget. I sign them, too, to show that we got them back from Mr. Leeper's office. Nobody ever asked me to tell them whether they are approved or not. Years ago I was told to file them, and that's what I did. There are other copies, too, so I'm not the only one that goofed. One of the three requests wasn't even sent to Leeper from this office, but I am the only one who got a nasty letter from Minad. I think the Policy Board guy insisted that he nail somebody."

Shortly thereafter, Mr. Minad apologized to Sally. He indicated that he realized that others were involved in the incident and that he had typed and signed the reprimand under pressure.

About a month later Sally had a chance to transfer to another division of the company and promptly did so. Her new job required considerable semi-independent administrative ability and was not at all secretarial. After several weeks, happy in her new job, Sally said to a confidant, "I didn't miss Leeper's signature on purpose. He writes with a big scrawl, and the 'L' did hit the 'Approved' space. The 'eeper' part was under 'Disapproved,' but we all saw that later. Mr. Minad never gave me a chance to explain. If it were to happen again, I might let it go intentionally."

QUESTIONS AND REQUIREMENTS

1. What elements of Mr. Minad's managerial style are likely to induce job satisfaction among his subordinates? What elements would give rise to dissatisfaction?

2. What further information do you need to evaluate whether or not Sally's reprimand was justified?

3. What steps might Mr. Minad have taken with respect to the policy board member and the junior executive? The president? The comptroller?

4. If you were Sally, would you have reacted as she did? Why?

5. If you were Mr. Minad, how would you have managed this incident and why?

PART IV
THE
TASK-SPECIALIZATION
PROCESS

The personnel management process of task specialization is similar to the management process of organizing. Generally, the management process of organizing consists of three main principles: (1) division of labor (specialization), (2) combination of labor, and (3) coordination (integration). Although the division of labor is as old as history, Adam Smith in his book *The Wealth of Nations* was the first economist to discuss and highlight the importance of this principle of organizing. He described the manufacture of a pin as his example of mass production and explained how the productivity of a given shop can be increased by having one person cut the wire, a second bend the wire, and still a third sharpen the wire.

Given this division of labor, there develops a need to arrange the tasks in a logical sequence or grouping to facilitate production. This combination of labor usually results in units or departments that are the structural basis for the business.

After a business has a division of labor and a combination of labor, it needs to integrate these activities into a system that maximizes output. For example, the assembly line was created to increase productivity; however, activities, procedures, work flow, and human resources require extensive coordination to produce a product.

Although the task-specialization process is similar to the management process of organizing, it is broader because it includes some of the more important aspects of personnel management. Actually the foundation of good personnel management is the task-specialization process:

In general, the task-specialization process consists of a sequence of events and activities somewhat as follows: (1) the determination of organizational objectives; (2) organizational planning, including organizational and job design based on the tools, machines, and systems technology to be used in achieving enterprise objectives; (3) job analysis; (4) the development of implicit or explicit job or position descriptions reflecting the resulting tasks to be performed; (5) the determination of human qualifications required on these jobs (job specifications); (6) the development of performance standards for each job; and (7) the establishment of work rules.[1]

Thus, the task-specialization process basically links these key activities together in a systematic way whereby activities are directed toward the objectives of the organization. As managers strive to direct the energy of the organization toward goal accomplishment, there are new developments, situational variables, and key issues that affect the task-specialization process. Some of these are:

1. *Federal laws.* All organization members and candidates must be given equal-employment opportunities because of federal laws. Further, as our society has become more concerned about the quality of life in organizations, the enactment of the Occupational Safety and Health Act of 1970 (OSHA) has had a tremendous impact on the task-specialization process by requiring employers to consider employee health and safety in task-design decisions. This act has been strictly enforced during its first six years of existence; violations of regulations range from the grounding of electrical equipment to the unsafe processing of dangerous chemicals.

2. *Technology.* Increasingly complex technologies require knowledge that can best be developed by teams of workers. Further, as our technology increases, workers are more educated and have higher job expectations. As our technologies become increasingly complex, personnel managers must be aware of the promises and pitfalls of such techniques as job enrichment, the four-ten plan, and flextime. At the end of this part of the book, we have recommended selected readings on each of these techniques.

3. *Unions.* Unions are an integral part of the task-specialization process, because they control admission to apprenticeships, oversee grievances, and have a significant voice in promotions through the seniority clause in labor contracts. Further, the union's reaction to any changes in technology must be anticipated and considered in the task-specialization process. Creative ideas, such as the Scanlon Plan, must be evaluated by personnel managers.

4. *Internal equity.* As personnel managers of the future react to federal laws, unions, and special interest groups (as indeed they must), they must also consider the impact of responding to external forces at the expense of internal equity. For example, special interest groups may successfully pressure enterprises to stop polluting; however, the decrease in pollution may be at the

---

[1] Wendell L. French, *The Personnel Management Process*, 3rd ed. (Boston: Houghton Mifflin, 1974), pp. 179–180.

expense of certain employees' jobs. From the employees' frame of reference this decision is perceived as inequitable.

Although this list of potential problem areas is not exhaustive, it does demonstrate that the personnel manager must recognize that the task-specialization process cannot be considered in a vacuum. When diagnosing the cases in this section, we recommend that you not only consider the task-specialization implications, but also consider the interrelationship with some of the other processes of personnel management.

SUGGESTED READINGS

Anderson, John W. "The Impact of Technology on Job Enrichment." *Personnel*, Vol. 47 (September-October 1970): 29–37.

Fleuter, Douglas L. *The Workweek Revolution*. Reading, Mass.: Addison-Wesley Publishing Company, 1975.

Ford, Robert N. "Job Enrichment Lessons from AT&T." *Harvard Business Review*, Vol. 51 (January-February 1973): 96–106.

French, Wendell L. *The Personnel Management Process*, 4th ed. Boston: Houghton Mifflin Company, 1978, Chapters 9–10.

Hackman, J. Richard. "Is Job Enrichment Just a Fad?" *Harvard Business Review*, Vol. 53 (September-October 1975): 129–138.

Hall, Douglas R. *Careers in Organizations*. Pacific Palisades, Calif.: Goodyear, 1976.

Reif, William E., and Fred Luthans. "Does Job Enrichment Really Pay Off?" *California Management Review*, Vol. 15 (Fall 1972): 30–37.

Scanlan, Burt K. "Determinants of Job Satisfaction." *Personnel Journal*, Vol. 55 (January 1976): 12–14.

Schneider, Benjamin. *Staffing Organizations*. Pacific Palisades, Calif.: Goodyear, 1976, 19–47.

Walters, Roy W. "Job Enrichment Isn't Easy." *Personnel Administration/Public Personnel Review*, Vol. 1 (September-October 1972): 61–66.

Whitsett, David A. "Where Are Your Unenriched Jobs?" *Harvard Business Review*, Vol. 53 (January-February 1975): 75–80.

Zawacki, Robert A., and Jason S. Johnson. "Alternative Workweek Schedules: One Company's Experience with Flextime." *Supervisory Management*, Vol. 21 (June 1976): 15–19.

19
METHODS ENGINEERING

MARGARET FENN

During the summer of 1973, I worked for a Division of the Airlines Company in a methods engineering group. Responsibilities of methods engineering included production scheduling, improvement of manufacturing methods, establishing engineered standards for production based on time/motion studies, controlling costs, and monitoring production efficiency.

PRODUCTION TECHNOLOGY

Airplanes are built by computers. Daily computer runs provided detailed descriptions of required work for each airplane. The computer also specified parts to be used and caused their release from stores. A moderate level of confusion was produced by this system. Due to the highly structured and detailed nature of the computer operations, the system often lacked sufficient flexibility to provide correct instructions under conditions of model changes, engineering refinements, and different customer specifications. As a consequence, incorrect parts were often supplied, or no parts at all, or units of work were omitted; all making it difficult for the shop to produce airplanes on schedule. So-called "improvements in manufacturing methods," created on paper by engineers and methods people, frequently had unanticipated effects when the shop workers tried to reproduce them in metal.

The shop personnel were divided into three job classifications: mechanics, riveters, and buckers. The mechanics were the most highly skilled group. They located and installed parts and drilled them for riveting using a wide variety of tools. Riveters were relatively unskilled and their work was highly repetitive. Buckers were unskilled workers who assisted the riveters by holding bucking bars behind the areas being riveted.

The work of the shop was highly standardized according to time/motion studies and the workers were subject to constant pressure to increase output and cut costs. Methods engineering was responsible for the administration of regular cuts in the number of man/hours each shop supervisor was budgeted. The basis was a set of learning curves, grounded on the theory that required time should decrease with experience.

The performance of a shop supervisor was evaluated primarily in terms of his ability to meet production schedules, often to the exclusion of other important objectives, including efficiency. In anticipation of these man/hour cuts, a supervisor tended to overstate the number of men required to complete assigned work on schedule. This practice left quite a cushion of man/hours on which he could rely when problems arose and still be able to stay on schedule.

Ben Johnson, the methods engineering supervisor, was in charge of a group composed of six methods engineers and a clerk/typist. Our office was located in the building which housed the manufacturing shops served by the group and was relatively isolated both functionally and geographically from other white-collar groups. Most members of the group were college graduates, and all had some college training.

The group acted as a liaison and organ of communication between the shop and other organizations such as planning and systems control. We checked the computer runs each day to ensure that all required jobs had printed for each airplane. If the shop had production problems, incorrect job sequencing, for example, or difficulty obtaining parts, the methods engineering group was responsible for taking corrective action.

When I reported for work, Ben told me that during my first two weeks I would be assisting Joe who was assigned to a shop assembling the tail sections. He told me that after I became familiar with the job, Joe would be transferred to another shop and I would assume sole responsibility for the tail-assembly shop.

I soon observed that there was a considerable amount of friction between methods and shop personnel, even occasional hostility. In general, methods engineers considered themselves to be part of higher management and were rather condescending in their attitudes toward the shop. Even though the shop supervisors were paid considerably more than the average methods engineer, most supervisors had worked their way up from production jobs and had not gone to college. A few days after I started work, my boss suggested that I should be somewhat skeptical of statements made by shop supervisors, mentioning several instances when supervisors had lied to him about the time required to perform a job or the feasibility of cutting man/hours.

The first thing Joe taught me was how to take the daily status report. It measured the percentage that the shop was behind schedule by comparing the number of jobs actually completed with those scheduled. Joe explained to me that the status report was a major point of contention between the shop supervisors and methods, a fact which was made clear to me the first morning I took status myself. The shop supervisor, Mike Barnes, came into the office shortly after I had distributed copies of the status report. The following conversation ensued:

MIKE: Who took my status this morning?

ALAN: I took it.

MIKE: Well, it's wrong. You got me down for five incomplete jobs in position three and there were only four.

ALAN: Well, I counted five.

MIKE: If you want to come out and look at the chart you can see for yourself that there's only four.

ALAN;   I'll take your word for it. What should I do about it?

MIKE: You'll have to write out another status sheet and change it. My job hangs on how good I look on the status.

This was only the first of a series of similar conversations. Several times I was quite sure that I had not made a mistake and that the jobs in question had been completed while I was taking status and distributing the report, rather than during the preceding day. Nor were there any complaints when I made a mistake indicating that the shop had completed more work than they actually had.

On another occasion, when Joe saw me in conversation with a mechanic, he took me aside and gave me the following advice, "It's not a good idea to talk to the workers any more than necessary. They usually can't understand what you're saying anyway and they have to stop working to think." The same day, another member of the group, upon noticing that I wasn't busy, made the following suggestion: "It's a good idea to spend all your free time out in the shop. You should keep moving around so they think you've got your eye on them. Carry your clipboard and stop and write something down every so often. It keeps them on their toes when they know we're watching them."

Early in September, Ben called a meeting of the methods engineers in our group. He announced that beginning the following Monday, the entire group would be conducting a five-day ratio/delay study. To take the study each methods man would go out to his shop and observe what activities the shop personnel were engaged in according to these categories: (1) working at work station (2) non-productive work (3) Look over/talk over with supervisor (4) Look over/talk over inspection (5) Look over/talk over with workers (6) idle (7) out of area. We were also told to indicate whether the shop supervisor was in the area. This was to be done eighteen–twenty times per day at specified randomly selected times. We were each given blank tally forms to be used in compiling the data (reproduced in exhibit 1). We were cautioned not to discuss the impending study with any shop personnel, especially the shop supervisors, in order to obtain the best possible reflection of normal conditions.

While the study was being conducted, the shop's reaction was both strong and negative. Productivity fell significantly while the study was in progress. Exhibit two shows the percentage that the shop was behind schedule before, during, and after the study as measured by the daily status report. The same data is presented graphically in exhibit three.

The shop came into the study 4.5% behind schedule. By the end of the first day they had fallen .7 percentage points further behind. The effect was more apparent at the end of the second day. The shop fell 2.1% further behind while the percentage of men "at work" rose from 66 to 74%. On the third, fourth, and

Exhibit 1   Ratio/delay study

Date 9-9	Shop	Tail Assembly		No. of Workers		43
	7:14	7:38	7:55	8:09	8:21	8:44
Working at work station	28	21	25	29	33	23
Non-productive work	6	4	1	3	0	8
LO/TO supervisor	0	0	0	0	3	0
LO/TO inspection	0	0	2	0	0	0
LO/TO other workers	3	8	5	3	0	5
Idle	2	4	3	4	4	5
Out of area	4	6	7	4	3	2
Supervisor in area	+	0	0	+	+	0

Exhibit 2   Ratio delay study and production

Date	Percent behind schedule	Percent of shop found at work station working during R/D study
8/28	4.7	
8/29	5.3	
8/30	5.0	
9/2	4.7	
9/3	4.8	
9/4	4.4	
9/5	4.5	
9/6	4.5	
9/9	5.2	66
——————— study ——————————————— begins ——		
9/10	7.3	74
9/11	7.5	72
9/12	7.8	64
9/13	7.9	59
———————study——————————————— ends ——		
9/16	7.4	
9/17	7.0	
9/18	6.7	
9/19	6.7	
9/20	6.4	
9/21	6.0	

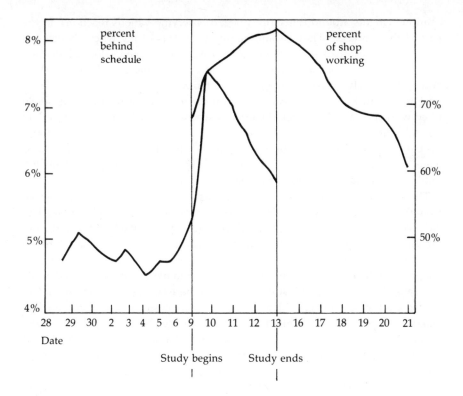

Exhibit 3   Graph of ratio/delay study and production

fifth days, the shop fell .4, .2, and .4% further behind respectively. The per-centage of men found working fell to 72, 64, and 59% during the third, fourth, and fifth days.

To the best of my knowledge, there were no unusual conditions present during this period that could explain the drop in productivity except that of the study itself. The other members of my group also felt this to be the case. Although it is impossible to draw firm conclusions based on such scanty data, the figures are supported by my own observations of the overall behavior of the shop during the course of the study (individual reactions varied greatly, how-ever).

The shop had no prior knowledge of the study, nor was any attempt made by methods to explain its nature and purpose during its progress. The riveters, buckers, and mechanics had no idea whether they were being rated individually or collectively, they didn't know what was being evaluated and they had no idea what use would be made of the information obtained.

About two hours into the first day of the study, after I had made five or six counting circuits around the shop, I began observing various reactions on the part of the workers. They became highly conscious of my whereabouts, but were totally absorbed in whatever they were doing when I looked in their direction. All conversation was suspended as I approached. Some workers became extremely nervous, trying to move too rapidly and consequently dropping tools and parts. This reaction was most frequent in women and newly hired workers. A young Black riveter was so disconcerted that he tried to rivet his index finger and had to go to the first aid station. For the first time, I saw people literally running around the airplanes. In general, the initial reactions were individual in nature; I saw no evidence of any collective group behavior until well into the second day of the study.

The second day I was the object of the most overt hostility I had experienced from the shop. I was trying to find the location of a particular part and asked an old mechanic who had previously been friendly and helpful where the part went into the plane. When he didn't respond, I asked again, thinking he hadn't heard me. Without looking up, he said, "I don't know where it goes." I had a blueprint of the part and when I tried to show it to him, he finally looked at me and said, "Why don't you just get away from here so I can do some work."

Also on the second day, Mike Barnes, the shop supervisor, came up and looked over my shoulder while I was filling out the sheet. He pointed to the "supervisor in the area" column and asked me what it was. When I explained he seemed very surprised and asked if he could see my entries. They indicated that he had been out of the area about fifty per cent of the time, and he said, "What are you trying to do to me? I haven't been out of the shop all day. You say at 11:38 I wasn't here. At 11:38 I was inside that plane right there showing one of my men how to put in a bracket. Anyway, just because I'm not here doesn't mean I'm not working; my job takes me all over the building."

By the end of the second day, each group of workers had organized their resistance and had appointed a lookout who warned the others when I approached. Initially, this system was applied quite surreptitiously, but as time passed it became flagrantly conspicuous. One vigilant worker shouted, "Look out you guys, the bastard's coming back again." Needless to say, everyone was industriously making airplanes when I got there. On the following day, whenever they saw me coming, another group of ten workers would sit down, light cigarettes, and start an animated conversation, ignoring me entirely.

On Friday, the fifth day of the study, I received a phone call from the supervisor of the group which inspected the work done in the tail assembly shop: "What's going on over there? The rate of rejection in your shop is higher than I've ever seen it. They're using the wrong-size rivets, they're leaving out parts and they're installing things in the wrong location. You know that mechanic named George Foster? We haven't had to reject one of his jobs for months, but we've done it five times this week. I don't understand what's going on. I think they're making mistakes intentionally."

QUESTIONS AND REQUIREMENTS

1. Did the ratio/delay study satisfy the organization's objectives? Why or why not?

2. How would you account for the decreased productivity during the study?

3. Compare the study performed in the Airlines Company with the Hawthorne studies.

4. As the personnel manager, how would you deal with the employees? What recommendations would you make concerning the conduct of the study?

20
GORDON FOUNDRY COMPANY

FACULTY SCHOOL OF COMMERCE
UNIVERSITY OF ALBERTA

Right after I had graduated from the Provincial Technical Institute I accepted a position with the Gordon Foundries, a medium sized firm located in a small town in one of the Eastern Provinces. It was a fine position for I was the assistant to Mr. Smith, who was general manager and president of the family-owned company. I was anxious to learn the foundry business, and since I was living alone it was not long before I literally lived in the foundry. We had many technical problems, the work was intensely interesting, and my boss was a very fine man.

The foundry workers were a closely knit group, and in the main they were older men. Several had spent a lifetime in the foundry. Many of them were related. They felt that they knew the foundry business from A to Z, and they were inclined to "pooh-pooh" the value of a technical education. When we discussed the duties and responsibilities of the position, the president had mentioned to me that no graduate of a technical institute had ever been employed in the Gordon Foundry. He added, "You will find that the men stick pretty well together. Most of them have been working together for more than ten years, which is rather unusual in a foundry, so it may take you some time to get accepted. But, on the whole, you will find them a fine group of men."

At first the men eyed me coldly as I went around and got acquainted. Also, I noticed that they would clam up as I approached. A bit later I became aware of cat-calls when I walked down the main aisle of the foundry. I chose to ignore these evidences of hostility because I considered them silly and childish. I believed that if I continued to ignore these antics the men would eventually stop, come to their senses, and see how ridiculous their behavior was.

One Saturday, about a month after I had started, I was down in the Enamel Shop. As I entered I observed a worker who was busy cleaning the floor with a hose from which flowed water at pretty good pressure. It was customary to "hose down" the Enamel Shop every so often. I was busy near one of the dipping tanks when, all of a sudden, I was nearly knocked down by the force of a stream of water. The worker had deliberately turned the hose on me. I knew that he had intended to hit me by the casual way in which he swung around as though he had never seen what he had done.

I was completely doused and I immediately decided that now had come the time for a showdown. I ran over to him and grabbed him by the neck. . . .

QUESTIONS AND REQUIREMENTS

1. How would you have reacted to getting doused?

2. What were the other employees trying to do with their cat-calls and other behavior?

3. The employees have obviously ignored some work rules. If you were the assistant to Mr. Smith, would you tell him about this incident? Why or why not?

4. If you were the personnel manager of Gordon Foundry Company and the doused employee reported this incident to you, what actions would you take and why?

21
LATEX PAINT COMPANY

DAVIS W. CARVEY AND BRUCE E. BONDY

Dave Richards, recently hired by the Latex Paint Company, was anxious to do well in his new position as personnel director. He realized he was fortunate to be working for an old established company known for its superior quality products and service. As he sat in his new office, he reflected on what great changes had taken place in his life in the last few years and how completely different the new setting was from the farm on which he grew up in Ohio. He was sure that the college degree he had finally obtained, as well as his experience as a part-time personnel interviewer for the state while he was in college, helped him in acquiring this new job. Having just graduated from the university, this was his first big chance to use all that he had learned. Dave had a strong desire to help people, but he was perhaps a bit idealistic.

Dave felt that one of his first tasks as personnel manager was to become acquainted with the 15 men working on the production floor. Considering that the majority of the work force had been with Latex Paint for a number of years, Dave thought that the workers would be able to contribute valuable information concerning past projects and procedures implemented by preceding personnel managers, most of whom had advanced in the company and then retired. Dave thought that by knowing this background he would be in a better position to encourage the positive programs and avoid those that had been proven unsuccessful.

Dave decided to begin by going on an extensive tour of the plant facilities. Latex Paint was still in its original building, although sales had increased substantially and employment had gone up five percent in the last two years. He started on the top floor where the managers had their offices, then ventured down to the second floor where the 15 union members worked. In addition to those in the main plant, Latex Paint had 25 salespersons working in 6 retail stores throughout the local area. They also handled contract work for a variety of nearby manufacturing concerns.

In touring the production area Dave was surprised to see that some of the original equipment was still in service even after 66 years of heavy use. He noted that it was still in good condition and had been somewhat modernized to increase production and incorporate new processes. While on the plant floor, the production supervisor, Oscar Lund, approached him and asked him if he was going to attend the bowling tournament that night since the company team was in the final competition. Dave replied, "I sure would like to go! But I thought only union members could participate since the tournament is sponsored by the local unions." The supervisor answered, "No, Mr. Richards, anyone from the company can join the team. It would be great if you'd come. We'd like to have the managers represented, too."

Walking back to his office Dave looked forward to joining activities of this type. He personally felt that greater management participation could help him build better relations between management and labor. He was also hopeful that this indicated that he was being accepted by the workers, especially since he had heard that many times older employees resented a young man stepping into such a position. However, he had noticed that at Latex Paint almost everyone seemed to be good friends with both managers and workers, congregating at breaks to discuss the bowling team results and to tell jokes.

Two weeks later, as he was busily working on setting up a new safety program, Dave received a phone call from Oscar Lund. In a frantic voice Oscar said, "Mr. Richards, we just had an accident in the holding tank that was being cleaned. Three men are hurt. I've called the fire department and an ambulance . . . Oh, they're here now. I'll give you the report later." It sounded to Dave like things were under control, and he assumed that the plant manager was already at the scene of the accident.

The next day, Dave Richards received the following accident report from the floor supervisor:

Accident Report

To   Dave Richards, Personnel Manager
From: Oscar Lund, Production Floor Supervisor
Subject: Industrial Accident on February 5, 1977, 3:30 P.M.

The accident occurred in the 1100 gallon holding tank located on the ground floor of the production area. The injured people were:

1. Don Merchant: Tank Washer
                   (29 year old ex-serviceman, one of our newest employees)
2. Mike Bussey: Observer
                   (45 years old, been with the company 15 years)
3. Roy Newton: Fork Lift Operator
                   (40 years old, been with the company 13 years)

Approximately 3:15 P.M. on the day of the accident, Don Merchant entered the holding tank to clean the inside. He was using a very toxic solvent when suddenly he had trouble with his face mask, which made it necessary to evacuate. However, as he tried to get out of the tank he threw off his oxygen mask and was immediately overcome by the fumes, and he collapsed while still inside the tank. The tank washer observer, Mike Bussey, saw that Don had collapsed. Mike turned and ran down the catwalk for help, but he had not been wearing his mask and as soon as he stood up and took a deep breath he, too, was exposed to the fumes. He collapsed approximately 20 feet from the holding tank. (See attached sketch.)

Almost immediately Roy Newton, the fork lift driver, noticed Mike on the floor and rushed to his aid. By this time several other employees had also arrived on the scene. Roy noticed the air hose going into the holding tank, and when he climbed up to the tank to investigate he found Don Merchant unconscious at the bottom of the tank without his air mask. Without thinking he headed into the tank after Don, but he was rapidly overcome by the toxic fumes and collapsed before reaching Don. About this time I arrived at the location and found that an accident had occurred. I took another respirator, which was located in the safety equipment box, and went down into the holding tank. I first carried out the tank washer, Don Merchant, and then the fork lift driver, Roy Newton.

Following this I called the fire department and an ambulance service, and I notified Mr. Brown, the Plant Manager, and Mr. Richards, the Personnel Manager. The fire department's rescue unit and the ambulance both arrived at approximately 3:45 P.M. All of the injured employees were treated by the rescue unit and taken to the hospital.

After the ambulance arrived it was necessary to disperse the group of fellow workers which had formed around the accident victims. I instructed the men to return to their work stations immediately. At this time I was wondering why Mr. Brown or Mr. Richards had not responded to my call. By the time the employees had resumed work, we had lost 30 to 40 minutes of production time. During this time production was at a complete standstill.

The injured men are now at Mountain Top Hospital.

Dave had heard through the grapevine that the supervisor had been quite upset because of the loss of production time and urged the men to make up for their lost time by working faster. He apparently told them to put the accident out of their minds and get to work.

Dave decided to look further into the accident situation. He found that the 1100 gallon holding tank is 8 feet high and about 12 feet across. The access hole is 2 feet by 6 feet. The job of the tank washer is to scrub the inside of the tank before changing colors of paint. Five gallons of toluol, a very volatile paint thinner, is used as a cleaning solvent. This requires the use of an oxygen mask which connects to an air hose running outside the tank.

Several days after carefully reading the report, Dave contacted the floor supervisor to find out if all of the injured employees had returned to work. Following a brief discussion, Dave found out that the observer and the fork lift operator had returned to work, but the tank washer was still in the hospital. Concerned about the situation, Dave tried to obtain more information about the employees involved, but the floor supervisor said that he had more important matters to attend to, especially since production had fallen off and the plant was not meeting the pre-determined production schedules. Oscar Lund attributed this production slowdown to the increase in machine breakdowns that had occurred over the last few days. Dave was puzzled at this sudden rash of breakdowns and the abruptness of the previously friendly supervisor.

After finding out that the tank washer, Don Merchant, was still in the hospital, Dave decided to drop by the hospital and talk with Don to see when he would be released and could return to work. Dave had already reviewed Don's personnel file and found that he had an excellent military service record and was considered a good worker but was sometimes a bit impetuous.

In visiting Don Merchant, Dave learned that he had no intention of returning to work. Don seemed to believe that both the company and his fellow workers would blame him for the accident and that his future with Latex Paint Company

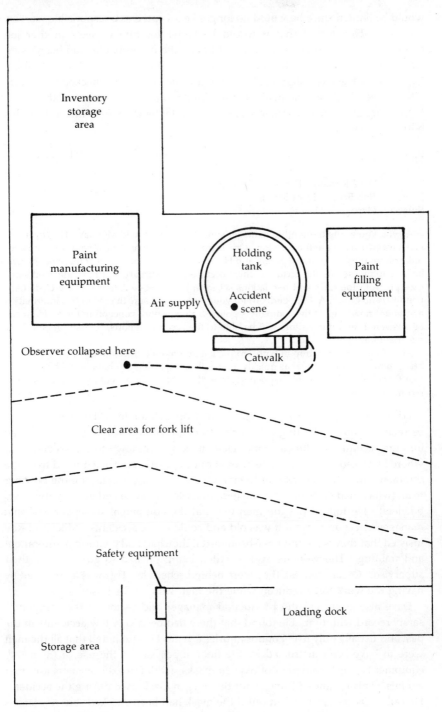

Latex Paint Company main production floor

would be limited since he would no longer be accepted as a responsible worker. Therefore, Don stated that it would be better for him to seek another job elsewhere. Don also made it clear that he felt the mask that he had been using was "no good" and that he was considering contacting a lawyer about taking legal action. Dave wondered to himself if the mask had been checked for defects after the accident, and he made a mental note to ask the supervisor about it.

Not long after Dave returned from the hospital he received a memo from his boss, Bob Bryant.

Memorandum

To: Dave Richards, Personnel Manager
From: Bob Bryant, Plant Manager
Subject: Manager's Meeting

As you know, the bi-monthly manager's meeting will be held Monday. However, we will have two visitors at the meeting. One is from the union, and the other is a compliance officer from the Occupational Safety and Health Administration. Both of these people will be here to investigate the accident which occurred on February 5. I have attached some excerpts from the rules and regulations set forth by the State Administrative Code (Appendix I) and O.S.H.A. (Appendix II) for your review. I'm sure that, with this information and your knowledge of the company's policies, all questions concerning the accident can be answered, and our visitors will be able to file accurate reports. Please prepare your material thoroughly.

Also, I have noted a drop in both production and morale since the accident; let's try to bring things back to normal as quickly as possible. Naturally we hope to take actions so that this kind of thing won't happen again in the future. I'll be looking forward to your recommendations.

Dave decided to probe this apparent drop in morale. At lunch hour the secretaries enjoyed chatting with each other and with the workers who ventured into the second floor lunch room. Dave took a walk down to the second floor where he talked to several secretaries about the workers. He gathered from the comments they had heard that the men were no longer discussing the bowling team (which had suffered from the temporary loss of Mike and Roy, the two lead bowlers). He found that the men felt that the equipment was poor and that management didn't care if it was old and could cause accidents. Mike and Roy insisted that they wouldn't have been hurt if they had had the proper equipment and training. The workers also resented being pushed to go faster by their supervisor, Oscar, because they were behind schedule. This was aggravated by having the work force reduced while the men were in the hospital.

Dave also contacted the production manager and reviewed the company's safety record with him. He found that there had been very few accidents in the past and usually only 3 or 4 minor injuries a year. He also noted that all the men were to have been instructed by the floor supervisor in the use of the safety equipment, which consisted of oxygen masks, foam fire extinguishers and first aid kits. This reminded Dave about the oxygen mask used during the accident. He called Oscar Lund to find out if the mask had been checked, but no defects were found other than that the air pressure setting was 20 PSI (pounds per square inch) instead of the normal setting of 100 PSI. He remarked that this could have resulted in hyperventilation causing Don to panic and throw off his mask, particularly since it had been Don's first holding tank cleaning assignment. Dave questioned Oscar on the instructions he gave Don. Oscar replied that he remembered that Don had told him he knew how to operate the mask, so Oscar allowed him to go ahead with the job. "As far as the other employees, well, they've been here for years. They know all about the equipment," Oscar commented. Oscar also mentioned to Dave that there was a rumor going around that Don had been fired as a result of the accident, since he had not yet returned to work. Dave assured Oscar that Don had not been fired, but he decided not to mention that Don was thinking of quitting because Don could change his mind once he left the hospital.

Dave wondered about the safety equipment on hand at Latex Paint, and he contacted the Purchasing Manager to find out when the equipment had been acquired. He found that the fire extinguishers had last been replaced 15 years ago and were normally checked twice a year. The first aid kits had been purchased 7 years ago and were refilled as needed. The masks were only 3 years old, and they replaced other masks which were basically the same design but were wearing out.

Dave checked back to the memo Mr. Bryant had sent containing the safety rules and regulation guidelines put out by the state and OSHA. He then began to put all his information together so that he would be prepared for the manager's meeting on Monday.

Appendix I
Excerpts from the *Washington Administrative Code*[1]

WAC 296-24-020 Management's Responsibility. (1) It shall be the responsibility of management to establish and supervise:
(a) A safe and healthful working environment.
(b) An accident prevention program as required by these standards.

WAC 296-24-025 Employee's Responsibility. (1) Employees shall coordinate and cooperate with all other employees in an attempt to eliminate accidents.
(2) Employees shall study and observe all safe practices governing their work.
(4) Employees shall apply the principles of accident prevention in their daily work and shall use proper safety devices and protective equipment as required by their employment or employer.

WAC 296-24-040 Accident Prevention Program.
(5) Accident prevention programs shall provide for employer-employee safety meetings and frequent and regular safety inspections of job sites, materials, equipment, and operating procedures.

WAC 296-24-073 Safe Place Standards.
(3) No employer shall require any employee to go or be in any employment or place of employment which is not safe.

[1] Title 296 Labor and Industry General Safety and Health Standards. Ch. 296-24

Appendix **II**
Rules and Regulations[2]

Subpart I—*Personal Protective Equipment*

*1910.132 General requirements.

(a) *Application*. Protective equipment, including personal protective equipment for eyes, face, head, and extremities, protective clothing, respiratory devices, and protective shields and barriers, shall be provided, used, and maintained in a sanitary and reliable condition wherever it is necessary by reason of hazards of processes or environment, chemical hazards, radiological hazards, or mechanical irritants encountered in a manner capable of causing injury or impairment in the function of any part of the body through absorption, inhalation or physical contact.

*1910.134 Respiratory protection.

(2) Respirators shall be provided by the employer when such equipment is necessary to protect the health of the employee. The employer shall provide the respirators which are applicable and suitable for the purpose intended. The employer shall be responsible for the establishment and maintenance of a respiratory protective program which shall include the requirements outlined in paragraph (b) of this section.

(3) The employee shall use the provided respiratory protection in accordance with instructions and training received.

(b) *Requirements for a Minimal Acceptable Program*. (1) Written standard operating procedures governing the selection and use of respirators shall be established.

(2) Respirators shall be selected on the basis of hazards to which the worker is exposed.

(3) The user shall be instructed and trained in the proper use of respirators and their limitations.

(4) Where practicable, the respirators should be assigned to individual workers for their exclusive use.

(5) Respirators shall be regularly cleaned and disinfected. Those issued for the exclusive use of one worker should be cleaned after each days's use, or more often if necessary. Those used by more than one worker shall be thoroughly cleaned and disinfected after each use.

(6) Respirators shall be stored in a convenient, clean, and sanitary location.

(7) Respirators used routinely shall be inspected during cleaning. Worn or deteriorated parts shall be replaced. Respirators for emergency use such as self-contained devices shall be thoroughly inspected at least once a month and after each use.

(8) Appropriate surveillance of work area conditions and degree of employee exposure or stress shall be maintained.

(9) There shall be regular inspection and evaluation to determine the continued effectiveness of the program.

(10) Persons should not be assigned to tasks requiring use of respirators unless it has been determined that they are physically able to perform the work and use the equipment. The local physician shall determine what health and physical conditions are pertinent. The respirator user's medical status should be reviewed periodically (for instance, annually).

(11) Approved or accepted respirators shall be used when they are available. The respirator furnished shall provide adequate respiratory protection against the particular hazard for which it is designed in accordance with standards established by competent authorities. The U.S. Department of Interior, Bureau of Mines, and the U.S. Department of Agriculture are recognized as such authorities. Although respirators listed by the U.S. Department of Agriculture continue to be acceptable for protection against specified

[2] *Federal Register*, Vol. 36, No. 105—Saturday, May 29, 1971.

pesticides, the U.S. Department of the Interior, Bureau of Mines, is the agency now responsible for testing and approving pesticide respirators.

(e) *Use of Respirators.*

(5) For safe use of any respirator, it is essential that the user be properly instructed in its selection, use, and maintenance. Both supervisors and workers shall be so instructed by competent persons. Training shall provide the men an opportunity to handle the respirator, have it fitted properly, test its face-piece-to-face seal, wear it in normal air for a long familiarity period, and, finally; to wear it in a test atmosphere.

(i) Every respirator wearer shall receive fitting instructions including demonstrations and practice in how the respirator should be worn, how to adjust it, and how to determine if it fits properly. Respirators shall not be worn when conditions prevent a good face seal. Such conditions may be a growth of beard, sideburns, a skull cap that projects under the facepiece, or temple pieces on glasses. Also, the absence of one or both dentures can seriously affect the fit of a facepiece. The worker's diligence in observing these factors shall be evaluated by periodic check. To assure proper protection, the facepiece fit shall be checked by the wearer each time he puts on the respirator. This may be done by following the manufacturer's facepiece fitting instructions.

(f) *Maintenance and Care of Respirators:* (1) A program for maintenance and care of respirators shall be adjusted to the type of plant, working conditions, and hazards involved, and shall include the following basic services:

(i)   Inspection for defects (including a leak check),
(ii) Cleaning and disinfecting,
(iii) Repair, and
(iv) Storage

Equipment shall be properly maintained to retain its original effectiveness.

QUESTIONS AND REQUIREMENTS

1. What caused the drop in morale at Latex Paint?

2. How could Dave Richards have prevented the drop in morale? Could he have prevented the accident? If so, how? If not, why?

3. What possible approaches might Dave Richards take in writing a report on this incident?

4. Comment on Dave's "style" as a new personnel director. After you graduate, how will you go about meeting people in your new job?

22
PARTS DISTRIBUTION DEPARTMENT

LARRY J. BOSSMAN, JR.

Corporate Personnel representative Bruce Pritchard has spent the afternoon observing operational characteristics of Parts Distribution Department and interviewing its manager, Bob Warren. Parts Distribution, together with Marketing and Warehousing, comprise the Operations section of Midwest Sales, a division of an electrical parts manufacturing corporation. A relatively small department of thirty people, Parts Distribution is responsible for coordinating the stock of primary parts/inventory for the corporation's warehouse and distributor operations throughout the United States.

Pritchard's visit from corporate headquarters was made at the request of Charlie Elsley, Operations Director. Elsley is perturbed with continuing signs of poor morale in Parts Distribution as well as with its failing reputation among the sister departments of Operations.

Before starting his afternoon of observations, Pritchard was made aware of Bob Warren's past history with Parts Distribution: Warren has been its manager for the past twelve years, having risen through the ranks of the department over a thirteen-year period. He now anticipates Charlie Elsley's retirement. With Charlie's retirement—certain within the next two years—Warren believes that he could become new Operations Director.

According to Warren, Parts Distribution has achieved an optimal organizational structure under his direction. The department's newest structure, he relates, allows him to make the most of the personnel who have "accumulated" over the years. "I've never been particularly happy with the supervisors; I've got to keep on their backs. But what do you do? They were the only ones available at the times we needed new supervisors." To compensate for individual weaknesses among the supervisors, he has reallocated certain tasks among them so that each might concentrate on those activities at which he is best.

Each supervisor typically oversees the work of two or three schedulers. The scheduler's job is core to the functioning of Parts Distribution. A scheduler (1) conducts a monthly survey on the inventory status of his assigned parts-line, (2) determines what should be purchased by part number, (3) executes purchase orders, (4) maintains warehouse contact by phone, message, or teletype, as well as supplier relations by telephone contact, expediting, and follow-up by phone. In addition, the scheduler maintains upgraded record sheets. This task accounts for over fifty percent of the scheduler's time. It is accomplished by hand-recording computer print-out data of end-of-month part stocks in the scheduler's book of monthly stock records.

Each scheduler receives from his supervisor a monthly turnover estimate which represents the number of times a parts-line is expected to be restocked to full inventory in an average month's time.

The monthly-turnover estimate, also used by the supervisor in his yearly estimate of each part-line's projected annual volume, originates from Bob Warren's office. Warren and his assistant, Harold Frain, compute the monthly-turnover figures, using market forecasts received from Marketing and inventory open-order data received from Warehousing.

Employment turnover among schedulers is a growing problem. Some seek transfers to the "more glamorous" Marketing Department. Others quit. Of the sixteen schedulers, nine are the college graduates of the department. In-fighting has occurred among some scheduler groups.

Warren's former strategy for promoting interest and morale among the department's personnel was to upgrade the job classifications, and thus the salary ranges, of both schedulers and supervisors. However, corporate Personnel Activity has not approved Warren's last four requests for higher classifications. In turn, Warren has implemented several organizational changes in the department. He believes that he has arrived at an optimal structure because greater promotional opportunities are provided for his people. He has assigned one of the younger schedulers to "Systems," a one-man operation, to debug computer errors in end-of-month inventory print-outs; he has created two "general supervisor" positions for Dave Wilson and Sid Ladimere such that the six remaining supervisors report to them; he has appointed Harold Frain, his right-hand man, as "assistant manager" to whom Wilson and Ladimere report.

In addition to their direct line involvement, Wilson and Ladimere are responsible for all plant visitations. They visit the operations of seventy suppliers—both within and without the corporation—to improve plant shipment times and order clearances.

Warren is proud of his reorganization design. In addition to rewarding some of his key men with higher positions, he has focused plant visitation responsibilities on two men who can handle themselves well in the field. As Warren related to Bruce Pritchard, "Plant visitations used to be the responsibility of each supervisor for his part-lines. But some of them were so damned lousy at it, I just couldn't trust them anymore."

Over dinner cocktails that evening, Bruce listens to Charlie Elsley reiterate his concern for the Parts Distribution schedulers. He admits that his own prior attempts to persuade Warren to reshape the department's activities have led to little, if any, improvements. Parts Distribution continues to carry its "Operation Ostrich" reputation among other divisional departments.

At one point, Charlie turns his thoughts to the topic of a brochure which corporate Personnel Activity had recently issued to the Divisions. Charlie states that he was impressed with the concepts of job enrichment described in the brochure, and saw their direct application to the Parts Distribution situation. After admitting that an enrichment project could "gain much . . . but lose little for that department," Charlie asks for Bruce's opinion.

After a pause, Bruce questions whether Bob Warren would accept an enrichment project. He is immediately assured by Charlie: "I've already bounced the idea off Bob, and he'll be willing to give it a try. That's why I've called you in, Bruce."

QUESTIONS AND REQUIREMENTS

1. What is the central issue in the parts distribution department?

2. In addition to job enrichment, what other techniques might solve the problems?

3. What are the pros and cons of job enrichment?

4. Do you think job enrichment will succeed in this management structure? Why or why not?

23
THE MIKE MOORE CASE

ROBERT L. TAYLOR

Mike Moore is an enthusiastic and energetic 25-year-old working for the accounting department of a major corporation. He has an unusual background in that his high school work was concentrated in the vocational subjects of business education, typing, shorthand, and the use of office machines. Immediately after high school he enrolled in a one-year course in a local business college where he improved his business skills to include key punch operations and the use of complex accounting machines. Mike then enlisted in the Air Force where for the next four years he served as a clerk-typist and secretary to high ranking officers. He greatly improved his business skills and was looked upon as one of the outstanding young enlisted people in the Air Force. Despite the opportunities available to him, he did not re-enlist. At the end of his four-year commitment he went to an employment agency which led him to his present job.

Mike is one of four secretaries to the corporation's ten auditors. He is the only one who can use a variety of dictating machines as well as take dictation by hand. In addition, Mike is familiar with all of the accounting machine equipment in the office and has done key punching when some of the auditors were pressed to meet a deadline.

After approximately four months on the job, Mike found that a smaller number of the auditors were giving him dictation. In fact, most of the work he was doing was overflow work from the other three secretaries, and he had less direct contact with the auditors. At the same time, the other three secretaries did not include him in their coffee breaks or lunch activities. Although this did not disturb him, he didn't feel a part of any of the office informal social groups.

After six months on the job, Mike was called into the head auditor's office and was told that the other auditors felt uncomfortable dealing with a male secretary. Although his skills were excellent, he was unable to work with and relate to the others in the office, and he was told that he would be released next week at the end of his probationary period.

Mike thoroughly enjoys his work and feels confident that he has the skills necessary to do an outstanding job. He is confused and hurt at this turn of events.

QUESTIONS AND REQUIREMENTS

1. What are the issues in this case?

2. How would you counsel Mike?

3. What should the head auditor have done to prepare the office staff for Mike's arrival?

PART V
THE STAFFING PROCESS

The continuous effective assignment of human resources to all organization positions at all levels is the objective of the staffing process. The activities needed to meet the staffing objective fall into three broad categories: preemployment planning, recruiting and selecting, and postemployment staffing and placement.

Human resources planning, a critical element in effective personnel administration, differs from planning in other functional areas of an organization; it deals in detail with factors that are both internal and external to the organization.

Sales growth and market forecasts can provide one broad planning parameter for the human resources planner, but these estimates need to be translated into needs for specific skills (using estimates of productivity and utilization for future periods). The potential availability of workers in the labor market also is required, but this estimate must take into account not only general external labor market conditions but also the organization's ability to compete for labor. Finally, these internally and externally derived estimates must then be adjusted to reflect attrition and movement anticipated within the organization during the planning period.

Human resources planning is closely linked to external events and conditions that tend to affect availability as well as those internal processes that tend to build labor resources (e.g., training, promotion, transfers) and affect employee satisfaction and consequent turnover. Among the latter are organizational leadership, organizational climate and justice, task design, compensation, and the grievance/arbitration process.

The linkage of these processes to human resources planning is particularly exemplified in the case entitled "The Corporate Policy." This case shows the

consequences of the system of planned rotation of job assignments for management development purposes. The "Birkenfield Furniture Manufacturing Company" case exemplifies some of the problems encountered in personnel planning and staffing in a restricted labor market, e.g., that of female second-income
earners.

Selection, a critical element in the pre-employment part of the staffing process, makes use of a number of devices (tests, application blanks, interviewing,
reference checks), which help the employer in reaching decisions. The process
is designed to enable the employer to hire those persons suitable for the work
and to reject those who are not. Care must be exercised in the use of these
selection devices to avoid illegal discrimination or the use of unreliable devices.
Devices that measure attributes that have little relationship to satisfactory performance on the job also must be avoided.

In general, the selection process uses a sequence of devices, each of which can
result in a rejection by the employer or the applicant. Normally the sequence
involves the completion of an application blank, interviews, tests for skills
and/or aptitudes, a medical examination, and reference checks.

In managerial selection, because of the importance of the position, the interviewing, testing, and reference-checking steps are more extensive. Whereas
some general evidence points to certain traits being associated with success in
managerial positions, a combination of more objective measures is a better
predictor of future success than any single measure or device. In addition to
making decisions regarding the identification of predictor measures, organizations may define success differently. The choice of success measures also tends
to affect the selection decision.

The "Belwood Lumber Company" case provides information on a number of
executives, each of whom might be a potential successor to Mr. Adams, who has
expressed a lack of interest in continuing as president of the company. Readers
might ask what characteristics Mr. Jones should look for in sizing up each
manager. What characteristics or attitudes would you look for in an interview?
What tests would you use in your selection? What measure of success do you
consider important for managers? In the selection process, these questions are
critical to framing an effective decision-making process.

The parts of the staffing process that deal with the effective placement of
employees include lateral and upward movement of labor through transfer and
promotion and downward movement by demotion. Movement out of the organization constitutes the last portion of the process and involves layoff and
separation.

These processes reflect the dynamic aspects of human resources management.
They serve the organization in the short run, for example, in transfers to meet
short-run employment needs, or aid in long-run shifts in resources to accommodate changes in the product/market strategies of the firm. The administration of layoff and separation processes deals with planned losses from retirement and unplanned losses from deaths and voluntary separations and assists in
the separation of persons whose performances are not acceptable.

"The Corporate Policy" case describes transfers that were planned to help develop and build organizational strengths. The incident "Reduction in Force" deals with a planned separation brought about by the research and development division's failure to meet company budget requirements. In each, the effects of plans are felt not only by the employees directly subject to the company action but also by those close to the affected employees.

As we examine these real life situations, we must ask how these unplanned consequences could have been anticipated and how, if possible, they might have been avoided.

SUGGESTED READINGS

Bassett, Glen A. "Manpower Forecasting and Planning: Problems and Solutions." *Personnel*, Vol. 47 (September-October 1970): 8–16.

Campbell, R.J., and D.W. Bray. "Assessment Centers: An Aid in Management Selection." *Personnel Administration* (March-April 1967): 7–13.

Carlson, Robert E., and Eugene C. Mayfield. "Evaluating Interview and Employment Application Data." *Personnel Psychology*, Vol. 20 (Winter 1967): 441–460.

Cox, A. "Personnel Planning Objectives and Methods: Presentation of an Integrated System." *Management International Review*, Vol. 8, No. 4–5 (1968): 104–114.

Deckard, N.S., and K.W. Lessey. "A Model for Understanding Management Manpower: Forecasting and Planning." *Personnel Journal* (March 1975): 169–175.

Dittrich, J.E., and D.S. Shannon. "Manpower Development." *Management Accounting* (October 1975): 29–32.

Domm, Donald R., and James E. Staffor. "Assimilating Blacks into the Organization." *California Management Review*, Vol. 15 (Fall 1972): 46–51.

Dunnette, Marvin D., and Wayne K. Kirchner. *Psychology Applied to Industry.* New York: Appleton-Century-Crofts, 1965.

England, George W. *Development and Use of Weighted Application Blanks.* Dubuque, Iowa: Wm. C. Brown Co., 1961.

French, Wendell L. *The Personnel Management Process*, 4th ed. Boston: Houghton Mifflin, 1978, Chapters 11–14.

Guion, Robert M. *Personnel Testing.* New York: McGraw-Hill Book Company, 1965.

Helfgott, Roy B. "Easing the Impact of Technological Change on Employees: A Conspectus of United States Experience." *International Labor Review*, Vol. 91 (June 1965): 503–520.

Loving, Rosalind, and Theodora Wells. *Breakthrough: Women in Management.* New York: Van Nostrand Reinhold Company, 1972.

Meyers, D., and L. M. Abramson. "Firing with Finesse: A Rationale for Outplacement." *Personnel Journal* (August 1975): 432–434, 437.

Miner, John B. "Psychological Testing and Fair Employment Practices: A Testing Program That Does Not Discriminate." *Personnel Psychology*, Vol. 27 (Spring 1974): 49-62.

Mintzberg, H. "Managerial Work: Analysis from Observation." *Management Science* (October 1971): 97-110.

Peskin, Dean B. *Human Behavior and Employment Interviewing.* New York: American Management Association, 1971.

Schneider, B. *Staffing Organizations.* Pacific Palisades, Calif.: Goodyear Publishing Company, 1976.

Shepard, David I. "Relationship of Job Satisfaction to Situational and Personal Characteristics of Terminating Employees." *Personnel Journal*, Vol. 46 (October 1967): 567-571.

Taylor, V.R. "A Hard Look at the Selection Interview." *Public Personnel Review*, Vol. 30, No. 3 (July 1969): 149-154.

Thompson, David W. "Some Criteria for Selecting Managers." *Personnel Administration*, Vol. 31 (January-February 1968): 32-37.

Wickstrom, Walter S. *Manpower Planning: Evolving Systems.* New York: Conference Board, 1971.

24
AFFIRMATIVE ACTION RECRUITING

ROBERT KNAPP

A year ago Culver College filed, with Federal government approval, an Affirmative Action Recruiting Plan to achieve certain broad objectives, including a maximum effort to hire minority and female faculty members. As a target to measure its progress, the college agreed to recruit sufficient minorities and women so that the percentage of these types of faculty would approximately equal the percentage of minorities and women among students.

Subsequent to approval of the recruiting plan, one additional faculty position was allocated to the Department of Economics at a salary range of $14,500 to $15,500.

Dr. William Wiley, the college president, personally reminded Dr. Sidney Smith, chairman of the Economics department, that the department had much progress to make in hiring women and minorities.

The department's faculty included 19 white males and one white female while 12 percent of the college's students were black and 22 percent were women.

President Wiley emphasized to Smith that the college could lose millions of dollars in federal funds if it did not achieve its recruiting commitments. He also said that government officials had singled out the Economics department as one that was "under-utilizing" women and minorities on its faculty and that he expected the department to meet the college's Affirmative Action goals.

In making extra efforts to reach women and minorities, Dr. Smith had expanded the usual search procedures. Announcement letters were sent to all major universities, advertisements were placed, and recruiting was conducted at three professional meetings.

After five months of advertising and searching, the recruiting process was entering its final stages.

Dr. Smith called a meeting of all department faculty to review the recruiting process results and to get recommendations as to which candidate should be offered the position. With most of the faculty present, Dr. Smith began by citing the traditional criteria for new faculty members hired at Culver College:

1. a doctoral degree in hand or near completion from a prestigious university;

2. experience, or at least promise, as a good teacher;

3. publications, or at least promise, as a scholar;

4. strong letters of recommendation.

He stressed that within these traditional criteria the college was committed to hiring minorities and women and that he had focused his recruiting efforts with that in mind.

Three major candidates surfaced from the recruiting effort, he said.

One candidate (A) was a white woman. She was about to earn her doctorate from a "Class A" university, she had two articles published, and she had a three-year teaching record. All her references said she performed outstandingly in the classroom and showed great promise as a teacher/scholar, and all expressed the wish that she would remain to join their faculty.

The second candidate (B) was a black male planning to graduate from a "Class B" university, and he had no teaching experience or publications. His references were mixed. Half indicated that they did not think he would qualify to teach at their school. Two said they were not sure he would ever finish his dissertation and graduate. However, two other references said the candidate had started late from a disadvantaged background, and while he was not fully qualified yet, he was "qualifiable" and might perform well if some experienced faculty members would work closely with him for a couple of years.

The third candidate (C) was also a black male who seemed outstandingly qualified in every way, certainly on par with the female. However, he had informed Culver College that he wanted at least $18,000 annual salary, which he believed he could obtain elsewhere, in private industry if necessary.

In response to a request from Dr. Smith for comments, a young professor who had been a civil rights activist said it was clear that one of the two blacks should be hired because they already had one woman on the faculty. He also said that he had heard that one present faculty member had accepted an offer from another school and would be leaving next year.

"Using some funds from this upcoming vacancy, we ought to make an offer of $18,000 or whatever it takes to get candidate 'C,'" he argued.

If this was not possible, he said that he would be glad to assist candidate "B" finish his dissertation after he arrived and assist him in other ways. A number of others nodded approval.

Dr. Knox, another faculty member, asked if Dr. Smith had turned up any qualified white males.

"Yes, there are some," said Smith, "but I think we ought to look first at hiring one of these."

The female professor said that candiate "A" clearly offered the best combination of credentials and availability. She had known candidate "A" for many years, could recommend her in highest terms, and had personally recruited her, she said. If an offer were not extended to "A," the professor said that it would only confirm her growing feelings of being the token woman on the faculty. Failure to extend an offer to "A" could only be viewed as blatant discrimination, and she would urge the Women's Caucus to bring legal action against the college, she concluded.

A fourth faculty member suggested another approach based on information no one else had. He had learned only yesterday, he said, that a highly qualified black who had been teaching for one year at another major school was dissatisfied and would probably seriously consider moving to Culver.

"I know he likes Culver and our city, and I think he would be satisfied with our stated salary," he said. "The only problem is that the professor is in the sub-field of macro-economics, whereas our opening is in mathematical economics."

Another professor quickly suggested that the department could go one year without filling the vacancy in mathematical economics. "We will be adding someone in macro-economics in a year or so anyway," he said. "Let's do it now, just a little early, and next year we will recruit again in mathematical economics."

Another comment suggested that a second faculty position should be requested from the college administration, thus permitting the department to hire in both sub-fields this year and to add a black and a woman to the faculty.

A variety of comments on the candidates and alternative courses of action followed for over two hours. Most focused on the pros and cons of the earlier suggestions, but no clear consensus emerged.

Finally, one faculty member, noting the late hour, said that it was time to compromise ideal principles and preferences. He recommended that an offer of $15,000 be made to candidate "C."

"We know he will reject it," he argued, "but we will at least show our good intentions."

After candidate "C" declined, they could extend an offer of $13,000 to candidate "B" for a "visiting" appointment for one year.

"We should be able to argue in the record that this low offer was justified because the candidate was clearly less than fully qualified," he said. "This would give us a year to evaluate his potential, after which he might be extended a regular appointment at full salary."

Someone commented that candidate "B" would probably refuse the offer anyway and thus save the college embarrassment if it had to terminate him after one year.

"Exactly," said the professor who had urged the compromise. "Then we could offer candidate 'A' a regular appointment at about $15,000 or $15,500."

This series of recommendations caused added discussion. Noting the late hour and improbability that a decision would be made, Dr. Smith said that he wanted to adjourn the meeting. He asked that the group think about all the matters discussed that day in preparation for a second meeting next week.

The next day, Professor Knox, who had asked about possible white male candidates, made an appointment to see Dr. Smith. When Knox arrived, Smith was surprised to see that he was accompanied by four other faculty members. None had spoken at the meeting, except for Knox's brief question.

Smith invited them to be seated and asked what he could do for them. "Dr. Smith, the five of us have discussed what happened at the meeting yesterday, and frankly sir, we are very distressed," Knox said, adding that they objected to the college's apparent policy to hire based upon racial and sexual quotas.

Smith quickly responded that the college had no quota policy, but that Affirmative Action required extra efforts be made to correct past hiring imbalances that led to under-utilization of certain groups on the faculty.

"It is the law, and President Wiley expects us to comply fully," he added.

A lengthy, and increasingly heated, discussion ensued. Finally, Professor Knox said that he didn't believe it possible for the group to reach a common understanding with Dr. Smith of what the law and equal opportunity really meant. Smith agreed that there was not much to be gained by continuing the discussion, adding that he also had another appointment to keep.

As they were leaving, one of the group said, "I think you should know, Dr. Smith, that since others are quick to suggest legal action charging discrimination, the five of us are thinking seriously about bringing action against what is clearly reverse discrimination."

QUESTIONS AND REQUIREMENTS

1. What is your understanding of affirmative action?

2. Are affirmative action and equal opportunity the same thing?

3. Do you think organizations should be required, either by law or by social pressure, to compensate for past discrimination by giving special preferences? Does it make any difference whether past discrimination is legally proved or only "subconscious"?

4. Which proposals discussed at the meeting would you favor and why? What other proposals could you recommend to hire qualified candidates and meet affirmative action commitments?

5. Which proposals at the meeting seem wrong to you and why?

6. If you were in an organization working under affirmative action commitments, what policies and procedures would fulfill recruiting responsibilities and also avoid the problems at Culver College?

7. If possible, bring to the class a real organization's affirmative action plan.

8. How would you resolve the argument that minorities tend to be underqualified because of discrimination and, therefore, can never become fully qualified without "allowances" being made for their deficiencies?

25

THE JOINING UP OF JANET MILLER

ROBERT A. ZAWACKI

Janet Miller is forty-seven years old, married, and the mother of two children in their twenties. Recently, Janet was hired to work in the Market Evaluation division of a large New York industrial firm. The Market Evaluation division has two sections: Research and Testing. Each section has approximately five women employees and a male supervisor.

The Research section consists of a homogeneous group of women who have worked together for over fifteen years. They range in age from forty-five to fifty-four, all have children, and some have grandchildren. They eat lunch together and use their coffee breaks to discuss, among other things, their children and grandchildren. Through the years, the group has become very close, and they often have family members visit the office.

When a vacancy occurred in Research, Mike A. Taylor, the section's supervisor, asked Personnel for the folders of qualified personnel seeking employment with the firm. He received five folders and asked the four female employees of Research to review them and select the top three applicants. After reviewing the five folders, the four employees ranked the top three and presented their decision to Mike. Mike agreed to interview the three candidates and asked Betty Grace, who had the longest tenure in Research, also to interview them. After the interviews, Mike and Betty both decided that Janet Miller was the most fully qualified and asked Personnel to process the necessary paperwork to effect her immediate employment.

When Janet started working, Mike explained to her that, although he was her supervisor, Betty would conduct her training program. He further explained that all five employees of the Research section must function as a team and that there was a general lack of structure and supervision because of the unique demands placed on the section by various research project officers.

Almost from Janet's first day of employment, her peers began to complain to Mike that Janet was slow, had a high error rate when computing statistics, and would sleep on the job for short periods of time. As the weeks passed and the complaints continued, Mike counseled Janet on her substandard performance. Janet denied that her work did not meet the minimum standards expected by her peers; however, she did admit that she occasionally "nodded" on the job because of the routine task.

Mike shared this personnel problem with his superior, the director of the Market Evaluation division, and both managers agreed to observe Janet's performance and make "memos for the record" if they observed an unacceptable attitude or behavior. Although the complaints continued, the two supervisors did not directly observe any unsatisfactory behavior by Janet during a two-month period. They did observe that Janet no longer went to lunch with the other group members and that she began to seek interpersonal relationships with people outside the Research section. As communication between Janet and her peers decreased, conflict continued to increase in the section, and Mike began to receive reports from other department managers that the effectiveness of Research was decreasing. Betty was observed discussing Janet's poor performance with the other team members; it was also rumored that she was discussing Janet's behavior with the Testing section. The situation finally deteriorated to the point where Mike decided that he had to terminate Janet's employment for the good of the Research section.

The morning after Janet's firing, George L. Kent, the supervisor of Testing, stuck his head in Mike's office and asked, "Who are the women going to pick on next, now that Janet is gone?"

QUESTIONS AND REQUIREMENTS

1. There was a rather serious conflict between Janet and her peers. What caused this conflict? Was it a personality conflict?

2. Analyze Mike Taylor's behavior. Was he an effective supervisor and counselor?

3. Discuss the overall joining-up process of the Market Evaluation division, and give your recommendations for increasing the reliability and validity of the process.

4. What is the predictive validity of the personal interview as a selection technique?

5. Was Janet Miller railroaded because she was new to the group? Could anyone be accepted by that group? If so, what type of person could be?

26
SUCCESSION IN MANAGEMENT
AT UNITED FOODS STORES, INC.

WELDON J. TAYLOR

John L. Fergeson, organizer and general manager of United Foods, the largest distributor of foods in the Atlanta metropolitan area, was confronted with a problem of whether or not he should name Don Franklin as his assistant. Such a move was tantamount to naming him to become his eventual successor as general manager. He was then 60 years old and planned on retiring at 65. Franklin was significantly younger than five other middle management men, all of whom aspired to the position and who felt that Franklin was Fergeson's favorite, yet had no better qualifications for the position than they had. Franklin came into Fergeson's office in the morning of September 15, 1964, and informed him that Superior Wholesale Grocery Company of Detroit, Michigan, had offered him an attractive executive position. He was disposed to accept it unless he could be assured that he would ultimately have a good opportunity to become general manager of United Foods Stores, Inc.

HISTORY

The United Foods Stores, Inc. was organized as a cooperative food chain in 1940. It was the independent merchant's response to the chain store movement which had experienced rapid growth through the 1920s. During the 1930s the problem of chain store dominance was aggravated by the depression. The public became more price conscious, and the chain trades promoted their price advantage vigorously. Some of the independent stores joined with other wholesalers in the Independent Grocers Alliance sponsored by the Greater Atlanta Wholesale Grocery Company. Others went with Ridges Incorporated, a wholesaler who franchised stores under the Red and White voluntary chain. By means of discounts for guaranteed volume, management services, and cooperative advertising, these two chains successfully took the cutting edge off the chain store drive for complete market dominance.

John Fergeson at this time was an attorney for the Atlanta Food Distributors Association. As an attorney well acquainted with the food distributing business,

Reprinted with permission of Brigham Young University Press, Provo, Utah, from a case by Weldon J. Taylor. Copyright 1973.

he was employed to assist in organizing the United Grocery Incorporated, composed of some of the leading merchants in the region. Subsequently he was invited to become the manager of this group and accepted the position. This system differed from the I.G.A. and Red and White since it was a cooperative type of organization in which the annual profits were returned as patronage dividends to the members.

CHANGING MANAGEMENT PROBLEMS RESULTING FROM INNOVATION AND GROWTH

From its inception the organization was successful. Several smaller wholesalers in the general Atlanta area were unable to compete with the marketing innovations of these new kinds of institutions and went out of business. Even Ridges, with its Red and White franchising program, although in a period from 1945 to 1955 reduced its operating margins from 10 percent to 5 percent of sales, was unable to compete successfully with the General Atlanta Wholesale Company with its I.G.A. and with Fergeson's group of United Grocers whose gross margin was below 4 percent.

The following statistics indicate the magnitudes of growth and the changing character of the business from 1945 to the projected goal of 1970 as viewed at the time of the problem.

Indexes of Growth of United Foods Stores, Inc.

	1940	1945	1964	Goals for 1970
No. stores	25	100	500	1000
No. of employees	100	200	600	1000
Sales in dollars	3,000,000	12,000,000	125,000,000	225,000,000
No. of items	1500	2000	5000	9000
Share of market in region	7%	25%	45%	50%

The above table outlines in quantitative dimensions the nature of the management challenges faced by Fergeson in this enterprise. From a small tightly managed unit with 25 stores it grew in every dimension. Each of the store managers, who theoretically under the cooperative philosophy had a voice in management, grew from 25 to 500. The employees increased from 100 to 600 in 1964. Tasks were divided and different positions were added such as departmental supervisors, division managers, and line departments within divisions. The divisions of Fruits and Vegetables, Meats, Frozen Foods, and Non-grocery items were added to the traditional grocery line of canned and packaged goods. Although the increasing lines and kinds of services proliferated in the food distribution trade throughout the nation, the growth of the market share of this Atlanta based group to 45 percent indicated that it anticipated these trends early and administered the innovations successfully into operations. It was, therefore, crucial to Fergeson that the unity of the organization be preserved and that his successor not only be accepted by the personnel,

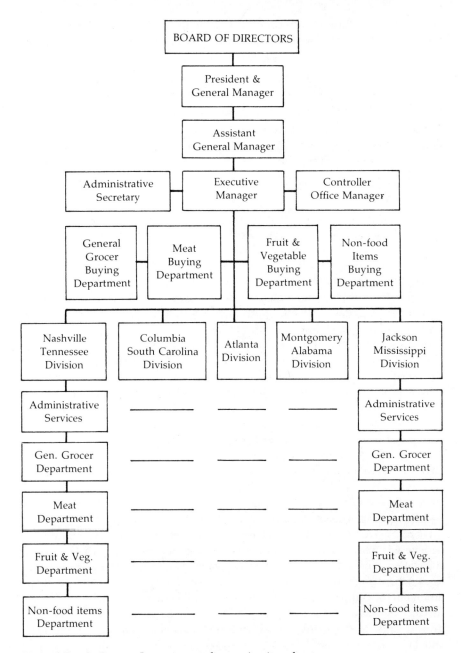

United Foods Stores, Inc. proposed organization chart

but that he have the ability to continue to build the organization. He was fairly certain that the goals for 1970, the year of his planned retirement, could be achieved.

DESCRIPTION OF PRINCIPALS

The description of the principals in the case will provide the intricate dimensions and the philosophy of each of the men involved and describe how they perceived the problem at the time.

JOHN FERGESON

John L. Fergeson was born in Atlanta, Georgia, and had a degree in law from Duke University Law School. He was the father of three boys and one girl. He began his career as indicated in private law practice. As would be expected from observing the growth of United Grocers, he was able to win, hold, and increase the support of the grocers in the Southern states and guide it into the building of the present unusually successful business. He was highly regarded in the community, a leader in Atlanta sports and recreation programs, and sat on the board of several leading business institutions.

Fergeson, by virtue of the basic pattern of the cooperative kind of organization, had to take an open stance as a manager. All financial information and company strategy was almost public information. He made no attempt to conceal profit on sales figures or any other data about the company. He worked well in this kind of environment. He was an open kind of person, and in any kind of organization would have had a strong commitment to human dignity and would have built a trust relationship with his associates.

In the selection of his successor, however, Fergeson confessed that he did not have the education and training necessary to achieve an optimum goal without serious conflict which might wreck the organization. As formal and informal leader of the organization, including the stockholder grocers, his influence was such that his selection of a successor would be formally accepted.

He recognized the need for preparing a successor in 1957, 13 years before he became 65, when he planned to retire. He selected five men who might be considered candidates for the top management post and placed them in positions where their management skill could be developed. He moved them around in the company to observe them under different responsibilities. In each instance he was concerned to give each of them an opportunity to maximize his growth and development. He described the qualifications which the man should have as follows:

There have been many advances in the field of Business Management during recent years. Many of them relate to the computer, to management science and the use of quantitative tools to achieve management goals. I haven't had the educational background which will enable me to give the kind of leadership the company must have if it is to achieve the goals we see as possible. The new manager must possess these qualities.

Another characteristic is one that we would expect from any manager: he must view the company and its operations as a unity. He must be able to spread his commitment from specialization to include all the company divisions and have a sincere concern for all the personnel and be accepted by them as a leader. Indeed, this latter, skill with people, is very important since there is some danger of dissonance arising from some of the men who aspire to the management position.

After three years in 1960 he perceived that each of these men had a talent in an area as division manager, or buyer, or warehouseman, or in some specialized area. But with one exception, the awareness of the general unity and inter-dependence of each division to the whole was not present. The exception was Don Franklin, who was 15 years younger than the average of the other four members. Franklin became interested in the company's future and accepted full-time employment with the company in 1953.

Fergeson confessed his weakness in handling this situation to prevent the resentment on the part of the four other men during the ensuing three years. The idea of succession was never discussed, and Fergeson attempted to avoid showing favoritism to Franklin. He did not place him in positions where he had status above the other men. He did, however, admit to consulting him on decisions when major issues arose because he respected his opinion and felt a genuine need for his advice. Fergeson had several positions in the trade and served as legal counsellor to the National Food Grocers Association for several years. On some occasions he would take Franklin with him to conferences to assist him in his administrative capacity. Franklin became known by the officers of the national organization and was asked to participate on programs. He performed well, and favorable reports of his presentations were published in the trade journals.

Reports on Franklin's triumphs filtered back to the company department heads, and they read the favorable reports in the trade magazines. They reacted negatively to these reports. They felt that if they had been given the opportunity and exposure that Franklin had, they could have performed as well or better. One of these men especially reacted with hostility. He began to backbite and bear tales about Franklin which evidenced, as Fergeson perceived it, considerable distortion. He solved this problem by transferring this man to a higher level position in the Nashville division.

Fergeson during this period perceived his program as a failure. He admitted that unthinkingly he might have shown slight favoritism to Franklin. He also thought that Franklin might have been unduly aggressive on some occasions and not thoughtful of his associates in terms of winning their respect. These indiscretions, however, did not change the nature of the problem. He still felt Franklin was the only man with the conceptual and other skills necessary to become manager.

Yet at the present time he perceived that the strong men in the company who had great influence and were strategic to the company's success were in no state of mind to accept Franklin as their future leader. This then was the dilemma faced by Fergeson when the Superior Wholesale Grocery Company, second largest food distributor in the nation, offered an executive position to Franklin; and he came in to discuss the issue with Fergeson.

DON FRANKLIN

Don Franklin was also a native of Atlanta, Georgia. His family was well known in business circles. Indeed, his father had done well in the real estate business and was eager to have Don join him. He had enjoyed his schooling in business at the Georgia State University, and found the part-time job at a department store which served as an effective supplement to his education. When he finished his school in 1953 he accepted a position with United.

From the beginning he shared Fergeson's enthusiasm about the company's prospects. Franklin was very eager to grow in stature in business and make his mark. He had no antagonism toward his peers in the organization but felt that it was legitimate for him to take advantage of every opportunity presented to show his better self and move up in the company. Although many of his triumphs and recognitions created jealousy among his peers, he felt that this was to be expected in business and a natural part of the game. He did not go out of his way to avoid such situations. He did, however, respect Fergeson and loyally accepted his leadership. Although he would have accepted an assistant managership at this point, he understood Fergeson's dilemma and felt no bitterness in his failure to appoint him. Such appointment would have been an overt admission of his being heir to the manager's position.

Franklin was very fond of the South as a place to live; he had many friends in Atlanta and really preferred to make it his home. Yet under the circumstances, he was disposed to accept Superior's offer and go to Michigan.

MICHAEL WILLIAMS

Michael Williams received his early training in the stock room for one of the small wholesalers in Atlanta. He went to night school and studied accounting and became office manager and chief assistant to the manager of the firm when Fergeson persuaded him to take a similar post with United when it was organized in 1940. Williams proved competent in every respect. He successfully integrated the accounting systems to include divisional and departmental operations and provided leadership in working out novel and efficient stock control and billing systems. Indeed, United was one of the first firms to have an ordering, accounting, and warehousing system completely coordinated so that ordering, loading, delivery, and billing could be perfectly integrated into a unified series of transactions.

Fergeson did not see in Williams, however, the spark of leadership that would hold the organization together and stimulate each man to be aggressive in his own calling and still be conscious of the activities of his associates in other areas. His competence and drive did not include these dimensions as Fergeson perceived him. It would be wrong to say that Williams did not aspire to the manager's position. Yet he accepted Fergeson's judgement and was not disposed to initiate any trouble.

ALAN HARDY

Alan Hardy also came to the company from the management of one of the large food chain units in Atlanta when the company was organized in 1940. He was appointed division manager of the Atlanta Division and worked in the home office. He was alert to company problems and opportunities. Fergeson, who came with his law background, needed considerable technical guidance in the food distribution field, especially in the initial years of the company's growth. He leaned on Hardy a great deal and counselled with him frequently. When he would leave the office, he would place Hardy in charge. Indeed for a period of years, without being specifically designated as such, Hardy served as assistant manager.

Yet Fergeson and Hardy's peers perceived him as a very jealous person. He was hypersensitive to criticism and found it difficult to accept suggestions. He required constant praise for his work. Indeed, his appetite for adulation was insatiable. Fergeson would compliment him on his performance, and he would always persist in enlarging on the compliment and seek additional praise. Hardy was completely unaware of these personal characteristics which others perceived as giving him problems, and he could not hear others when they tried to inform him.

In spite of his quickness and competence in many areas, in other areas on the spectrum of his qualities he was rigid and opinionated. For example, early in the history of the company when the frozen foods division was proposed with some empirical evidence for its success, he fought the adoption vigorously and was not open to consideration of the data which predicted large volume sales.

In view of his senior position in the company he expected to become general manager. He was jealous of anyone who rivalled him in these expectations. When Franklin began to emerge as a candidate, he spread talk around the Atlanta office about him and enlarged on what he perceived to be Franklin's faults to his associates. The tension around this relationship developed to such a degree that Fergeson placed him in charge of the Nashville Division. Hardy accepted this assignment gracefully since the Nashville Office was the largest outside of Atlanta. The manager there had more autonomy than the Atlanta division, which operated out of the main office of the company.

Although the employees of the company fully expected Hardy to become the president and general manager because of his seniority and Fergeson's one-time dependence on him, they would have resented his leadership.

BURTON KELLEY

Burton Kelley came to the company as a young man who had been raised in the grocery business. His father had been a successful merchant. His father's store had grown from a mom and pop, one-man operation to a modern supermarket.

Burton had worked part-time while in high school and college and was therefore quite aware of the nature and operations in the food distribution business. His father was a member of the board of United Grocers and encouraged Burton to take a position in the warehouse that was open at the time, 1954, when he finished his college training at the University of Georgia in business administration.

He was successful in his assignment and showed up well as promotion manager and buying and merchandise manager of a product division. He was flexible and could adapt quickly to any assignment he was given. He was technically prepared. In addition to his skill in promotion, he was also competent in the quantitative skills and the use of the computer.

Kelley seemed to have all the characteristics that Fergeson was seeking in a manager. Yet there was one aspect that worried Fergeson. He actually appeared to want promotion; and while it was not explicitly discussed, Fergeson felt that he would want and may even expect an appointment that would be in line for the manager's post, especially when Alan Hardy was transferred. Yet Fergeson perceived that he was not willing to pay the price. He often failed to give the extra effort to see a task completely through and give the necessary attention to details. He had an attractive wife who demanded his time and attention. She was not satisfied with the progress he was making. Their social life was important to him. These activities made it even more desirable for Kelley to get promoted to general manager. Yet it appeared to Fergeson that he would often place his social commitments ahead of his commitments to the company.

To observe him more thoroughly, Fergeson placed him in charge of one of the buying divisions where he had ultimate responsibility for getting a rather intricate job done supervising the activities of many buyers and their staffs. He did not do well in this position, and many of the men in the division tended to adopt his characteristic of failing to follow through until a desirable degree of excellence was achieved.

Kelley was not aware of his weakness. He was not prepared to listen to those who might have given him helpful feedback. In view of this characteristic, Fergeson could not place him in a position where he would become manager. Yet he expected him to make trouble if someone whom Kelley perceived as less capable was promoted ahead of him. At the present time Kelley seemed to give the impression to Fergeson that he was being overlooked.

FERRELL SCOTT

Ferrell Scott was 56 years old. He had previous experience in another company before coming to United and came with strong recommendations. He was capable, strong, level headed, and very loyal to the company. He was aware of the vying for position of the other members of the staff, but took an aloof and philosophical view of the contest. In the event that Fergeson had for any reason left the company, Scott would have been a natural replacement. He was, however, only four years younger than Fergeson. Therefore, Fergeson felt that it would not be in the best interest of the company for him to be appointed.

SUMMARY STATEMENT

Fergeson hoped that he would have another two or three years to make a decision. Franklin appeared to have the potential for the position. But his own attitude needed further seasoning and maturing. For this reason as well as the personal ambition of the other men who themselves were valuable to the company and who wielded significant influence with other strong people, he hardly felt safe in granting Franklin the position that would have placed him in direct line for the general manager's job. He was very much against and felt the men would be against bringing in someone from the outside. Franklin indicated that he would delay his answer to Superior Grocery Company for five days.

QUESTIONS AND REQUIREMENTS

1. How should Fergeson have handled the conflict between Franklin and the others?

2. List the strengths and weaknesses of each candidate for general manager.

3. Whom would you choose? Why?

4. If you deferred the decision, what would you do until then?

5. Does promoting someone from within the organization, without a national search, violate the law regarding affirmative action?

27
BELWOOD LUMBER COMPANY

RICHARD C. JOHANSON

BACKGROUND

In July, Mr. Fred Jones, Division Vice President for Georgia-Atlantic Company, sat in his office in Atlanta, Georgia, reviewing the results of a meeting he conducted the previous day with the management of the Belwood Lumber Company. Since Georgia-Atlantic had just acquired the Belwood firm, it became the responsibility of Mr. Jones to integrate this new acquisition into his Eastern Division of Georgia-Atlantic Company.

During yesterday's meeting with the management of Belwood, Mr. Jones had observed that a great amount of time was taken up by Mr. Adams, President of Belwood, defending the way he had managed and operated Belwood. The meeting with the management team of Belwood also revealed that the persons who serve under the President are provided minimal opportunity to participate in managing the affairs of Belwood. Mr. Jones felt that there was a lack of delegation due to the highly centralized style of leadership carried out by Mr. Adams.

To lay the groundwork for becoming better acquainted with Belwood's management personnel, Fred Jones developed, informally, a personal profile of each top-level person in the Belwood organization.

MANAGEMENT PROFILES

S.D. ADAMS, PRESIDENT

Joined Belwood in 1925 as one of the two founders and has served as the Chief Executive for the past 42 years. His main objectives have been to acquire for Belwood a strong raw material base, plus maintaining up-to-date manufacturing facilities, and the way this could best be accomplished would be to take the job on himself since his chief interest lay in mechanical efficiency; and, if you had this edge on competition, then it wouldn't be necessary to spend considerable time on management functions. While Adams had a lot of management talent working for him, it was evident that he desired to continually tell each person what to do and how to do it. Adams made all the major decisions with respect to

166

purchase of raw materials, methods of manufacture, products to be manufactured, plus numerous minor daily decisions. In fact, on a typical day you would find Mr. Adams in the plant assisting each department head in the performance of his duties. Adams' philosophy of how you run a lumber company is to place most of the emphasis on efficiency of operation to allow for low-cost production. In conversation with Mr. Fred Jones of Georgia-Atlantic, Mr. Adams noted that the formula for success was that the woodlands department's function was to keep the mill supplied with logs at the lowest possible cost, the mill's function was to produce lumber from these logs at the lowest possible cost, and the responsibility of the sales department was to sell the production of the mill at the lowest possible cost.

STRENGTHS   Experience, technically competent, knows the business from the ground up, knowledge of the company's operations, knows the employees.

WEAKNESSES   Has more technical knowledge and experience than administrative management; fails to delegate work, authority, and responsibility; due to his age, he is not very energetic and desires to retire.

EVALUATION AS A MANAGER   "No comment."

SAM MARTIN, PLANT SUPERINTENDENT

Sam first became interested in the lumber industry upon graduation from high school, and he has spent his whole career in this industry, with the last 40 years in association with Belwood.

STRENGTHS   Loyal to the company, knows the workers very well, also has good understanding of Belwood's equipment and facilities.

WEAKNESSES   Inability to learn new things, doesn't have the drive and energy necessary for a line production job, had a heart attack five years ago.

EVALUATION AS A MANAGER   Poor.

JOHN FRY, CHIEF FORESTER

Joined Belwood in June, 1939, after completion of the requirements for a Master's Degree in Forestry. John was hired as a Forester by Mr. Adams and was promoted to the Chief Forester position some fifteen years ago.

STRENGTHS   Technically competent in forestry and highly motivated; is well liked by his associates; and has been active in the local chapter of his professional organization, plus his church.

WEAKNESSES   Prefers special research projects over administrative management duties; he hasn't acquired a broad insight into the total of Belwood's operations.

EVALUATION AS A MANAGER   Satisfactory to fair.

MIKE FLEMING, CHIEF ENGINEER

Mike was hired in June, 1959, after graduation from the University of Georgia, where he earned a degree in mechanical engineering. Since his father had been associated with the lumber industry for many years, Mike became interested in having an opportunity to contribute to the greater mechanization of the various facets to the lumber business. On various occasions, Mike would experience difficulty in selling Mr. Adams on a new innovation for Belwood.

STRENGTHS   Very productive, graduate engineer and technically competent, personally ambitious, good follow-through when given a job to do, very personable and cultured.

WEAKNESSES   May be overly ambitious, limited experience in management, youngest member of the management staff.

EVALUATION AS A MANAGER   Satisfactory to good.

BOB MEYERS, SALES MANAGER

Joined the company in 1942; and, prior to this date, Bob earned a Master's degree at Georgia Institute of Technology and spent eight years selling machinery and supplies to the lumber industry. Since Mr. Adams placed such emphasis on technology and production, Bob Meyers did not occupy a favored position on the management team at Belwood.

STRENGTHS   Good salesman when supported by top management, personality helped him to develop good relationship with customers, personally ambitious.

WEAKNESSES   Very prestige conscious, argued with Mr. Adams at times, limited managerial experience.

FRED JONES' SUMMARY

Fred Jones reviewed the personal profiles of Belwood's top-management people and jotted down the following conclusions:

1. Of the top five positions filled in the organization, including the position of President, two persons need to be replaced due to age and one person who is at a more junior age has a minimum of experience in management.

2. It appears that none of the managers can be rated above "good" in their managerial performance. Some are technically competent to a high degree, but currently lack the managerial and administrative skills so necessary to assure the survival and growth of a company.

3. Of the managers now holding the key positions, all felt that they were doing a very satisfactory job, and Mr. Adams had recently given each a substantial raise in salary.

4. The management and administrative system at Belwood was based upon the centralized and autocratic style of management practiced by Mr. Adams over a very long period of time.

5. The organization conflicts between engineering and production and between sales and Mr. Adams were hurting the company in general.

Fred Jones, Eastern Division Vice President for Georgia-Atlantic, realized that he was responsible for the future growth, success, and failures of the Belwood operation. Also, that he had the responsibility and authority to take whatever action was necessary to the survival and growth of this newly acquired operation.

HISTORY OF BELWOOD

The Belwood Lumber Company was organized in 1925 by Mr. S.D. Adams, who was then a young man in his late 20's. Also assisting in founding the company was S.D.'s brother, who is no longer active in the business. Initially, the two brothers installed a small circular sawmill and began buying timber, cutting lumber, and selling it green and air-dried in the southeastern part of the country from their base of operation in Georgia. The company experienced gradual growth over a 40-year period and by the mid-1960's was producing 30,000,000 feet of lumber per year. To provide a source of raw material supply, they amassed 160,000 acres of excellent pine timberland in South Georgia.

Since Mr. Adams was more interested in developing a raw material base, plus developing modern manufacturing facilities, the profits were about average over this 40-year period.

As the company grew, so did the number of employees; and by the mid-1960's total employment was 235 persons.

Ownership of the company after the founding experienced a slightly broadening base, with Mr. S.D. Adams retaining 72 percent of the common stock. The balance of the common stock was divided among a few other members of the family and a few key employees.

Mr. Adams, upon reaching age 67, came to realize that an estate problem was imminent; thus, he decided to sell the business, and Georgia-Atlantic was successful in negotiating the acquisition of the Belwood Lumber Company by agreeing to pay the shareholders $25 million for their interest in Belwood. The chief asset of Belwood was the 160,000 acres of well-stocked timberland, which would on a sustained-yield basis support production considerably in excess of that produced by Belwood. Upon selling the company, Mr. Adams told the Georgia-Atlantic officials that he had no interest in remaining with Belwood in a managerial capacity.

Belwood Lumber Co. organization chart

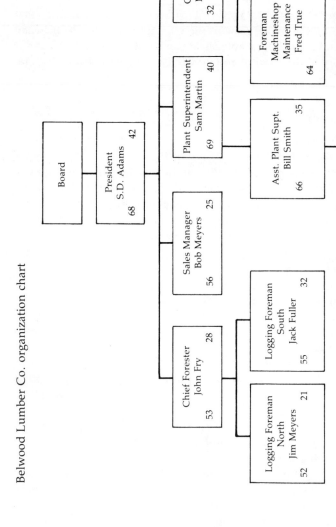

NOTE: Within the boxes, the number on the left refers to the person's age; the number on the right refers to length of service.

Belwood Lumber Company, Balance sheet, December 31

	Previous year 12/31	Recent year 12/31
Assets:		
Cash	725,613	769,150
Mkt. sec.	392,763	416,329
Acct. rec.	2,170,182	2,300,392
Inventories	3,075,534	3,260,066
Prepaid expense	292,908	310,483
Total current assets	6,657,000	7,056,420
Properties: timberlands, buildings, machinery & equipment	21,303,020	22,649,995
Less: accumulated depreciation	7,779,020	8,314,555
Net properties	13,524,000	14,335,440
Investments in affiliated companies	399,000	422,940
Other investments & receivables	378,000	400,680
Deferred changes	42,000	44,520
Total assets	21,000,000	22,260,000
Liabilities:		
Trade accounts payable	1,709,400	1,811,964
Accrued taxes	267,960	284,038
Dividend payable	198,660	210,579
Long-term debt due in 1 year	133,980	142,019
Total current liabilities	2,310,000	2,448,600
Long-term debt	4,452,000	4,719,200
Deferred income taxes	1,281,000	1,357,860
Reserve for SEIF insurance	231,000	244,860
Minority interests	210,000	222,600
Common stock	2,835,000	3,005,100
Earned surplus	9,681,000	10,261,780
Total liabilities & net worth	21,000,000	22,260,000

Belwood Lumber Company, Statement of income (loss) for the year ending December 31

	Previous year 12/31	Recent year 12/31
Income:		
Sales	15,000,000	15,900,000
Cost of goods sold	11,460,000	12,147,600
Gross margin	3,540,000	3,752,400
Operating expense:		
Selling & administrative expense	1,410,000	1,494,600
Net profit before taxes	2,130,000	2,257,800
Taxes	1,022,400	1,083,744
Net profit	1,107,600	1,174,056

QUESTIONS AND REQUIREMENTS

1. Where are the strengths and weaknesses in Belwood's top management? Where do you see potential?

2. What changes would you make in Belwood's top management? Whom would you terminate or transfer?

3. If you were given the job of training director for Belwood's top management, what kind of program would you design?

28
WHO SHALL IT BE?

W.D. HEIER

At the fall meeting of the Board of Directors, President James Fowler, who will be resigning his position next summer to accept a position with a national foundation, presented the names of the five logical candidates for the president's job to the board members. In the discussion that followed it was quickly agreed that all five men were acceptable with respect to their ages and health. Having agreed upon those items the board members turned their attention toward the investigation of the candidates' backgrounds. As the question and answer session proceeded, it became evident that some board members were increasingly upset that among the individuals being discussed there did not seem to be a single candidate with all of the desired presidential qualifications. President Fowler was pointedly asked how such a situation could have developed during his eight years as president. In attempting to "capsulize" the experience the candidates had received, President Fowler made a statement about each of them:

(A) *Alfred Ashe,* our Vice-President of Production, thoroughly knows the production side of the business. He came to us twenty years ago because he wanted to be with one of the big companies in the industry. We have maintained our status as a leader in this industry, and Ashe has helped us. Since he came to us as plant superintendent, he has had only one promotion to V.P., but he does know the job "inside out." He is a hard-working, driving guy who expects his men to work as hard as he does. It is true that, as a high school graduate, he may lack formal education, but his years of experience compensate for this lack. I have suggested several times that he would be most welcome at our executive sessions, and he has attended once or twice. Of course, as he says, he is pretty busy and doesn't have a lot of time for other than production meetings. If Al has one fault, I would say that it is a tendency to be a trifle intolerant, maybe even harsh, toward anyone he believes does not work as hard as he. He runs things and does them well in his area. We may have done Al a disservice by permitting him to stay in his own "bailiwick" so to speak. Maybe we should have dragged him out of his empire and broadened his outlook. It might have been good for Al, but, on the other hand, he might have resented it. You really cannot tell in advance how people will react to this type of thing.

(B) *Bob Black,* the Personnel Director, has done an outstanding job in his area. You all know we had quite a mess with the union six years ago when Bob came with us, and he straightened things out beautifully. We have one of the most efficient personnel departments in the industry. Bob has the ability to take programs other companies have used and make them work for us. You gentlemen know how hard he has pushed for skill-training programs for our employees in all branches of the company. If you will recall, he was also the "guiding light" in our adopting a program for our management people to attend college after work hours. Bob has done an excellent job in making personnel a first class operation.

With respect to a remark made earlier that the personnel department seems to have gone "overboard" on testing and time and motion study, let me say that this is a scientific age, and I agree with Bob Black: we must use all the tools available to us in doing our jobs. As one of you stated, there may have been some abuses and some lapses of judgment in the early stages of these programs, but it seemed better to be quite strict at first and then to relax the standards a little later. Bob told me that this philosophy had proven to be the best approach at the Knowonze Company where he worked previously. He's a good man with a college degree in his specialty. This company needs more men like Bob Black.

(C) *Charles Coke*, our Controller, did a brilliant job of setting up our cost system. Unfortunately, he wasn't too popular while the program was being instituted, and a lot of noses were "bent out of joint." Well, we hired him five years ago to do that job, and he did it. Can we now hold it against him that he had to push a program that wasn't popular? He had my backing all the way, and everyone knew it; but Charlie received all of the abuse from Sales, Production, Personnel and all of the other divisions. Even Accounting had a few words to say about the program, which was somewhat of a surprise to me. I thought at least the Accounting Division would appreciate the necessity for a good cost program. But, of course, that is all in the past now. The cost program runs well and has helped this company remain a strong competitor in both the cost and pricing areas.

As you gentlemen are aware, Charlie has placed our finances in fine condition. I dare say that no company in the industry is in better shape, financially, than we are. Furthermore, Charlie has taken an active interest in the affairs of other divisions in the company. For example, Charlie talked to me last year about the possibility of starting a junior manager cross-training program for our on-board college graduates. It seems he went through one of those after he got out of the university. I talked about the idea with Bob Black in Personnel, and he said he would look into the matter and let me know. He hasn't mentioned it since, and, frankly, I haven't remembered to ask him about it.

Anyway, as you can see, Charlie Coke is a good man who has proven to be a real asset to the company. It is really a shame that his job is to sit on the purse strings of the company since that is an unpopular position to have. I also think that the other division heads tend to look down on Charlie's division because it has the fewest employees of any of the major areas. I guess I would have to agree that Charlie has considerable power but not much prestige—or should I say respect? That may be partially my fault because I did not feel I should deliberately go out of my way to equalize the status of our top staff echelon. Maybe I could have done more along those lines, but I am not really sure how it would have worked out.

(D) *Dick Doss*, the Sales Manager, who has been with the company since he was nineteen years old, will complete his thirtieth year of service next month. Dick has worked in every department in the Sales Division. I said that Al Ashe knew Production "inside out." Well, Dick knows the sales job in this company "upside down" as well as "inside out." There is no question of his knowing more about our sales program than anyone we have ever had. He personally runs the entire operation. I have told him many times that he works too hard. For example, I returned from Chicago at 11:00 P.M. last Thursday night and came by the office to drop off some papers for my secretary to type Friday morning. Dick was in his office at midnight. When I asked him if anything unusual had come up he told me that he was just going over some old sales charts to see if they showed anything of interest. Dick has done this kind of thing for years. His wife told mine that he works at least four nights a week, every Saturday, and many of the Sundays he is in town.

We have had our problems in sales, but we have done remarkably well considering the rather large turnover of personnel in that area. I asked Bob Black to try to find out why we had such a turnover there. Bob said the exit interviews indicated that the salesmen obtained better paying jobs with other companies. I don't see how that could be since we pay as well as, if not better than, similar companies in the industry.

You know, for a while I thought it might be Dick himself who was the cause of this turnover. He has had four assistant sales managers since I came here as President in 1968. But I found that Dick is most anxious to help his people. One of the reasons he is in the office so much is that he spends lots of time with his assistant showing him just how he wants things done. He seems to do all of this extra training in the kindliest manner. He is never impatient with his people. They know exactly what is expected of them. Dick must be an easy man to work for, and he certainly is an expert in his area. His people are well trained for promotion. Still, I wonder why so many quit? Maybe salesmen are just restless these days.

(E) *Edward East*, our Director of Research and Development, has charge of the twelve scientists in our laboratory. We have spared neither money nor effort to see that we have the best qualified men available. Mr. East has often commented that R&D is the basic product of the company. This statement is at least partially correct for our industry. We must have research to remain competitive.

As you are aware, Mr. East has no assistant. He oversees the laboratory work himself and prepares reports for me on progress in current programs. We have had only one scientist leave our employment since the laboratory was completed in 1958. We have never had even the first complaint from that area, and I think we must give Mr. East credit for that. I do not know how I would do in his job, but he seems to have a "knack" for getting along with those people. If you are looking for a president who gets along with people, Mr. East would certainly appear to qualify on that score. I do not know what we would have done if he had left suddenly. We might have replaced him with one of the lab men, but I suspect we would have had to go outside the company for a man.

I must state that I am uncertain as to how Mr. East would do as president of this company. He appears to have the qualities you gentlemen want, but I have not worked as closely with him as I have the other four candidates. Therefore, I would be reluctant to recommend him for the job. His name is before you because he is a top staff man, has eleven years with the company, has an excellent record as a manager, and has run a productive and stable division. Nevertheless, for the reason stated, I would have to withhold my recommendation of Mr. East.

Gentlemen, I think you can see that our candidates are very experienced in their jobs. We conduct many types of training for our employees in order to qualify them for promotion. Perhaps we could have done more. You have six months before I must vacate the president's job. If you can tentatively pick my successor, I will do everything in my power to see that he knows the job thoroughly before I leave. Better still, perhaps you can offer some suggestions as to the way I should proceed. I await your pleasure.

QUESTIONS AND REQUIREMENTS

1. Accepting the fact that the age and health of each applicant is satisfactory, how would you evaluate the five candidates in terms of educational background, job knowledge and experience, team-building potential, and probable motivation and drive to be president?

2. Based on the evaluation made in question 1, who is your choice for president?

3. Based on your choice for president, what action should be taken to qualify your candidate for the presidency?

4. What insights do you gain about the management styles and skills of each applicant? How might the styles and skills affect the ways in which the applicants would manage the company?

5. Would an assessment center be appropriate for selecting a president? Why or why not?

29
A DIFFICULT DECISION

ROBERT L. TAYLOR

You are the supervisor of nine people in the accounting and reports section of a medium-sized company. Most of your people have been with you for several years, although two individuals joined you at the entry level within the last six months. The individuals in your section are all white-collar employees and do not belong to any organized bargaining or professional unit.

Your operation is essentially one of condensing data from distributors, salesmen and customers and then recording the information in ledgers. Summary reports are prepared from the ledgers for top management personnel. For the last several weeks a contractor has been in your office area installing a new computer system. Last week you asked your boss, Mr. Jarmon, if the computerized system would have any effect on your manning. He seemed to think that the manning problem would be handled by attrition (i.e., retirement, resignation, etc.).

Last Friday you spoke with the individual in charge of the computer installation. He told you that in the last site where he had installed this unit, five of the ten people working in that organization were dismissed. Some were reassigned to lower grade jobs or asked to retire early, and others were simply released.

This morning Mr. Jarmon called you in and asked you to select four of your people for computer training in the new accounting techniques. Further, he indicated that the tests were running well ahead of schedule and that he may have some difficult manning decisions to make with respect to your unit shortly after the first of the year. He would like your nominations this afternoon.

Until now, you and your people have felt fairly confident that there would be job security in this company. You really begin to wonder what's going on. However, your mind moves quickly to the people in your group as you think about whom to send to school:

1. Martin Cole, age 55, married, has one son in college. Although he is a very faithful worker, he would probably have great difficulty in going back to school to learn computer techniques. He has been with the group for nearly 30 years, and he is well skilled in company procedures and methods.

2. Alice Moore, age 49, like Martin has been with the group a long time. She is very skilled, has always been punctual, and, since she is not married, the job has apparently been the center of her social life as well as her career. She has been very critical of the computer installation, and you sense that she feels threatened by it.

3. Ron Stamp, age 48, is married with three children. He is a very enthusiastic employee whose energy surpasses his capabilities, although his performance has been adequate. You wonder whether he could grasp the more technical computer skills necessary, but he seems like the type who would certainly be willing to try.

4. Mark Hannah, age 50. Since his divorce, Mark has been one of the most dedicated workers, spending a great deal of extra time in the evenings and on weekends at the office. He has recently gone back to school to study for his masters degree in business administration. He is very skilled at his job.

5. Cara Hamm, age 39, is married with two children. Cara is an exceptionally talented individual who has been frustrated in her job because of the lack of promotion opportunities. Although her income is necessary to maintain her family's standard of living, Cara is the kind of individual who appears to be able to handle any task. She has been very inquisitive around the computer installers, and you have often seen her at the console participating in the tests.

6. Stu Kirt, an affable and friendly bachelor of 35. Your group's social scene is centered around Stu, who is always coming up with good ideas. He is an extremely competent worker as well. However, he has voiced objections to the new computer installation because he isn't convinced it is a better replacement for current methods.

7. Jack Morgan, age 34, is a very close friend of yours. You spend a lot of your outside time with each other's families, and, although he is certainly not the most productive person in the group, you have enjoyed his company a great deal. You suggested that he might go to the local business college to take computer programming, but his response was that you would never replace a good friend like him with a computer.

8. Sylvia Hanson, age 21, is a recent college graduate and is working to support her husband while he is in medical school. Despite the fact that she has been with you only a short time, she is easily the most talented and productive individual on your staff. In addition, she has suggested a number of changes which resulted in the computer testing period being considerably shortened.

9. Rob Henry, age 21, is also a recent addition to your staff. Although he appears to be a competent individual, you get the feeling that he is working in this job until he can find something better. He has been the least disturbed about the computer installation and has been heard to remark that the computer will replace all the "dead wood" around here.

QUESTIONS AND REQUIREMENTS

1. What would you ask Mr. Jarmon before you initiated the selection process?

2. What criteria would you use in selecting individuals for computer training?

3. What responsibilities do you have to those who are not selected?

4. What role should the personnel department have in the selection process?

30
VALIDITY OF SELECTION DEVICES

WILLIAM L. TULLAR

Smythe Textiles, a large manufacturer of sheets and pillowcases, is located in the southeastern United States. Smythe has been considered a progressive employer in its area for many years. The personnel department has historically been able to take only half of the individuals who apply for production jobs at Smythe.

Recently there have been a number of sewing machine operators hired who did not meet minimum production and quality standards, even after extended training. As a result, Bob Browning, the Personnel Director at Smythe, has decided to use a test to select sewing machine operators. After a job analysis and much deliberation, Browning decided to use (among other things) a perceptual speed test. He knows, however, that he must validate the test, so he hires twenty new sewing machine operators who have taken the test but for whom the test was not part of the selection decision. Three months after the sewing machine operators were trained, Browning received data on each operator's average daily production.

As a personnel man wise in the ways of EEOC, Bob Browning knows he must have data on more than twenty sewing machine operators before he can draw conclusions about the validity of the perceptual speed test. However, Bob wants a preliminary indication of validity. So he assembles all the data found in Table 1 (on p. 179). Bob included the other biographical data to check on the possibility of differential validity—that is, to see if the test is more valid for one subgroup of his sample than it is for the whole sample.

Bob used the Spearman Rho correlation coefficient* to calculate his correlations.

QUESTIONS AND REQUIREMENTS

1. Did Bob find a strong relationship between scores on the test and units produced?

2. Did Bob find any evidence of differential validity?

3. If you set up a selection program for sewing machine operators, would you be able to use this test? If so, how would you use it?

*Students unfamiliar with this method should read Sidney Siegel, *Non-parametric Statistics* (New York: McGraw-Hill, 1956), pp. 202–213.

Table 1

Employee	Age	Education	Marital status	Ethnic origin	Perceptual speed test	Units produced
1	30	10	S	NW	31	40
2	39	9	M	NW	62	42
3	31	12	D	NW	79	58
4	19	12	M	W	60	60
5	27	12	M	NW	50	31
6	20	10	D	W	53	53
7	24	9	S	W	50	50
8	33	9	M	W	47	48
9	23	12	M	W	49	45
10	36	12	M	W	42	45
11	26	10	M	NW	46	31
12	34	9	D	NW	40	53
13	28	11	M	W	40	40
14	25	12	S	NW	39	55
15	33	12	M	W	36	42
16	36	11	S	NW	35	59
17	22	10	S	NW	78	50
18	24	9	D	NW	40	56
19	32	9	M	W	62	59
20	35	12	S	W	48	32

Age: years at time of employment
Education: grade completed
Marital status: S = Single, M = Married, D = Divorced
Ethnic origin: W = White, NW = Non-white
All of these employees were female.

31
PERSONNEL TESTING AT WESTERN HEMISPHERE

WENDELL L. FRENCH

Dr. Anthony ("Tony") Simmons, recently appointed Director of Manpower and Organizational Development for Western Hemisphere, Inc., approached Dr. Stanley ("Stan") Smith, a former academic colleague, about the possibility of Dr. Smith's undertaking a consulting project relative to current and potential uses of tests at Western Hemisphere. Tony had felt that this was an area of personnel technology that ought to be considered and evaluated. Furthermore, it was evident that tests were being used to some extent in various parts of the corporation and that there was a need for a review of these practices.

Dr. Simmons and his subordinates visualized the Department of Management and Organization as being broadly concerned with human resources selection, development and utilization. Their "1970 Strategy Summary," which emerged from a two-day session between Tony and his staff, is shown in Figure 1.

Figure 1   *Manpower & Organization—1970 Strategy Summary*

Function

To provide Western Hemisphere management with leadership, support and focus in the:

1. Identification, development and utilization of manpower resources.

2. Design of management and personnel systems to maximize individual, organization and corporate growth and effectiveness.

3. Creation of a motivation climate to encourage employees and organizational units to achieve more.

4. Development of community relationships, attitudes, and capacities supportive of local Western Hemisphere operations.

5. General utilization of the behavioral sciences in the implementation of planned organizational change and development of problem-solving capacities.

In our relationships with other support and operating units, our major role will be, in essence, that of change agents. Such a role involves several kinds of interrelationships with other support and operating units in implementing the functions described above:

1. Diagnostic—Collection of data about organizational functioning and feedback of such data to "client managers." Building acceptance of feedback (research) within the organization and relating this feedback strategically to management.

2. Consulting—Providing guidance to managers in responding to identified problems. Beginning with the "presented" symptom, articulating it in such a way that the underlying and changeable factors of the problem are understood, and then suggesting remedial alternatives.

3. Training—Development of managers and organizational units in problem-solving through self-examination of present behavior and experimenting with more effective behaviors in consultation with M&O staff.

Regardless of the specific relationship involved, nearly all of our activities will reflect a collaborative effort aimed at the improvement, development and measurement of organizational effectiveness. Such efforts necessitate: (1) initiating upon, as well as responding to, "client" and top management; (2) looking at "client" organizations as total systems rather than as collections of individuals; and (3) dealing with both technical and social content. In addition, we expect to exercise a substantial responsibility in regard to the personnel functions of the operating divisions. This responsibility may range from involvement in hiring decisions in this area to the auditing of personnel procedures and practices.

Five-Year Goals

○ To establish within Western Hemisphere a recruiting, selection, identification and development process which will enable us to fulfill the immediate and long-range manpower needs necessary to achieve strategic goals. Such a process must consider and include all potential manpower, i.e., minority, foreign and unskilled groups as well as the "regulars."

○ To establish the capacity to diagnose and respond to personnel and organizational development needs, i.e., a limited in-house consulting service drawing on professional skills in the behavioral sciences, plus experienced in-house operating management.

○ To provide a continuing appraisal of current and future management systems, e.g., compensation, fringe benefits, budget, etc., in light of their impact on effective organizational and individual performance, as well as to determine competitive standing. To provide guidance in correcting current systems or establishing new systems and procedures where required; thereafter, monitor and recommend as needed.

○ To provide a continuing organizational planning activity, one designed to respond to expansion and strategy development.

○ To bring systems technology to bear on the human informational needs of Western Hemisphere management. To have the ability to "map" and provide feedback to management on organizational "health" in much the same manner as financial results are reported.

○ To increase our efforts at strengthening the communities in which Western Hemisphere organizations are located through making the town a better place in which to live and work and better able to cope with its dependence on Western Hemisphere.

○ To provide Western Hemisphere management with the capacity to more realistically evaluate the "ROI" of non-operating units, i.e., what is a manpower organization worth, how can we assess the return on advertising, public relations, training, finance, etc.?

Specific 1970 Goals

1. Recruiting, Selection, Identification and Development

A. Have operational a manpower planning system which, on a corporate-wide basis, will allow Western Hemisphere management to prepare replacement and development plans for key management personnel, e.g., four levels beneath the Council.

B. Design and begin installment of an effective performance appraisal system for exempt employees which will serve as the basis for:

1. Identification of high and low potential employees.

2. Identifying and responding to individual development needs.

3. Increased management involvement in development process.

C. Complete a review of our current psychological testing practices, recommend and introduce needed changes.

D. Develop the manpower planning, recruiting and selection proficiency of all management levels through a company-wide educational program.

E. Develop a clearing-house system to begin to expand the matching of qualified applicants and current employees to job opportunities *throughout* the company.

F. Begin evaluation and coordination of recruiting advertising and employment agency usage to assure a more cost-effective recruiting effort.

G. Evaluate and manage *all* campus recruiting activity, including selection of schools, selecting, training and coordination of campus recruiting teams. A special effort will be made in 1970 to recruit at black campuses and to recruit minority bachelor and masters candidates.

H. Attempt to determine a "success profile" based upon common characteristics of past and present high potential WH employees and apply this profile to future selections.

I. Incorporate manpower planning into overall corporate strategy, as it relates to numbers and types of personnel required to support the strategies of staff and operating groups. Assist Western Hemisphere management in designing and implementing programs to meet these requirements.

2. Improve Capacity to Diagnose and Respond to Personnel and Organization Development Needs

A. Conduct a needs-analysis survey of Council members, group managers and major division and department heads to determine personnel and organizational development needs as perceived by them. Introduce survey technology to assist in this analysis by broadening participation.

B. Develop internal and external programs to meet identified needs.

C. Continue and expand on work currently being done in the old WR&S organizations, Packaging, Paper Sales and Manufacturing, and Western Hemisphere Building Company, as well as servicing new requests.

3. Examine Impact of Current and Future Management Procedures on Performance

A. Initiate research projects in conjunction with an outside resource, as well as relevant management groups, on two systems. The systems proposed to be studied are the budgeting and AFE procedures.

B. Respond to the questions of the structural implications of the company's strategy decisions. Particular attention must be given the Timber & Building Products group as it relates to the Shelter function and to the need for increased staff activities.

C. Conduct surveys on compensation programs to determine our competitive standing plus employee reactions to current practice.

D. Provide support services to the Compensation Committee.

4. Systems Technology

A. Design and implement an Employee Information System which will allow management to analyze such things as turnover, education and experience of personnel, and salaries and their interrelationship, as well as to perform forecasts, e.g., given a turnover rate for various locations, manpower needs by skills, locations, management level, etc., can be predicted. Such a system will have the capacity to perform personnel skill searches.

B. Devise qualitative and quantitative methods for determining human resource requirements for acquisitions, expansion and other alternate investments and for the preparation of related manpower budgets.

5. Community Relations and Equal Employment Opportunity

    A. To strengthen the WH Affirmative Action program by:

        1. Developing company-wide awareness and understanding of EEO requirements.

        2. Providing assistance and guidance in meeting EEO requirements.

        3. Monitoring Affirmative Action plans and progress.

    B. Expand the manpower pool from which the company draws its employees through upgrading of present unskilled employees and by employing and training between 300–400 disadvantaged. Specific goals for upgrading include the training of 350 employees and some form of supportive supervisory training at the following plants, as well as others: Hillcrest, Hartford, Waterbury, St. Petersburg, Los Angeles Plastics, International Falls, St. Helens, Allentown, Fort Worth and Ogden.

    C. Conduct seminars in community management and development, starting with the largest company towns.

    D. Support the Shelter Group on low-income housing packages whereby housing bids are combined with programs to meet other needs—employment, transportation, education, health and effective government.

As shown in Figure 2, Western Hemisphere, Inc., is an extremely rapidly growing organization. Dr. Simmons was particularly concerned that any unique cultures of the various sub-parts be preserved where local practices and customs seem to be working well. As a result, he indicated to Stan Smith that he did not wish to disrupt practices of newly acquired companies unless there were good reasons to do so.

Figure 2

Since 1957 Western Hemisphere has grown from a lumber-oriented company with annual sales of $34 million to a diversified corporation with sales over $1 billion in seven major markets. These markets are building materials, shelter, packaging, paper, office supplies, recreation, and urban development. We are increasingly dedicated to these markets, and have recently added an eighth: construction engineering in the utility field. Our operations in the Western Hemisphere and elsewhere are expanding as opportunities appear in this era of fast-moving technology and change.

    To attain and hold a dynamic and profitable position as a growth company requires skillful, imaginative people. Western Hemisphere believes that people are most productive when they are properly motivated and provided with an environment which encourages them to work in their own individual way. The men and women of Western Hemisphere thrive on new challenges and carefully observe every new opportunity created by change. This spirit is one of the keys to our growth.

    Today our major markets include 200 million Americans and 20 million Canadians. By 1975 these markets will increase to almost 250 million people, and by the year 2000 the total will be 330 million. Western Hemisphere aspires to serve these growing markets as well as other selected markets in the various countries of Europe, Central and South America. Each major division, therefore, provides prompt information to all who wish to buy the products we sell, and we cordially invite you to call upon us whenever we may supply your needs.

From a May 1969 pamphlet.

During their discussion, Tony suggested to Stan that the latter visit several diverse company sites and that he talk with a number of managers at different levels. In addition, Tony and Stan agreed that any report would be a preliminary "working paper" to be used as a mechanism for a more extensive dialogue about the relevance of testing to the Company.

The results of Dr. Smith's brief investigation are shown below in the form of a report submitted several weeks later.

Preliminary Observations and Recommendations
About the Use of Tests at Western Hemisphere, Inc.

The basic intent of this report is to make some general recommendations about the use of tests in the context of Western Hemisphere evolving climate relative to human resources administration. The first parts of the report will focus on the present situation with regard to organizational environment and the use of tests. A later part will deal with problems and dilemmas in the use of tests. Finally, recommendations will be made.

"Tests," in the meaning of this report, include a wide range of pencil-and-paper instruments or performance measures, including devices for measuring intelligence, interest, personality, aptitude, knowledge and skill.

The Current Situation

MANAGERS INTERVIEWED. During a two-day period, personnel and labor relations executives and subordinate personnel were interviewed in the General Offices. In addition, several top executives and middle managers in diverse fields outside of the personnel area were interviewed.

A third and fourth day were spent interviewing managers at three sites: a lumber mill, a pulp mill, and a large sales and accounting office.

Thus, the comments which follow should not be construed as being based on an exhaustive sampling of the range of practices and attitudes regarding tests at Western Hemisphere. However, the interviews were invaluable in obtaining a preliminary feel of the culture of the organization, and in pointing up some of the dilemmas and issues surrounding testing.

RELEVANT ORGANIZATIONAL CLIMATE FACTORS. The interview suggested that the following organizational climate is emerging, at least in the management hierarchy, and that there is a conscious effort to enlarge upon it. This climate is consistent with the kind of climate advocated by contemporary behavioral scientists, and is one to which I subscribe as having the most promise for organizational effectiveness in the decades ahead. It is a climate in which there is:

a. Substantial opportunity for subordinates to make inquiries and to express their feelings across a wide range of matters, including organizational objectives and job choice.

b. Assignment of additional responsibilities as rapidly as organizational members demonstrate their capabilities.

c. Strong interest in and support for personal growth and development.

d. Emphasis on open communications—laterally, diagonally, vertically.

e. Flexible job boundaries.

f. Protection of organizational subcultures when effective, i.e., avoidance of central direction simply for the sake of standardization.

g. Central guidance and direction when regional practices appear that are less than optimal.

PRESENT SELECTION PRACTICES.   It appears that in few, if any, instances are there systematic validation procedures, with regard either to testing or to other personnel selection and placement devices. It is important to recognize that tests, as defined above, constitute only one class of devices that are commonly used in the selection process. The application blank, the interview, the reference check, employment and job performance histories are other devices about which questions of reliability (consistency) and validity (predictability of job performance) must be asked. Not only are questions about instrument reliability and validity important, but questions about the interrelatedness and the validity of the use of such instruments in conjunction with each other are also important.

Practices in the use of tests appear to vary widely across the many segments of the company. The use of other selection devices also varies; e.g., in one location references are checked by mail—in another location, by telephone.

PRESENT USE OF TESTS.   Interviews indicated at least the following use of tests:

a. Intelligence testing of hourly candidates at some of the larger mills, and some use of mechanical aptitude tests.

b. Use of a test battery, including personality and intelligence tests, in the case of pulp mill production workers wishing to move up the ladder.

c. Some testing of millwright trainees.

d. Aptitude and intelligence testing of candidates for E.D.P. programming jobs.

e. Aptitude testing for candidates for keypunch jobs.

f. Some use of state employment services (U.S.E.S.), including preliminary testing through such agencies.

g. Some use of private employment agencies, including their testing practices.

h. Some testing of candidates for office-clerical positions including typing, spelling, vocabulary, arithmetic, and clerical ability tests.

Most of the testing appears to be of the intelligence, aptitude, and achievement varieties. There appears to be some use of personality and interest tests, however. In terms of employee categories, current usage focuses on production operators, craftsmen, and some nonsupervisory salaried employees. There appears to be no use of tests in selecting salesmen, professional-technicians, foremen, other first-line supervisors, middle managers, and higher managers. There appears to be no use of testing for counseling and career planning purposes.

The Corporation appears to have little data about the validity of the above test usage in specific instances. At least one practice, on the face of it, however, is of doubtful merit. This is the practice of sending tests away to a consulting firm for scoring and interpretation. Such "long distance" procedures which do not involve an interview by the person interpreting the tests maximizes the possibility of undue emphasis on a test battery, and prohibits a psychological assessment based on a wide range of data.

PRESENT RANGE OF ATTITUDES ABOUT TESTING.   The following, while not exact quotes in each instance, convey central attitudes about the use of tests expressed by the managers interviewed. A wide range of attitudes is evident:

o "I am 'gun-shy' about tests at salaried levels, but they are useful at hourly levels."

o "Testing is likely to be relevant for assessing management potential, but not useful for recruiting accountants."

o "I am suspicious of tests in the sales field; I'm afraid of how salesmen will react."

o "Production candidates are nervous about testing."

o "Tests could be a valuable guide, but they have been misused in some parts of the Company."

o "I have found the Wonderlic to be a useful tool."

o "Testing has been useful to me, but the Company should do some validation research."

o "Testing for promotion could be interpreted as showing lack of confidence in the candidates; however, if tests were sound, test results should be only one of several measurements, and there should be feedback of results. Tests could have some additional value in a counseling context."

o "I don't believe in testing."

o "I am currently giving some tests, but I don't really believe in them."

Problems and Challenges in the Use of Tests

At the negative end of the spectrum, tests can be used to screen out people who would have made a higher contribution than those selected. Also at this end of the spectrum can be the situation in which there is reliance on tests scores which are essentially random measures having no relationship to job performance, thus minimizing the effects of other devices which might have some positive validity, e.g., interview impressions. On the positive side, if used properly, research results indicate quite clearly that testing programs can improve a company's "batting average" in the selection process.

Test usage can also support a static, mechanistic kind of organization. Or tests can be used in such a way as to be congruent with and support a more dynamic, organic, open system. To give a hypothetical illustration of a mechanistic use of tests, a mechanical aptitude test could be the focal point in the selection of maintenance foremen in a mill, while in reality much more important skills at that level in this particular mill might be in the leadership and planning areas. Conversely, in an organic, open system, predictor variables including test scores must be related to a continuous analysis of dynamically changing job structures and organizational needs.

Arguments that tests inherently create a static organization are fallacious. Intelligence tests which measure major components of problem-solving capability are indicators of adaptability. Personality tests which measure such dimensions as a need to dominate versus attitudes of tolerance and support can identify qualities which lend themselves to effective communication and to a participative leadership style.

Research indicates that intelligence tests tend to be the most reliable and valid of all psychological tests; various aptitude tests are in the middle range; and interest and personality tests are the least reliable and valid for selection purposes. The latter are notoriously subject to faking, although some are better designed than others. Personality tests frequently are more useful in screening out potential problem employees than in identifying the probable range of success among acceptable candidates. However, at least one personality inventory has been found useful in making positive predictions in some situations.

Further, development of adequate criteria of job success is an extremely difficult proposition, and will reflect basic managerial assumptions about what makes for organizational effectiveness. Thus, an effective testing program must be designed and developed relative to a particular organization and its subunits.

Recommendations: Long Range

Perhaps it would be well to start with a recommended long-range state of affairs for testing in the Western Hemisphere organization. We can then work backwards toward intermediate and preliminary steps.

For the long range it is recommended that the Corporation evolve a Career Planning and Assessment Center at headquarters. This Center would be an amalgamation of the assessment center concept which is in use in some large corporations and the career planning programs of still other firms. Such an amalgamation would require a high level of openness and trust in the organization and a high level of professional capability at the headquarters level. Elaboration of these concepts may be helpful:

THE ASSESSMENT CENTER CONCEPT. A number of large organizations have had successful results with assessment centers as a means to identifying promotion potential from among rank-and-file employees, first-level, or higher supervisors. Probably the most well-known such program originated with the American Telephone and Telegraph Company in 1956 and has been in operation in a number of the Bell System companies since then.

The typical center processes a dozen candidates per week, with each group of candidates spending two and one-half to three days in the center. The remainder of the week is spent by the staff in discussing results, making ratings, and writing reports. Candidates for the center are nominated by line managers.

The devices which are used are extensive interviews, tests of mental ability, reasoning, and current affairs, and simulation exercises. One such exercise is the "In-Basket" exercise, another involves a business game in which teams of six candidates "run" a toy company, and still another is a leaderless group discussion preceded by presentations by each member of the group. Staff members are present during these exercises.

The data reported in the literature suggest that the assessment centers have increased the proportion of successful to unsuccessful supervisors and higher managers. One longitudinal study, which did not reveal the results of the assessments for use in advancing candidates, found that, of those young, first-level supervisors predicted to reach middle management within ten years, 78% had reached this level within eight years. Of those assessed as not having potential for advancement, 95% had not progressed beyond their first-level assignments. Other studies have shown that the quality of supervision is increasing as a result of assessment center assistance in selection.

In considering this concept, it is recommended that an assessment center be considered initially for identifying candidates for promotion to first-level supervisory positions and only as one route to advancement. Candidates for promotion need not have gone through the center. In addition, "failure" at the center does not necessarily preclude advancement.

THE CAREER PLANNING CONCEPT. As used here, this concept is essentially synonymous with modern vocational and educational testing and guidance, but embraces "clinical" counseling of normals. In contrast to the assessment center concept, the main thrust of career planning activities should be geographically decentralized so that rank-and-file employees would have convenient access. Policy direction and coordination of resources and research, however, would stem from company headquarters.

The amalgamation of this concept with the assessment center notion stems partly from the fact that some of the necessary professional skills and insights are common to both. A second reason for the amalgamation is the selection process needs to be developmental, given the type of environment described earlier. Selection and development can be contradictory unless an intense effort is made toward their reconciliation. Some difficult problems pertaining to the degree of confidentiality of data would need to be resolved, but can be worked out.

Recommendations: Short Range

For the immediate future, it is recommended:

a. That if not already completed, a detailed comprehensive survey be made of the testing practices at all sites.

b. That the Corporation hire a psychologist or a part-time consultant to visit a substantial number of sites (perhaps all) where tests are used and to counsel local personnel on test usage and on the design of validity studies where validity data are not adequate. This matter is particularly critical with respect to minority employment.

c. That the corporation move in the direction of hiring a full-time psychologist who has skills and interests across traditional industrial and personnel psychology, counseling psychology, social psychology, organization development. This is a tall order, but can be accomplished.

The psychologist (eventually more than one person) could be responsible for validity studies pertaining to the total selection system including such devices as interviewing and reference checking, and for training in their use.

Further, the psychologist could assist in "action-research," i.e., working with managers in data gathering and feedback, and in problem discussions in a team context. If properly selected and given the opportunity, such a person could become an important part of the organizational development efforts.

d. That the initial long-range testing activities of this new staff member, in addition to item b above, be in the following directions:

Recommended Phases in a Testing Program (by Employee Category)

	Initial program	Intermediate program*	Long-range program*
Selection for beginning employment	Production Craft Clerical-secretarial Programming, key punch	Foremen First-line super. Technical sub-prof.	Managers Salesmen Management trainees
Training Educational opportunities Transfer		All categories The career planning concept	
Promotion to higher-paid non-managerial positions	Production Craft	Salaried, e.g., technician	
Promotion to beginning or to high managerial positions		To foremen or first-level supervision The assessment center concept	Middle management

* As acceptance, professional skills, and research studies warrant.

Summary

The central point of this report is that testing can facilitate organizational goals and the kind of organizational climate which appears to be emerging in Western Hemisphere. However, test usage, including criterion development and research, will need to be much more imaginative than is the case in most companies. The major dilemma is to marry personnel selection with personnel development. This will require a high order of professional skill.

Specifically, it is recommended that a well-selected psychologist begin to improve upon present testing practices, as well as all selection practices, and to move in the direction of establishing a career planning and assessment center concept in the corporation.

It is essential that the efforts of the psychologist be integrated with broader personnel and organizational development activities. Further, it is important that continuous efforts be made to examine the underlying assumptions and effectiveness of all personnel practices and procedures so that all segments of the total personnel and labor relations system be congruent and mutually supportive.

Finally, the support of General Office, regional, and local managers will be indispensible in the development of improved selection and development procedures. This argues for responsive innovation and interaction, rather than massive programs.

QUESTIONS AND REQUIREMENTS

1. Why are certain employee categories tested and not others?

2. Comment on the strengths and weaknesses of: (a) testing alone, (b) interviewing alone, and (c) testing plus interviewing.

3. Can the use of testing be reconciled with the contingency approach to management? Discuss.

4. Do career planning and assessment centers specialize in self-fulfilling prophecies (see prediction results under "The Assessment Center Concept")? Explain your answer.

5. How would you upgrade this organization's testing program? Be specific in your answer.

PART VI
THE APPRAISAL AND TRAINING AND DEVELOPMENT PROCESS

"The process of performance appraisal is the continuous evaluation of the contribution of individuals and groups within organizations."[1] Performance appraisal is a required function of management that aids in the selection, reward, justice determination, task-specialization, leadership, collective-bargaining, and organization development processes. As shown in the accompanying diagram, there is a complex interdependency between these processes and performance appraisal.

"The training and development process is a complex amalgamation of many subprocesses aimed at increasing the capability of individuals to contribute to organizational goal attainment."[2] The training and development process is also highly interrelated to the performance appraisal process. When we appraise people, we ask such questions as: Why do we appraise personnel? How do we appraise personnel? When the appraisal is then communicated to the ratee, we are concerned with questions such as: What does negative feedback of performance do to people? How can supervisors reduce resistance to performance appraisal? Thus, communication, training, and development processes are inseparable from performance appraisal and development process (PADP) in this book.

Research and writings on PADP can be classified into one of two categories: traditional or collaborative. The traditional approach to performance appraisal consists of numerous devices including: graphic-rating scale method, rank-order method, forced-distribution method, paired-comparison method, critical inci-

---

[1] Wendell L. French, *The Personnel Management Process*, 3rd ed. (Boston: Houghton Mifflin, 1974), p. 54.
[2] Ibid.

191

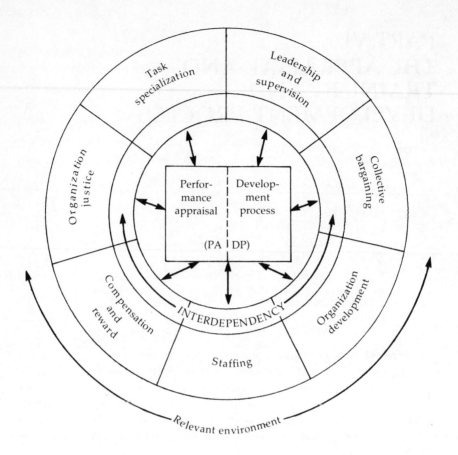

Figure **VI-1** PADP and personnel management

dent method, forced-choice rating method, and peer ratings.[3] Traditional writers normally use statistical tools in trying to remedy consistency problems such as rater inflation, the halo effect, and improving the predictive validity of the rating scales.

The collaborative approach to appraisal consists of such techniques as behavior-anchored rating scales (BARS) and management by objectives (MBO). The leading advocates of the collaborative approach to appraisal are concerned not only with the problems of the traditionalists, but also with developing people and organizations. They make a normative argument for increased feedback of performance. This communication is focused on joint goal setting in a coaching environment.

[3] For a description of each method see French, *The Personnel Management Process,* pp. 361–367.

A recent study[4] of industrial firms, life insurance companies, utilities, and banks indicated an almost even split between the traditional and collaborative approaches to appraisal. Of the responding organizations, 35 percent used a graphic-rating scale and 7 percent of the firms had a forced-distribution system. Of the responding firms, 56 percent use a results-oriented appraisal system, and another 15 percent plan shortly to change to a collaborative approach. As you read the incidents and cases in Part VI, determine whether the organization has a traditional or collaborative appraisal system and try to analyze the consequences of the system for the organizational participants and the organization. For example, does the organization have a PADP that encourages competition at the expense of cooperation? Does management have a PADP that is congruent with management philosophy and the other subsystems of personnel?

In addition to the problems just addressed, the overall performance evaluation systems in organizations are receiving more than just passing attention from EEOC, OFCC, and the courts. The problem is that appraisal systems are often biased, not reliable, and not demonstrably job-related.[5] Further, imperfect appraisal systems are often used as part of the validation evidence for selection tests. More and more, we see evidence that indicates that EEOC, OFCC, and the courts are concluding that performance appraisal systems fall under the purview of the EEOC "Guidelines on Employee Selection Procedures."[6] This problem must be addressed when validating selection devices. In Part V, the "Validity of Selection Devices" case is an excellent example of the problems associated with validating a selection device related to performance appraisal.

The eight cases and incidents in Part VI are primarily concerned with the problems of performance appraisal, training, and the development of management and employees. The incidents and cases provide a vehicle for applying theories and concepts taught in previous personnel management courses.

SUGGESTED READINGS

Conant, J.C. "The Performance Appraisal: A Critique and Alternative." *Business Horizons,* Vol. 16 (June 1973): 73–78.

Cummings, L.L., and Donald P. Schwab. *Performance in Organizations.* Glenview, Ill.: Scott, Foresman and Company, 1974.

French, Wendell L. *The Personnel Management Process,* 4th ed. Boston: Houghton Mifflin Company, 1978, Chapters 15–18.

———, and Robert W. Hollmann. "Management by Objectives: The Team Approach." *California Management Review,* Vol. 17 (Spring 1975): 13–22.

[4] Robert A. Zawacki and Robert L. Taylor, "A View of Performance Appraisal from Organizations Using It," *Personnel Journal* (June 1976): 290–299.
[5] William H. Holley and Hubert S. Field, "Performance Appraisal and the Law," *Labor Law Journal* (July 1975): 423–430.
[6] Ibid., pp. 424–425.

Holley, William H., and Hubert S. Field. "Performance Appraisal and the Law." *Labor Law Journal*, Vol. 18 (July 1975): 423–430.

Ivancevich, J.M., J.H. Donnelly, and J.L. Gibson. "Evaluating MBO: The Challenge Ahead." *Management by Objectives*, Vol. 4 (1975): 15–23.

McConkey, D.D. "MBO—Twenty Years Later, Where Do We Stand?" *Business Horizons*, Vol. 16 (August 1973): 25–36.

McGregor, D. "An Uneasy Look at Performance Appraisal." *Harvard Business Review*, Vol. 35 (May-June 1957): 89–94.

Miner, J.B. "Management Appraisal: A Capsule Review and Current References." *Business Horizons*, Vol. 11 (October 1968): 83 +.

Patz, A.L. "Performance Appraisal: Useful but Still Resisted." *Harvard Business Review*, Vol. 51 (January-February 1973): 74–80.

Raia, Anthony P. *Managing by Objectives.* Glenview, Ill.: Scott, Foresman and Company, 1974.

Taylor, R.L., and W.D. Wilsted. "Capturing Judgment Policies: A Field Study of Performance Appraisal." *Academy of Management Journal*, Vol. 17 (September 1974): 440–449.

Thompson, P.H., and G.W. Dalton. "Performance Appraisal: Managers Beware." *Harvard Business Review*, Vol. 48 (January-February 1970): 149–157.

Zawacki, Robert A. "The Performance Appraisal and Development Process: A Trend toward Increased Communication." *Academy of Management Proceedings* (1974), 62.

———, and Robert L. Taylor. "A View of Performance Appraisal from Organizations Using It." *Personnel Journal*, Vol. 55 (June 1976): 290–299.

32
DIGITAL ELECTRONICS, PART I

JAMES L. HALL AND JOEL K. LEIDECKER

BACKGROUND

Digital Electronics started on the East Coast in the 1930's. During the company's early years, it was primarily a defense contractor and manufacturer of radio equipment. In the 1950's Digital Electronics began to diversify and expand its operations to various electronic products, including semiconductors. In 1962 the corporate headquarters was relocated to the West Coast. As the demand for electronics technology continued to expand, Digital Electronics responded with worldwide expansion and rapid growth during the 1960's.

Since 1969 the company has followed the cyclical fluctuations within the electronics industry while continuing to grow. The general trend has been an increase in sales, number of employees and profits. However, in this five year time period there have been layoffs, sales declines and short run periods of running in the "red." At this time, the company is one of the five largest sellers of electrical components in its field and, technologically, Digital Electronics is the most advanced of the five major producers. (Digital Electronics' current employee population, worldwide, is 16,000.) The industry is in a decline phase while Digital's sales have been stable over the last few months.

Ralph Duncan became president of Digital Electronics in the early seventies. An electrical engineer in college, he had spent most of his career in the electronics semiconductor field and came to Digital from one of their competitors in 1964. Ralph was an extremely bright individual who had developed many patented products early in his career. Ralph was considered a no-nonsense hard driving executive. His staff were pushed and challenged and he expected everyone to perform at 101 percent. He was open and approachable. Almost any idea or program could be implemented if it was economically feasible and thoroughly planned and developed. In the last few years Ralph had concentrated his self-development in the area of management instead of in the engineering field. Around the company he had come to be known at the Resident Management Philosopher. Some of his ideas and broad areas of concern are noted in an excerpt from last year's speech at the stockholders meeting.

. . . The realization of Digital Electronics' full participation in the opportunities that lie ahead is the availability of skilled and experienced people to assume the management of our future. Bricks and mortar won't accomplish the growth we have projected for ourselves in the next decade; trained and talented people will. One of the major commitments a company makes and must make is to pledge to provide the training, education and experience which will develop today's engineers, administrators and assemblers into tomorrow's skilled managers at all levels. Without this commitment, any company restricts its future.

Bill Carson has been the Personnel Director at Digital Electronics for the last four years. A Liberal Arts undergrad, Bill graduated with an M.B.A. from a major west coast university in the late fifties. His early career experiences centered around a series of line positions with a large industrial product manufacturer. In 1962, Bill accepted a position with the Personnel Department of a large transportation firm and grew rapidly in the field. In 1970, he was an officer of the west coast chapter of the association training and development directors. That same year, he left his position of Assistant Director of Management and Career Development with the transportation company to accept the position of Personnel Director at Digital Electronics.

The first few months at Digital were difficult ones for Bill. He became part of an executive staff who, with the possible exception of Ralph Duncan, were highly sceptical of the contribution of the Personnel Department to overall profitability. The atmosphere has changed somewhat, but this has come about only through Bill's well-organized programs and his dogged determination to make the plans he has initiated work. Most of the changes he has had adopted are in specialized areas such as: fringe benefits, employee compensation, up grade wage and salary reviews, and in-house technical training programs. In the last two years the company has not embarked on any major changes in the area of management or employee development.

Last Thursday Ralph called Bill and asked him to come to his office today. He told Bill on Thursday that he wanted to discuss with him some of the broad management ideas he had outlined in his speech to the stockholders the previous week. Bill was a little apprehensive. Most of the previous meetings with Ralph had been strictly business focused on amplifying points about specific programs or attending the weekly executive staff meetings. As Bill walked into the executive suite, he wasn't sure what would take place.

After Ralph greeted Bill, the following discussion took place.

THE MEETING

RALPH DUNCAN: Bill, I've been stressing the importance of human resource development in several talks that I've given in the past year. As you know, this theme was the keynote of my talk at the last stockholders' meeting. I thought it was time to talk with you and find out just where Digital Electronics stands in this area. In fact, I'm wondering if we need to do some work here. Although we are tops in our field technically, we have been having some problems with declining sales and with meeting production deadlines. It has occurred to me that perhaps some of the cause is attributable to a lack of managerial skills and to a lack of employee motivation.

What are we doing to upgrade the level of managerial skills possessed by our managers and supervisors?

BILL CARSON: Well Ralph, we've been trying several programs to build the competence of our managers and supervisors. For several years we have sent some of them to management development programs run by a local university. The managers who have attended tell me that the program has given them a broader perspective of the managerial role.

The company also has a tuition-reimbursement program with which we encourage our employees with technical education to take course work designed to give them "management" knowledge. As a result, we have twenty-four employees who are now enrolled in M.B.A. programs or taking selected business courses.

We have run some short training programs on-site at Digital Electronics to familiarize our managers and supervisors with changing government regulations that affect our defense contracts. As you know, we recently completed an in-house technical training program for foremen that our industry thinks is a major breakthrough.

I think that our employee, supervisory and manager education programs are as good as any in the industry. They provide exposure of management concepts to all personnel who want to take advantage of our programs.

RALPH DUNCAN: Bill, is the understanding of management concepts that our managers attain helping them to be more effective with subordinates? Is this exposure to management concepts paying off in productivity and profits? Is this kind of management training sufficient?

BILL CARSON: We don't have any direct measure of its pay-off, but we do think that our management team has led us to success in the past. Morale measures tell us that our employee satisfaction is similar to that in our industry. Turnover is high, but that reflects the cyclical nature of the industry.

RALPH DUNCAN: Specifically Bill, in your estimation, what are the key areas— the concrete things we do in this company—that have an impact on profitability, productivity, and morale? Give me your realistic assessment of where Digital Electronics stands in these areas. Level with me—let's be candid and open about this.

BILL CARSON: Here are the areas in the company—not all are under my control—that have a major impact on profitability, productivity, and employee morale or satisfaction:

o Compensation and fringe benefits
o Security and advancement
o Performance appraisal program
o Training & development program
o Working conditions
o Communication: managers are accessible to employees

RALPH DUNCAN: Well, where do *we* stand—how do we compare to other companies in our industry? How are we doing compared to your own standards and expectations?

Table 1 summarizes Bill's comments, showing how, in Bill's opinion, Digital Electronics is doing in the six areas Bill has identified as having a major impact on profits, productivity, and employee satisfaction. Table 1 compares Digital Electronics to other companies in the industry, and also to Bill's own standards. Each area is ranked on a basis of 1 (High) to 5 (Low).

RALPH DUNCAN: Bill, this is really helpful. I'm curious, however, why you think we need to improve if we are up there with the best in the industry. Tell me more about those areas that don't meet your standards or expectations. I'm especially interested in hearing your thoughts on our performance appraisal program.

BILL CARSON: One thing that concerns me about our appraisal program is that a number of managers seem to give it minimal time and effort. I'm thinking in particular of some managers and supervisors who never hand in their appraisal forms on time. They always have to be reminded more than once.

RALPH DUNCAN: Does this mean that these managers don't find the performance appraisal program to be an effective managerial tool?

BILL CARSON: Well, that may be. In addition, some supervisors and managers complain that they always have to spend a lot of time defending their evaluations to their subordinates. Not only does this take-up valuable time, but also it sometimes causes bad feelings between the manager and his subordinate.

RALPH DUNCAN: You know, Bill, it seems to me that what you have just said also helps to explain why Digital Electronic's programs in Security and Advancement and in Communication are not up to your standards either.

Specifically, how does our Performance Appraisal program operate, and what causes the weaknesses that you think exist?

BILL CARSON: Most performance appraisals try to accomplish three objectives:

1. review past performance
2. establish wage or salary levels, based on performance
3. work on the development or growth of the subordinate

As you know, we have been using a standard form (Appendix A pp. 205–206) which asks the manager or supervisor to rate each subordinate on various aspects including personality traits, promptness, etc. The skill level of the subordinate is rated with respect to the job he holds. The employee is also rated on interpersonal relationships; that is, how well does the employee get along with others? Also each supervisor or manager is asked to comment on the future development of the employee.

Some of these aspects that are rated can be related directly to performance; others we're not sure about. Every manager and supervisor is required to fill out one of these forms on each of his subordinates once a year.

Table 1

Areas having a major impact on productivity, profits, morale	Bill Carson's rating of Digital Electronics:	
	Compared to other companies in industry	Compared to Bill Carson's standards
Compensation & fringe benefits	1	1
Security & advancement	1	2
Performance appraisal program	1	3
Training & development program	1	1
Working conditions	1	1
Communication: managers are accessible to employees	1	2

Upon completion of the form, the supervisor sends it to the Personnel Office where it becomes a permanent part of the subordinates' file. Based on a comparative evaluation of all employee evaluation forms, merit increases are then recommended by my Wage and Salary staff.

Ralph, you expressed concern earlier about the link between managerial skills and profits. In your opinion, where does the performance appraisal fit in? Is it an important part of "managerial skill"?

RALPH DUNCAN: In my mind, "managerial skills" refers to motivating people, developing commitment, and getting the most out of people. I've never really thought about where performance appraisals fit in. Most companies, including Digital Electronics, run their performance appraisals pretty much the same. I never really thought about how the performance appraisal can be used as an effective tool to help improve the company's performance.

What do you think, Bill? How do you see it related to profit, productivity and employee morale? Is it important? If so, what changes need to be made?

BILL CARSON: Well, from research in motivation we know that most people want to know where they stand and want a chance for advancement; that is, they also want to know where they stand in terms of future opportunities. They want to know what's expected of them, and they want timely feedback. One last thing that is worth mentioning in this connection is that money can be an effective motivator of performance if it is closely linked to performance.

RALPH DUNCAN: Do we know how effective we are in tying dollars to performance?

BILL CARSON: I think we could be more effective than we are. But that might mean giving managers more discretion in distributing dollars. Would you be willing to back a program that distributed a pile of money to each manager and allowed him to decide how the money would be divided up among his subordinates?

RALPH DUNCAN: It's worth thinking about, Bill. Something else has also occurred to me. You indicated earlier that communication was an area that could be improved. It seems to me that our current performance appraisal system is completely one-way communication. Let's start thinking about how to make it two-way communication.

BILL CARSON: The more I think about the motivational points I mentioned earlier, the more convinced I become that a major means of implementing these motivation points is either through the formal performance appraisal or under guidelines set up during the formal performance appraisal. However, I don't think that our present appraisal system, including the form, contribute as strongly as I believe they should. For example, an employee looks for frequent feedback but gets it only once a year from his foreman.

RALPH DUNCAN: But don't foremen give feedback informally on a daily basis?

BILL CARSON: Ralph, you would be surprised at the number of times, during exit interviews, employees state that the only time they received positive or even negative feedback was during the formal, annual performance appraisal. I think we need to change our present thinking and get all managers or supervisors to view performance appraisal as a continuous, on-going process.

RALPH DUNCAN: Does this mean that, to give timely feedback, we have to provide formal performance appraisals more than once a year? Won't this take the manager away from other, equally important, functions?

BILL CARSON: I really don't have a position on that. I am firmly committed to the need for having performance appraisal more than once a year. But I also believe that time is vital to the manager.

This raises another question in my mind. Do we need different frequencies of performance appraisals for different levels (managers, supervisors, other employees) of employees? Maybe we also should use different forms for these different levels.

RALPH DUNCAN: Those are interesting points. I'd like to comment on the form. In our appraisal form, the employee's needs or goals are discussed last. Is this one of the aspects that you think needs improvement if we are to upgrade the management development dimension of the performance appraisal?

You know, one of the management seminars I was in last year was concerned with the link between performance appraisals and the Management-By-Objectives approach. Maybe that is something we should look into also.

BILL CARSON: Maybe so. Something I think needs to be emphasized is that when subordinates are being evaluated, supervisors should evaluate aspects related to job objectives. This may require that we take another look at our appraisal form and may involve adding employee inputs in the setting of objectives. If we did this, I think it would help to build the two-way communication you mentioned earlier.

RALPH DUNCAN: Perhaps we need to take a hard look at the measures we are now using to evaluate employees. If you believe that feedback on actual job performance is the key to productivity increases, should we continue to focus on the evaluation of personality characteristics or skill-levels?

BILL CARSON: We certainly need to ask ourselves if our appraisal form is helping us to achieve the objective of our performance appraisal program.

Another weakness in our current appraisal system is in the way individual managers rate their subordinates. It seems to me there is a lot of inconsistency—some managers always rate high, others tend to rate low, and so forth.

RALPH DUNCAN: What do you suggest, Bill?

BILL CARSON: It might be a good idea to develop policy guidelines and a training program to help our managers and supervisors effectively administer a performance appraisal.

RALPH DUNCAN: That's interesting, Bill. I thought you were completely satisfied with your training effort. But now you suggest that more training—to develop managerial skills in giving performance appraisals—is needed.

BILL CARSON: I think this discussion is directing our attention to several matters that need more work. However, the key to a successful performance appraisal program, as in any change effort, is the commitment from top management. Ralph, are you and your staff ready to support this kind of program and emphasize its importance to all the employees? The only way we can change the climate is if you and your staff are as committed to the performance appraisal program as you are to profits and productivity.

In my mind it is inconsistent to be committed to profits without giving equal commitment to a strong on-going performance appraisal program. In practice, we seem to have a high concern for getting products out the door, but a low concern for people development.

RALPH DUNCAN: This has been an enlightening discussion, but I can't commit money and other resources to ideas that are so general. I need to see specific policies, specific forms. I need to see the reasoning, the logic, as to how this performance appraisal program will be linked to productivity.

I like the idea. Now let's develop specifics.

BILL CARSON: Do I hear you correctly? You want me and my staff to develop a new performance appraisal policy and forms, for Digital Electronics?

RALPH DUNCAN: Yes. You have the ball. Let's see what you can do with it.

ASSIGNMENT

You are a member of Bill Carson's staff. Bill has given you the assignment of developing a new performance appraisal system for Digital Electronics.

DIGITAL ELECTRONICS, PART II

In Part I of this case, Bill Carson (Personnel Director) and Ralph Duncan (President) were discussing ways of improving the company's productivity and profits. Ralph Duncan gave Bill Carson's Personnel Department the assignment of developing a policy and appropriate forms for a new or revised performance appraisal program at Digital Electronics.

The new policy and forms have been developed by Bill Carson and his staff. The material that follows describes three company employees (Fred Beale, Baxter Davies, and Jason Forrester) and their attitudes toward performance appraisals. These viewpoints seem to represent the attitudes of most of the employees at Digital Electronics. Personnel now is interested in receiving feedback on the Performance Appraisal Program and developing a plan to implement the program in the company.

REPRESENTATIVE ATTITUDES TOWARD PERFORMANCE APPRAISALS

FRED BEALE

Fred is supervisor of foremen in the Assembly Section of the Semiconductor Division. He is 53 years old, has a high school education and is married with four children. He had been with Digital Electronics for twenty-two years, including fourteen years in supervisory positions. Fred has held his current position for the last six years.

He has a reputation among fellow employees as a conscientious, loyal, capable employee. Fred has seen many new management ideas introduced and fail to be effectively implemented in the production sections of Digital Electronics. He is known to have a high concern for getting the product out the door, and tends to be crisis oriented. Fred has a negative view of the existing performance appraisal system. According to him, it accomplishes very little in terms of motivating employees. In fact, he sees it as a set of paperwork required by Personnel to help justify the Personnel Department's existence in the Company.

Fred administers performance appraisals to seven foremen, and is also responsible for reviewing the appraisals administered by each foreman. These foremen respect Fred, and consider him to be fair. Fred usually completes his performance appraisals only under pressure from the Personnel Department.

He spends no more than thirty minutes in each appraisal session which is a one-way communication process in which Fred points out the strengths and weaknesses that he sees in his foremen.

The productivity, quality, turnover, and absenteeism records of Fred's Assembly Section compare favorably with other assembly sections in the Semiconductor Division. Movement of employees from Fred's section to higher positions in the Manufacturing Department has not been high.

The following quotes are characteristic of Fred Beale's attitude toward performance appraisals in general:

"Performance appraisal is basically a waste of time because all we do is fill out the form, send it to Personnel, and then we never see it again."

"I don't need a form to evaluate my subordinates' performance. I can do that in my weekly section meeting or when I see them on the shop floor."

"I guess performance appraisal forms do serve a useful function in helping Personnel to make merit ratings throughout the company."

"Employee development? I don't need appraisal forms for that. I can spot workers who have potential for advancement in their first six months of employment."

BAXTER DAVIES

Age 42, Baxter is married, with two children, and has a B.S. degree in Electrical Engineering. Baxter is a Section Chief in the Design Engineering Group. He has three lead engineers reporting directly to him, and has responsibility for a total of eighteen employees. Although Baxter has been with Digital Electronics for only six years, he has worked in the electronics industry with two other firms since graduating from college in 1954.

Five years ago, Baxter made a decision to move up the administrative or management ladder, rather than the technical ladder. Often considered a realist by his peers, Baxter decided that, at Digital Electronics, advancement possibilities were greater on the administrative side than on the technical side. Prior to that decision, all his experience had been engineering design work. His work was considered to be of superior quality by his peers and superiors.

He has moved rapidly in engineering administration, and is being groomed for a higher-level administrative position. While Baxter's formal education has been in engineering, during the past five years he has taken advantage of Company sponsored management courses (in-house), and also attended management development seminars offered by a local university.

Baxter's management philosophy is based on the following three tenets:

1. An individual should have clearly defined work objectives.

2. Organizational rewards (salary increases and promotions) should be based primarily on performance-related accomplishments.

3. Most employees have the potential to progress within the company, but management's responsibility is to continually look for and foster that potential.

Baxter is a strong believer in performance appraisal and regularly schedules them for his subordinates. He uses the company appraisal form, but also adds subjective comments on areas not covered by the form. The annual performance appraisals he gives generally take one hour, and occasionally have taken two to three hours. During the appraisal session, Baxter feels that he actively solicits his subordinates' ideas, and believes that he and his subordinates level with each other.

Baxter's management record shows effective teamwork, high productivity, and that his groups have a high spirit of cooperation.

Following the last performance appraisal, Baxter was very upset, and complained to Personnel that some of his outstanding subordinates were not adequately rewarded by Personnel for their prior year's performance.

The following quotes are characteristic of Baxter Davies' attitude toward performance appraisals:

"Employee development is to be accomplished during performance appraisal, but time and support from higher management and Personnel is non-existent."

"All the companies I've been with pay lip-service to employee development, but I have found that it only gets done if the individual employee works at it on his own. It's usually non-existent in the performance appraisal process."

"Most of the engineering managers at Digital Electronics do not have the experience to provide the support and guidance necessary to develop work-related objectives and help develop employee potential. Sometimes I think that many of the engineering managers feel uncomfortable in giving performance appraisals. Maybe it's because they find themselves going on the defensive after giving criticisms."

"Even though I think the existing system needs improvement, I'm not sure that an increased time demand on the manager would be worthwhile in terms of the trade-off."

JASON FORRESTER

Jason is 34, has a B.S. degree in Psychology, and is single. He has been with Digital Electronics since he graduated in 1964. Jason started as a sales trainee, and graduated first in the Company's Sales School. Within three years he was one of the Company's most successful salesmen. After a one-year assignment on the President's staff, Jason was named Divisional Sales Manager four months ago.

Always an exponent of personal selling, three years ago Jason was involved in an In-House training program that increased his interest in Interpersonal Relations. He has pursued this area of interest on his own by involvement in sensitivity training and encounter groups run by reputable groups in the area.

Although Jason has not given any performance appraisals since becoming Sales Manager, he has in the past been critical of the Company's performance appraisal system. He finds most appraisal sessions are one-sided, non-human, and emphasize negative factors rather than positive, growth factors. Often he has commented that when he gained responsibility for giving performance appraisals, he would concentrate on the development of personal growth and focus on personal work objectives.

The following quotes are characteristic of Jason Forrester's attitudes toward performance appraisals:

"The human resource is the most important resource any company has. A manager's prime responsibility is for the growth and development of this resource."

"I believe that the performance appraisal system can be an important tool for motivating employees. The time spent for performance evaluation can be the most important time spent by the manager. Therefore, the manager must be interpersonally effective. This means the manager must know himself, be trusting, and be able to be open with his subordinates on any matter that might affect performance."

"It wouldn't bother me to spend two days giving a performance review."

"One of the things wrong with our existing system is that the subordinate is not involved in his own evaluation. The subordinate has a major role to play in the performance appraisal."

ASSIGNMENT

As a member of Bill Carson's Personnel staff, you have developed a new Performance Appraisal policy and form. Keeping in mind the attitudes of Company employees, as represented by the three viewpoints described in Part II:

1. Identify any changes you would make in your performance appraisal program.

2. Develop a *plan for implementing* the new performance appraisal policy and forms.

Appendix **A**   Digital Electronics annual performance appraisal form

_____ Employee's Name	Rating Period: Year Ended Dec. 31, 19____			
Present Position	Code	Position Grade Level	Department Section # Division	

	Below Standard	Satisfactory	Outstanding
1. ADAPTABILITY—Adjusts easily to changing conditions and assignments.	☐	☐	☐
2. APPEARANCE—Suitability in relation to the position.	☐	☐	☐
3. TEAMWORK—Cooperation with the fellow employees, works well with others.	☐	☐	☐
4. DEPENDABILITY—Degree to which employee can be relied upon to meet deadline without close supervision.	☐	☐	☐

	Below Standard	Satisfactory	Outstanding
5. DISPOSITION AND ATTITUDE—Obedient in carrying out orders; willingness to accept suggestions for work improvement; gives constant support to the organization.	☐	☐	☐
6. INITIATIVE—Has seen what needed to be done, and has shown initiative when the occasion called for it.	☐	☐	☐
7. JUDGMENT AND COMMON SENSE—Thinks clearly, weighs each problem, handles each situation with a minimum of supervision and readily adapts himself to meet the problem.	☐	☐	☐
8. SKILL LEVEL—Has skills required for present position.	☐	☐	☐
9. QUALITY OF WORK—Accuracy, completeness and neatness in performing special tasks.	☐	☐	☐
10. QUANTITY OF WORK—Amount completed in relation to job requirements.	☐	☐	☐
11. WORK HABITS—Punctuality, organization of work, care of equipment, and attention to safety.	☐	☐	☐
12. MORALS—Strength of morals and character.	☐	☐	☐
13. DEVELOPMENT—Potential shown for advancement and development.	☐	☐	☐
14. EMPLOYEE NEEDS & GOALS—Are employee needs and goals being met?	☐	☐	☐

Appraised by: _____   Date: _____

Appraisal review by: _____   Date: _____

QUESTIONS AND REQUIREMENTS

1. How is this organization using performance appraisal? Can the performance appraisal system be improved?

2. Discuss Bill Carson's contention that "money can be an effective motivator of performance if it is closely linked to performance."

3. How would you close the information loop of goal setting and performance?

4. Describe the difference between traditional and collaborative performance appraisal systems.

33
SAFETY TRAINING (A)

PHILLIP H. BIRNBAUM

BACKGROUND

Los Diablos County is one of the largest centers of population in the southwestern United States. The County government employs over 50,000 people and provides fire, police, highway, probationary, charity, and judicial services for all of the unincorporated cities within its boundaries and all but fire and police services for the incorporated cities.

Industrial accident prevention management had been centralized, except for the Sheriff and Fire Departments, in the County's Chief Administrative Office under the title of the "Los Diablos County Safety Division." The Safety Officers operated a fleet of black and white radio-equipped cars with red lights and sirens similiar to regular police vehicles. They were used by the Safety Officers to respond to the scene of industrial or automotive accidents involving County employees or equipment and also to provide general transportation as required by their other duties.

The Safety Division was made up of nine Safety Officers and one supervisor (also a Safety Officer) who reported directly to the County's Chief Administrative Officer. These men were all in their forties to sixties, were high school graduates, and had a variety of backgrounds and work experiences prior to their work in the Safety Division. Some had completed twenty or more years of military service and upon retirement had joined the Division. Others had held a variety of jobs, usually in law enforcement agencies or fire departments. None had received any formal training for their position other than in the military. They were men who had been around safety programs for many years and had informally picked up their expertise.

John Killingsworth, their supervisor, had often been heard to remark that, "the CAO (Chief Administrative Officer) didn't know his . . . from a hole in the ground when it came to safety and had no idea how valuable a resource he had in his Safety Division." It was John who had insisted on and finally obtained the black and white cars for his officers. He felt that the cars gave them status in the eyes of the other County employees and helped in "getting the facts" after an accident because of the authority associated with black and white cars. The other Safety Officers shared John's attitude toward the Chief Administrative Officer and toward the value of their specially equipped cars.

On January 1, 1972, the safety function was decentralized and the former Safety Officers were transferred to several County departments. Some were transferred to the Mechanical Department, some to the Personnel Department's Employee Development Division, and still others to the Probation and Charities Departments. As a result, John Killingsworth and one other Safety Officer retired. Although divided, the remaining members of the former Safety Division still continued to meet together for lunch and coffee even though their offices were several miles apart.

Under the reorganization, the Chief Administrative Office retained budgetary control over the workmen's compensation obligations of the County and continued to serve as the centralized coordinating agency for the decentralized safety activities. The Personnel Department was assigned the responsibility for conducting safety training, for developing a safety policy guide to attempt to standardize departmental safety policies, for maintaining accident records in accordance with the State's workmen's compensation requirements, and for initiating an incentive awards program which, although funds were not available for monetary rewards, was to provide some form of recognition to employees for good safety records. Each County department was to develop its own safety policy statement along the lines of the safety policy guide published by the Personnel Department and was to implement an effective safety program. Where assigned, the former Safety Officers were to coordinate safety for their department and provide their safety expertise to the department head as required. The centralized staff functions of the Chief Administrative Office and the Personnel Department were made available to departments for assistance upon request.

Within the Employee Development Division of the Personnel Department there were a total of twenty-four people assigned with the largest section consisting of the safety training group. This group consisted of four Personnel Analysts, two former Safety Officers, one Statistician, and two Statistical Clerks who were assigned to provide safety management training, driver training, and to maintain the records required by the state's workmen's compensation laws and by the County's private insurance company. The four Personnel Analysts were all college graduates. Jason, the supervisor of the group, had received his bachelor's degree and one master's degree in anthropology and a second master's degree in public administration. Dick had received his bachelor's degree in political science, Joan her bachelor's degree in anthropology, and Lou his bachelor's in psychology. Both Joan and Lou were recent graduates of a large western university and were only recently employed, this being their first professional job. Frank, the Statistician, had received his bachelor's degree in mathematics and was a long-time County employee. Michiko, the Chief Statistical Clerk, and George, her assistant, were both long-time County employees and were attending night school classes to earn their bachelor degrees. Howard and Russ, the two former Safety Officers, made up the rest of the training staff. The training was divided so that Howard and Russ were responsible for only developing and conducting driver training courses and Dick, Joan, and Lou for developing and conducting the safety management training course for supervisors.

THE TRAINING

It was the Employee Development Division's policy to train departmental trainers who would then conduct the actual employee training. This division had supervisory training programs already underway in the areas of basic management for supervisors, written communications, and a home-study programmed instruction course for executives in current management theory. In addition, they administered the County's tuition reimbursement program and several other training-related programs.

The Safety Management course was prepared from specific educational objectives considered crucial to the job performance desired. The training was divided into five sessions: (1) supervisor and safety, (2) task analysis, (3) training and inspection, (4) accident investigation and injury reporting, and (5) evaluation and motivation.

The first training session was concerned with orienting the trainees to the Safety Management program by giving them an overview of the course, pointing out their responsibilities as students, and giving them an appreciation of the problem by providing them with information on their recent safety record and the type of accidents which most frequently occurred.

The second session was aimed at each trainee mastering the essentials of a task safety analysis (Appendix I). This involved first identifying those jobs which had experienced the greatest number of accidents and then breaking those jobs down into their individual tasks and analyzing each task to determine how it could be made safer. This was the key session in the training and, because of its newness to most trainees, it was presented early in the training to allow time for them to see how it could be used as the basis for an effective safety program. To aid in lessening any resistance to this time-consuming procedure, it was introduced not only as an aid in accident prevention but also as an aid in training, performance evaluation, general job improvement, and morale building.

The third session was intended to give the trainees the principles of how to train employees in safe work procedures and how to inspect the work place for safety hazards.

The fourth session was aimed at teaching the trainees how to properly investigate an accident so as to gather key facts that could be used to prevent its recurrence. Trainees were also introduced to how the County's accident-reporting system worked and what part they as supervisors played in it.

The fifth session was concerned with using the performance evaluation procedures of the County as well as social science principles to motivate employees

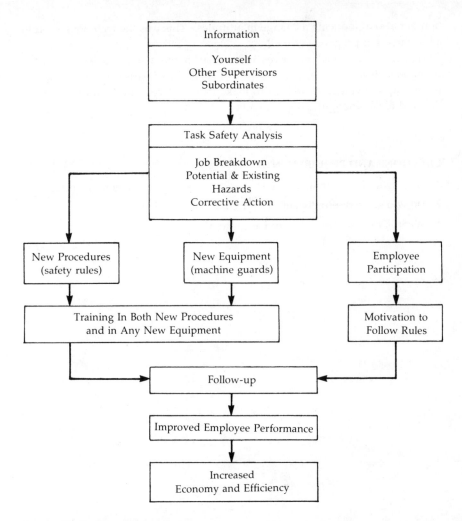

Appendix I The task analysis

to follow safe work practices. Techniques such as getting employee participation in the safety program and appealing to their psychological needs were discussed.

The program was developed around a trainer's manual which was constructed in such a way that the trainer was prompted as to what topic to cover and material to discuss but not so that he could read the material directly to the group. The intent was to prevent straight lecture but to allow the trainer to present material in his own words and to then encourage class participation in discussions and class examples with the idea of not only imparting new information but also of inducing a change in attitudes. This was the technique used in all of the other programs as well.

After the educational objectives and course content had been developed, the program's developers began a series of shakedown sessions to attempt to tighten up the course as well as to make its existence known and to build up demand for it among the departments.

QUESTIONS AND REQUIREMENTS

1. How would you evaluate the format of the safety management course?

2. Do you see any pitfalls with the training methodology?

3. What is missing from the course content?

34
SAFETY TRAINING (B)

PHILLIP H. BIRNBAUM

Based on the accident records available, the Department of Charities was selected for the initial training sessions even though their policy statement on safety was not yet finished. The County had eight large hospitals administered by the Charities Department. Two hospitals with the highest accident rates were selected, one primarily a physical rehabilitation hospital and the other a geriatrics hospital. In each case, the hospital's attendants had the greatest share of the accidents for their numbers, usually back injuries as a result of having to lift patients (Appendix II). Lou was selected as the trainer to conduct these first sessions.

The training began with a two-hour session covering the basic content and objectives of the training to allow the hospital's top executives to become familiar with the material and to improve its relevance. Working from the top down, the training was then given to each supervisory level of the Nursing Division. At each succeeding level the material was presented in greater depth and detail.

In the last groups trained, there were a total of 55 Registered Nurses. Each Registered Nurse trained was either a first-, second-, or third-level supervisor. They represented two employee classifications: Graduate Nurses and Head Nurses and were responsible for the supervision of Attendants, Senior Attendants, and Vocational Nurses. This group of attendants and Vocational Nurses represented approximately 91 percent of the total Nursing Division's employees and yet made up over 97 percent of their industrial accidents. The Graduate and Head Nurses trained averaged 41 years of age, had all held their present positions for over one year, and had either been graduated from a two-year college nursing program or had received their bachelor degrees in nursing.

In order to evaluate the success of the training program, both a pre- and post-test were administered to the Nursing Division supervisors. The test battery consisted of an already on-hand commercially prepared standardized safety attitude survey known as the "Industrial Safety Attitude Scale for Male Supervisors" and an internally prepared course content examination. The training had as its stated objective: The improvement of supervisors' attitudes toward safety as well as an increase in the skills associated with the reduction in industrial accidents.

At the end of the training, the results were evaluated for each hospital. In

Appendix II   Industrial Accident Summary

Geriatrics Hospital

Attendants: — Represent 13% of the total Nursing Division's employee population while accounting for 65% of the industrial injuries.

Non-probationers: — Only 19% of the industrial injuries of the Nursing Division are attributable to probationary employees (less than 6 months' service). All 19%, however, are attendants.

43 Years Old: — The mean age for an industrial injury in the Nursing Division is 43 years old.

6:01 A.M. to 6:00 P.M.: — 58% of all industrial accidents occur between these hours. The largest single percentage occurs between 6:01 A.M. and 12:00 A.M.

Back Injury Caused by Someone Else: — The most commonly occurring injury to Nursing Division personnel is a strain or overexertion to the back caused by someone other than the injured and resulting in a sprain or dislocation.

Physical Rehabilitation Hospital

Attendants: — Represent 59.6% of all industrial injuries to Nursing Division personnel while making up 32% of the Nursing Division employee population.

Non-probationers: — Only 13.5% of the industrial injuries of the Nursing Division are attributable to probationary employees.

41 Years Old: — The most commonly occurring age for an industrial injury is 40 years whereas the mean age is 41 years old.

6:01 A.M. to 6:00 P.M.: — 54% of all industrial injuries occur during these hours. The largest single percentage (32%) occurs between 6:01 A.M. and 12:00 A.M.

Back Injury Caused by Someone Else: — The most commonly occurring injury to Nursing Division personnel is a strain or overexertion to the back caused by someone other than the injured and resulting in a sprain or dislocation.

each case, the results indicated a slightly improved attitude and knowledge score but not sufficiently improved to be considered statistically significant.

At follow-ups of six and twelve months later, no appreciable difference was noticed in the hospital's accident rates.

DISCUSSION QUESTIONS

1. Imagine you are a newly employed Personnel Analyst and are asked to take over the further development of this safety management training program. What actions would you take and why?

2. Imagine you are the newly appointed Chief Administrative Officer and have the authority to make whatever changes are necessary to improve the County's industrial accident program. What problems do you see in the Personnel Department's training program and how would you recommend correcting them?

3. Imagine that you have just been hired as an outside consultant to study the County's training program You have come across the facts in this case in the course of your investigation. What recommendations, if any, would you make?

35
THE CORPORATE POLICY

JOHN WHOLIHAN AND K. MARK WEAVER

Sands Manufacturing Company, a fifty-year-old company, has grown from a small manufacturing concern to a leader in its industry with a complete line of material handling equipment. Over the years some engineers have become product experts of unquestioned caliber. The company finds however, that these experts are not able to easily adapt when transferred to a new job situation. This has hurt the company in the last ten years because of the tremendous growth and resulting need for older, experienced engineers to take over supervisory roles in new product areas. To give these personnel a broader background and experience in new job situations the vice-president of engineering has instituted a policy to encourage engineering personnel to be more mobile within the company's various branches of engineering.

John Turner, three years out of college, has been working as a design engineer under Lawrence Conner, Supervisor of New Products in the Product Design Division. John has done moderately well, but really doesn't enjoy design work as much as he thought he would. Instead he feels he would prefer to "get my hands dirty" in one of the Test Division labs.

Don Sutter, a project engineer in the Test Division, has been in the same department since he graduated from college twelve years ago. He has worked his way up from test engineer to his present position and would be next in line for promotion to supervisor. The current supervisors, however, don't show any sign of either moving to another area or being promoted to another job. For this reason Don sees his chance of being promoted to supervisor in this department as very limited now. Don feels he should take advantage of the new policy encouraging mobility so he requests a transfer to a design area. The request is given considerable attention and a trade is negotiated between the managers of the Test Division and the Product Design Division. Now Don, a project engineer with only test experience, is assigned to work for Lawrence Conner. John Turner, formerly a design engineer, is assigned to work as a test engineer in the group Don came out of.

John begins work in his new capacity and in a few months is quite satisfied with the move. Don, on the other hand, has encountered some problems which he hadn't anticipated. Don's new supervisor, Lawrence Conner, is less than happy with the trade since he had spent nearly three years developing John Turner as a design engineer and now finds he has lost him and gained a highly paid project engineer who has no design experience or knowledge of the design process.

Don also finds that his co-workers are not pleased to see another project engineer added to the group. Lee Jones, a project engineer himself, has felt that he would be the next candidate for promotion to supervisor within the Design Division. Will Round, senior design engineer, felt that he would soon be promoted to project engineer. He now feels that this will not occur while there are two project engineers in the group. Both Lee and Will see Don as a threat to their anticipated promotions and privately vow to give Don as little help as possible. The other design engineers and draftsmen also realize Don's design background is limited. They are not overly anxious to have to work with a weak project engineer and casually let it be known.

Lawrence, not knowing how else to use Don, assigns him to concept a new material-handling product modeled after one currently on the market. This includes contacting the company's marketing and manufacturing groups to solicit their input, doing an extensive review of advertisements and sales brochures of the products currently on the market, and traveling extensively to talk with potential customers. (Contact within the design department is minimized during the concept phase of a design.)

After nearly a year Don concludes that this new product has great potential and reports this to his supervisor Mr. Conner. The marketing and manufacturing groups deliver similar reports to their respective Divisions and the company product committee decides that a prototype machine should be built.

At this point Conner would normally have assigned the project engineer who had worked on the original concept to lead the prototype design effort. In this case, however, he decides that Don really wouldn't be able to handle it. Instead he assigns Lee Jones as the project engineer to lead the prototype design effort and has Don report directly to Lee. Lee, not wanting the project to be slowed down, assigns a menial job to Don and proportions the rest of the work to the others in the group. In the following months Don finds it harder and harder to accept his situation. He is responsible for an insignificant part of the project which he had originally concepted. Lee somehow never has time to listen to Don's suggestions regarding the overall development of the project. Will Round, the senior design engineer, has not only kept back information from Don, but has gone out of his way to make Don's job harder and to discredit Don's design efforts. The design engineers and draftsmen don't make things any easier for Don either.

After two years in the Design Division Don feels completely out of place and defeated. He can't seem to get any cooperation from the rest of the group, only an occasional joke about the quality of his work. He has learned practically nothing as a designer, he feels, and has been frustrated in his attempts to participate as a project engineer this past year. At the same time he sees the Test Division, where he was once highly regarded, being rearranged. With this he feels that he has no doubt lost any chance of returning to his former position.

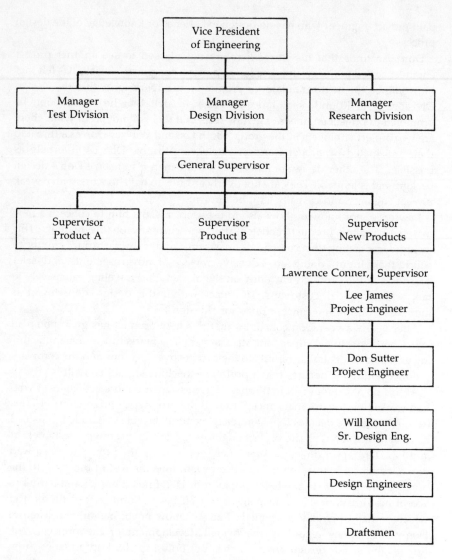

Exhibit **I**   Organization chart for Engineering Department Design Division Personnel New Products Department

Exhibit **II**   Job descriptions

Engineering Supervisor:	Has first-level line responsibility in the engineering department. Reports to General Supervisor.
Project Engineer:	Has responsibility to set up and direct work on engineering projects. No line responsibility. Reports to the Engineering Supervisor.
Senior Design Engineer:	Has responsibility for major portions or projects. Provides

	technical assistance to younger engineers. Reports to the Engineering Supervisor.
Design Engineer or Test Engineer:	Has responsibility for specific parts of components of a design or for specific tests. Reports to the Engineering Supervisor.
Draftsman or Technician:	Has responsibility to assist Design or Test Engineers. Reports to the Engineering Supervisor.

Exhibit III   Key people in the case

Supervisor Lawrence Conner	55 year old man, started in shop at the age of 16, somewhat a theory X type supervisor, has little chance for advancement himself.
Project Engineer Lee James	37 years old, worked his way up from draftsman, distrustful of college graduates and seldom gives help to anyone.
Project Engineer Don Sutter	34 years old college graduate, an upward mobile, has experience in test division only.
Senior Design Engineer Will Round	36 years old, got his degree at night school, rapidly becoming aware of diminishing chances of promotion.
Design Engineer John Turner	25 years old, college graduate, worked in design department 3 years and would like a chance at test work.

QUESTIONS AND REQUIREMENTS

1. As personnel director, how would you deal with Don Sutter?

2. Describe the general organization climate in the firm.

3. How would you work with Conner to prevent this situation from deteriorating? How would you work other engineers in the product design division?

4. Do engineers have a unique set of values? Describe what most engineers want from a job.

36
NORTON CONSOLIDATED

DAVIS W. CARVEY

Douglas Downing, purchasing manager for Norton Consolidated, a large defense contractor, was startled by the phone ringing at his elbow. He had been deep in thought as he tried to find an answer to the growing problem of supervisor turnover at Norton. Not that this was anything new, of course, but higher management was becoming more concerned due to the increasing realization that in many cases it was the better people who were leaving. . . . "Hello. Yes, this is Doug Downing. Oh, Hi Frank; how are things in personnel these days? What can we do for you? Hmmm. Well, I guess you might as well send the authorization on through to corporate: Ray is a good man and I think he would benefit considerably from this type of graduate study. I do have the budget to cover it, and you of all people know that I encourage my employees to continue their education, particularly where an evening program is available."

Doug hung up the phone with mixed feelings. On the one hand he knew that Ray would be better off in the long run by completing his MBA program; on the other hand, he also knew that from the company's standpoint it meant losing another promising young manager. He had seen the same pattern develop time after time and he knew that graduate work was only one more step in the process that began with the promises made to these men when they were recruited to work for the company. He knew all too well that the "stimulating environment" and "rapid advancement" would soon disappear into the drab work-a-day world of reality. Given the inevitable, somehow it seemed a shame to offer the encouragement of graduate school knowing full well that the company had no real plan for either utilizing or continuing their development. The really unfortunate part was that many managers in the company recognized the need to retain the talent available through such men, but were unable to offer more than personal encouragement—which was not reflected in any tangible manner by the company. Frequently this meant that opportunities did not meet even the minimum expectations of these individuals concerning their personal growth and growth opportunities. As a result, most of them would soon find it necessary to choose between a long-term "seasoning" process based primarily on chance, if they chose to stick it out, or leaving Norton for the immediate challenge of a new job with another firm. The ironical part is that the greater an individual's potential, the more likely he is to leave—and probably the sooner.

Doug was well aware of the pressures that would develop since he, too, had found it necessary to change companies in order to achieve what he considered to be reasonable growth in his work. He had even been idealistic (or naive) enough to think that his leaving might have some impact toward improving the system at his previous company. He had come a long way since then, mostly in spite of the system. On the other hand, now he was the system—or at least part of it. Maybe this was the time to put some of those earlier thoughts into practice.

The next day Doug dictated the following memo to the vice president of personnel and industrial relations. The memo outlined what he felt was a positive program to develop and encourage those individuals in his department with management potential.

Memorandum

To: Richard Chapman, Vice President, Personnel and Industrial Relations
From: Douglas Downing, Purchasing Manager
Subject: Proposed Management Development Program

As you know, the Company is currently encountering a two-faced dilemma. On the one hand, business is slack with resultant open capacity—both facilities and manpower. On the other hand, potential business opportunities necessitate that capacity, even though currently in excess of requirements, be kept available for future ventures.

Traditionally, this situation has been resolved primarily through Management inaction, that is by attrition, which does, in fact, reduce manpower to acceptable levels based on a "head count" philosophy. Along with attrition, some effort is usually made to utilize facilities through a change in the make-or-buy structure of our programs and a variety of make-work programs.

Unfortunately, this approach seriously hampers our ability to recover from periods of reduced activity as we, in effect, compound the problem. What is not considered is that individuals with education, foresight, drive, ability and other desirable leadership attributes are those that often resign during these periods. This is the type of person that should be most encouraged to remain with Norton for planning, developing and staffing future programs.

It appears that a limited attempt is being made at this time to work the problem by offering lateral "experience transfers" to a few employees with potential. This, while a step in the right direction, is certainly inadequate to significantly reduce the loss of good personnel.

Based on the present situation, it would seem that an effective and appropriate course of action would include the following steps:

1. Designate a number of potential Management employees to be included in an advancement/training program.

2. Discuss the program with these people on at least a Department Manager level and let them know that they are part of the program, possibly even in writing.

3. Pay the designated personnel increased salaries to the point of making it worth their while to become personally committed to their own development.

4. Lay off less productive employees in sufficient number to make up the budget money used for Step 3.

5. Give these individuals as much experience as possible, including frequent job changes, management exposure and formal training.

6. Establish "innovation sessions" as part of the training program with the purpose of acting as a group to establish new and/or better systems, organizations or work methods.

These sessions should be free flowing and include management participation on an as-required basis. Constructive ideas resulting from these sessions should be examined objectively and implemented whenever possible.

7. Each participant should be promoted as appropriate with others added to the group as required and/or are available.

All promotions should be based on merit; thus the plan would involve no Company commitment other than to put the individuals into the group and give them sufficient encouragement, including money, to remain with Norton.

The approach suggested will decrease the number of employees, yet at the same time upgrades the quality of the manpower pool available for future expansion. Part of the training group assignment could also be to develop new business and facility usage ideas, thus helping solve the excess capacity problem as well.

I would appreciate your comments concerning this proposal since we are planning to implement it on an experimental basis in the purchasing department as soon as we work out the details.

Once the approach proves successful in our department, it could then be expanded to include other departments in the near future.

QUESTIONS AND REQUIREMENTS

1. What is management development? How does it fit into an overall scheme of personnel planning?

2. What are some of the possible *negative* effects of proceeding with the plan suggested by Douglas Downing?

3. What are some of the possible *positive* effects of proceeding with the plan proposed by Mr. Downing?

4. How might this plan be implemented most effectively to maximize the positive results while minimizing negative impact?

5. What are some practical alternatives to the plan proposed by Downing? How might these alternatives be integrated into a realistic overall human resources plan?

37
SELECTIVE TRAINING—GOOD OR BAD?

W.D. HEIER

The four guests and their host, Arnold Ames, sat at a table in one corner of the private dining room. They had finished an excellent lunch and were waiting for their host to begin the monthly discussion period. At their last meeting the subject of management development had arisen just as the five were starting to leave for their offices. Therefore, although it had been tacitly agreed that the host for the month would select the luncheon topic, it was no surprise to hear Arnold Ames state that the subject for the day was to be management development. As was the custom, the host spoke first:

ARNOLD AMES (President of a large electronics company): Well, ladies and gentlemen, as we are all too often painfully aware, there seem to be periodic cycles in the supply of managerial talent. I can recall when there were plenty of sources, other than from your organizations of course, where we could pick up a good, well-trained executive. But no more! Now we are almost forced to do our own training. But you know, I don't think we save any money. We train a man and then have to give him a big salary increase to hold him because now that we've increased his potential he can get a job elsewhere very easily. We have trained many executives for other firms since I've been president. But, as I said, we don't have any good alternatives. It's a vicious circle from that point of view.

With respect to the kind of training we do, we concentrate our efforts on our managers who have already proven that they have high-level executive capacity. We do several things to broaden their scopes of operations and their general business outlooks. Further, we have one special program that seems to work exceptionally well for us. This is a series of bi-weekly programs held in my personal conference room. My personnel manager, executive vice-president and I act as a screening committee for candidates. We select five people who are just under our top level and hold school for them every other Friday afternoon for approximately an hour and a half. Our top executives talk to them about the activities in their specific areas of expertise. I'm told that they don't hold back much at those meetings. We feel that these trainees are an important feature in our company's future, and we let them know it. However, I have had to sit on a couple of our top people who were trying to pull a few political tricks to get one of their protégés in the program.

Oh yes, I forgot to mention that the program lasts from October until May. We have found that this eight month period gives us plenty of time to have our top level people cover their own areas and to have some eight or ten speakers from outside the company come in to speak. For example, last year we brought in an economist, a statistician, an operations research man, and a systems analyst from the university to talk to our trainees. My personnel manager, who sits in on most of the meetings, advised me that those sessions are very well received by the trainees. At one time I considered the idea of expanding that phase of the program, but, since we hire only college graduates in managerial positions, it didn't seem to offer too much in the way of a return for the dollars expended, so I decided against it.

Well, gentlemen, that's about it from our viewpoint. How about your development program, Bob?

BOB BROOKS (President of a construction supplies manufacturing company): Arnold, I think you have a good program going there. I may even start one in my company, if you don't mind.

Right now our current program is quite different from Arnold's operation. Since we sell almost exclusively through manufacturers' representatives, we are very production-oriented. Therefore, we don't have the capability in our personnel department to do any real internal training except the low-level skill improvement type. So we look to outside sources for ways to improve our managers' skills. For example, we have specifically designated a number of college courses a manager in a particular department may request to take, at our expense of course. Our accounting managers can take courses in Corporation Taxes, Governmental Contract Accounting, Auditing, Budgeting and Controllership. Our computer division managers can take System Analysis. The production managers can take Time and Motion Study, Advanced Production Management, and a couple of others whose names I've forgotten. The managers in personnel have a number of courses they are permitted to request. In view of the costs, and also to insure that proper control is maintained, I approve all such course requests myself. In doing so, I try to be objective as to whether the course fills a company need.

So you see, like Arnold, we, too, have some "outside" course training. I guess the primary difference in our program is that we make it available to everyone we designate as a manager, whereas the training Arnold spoke of is confined to his future top managers. We have to do more than that since we do not have a policy of hiring only college graduates. How about your program, Carla?

CARLA CAMAN (President of a state-wide banking organization): Our development program is really quite simple. We hire almost everyone at the bottom, and they work up, and grow up, in the business. We get everyone at the teller level, or equivalent, teach him the business ourselves, and, if he has talent, promote him. Like Arnold, we do subsidize a little outside training, some of it at universities, for our higher-level managers. But none of it is actually what you would consider classroom college course work. Our outside training consists of sending managers to Executive Training Conferences, Financial Seminars, and professional banking meetings.

We did try one special course for our lower-level management people. Our national banking association published a textbook for bank managers, hired a teacher and held the classes one night a week for three hours each night. Six of our employees attended. I've tried to find out whether their bosses thought it was worthwhile, but I never did get a good report. I suppose it didn't hurt them any, but that is hardly a good basis for a training program. I'll probably never be sure on that one.

At any rate, our training requirement is mostly an internal development problem, and we handle it that way. Maybe it isn't complete in some respects, but it seems to produce our kind of managerial talent. When it fails to do this, we'll be the first to change to something else. Don, I guess it's your turn to take the floor.

DONALD DOBBS (President of a national chemical manufacturing organization): I briefly discussed our management development approach with Bob after our meeting last month. As I told him then, we have a training department in the personnel division that gives internal training programs any time they are requested. For example, let's say that my office manager feels his work flow is "bogging down" some place. He may ask the training director to give a program on work simplification, forms control, reporting procedures or filing. If the training director has someone who can do the job, he will outline the program, get it approved, and run it. If he has no one qualified, he must get permission to go outside the firm and hire an instructor. Since this does not often happen, I can't remember ever refusing such a request.

We think that each individual manager is responsible for training his people. Therefore, the key to our program is that the manager, himself, requests the training for his people—as he should! We have a department to train our people, and our managers know we want them to use that service.

Our training department also arranges for lecturers to come in and present talks on both technical and general business subjects. We have had two special day-long workshops on marketing and credit management. I went to the opening ceremonies and stayed for the first session each time. The marketing seemed to have some relevance to our operation, but I think we could have done without the credit management program. I'm sure it was "broadening," but since a manager can't use this information in our company, I wondered if we weren't really training these men for jobs with some other company. That's a rather discouraging thought, isn't it? I'll stop with that and let Elaine carry on.

ELAINE EASTERN (President of a major paper-goods manufacturing company): I'll just stick to what we call the on-the-job training for our managers. Let me say, first, that we used to have a job rotation program, and it probably was worthwhile—but I couldn't prove that it was any good! It certainly gave our trainees a fine understanding of the company organization, but I kept getting little hints and remarks from division managers that they couldn't really use a man who was only going to be in a job a few months. So we finally stopped it.

We use committees a lot as training grounds. If we have a problem that we can give to a committee, we put a couple of the younger managers on with several of the more experienced executives. This gives the youngsters a taste of how higher level managers think and work. Our results here seem to have been very good. Others of you probably have several standing committees of your own. Just slip an extra youngster or two in on them and see how it works out for you.

We have also found that giving special assignments to younger executives works well for us. We may ask a man to re-do all of the job descriptions in his department and make recommendations for changes if he thinks any modifications are desirable. Or, he may be asked to evaluate the reporting procedures used with a view toward eliminating unproductive reports. There are many possibilities for training in this area.

Philosophically speaking, we believe every manager should prepare at least one subordinate to take his place. We never know when that subordinate may suddenly be called upon to step into his superior's shoes. He had better be ready! We also give our managers who haven't finished college the opportunity to finish their degrees, partially at our expense. We do not pay all of the cost because we feel that a man may be motivated a little more if part of the money he's spending is his own. That about does it for our management development program.

Sorry, I've got to run. Next month lunch is my treat.

QUESTIONS AND REQUIREMENTS

1. What are the various management development training programs mentioned in this case?

2. What are some of the strengths and deficiencies of the programs being offered?

3. How would you improve the programs?

38
THE FIRST RATING

ROBERT L. TAYLOR

Ann is a newly hired member of a state government office secretarial pool. Young and exceptionally hardworking, she is trying to make a good impression in her first job. Because of proposed work force reductions, not all newly hired employees will be able to stay on, and Ann is very concerned about not being retained.

Other than her initial meeting with Tom Mitchell, supervisor of the secretarial pool, she has received no formal feedback on her performance. However, many of the people for whom she works are highly complimentary of her efforts and her attitude. In fact, the senior secretary in the pool took time to write a letter on Ann's behalf praising her service, citing her "cheerful attitude, unusual motivation, and the usefulness of her many ideas for improving the flow of work."

Ann's first performance evaluation is due today (the anniversary of her first year of service). For each of ten categories, one of three ratings is possible: outstanding, satisfactory or unsatisfactory. The ten categories rated include: compliance with work schedules and deadlines; attention to details and close accuracy; reliability of work habits and dependability in attendance; maintaining, using and updating files; maintaining good relationships with co-workers and superiors; retaining necessary information regarding correspondence, regulations and directives; accepting authority and direction from others; accepting responsibility for assigned work; minimizing errors and reducing waste; and planning and accepting work priorities. Ratings in the extremes (outstanding or unsatisfactory) require specific written justification; satisfactory ratings need no written comment.

When Ann is called in to Mr. Mitchell's office for her performance appraisal review, he hands her the completed rating form and asks her to sign it at the bottom acknowledging that she has seen the rating. He rated her satisfactory in each of the categories.

Somewhat rushed, Mr. Mitchell becomes annoyed when Ann asks why she received the ratings. Mitchell replies that he never rates anyone other than satisfactory on the initial rating. His rationale is that a new person does not have the experience necessary to be outstanding, and, if her performance was unsatisfactory, he would recommend dismissal. Besides, he sees this as a way for her next rating to show improvement.

Tears form in Ann's eyes when she asks what she needs to do to be a better secretary. Mitchell states that her performance has been better than most of the career girls; everything is just fine and everyone is pleased with her work. She asks him about specific categories, but he is unable to offer recommendations as to what she might do to earn an outstanding rating. He quickly closes the meeting by stating, "For a first rating, it is an excellent one. However, if you want to discuss this further, I will be happy to talk to you tomorrow."

QUESTIONS AND REQUIREMENTS

1. Should Ann request another interview for tomorrow?

2. How could Tom Mitchell have better conducted the appraisal interview?

3. What should Tom Mitchell have done to prepare himself and Ann for this first appraisal?

4. As a result of the appraisal interview, Ann's performance might be expected to change. What would you predict? Why?

39
THE SCIENTIST WHO QUIT

WENDELL L. FRENCH

On Tuesday morning, Elliott Merrill, a Ph.D. in metallurgy and a researcher with a large defense contractor in California, was shocked to see the following written across one of his technical reports:

"This is ridiculous. Your hypothesis is not plausible, and your conclusions are equally implausible. Start over.

(Signed) A.M.

A.M. was Dr. Andrew Mackenzie, Vice President in charge of Research, and Dr. Merrill's boss.

During lunch with a colleague that day, Dr. Merrill was quite agitated, and stated that he was "sick and tired of Andy's high-handed methods," and that he wasn't going to "take it any longer." The colleague agreed that Dr. Mackenzie was "an abrupt, cold fish," and tried to reassure Dr. Merrill that Dr. Mackenzie treated everyone that way.

Late on a Friday afternoon, two and one-half weeks later, Dr. Merrill wrote out his resignation, which stated that he was going to work for a competitor and which gave two weeks' notice, walked into Dr. Mackenzie's office, handed the resignation to him without comment, and walked back to his own office. Shortly thereafter, he left the plant for the weekend.

On Monday morning, about a half-hour after Dr. Merrill had arrived at his office, the telephone rang. It was James Black, Personnel Director. "Elliott," he said, "I'm sorry to hear about this unfortunate business, but Andy and I think you might as well leave today. We'll pay you the two weeks' pay, of course. You can pick up your check from me as soon as you've cleared out your desk. I'll expect you in a half hour."

QUESTIONS AND REQUIREMENTS

1. What does this incident tell you about the relationship between Dr. Merrill and Dr. Mackenzie? About Dr. Mackenzie's leadership?

2. How do you feel about how this matter was handled?

229

PART VII
THE COMPENSATION
PROCESS

In personnel administration, compensation refers to those processes aimed at paying people both for the services they provide and as motivation for them to achieve desired levels of performance. A number of techniques have been developed to assist in the process of administering compensation. In all of these techniques, information gathering is critical. Compensation specialists need to gather detailed information on the content of each job. They must describe this content in terms that are clear and in common use throughout the organization. Job analysis and description, therefore, are fundamental elements in information gathering. Information is also needed in order to determine the "price" for personnel resources in any given labor market. Wage and fringe benefit surveys, conducted either by government or business organizations, serve to determine pay rates for a wide range of jobs described in standardized terms.

Job evaluation involves a systematic analysis of each job and a comparison of jobs for relative importance. In addition, job pay rates are compared with external rates of pay to assess the extent to which the organization is meeting area and/or industry pay standards for various job categories.

The compensation process is intimately related to the concepts of organizational justice covered in Part III. Employees compare their compensation and work demands with those of others within and without the organization. Thus, they arrive at their perceptions of the fairness of the organization—perceptions that have important organizational consequences. In a recent research study in a large government clerical office, internal pay comparisons were very closely and significantly related to feelings of employee job satisfaction. External pay comparisons, on the other hand, related very closely to departmental absence and turnover rates.[1]

Following the description and evaluation of jobs and the establishment of fair pay rates, the compensation process calls for a compensation plan to provide rewards in a consistent and logical manner. Across-the-board increases, cost-of-living escalators, merit-rating systems, and selective "cafeteria-style" compensation schemes are types of compensation plans that might be employed. Each, of course, might be appropriate in some circumstances and not in others. All, however, should address the issues of competition for resources in the external labor market, equity in the relative treatment of employees within the organization, and whether that compensation serves as a motivating factor to support and encourage acceptable forms of employee work behavior.

"The Apex Case" provides an opportunity to discuss the results of a job redesign. A change in work method was used as the basis for a change in pay. Readers should think not only of the job study aspects of this case, but also of the issues of equity in compensation and the effect of the job change on the motivation of the affected workers. Equity is also a key element in the case entitled "Salary Adjustment." Here, the administrator has been instructed to communicate reward information to employees by letter without providing information that might enable the employee to compare his rewards with those received by others.

The "Hoerner Waldorf vs. IBPS and PMW" case illustrates some of the complexities involved in the administration of wages. In this case, a complex overtime premium pay question has resulted in the employee filing a grievance and in the union taking the grievance to arbitration for resolution. Here the reader can see the issues of compensation, equity (as a distributive justice) relative to the payment of a premium for overtime or holiday work, and (as corrective justice) the employee pursuing a grievance through due process to arbitration.

SUGGESTED READINGS

Andrews, Robert, ed. *Managerial Compensation.* Ann Arbor, Mich.: Foundation for Research in Human Behavior, 1965.

Atchison, T.J., and D.W. Belcher. "Equity, Rewards and Compensation Administration." *Personnel Administration,* Vol. 34 (March-April 1971): 32–36.

Bassett, Glenn A., and Harlow A. Nelson. "Keys to Better Salary Administration." *Personnel,* Vol. 44 (March-April 1967): 23–30.

Cassell, Frank H. "Management Incentives and Management Style." *Personnel Administration,* Vol. 31 (July-August 1968): 4–7ff.

---

[1] J.E. Dittrich and M.R. Carrell, "Dimensions of Organizational Fairness and Job Satisfaction as Predictors of Employee Absence and Turnover," *Academy of Management Proceedings* (1976).

French, Wendell L. *The Personnel Management Process*, 4th ed. Boston: Houghton Mifflin, 1978, Chapters 19–21.

Gordon, T.J., and R.E. LeBleu. "Employee Benefits, 1970–1985." *Harvard Business Review*, Vol. 48 (January-February 1970): 93–107.

Griffes, Ernest J.E. "What's Happening to the Private Pension System?" *The Personnel Administrator*, Vol. 16 (September-October 1971): 29–32.

Grinyer, P.H., and S. Kessler. "The Systematic Evaluation of Methods of Wage Payment." *The Journal of Management Studies*, Vol. 14, No. 3 (October 1967): 309–320.

Hickery, Joseph A. "Workmen's Compensation: Administration and Provisions." *Monthly Labor Review*, Vol. 90 (December 1967): 29–39.

Jaffee, William A. "Paying Salesmen Properly." *The Personnel Administrator*, Vol. 17 (May-June 1972): 30–32.

Lawler, E.E., III. "The Mythology of Management Compensation." *California Business Review*, Vol. 9, No. 1 (Fall 1966): 11–22.

Lesieur, F.E., and E.S. Puckett. "The Scanlon Plan Has Proved Itself." *Harvard Business Review*, Vol. 47, No. 5 (September-October 1969): 109–118.

Lewellen, W. G. *Executive Compensation in Large Industrial Corporations*. New York: National Bureau of Economic Research, 1968.

Matthies, Mary T. "The Developing Law on Equal Employment Opportunity." *Journal of Contemporary Business*, Vol. 5 (Winter 1976): 29–46.

Nash, Allan N., and Stephen J. Carroll, Jr. *The Management of Compensation*. Monterrey, Calif.: Brooks/Cole Publishing Co., 1975.

Opsahl, R.L., and M.D. Dunnette. "The Role of Financial Compensation in Industrial Motivation." *Psychological Bulletin*, Vol. 66 (1966): 94–96.

Paterson, T.T. *Job Evaluation, Volumes 1 and 2*. London: Business Books, Limited, 1972.

Patton, Arch. "Why Incentive Plans Fail." *Harvard Business Review*, Vol. 50 (May-June 1972): 58–66.

Scanlan, Burt K. "Is Money Still the Motivator?" *The Personnel Administrator*, Vol. 33, No. 3 (July-August 1970): 8–12.

Showengerdt, R.N. "How Reliable Are Merit Rating Techniques?" *Personnel Journal* (September 1975): 496–498.

Todd, J.O. " 'Cafeteria Compensation,' Making Management Motivators Meaningful." *Personnel Journal* (May 1975): 275–281.

Zollitsch, Herbert G., and Adolph Langsner. *Wage and Salary Administration*. Cincinnati: South-Western Publishing Company, 1970.

40
THE PUZZLED MANAGER

WENDELL L. FRENCH

Tom Hoffman, department manager of the packaging department for the High-Grade Pharmaceutical Company, sat in his office and stared out of the window. He had just come back from having lunch with Arnold Clark, the personnel director, and was thinking over their conversation about incentive systems. His thoughts ran as follows:

I think our employees could package a lot more materials each day if we had the proper incentives. We have this constant pressure for getting things out faster, and I'm not sure it's economical to keep adding employees. Of course, we are gradually adding better equipment which helps a lot. Maybe if we really got our packaging automated we could cut costs a good deal.

Arnold argues against incentives because incentive plans are always such a headache to administer and because the union is always on your back if you try to change standards. He also says we'll really have problems if we install an incentive system and then bring in new equipment.

I think what Arnold wants is a merit-rating system instead of a single rate for each job, but he's naive if he thinks that won't produce just as many hassles with the union. I sure wish I could figure out what to do. We've got to do something.

QUESTIONS AND REQUIREMENTS

1. If you were called in as a consultant, what considerations would enter your recommendations?

2. List the advantages and disadvantages of various compensation plans.

41
THE NEW YEAR'S BONUS

WILLIAM F. GLUECK

Ezell Musical Instrument Company (EMI) is located in Frederick, Maryland. It is a middle-sized operation which has grown out of a family-owned company. Like many companies it has to face tough competition at home and abroad. M.G. Ezell III is now the president of the firm.

Several years ago, when Ezell first took over, he thought about how he might build morale at the works. He felt that the company had good workers, and he'd like to reward them for past services to encourage them to be more productive. EMI was not unionized. He hesitated about raising base wages because it might make the firm uncompetitive if foreign competition increased.

EMI was having an exceptionally good year, both for sales and profits. As a result, Ezell thought that the best way to reward the employees was to give them a Christmas–New Year's bonus. As he said to Abe Stick, his personnel manager: "Nothing like the old buck to make a man work harder." His bonus system was as follows:

Wages or salary	Bonus
<$6,500	$500
$6,501–7,500	$600
$7,501–8,500	$700
$8,501–10,000	$800
>$10,000	8% of salary or wage

The bonuses were well received. Many people thanked the president and Stick heard lots of good comments from supervisors in January about how much harder the employees were working.

The next year, more foreign competitors entered the market. Materials were harder to get and more expensive. Sales were down 5 percent and profits down 15 percent. Ezell didn't feel he could afford the same bonuses as last year. As a result, the bonuses were decreased as follows:

Reprinted with permission from *Cases and Exercises in Personnel* by W.F. Glueck (Dallas, Texas: Business Publications, Inc., 1974 c.) pp. 95–97.

Wages or salary	Bonus
<$6,500	$250
$6,501–7,500	$300
$7,501–8,500	$350
$8,501–9,500	$400
>$10,000	4% of salary or wage

This time, Stick heard little from the supervisors about increased productivity. He asked Harry Bell, one of the supervisors, what the reaction was to the bonuses.

BELL: To tell you the truth, Abe, I have morale problems. My people worked hard this year. It wasn't their fault sales or profits were down. Many expected last year's bonus or better. So they spent most of the old figure for Christmas gifts. When they got that letter from M.G. telling them they were getting only half of last year's on December 27, there was gloom and doom and some mumblings. Some of my people seem to be working less hard than at any time I can remember.

STICK: But that's not fair, Harry. They never received any bonuses before. Now they should be glad they received anything.

BELL: That's not the way they see it!

Stick decided not to discuss the matter with Ezell. Stick figured the problem would blow over. But, this year was even worse. Sales held but were not up to the prior years' levels. But, profits were almost nonexistent. The board of directors has decided to omit the dividend.

Now, Ezell has come to Stick. Ezell says: "Abe, I don't see how we can pay any bonus this year. Do you think we can get by without causing a big drop in morale?"

QUESTION AND REQUIREMENT

1. It is December 1. You are Stick. What do you advise Ezell? How do you suggest he handle the situation? When do you inform the employees?

42
THE APEX CASE

DAVID KUECHLE

The Railroad Products Division of R.G. Budd Company manufactured gal-
vanized steel-grated walkways for freight cars and diesel locomotives and sold
them exclusively to the Apex Railroad Products Company in the United States.
Aside from adjustments needed to accommodate differences in width and
length the various walkway sections were manufactured in the same manner.
Steel sheets were sheared and notched by a press to produce strips ranging in
height from two to two and one-half inches, in thickness from ³⁄₁₆ to ⁵⁄₁₆ inch, and
in length from one and one-half to four feet. One edge of each strip was flat; the
other had scallops designed for firm footing. The strips—called beam bars—
were fitted in criss-cross fashion with somewhat heavier, non-scalloped, cross
bars. The bars were nested in pre-formed notches cut on both bars at three-inch
intervals. A press forced the bars together, and the galvanizing operation—
following straightening and grinding—served to weld them sufficiently for the
purpose they would serve.

The key operations in production of walkways were called "assemble and
press." These had been essentially unchanged for the past 24 years. Two men,
one working on each side of an assembly table, placed the cross bars and beam
bars into a jig, which was adjusted from time to time for differences in size.
There were identical assembly tables on two sides of a large ram press. When
the assembly of a section was completed, one of the operators pushed a button
to move his table underneath the press. Then he pressed another button to
activate the press—forcing the bars together via the notches—and a third button
to move the table from under the press so that the assembled walkway could be
removed from the jig. Work was then begun on a new assembly. The controls
of the assembly tables were wired so that it was impossible for the tables on
opposite sides of the press to be activated at the same time.

Operators on the assembly tables were instructed by their foremen to activate
each of the three buttons only after the prior operation was completed. Thus,
the button to lower and raise the press was to be pushed only after the assembly
table had moved in under the press and stopped. Times were assigned to the
three button-pushing operations as follows: Table in, .155; Press, .080; Table

out, .130.[1] Industrial engineers recorded those times based on stop-watch observations. The total time for the three operations was .365 minutes.

Soon after the "assemble-and-press" operation was inaugurated the operators modified the prescribed technique in order to activate the press, thus starting the downward action of the ram while the assembly table was moving into position under the ram. A highly-skilled operator could time action so that the press ram made contact with the grating just as the table came into full position. Then, just before the pressing had been completed, the button initiating the "table-out" action was activated. Thus, the table began to move from under the press at about the instant that the ram was released. As a result of their skill in exercising these short-timing techniques, some operators were able to reduce the total time for the combined three elements to as low as .250 minutes. Consequently earnings on the "assemble-and-press" operation were extremely favorable. First-shift operators during the past year realized earnings averaging $4.60 per hour; 44 per cent over normal; second-shift earnings were $4.56, 42½ per cent over normal; and third-shift earnings were $4.00, 25 per cent over normal. Third-shift earnings under the synchronized method were considerably below those of the first two shifts, because the third shift operated only two or three months; cumulatively, in each year, and operators on "assemble and press" had little time to become accustomed to the job before facing layoffs.[2]

The synchronized method of "assemble and press" was observed and acknowledged by supervisors in the shop and by the industrial engineers. No one discouraged it or attempted to change it. This was a favorite job in the division—one with steady employment characteristics, less than average difficulty in performance and high earnings. The only time it caused trouble was when an operator failed to time the buttons correctly so that the press ram reached the bottom of its stroke before the assembly table was in position. Sometimes this resulted in considerable damage to the table, but most often it simply caused spoilage of the walkway section to be pressed. Repair bills caused by damage from improper synchronization of the press average $3,212 each year for the past ten years. Repairs to the press and table from such damage resulted in an average of four days' down time each year. Because of this, foremen in the division always instructed new operators to activate the three buttons as prescribed by the original time study.

THE SUGGESTION SYSTEM

Approximately one and a half years ago R.G. Budd Co. initiated a suggestion system designed to tap the ideas of all employees for improvements that would save the company money. It was an attractive plan—providing 25 per cent of

[1] Times are expressed as fractions of minutes.
[2] Time-study policy at R.G. Budd was informally acknowledged to allow 30 per cent earning opportunity on all jobs. Consequently a 30 per cent factor was added into all machine-controlled operations where operators were not able to exercise skill and effort.

the first year's estimated savings to the successful suggestor. All employees were eligible to make suggestions, except eligibility did not extend to those whose suggestions could be considered within one's direct area of responsibility. The Industrial Relations Director, for example, could not receive an award for a suggestion to change the wording of a collective agreement which he had responsibility to negotiate. Eligibility for awards under the suggestion plan was decided upon by a committee of three—headed by the Industrial Relations Director. Whenever in doubt the committee decided questions of eligibility in favor of the suggestor—thus endeavouring to preserve the attractiveness of the suggestion system.

Last June 5 the committee received a suggestion from Mr. Philip Evans, Industrial Engineer assigned to the Railroad Products Division. It was a scheme for rewiring the electrical circuits for the assembly tables and press so that a fool-proof synchronized operation would result. Under Mr. Evans' suggestion, the assembly operator would push only one button—not three. When the assembly table reached a predetermined spot, the press would be automatically activated so that the ram would meet the assembled grating at the precise moment the assembly table stopped. Then, as soon as the ram released from the grating, the assembly table would automatically return to its former position. With the new system, pointed out Mr. Evans, the company would save damage caused by improper synchronization of the three buttons, would raise production of inexperienced operators, and most important, would save the company the high incentive wages which served to make "assemble and press" such an attractive job through the years.

The suggestion committee turned over Mr. Evans' suggestion to Mr. Harry Bateman, an industrial engineer, whose job it was to investigate and determine feasibility of cost savings ideas that were submitted. Mr. Bateman consulted with Mr. Edward Artz, Superintendent of the Railroad Products Division, and the two men lost little time in recommending that the suggestion be adopted. The total cost of rewiring the tables and press was estimated at $600. The total savings in repairs caused by improper synchronization of the buttons were estimated at $3,200 per year, and the savings on wages were estimated at $400 a year. This latter figure was, at best, a rough estimate, because neither Bateman nor Artz could know exactly how much in wages would be saved as a result of the change. Clearly the attractiveness of the job would diminish, and the company, through the years, had benefitted from the skill of assemblers staying on the job year after year. Mr. Artz observed that time used by moving assembly tables under and out from the press and by activating the press itself constituted less than $\frac{1}{12}$ of the job. Each of the two tables was activated every four minutes, on the average, with the press coming down every two minutes. Since the total time allowed for activating the table and press was slightly over $\frac{1}{3}$ of a minute (.365), the men were occupied in manual assembly operations for approximately $\frac{11}{12}$ of their time—time unaffected by this change.

THE GRIEVANCE

"If the division could save on repair costs alone, the suggestion is worth adopting," said Mr. Artz. Consequently he assigned an electrician to rewire the activating mechanisms of the tables and press, and on Monday, June 15 the new system went into effect. Mr. Evans timed the tables and press that day and assigned .260 minutes—a reduction of .105 minutes from the previously-assigned time. The operators immediately filed a grievance claiming an illegal rate cut. "We've been running this job through our own skill at .250 minutes," pointed out one operator. "Now you make an 'improvement'—adding .01 to the actual time and you want to cut our rate! This is outrageous."

Mr. Joseph Majda, Contact Board Representative of the Union, was summoned to the division and, after talking with operators, went to see Messrs. Evans and Artz. Mr. Majda pointed to Section 12 of the Time Study Policy of the Collective Bargaining Agreement. He said that by changing the rate, the company was in violation of this section.

Section 12

Established standards and rates will remain in effect for the life of the contract unless there is a change in methods, procedures, feeds, speeds, dies, machines, jigs, fixtures, products or materials which tend to increase or decrease production. In these cases, a restudy will be made and only those elements affected by the change will be ajdusted. If it appears on examination that the resulting rate is clearly out of line, a conference will be called between the Contact Board representatives for the area and management to review the factors involved in the rate to determine the best procedure for adjusting the rate.

The above procedure for changing standards is based on the principle that where proper standards exist, any changes will permit the same earning opportunity as existed under the original standard.

Section 12, in its present form, had been adopted by the company and union 11 years ago. It had been the subject of repeated grievances since then—the union consistently claiming that any change of rate that reduced earnings on a job was a violation. Company representatives, on the other hand, were inconsistent in their interpretation of the Section. Some agreed with the union. Others contended that earning opportunities referred to a "normal" worker expending "normal" effort on a job he could do well under the prescribed method. Such a worker, they said, should earn 100 per cent of the assigned rate. In their support these company people pointed to Section 8 of the Collective Agreement's Time Study Policy.

Section 8

One hundred (100) per cent shall be considered normal. The levelled time shall reflect the performance of the average worker working efficiently at a job he can do well, working at normal effort under the prescribed methods to produce the production standard (yield) under the conditions.

Other company representatives argued that Section 12 was designed to prevent wholesale rate cutting—that rates could be changed only when bona fide methods changes occurred: this, even though both company and union agreed the rate was out-of-line because of sloppy time study practices or lucrative because operators had devised effective short cuts. Until the Apex Case arose in June this latter view had prevailed. Section 12 had never been challenged in arbitration.

Upon receiving his report from Mr. Bateman, the Industrial Relations Director had to consider three questions—all three of which were related.

QUESTIONS AND REQUIREMENTS

1. Should a suggestion award be tendered to Mr. Philip Evans?

2. If an award to Mr. Evans is made, what should be its amount?

3. Should the incentive rate on the assemble and press operation be reduced as a result of the rewiring?

43
SALARY ADJUSTMENT: EQUITY AND MORALE

ROBERT KNAPP

It was faculty salary increase time. Dr. John Suverman, Dean of the Pharmacy College, had recently sent notices of salaries for the forthcoming year to all of his members.

Since he was new to the Dean's job, Suverman had asked University President Hadley what information to include in salary announcement letters. He was particularly concerned if he should inform each faculty member of the average increases for the entire college and for the University so that each professor would be able to compare an individual salary with the average.

President Hadley told Suverman to include in the letter only the salary for that faculty member, and this Suverman did.

Two days after announcement letters were issued, Professor Wick visited Dean Suverman's office. Suverman saw immediately that Wick was tense and upset.

"I would like to discuss my new salary—there must be a mistake in the announcement letter," Wick said. After a brief conversation concerning the contents of the letter, Suverman confirmed that the salary figure was indeed correct.

"But I thought my teaching and research performance this past year were excellent, and I am shocked that you awarded me only a seven percent increase," Wick said.

Believing that Wick was an above average professor whom he wanted to keep, Suverman explained that the legislature had not been very generous with faculty salary increases this year. He also said that no professor had received a great increase.

Wick wasn't satisfied. He asked whether his performance was lacking in the eyes of the University and what the average increase was for the entire faculty so that he could determine how he did relative to his colleagues.

Suverman declined to release any more information than was in the announcement letter.

"I can't understand that," said Wick. "You have a well-deserved reputation for always being open and frank with the faculty."

The telephone rang, and Suverman picked it up.

After waiting impatiently for a few minutes, Wick hurriedly arose from his chair and started to leave the Dean's office. As he did so, Suverman, still on the

243

phone, called out to Wick that he would finish his call shortly. The door was closing behind Wick, and Suverman wasn't sure his message was heard.

After finishing his phone conversation, Suverman pondered what to do. Wick was doing a good job, and Suverman didn't want to see such a valuable professor become dissatisfied and unmotivated. If Wick knew that the average increase was only 4% and that he had received the third highest increase among the 23 faculty members, Suverman felt that Wick was reasonable enough to gladly accept that situation. Perhaps, he thought, he should just tell Wick this privately and ask him not to reveal it.

Suverman also realized that Wick apparently did not know that, because the University was a public institution operating under an "open information" law, all faculty salaries were published in a roster available in the library to anyone who requested it. While the University did not hide this fact, it did not advertise it either. Consequently, many newer faculty members did not know of the existence of the roster.

Perhaps, Suverman mused, he should send a letter to all the faculty telling them about the roster. On the other hand, this might distress President Hadley, and, anyway, the roster wouldn't be available for another month.

He thought it would be even more risky to announce in a memo or in a faculty meeting the average salary increase awarded by the college. Although he felt this was the fairest approach, Suverman was certain that if he asked for Hadley's permission in advance, it would be denied.

Better to just go ahead and do it, he concluded. Hadley might never find out. If he did, Suverman believed he could defend his action by arguing that the University secrecy policy was wrong and should be changed, and by explaining to the President his desire not to discourage a good faculty member. He could also point out that accounts in local newspapers and in-house newsletters had fairly accurate estimates of the average compensation allocated to the University. Some faculty members read these and some did not, and no one was really sure how accurate they were.

Instead of going that route, perhaps the safest approach would be to do nothing and hope that Wick would get over it.

Suverman finally decided to wait a few days, watch Wick carefully, and see if anyone else complained.

QUESTIONS AND REQUIREMENTS

1. How would you evaluate and possibly change the university's policies?

2. Which actions would you recommend for Dean Suverman? Why?

3. Would your answer to question 2 be any different if the average faculty salary increase was 10 percent instead of 4 percent?

4. What should Dean Suverman have done when Professor Wick walked out of his office?

PART VIII
THE COLLECTIVE-BARGAINING PROCESS

In our work culture, collective bargaining establishes the price of labor and fixes working hours and working conditions. It introduces an element of democracy, a counterbalance of economic power, and a system of what has been called "industrial jurisprudence."

Collective bargaining is very closely related to the concepts of organizational justice covered in Part III. The legislation that authorizes and governs the conduct of employee-employer bargaining reflects the desires of society for order, for justice in the distribution of the economic gains of our technology, and for justice in correcting the misapplication of economic power.

Three major processes are involved. The unionization process—the circumstances and events leading to the formation and recognition of a bargaining agent—is first. Second are the processes involved in the negotiation between the employer and the authorized agent of employees in a contract covering wages, hours, and working conditions. The final processes are those involved in the administration of the contract. The mechanism for addressing alleged abuses of the contract can be seen as the exercise of due process in employee-employer relations.

Various stages of unionization are carefully regulated by the National Labor Relations Board (NLRB), under the provisions of the National Labor Relations Act of 1935 (the Wagner Act), and its amendments (the Taft-Hartley Act of 1947 and the Landrum-Griffin Act of 1959). Generally speaking, the Act requires that neither the company nor the union shall interfere with the exercise by employees of their right to organize and to bargain collectively. The NLRB has the authority to determine the appropriateness of a bargaining unit, to supervise the election, and, upon receipt of a majority vote, to certify or decertify a union as the bargaining agent.

While the perceived need for and the presence of labor unions in some areas and occupations are accepted parts of the culture, in others unions are not well received.

Inept management is frequently found to be the impetus for a union-organizing campaign. Indeed, adequate attention to the human aspects of the organization is often viewed as the best deterrent to the growth of unions. Thus, the presence of a strong and active labor movement can serve to directly encourage good management practice in unionized industries and occupations through negotiations and contract administration. A strong labor movement indirectly influences nonunionized industries through its potential influence as a bargaining representative.

In the "Knoll Kakery" case, the reader should think of the factors that may have caused the unionization campaign to start, and of the extent to which both management and union actions are covered by NLRB regulations. "Vann Engineering Unionization" is another case involving the unionization of a company. Again, the pervasive influence of the NLRB is seen in all stages of the unionization process. In this case, one might ask what kinds of relationships might evolve from this unionization attempt, and what effects this may have on organization climate, leadership style, and employee morale.

The process of negotiation between company and bargaining agent typically involves bargaining teams from each side. It has been described by Walton and McKersie[1] as being comprised of four identifiable elements: distributive bargaining, attitudinal structuring (between the parties), integrative bargaining, and intraorganizational bargaining (between the teams and their respective constituencies).

While a common tactic employed in bargaining is that of "horse trading," some forms of bargaining tactics are prohibited by the NLRB because they represent a refusal to bargain in good faith (e.g., no offers or no meetings, or Boulwarism—the issuance of a single, final offer, and a refusal to move from that position).

The process, in many respects, is characterized by a high degree of ritual. It contains, however, many complex underlying networks and facets of power relationships, favors asked and given, unwritten understandings among individuals and institutions, hopes, expectations, grudges, and old scores to settle.

The grievance-arbitration process often brings to light these understandings as they become outmoded or as their originators move into other jobs. The "Hoerner-Waldorf v. IBPS-PMW" case is an example of a situation in which the contract language was unclear and did not seem to serve either the company or its employees adequately. The problem presented to the arbitrator might well be a major issue in a subsequent negotiation.

---

[1] Richard E. Walton and Robert B. McKersie, *A Behavioral Theory of Labor Negotiations* (New York: McGraw-Hill, 1965).

The complexity of the issues faced by negotiators is pointed up by two cases drawn from the public sector: "New York Teacher's Walkout, 1967" and the "Atlanta Sanitation Strike." In both cases, negotiators not only must deal with the problems raised by the parties, but also must do so in a highly publicized arena, within the boundaries of unclear and generally untested laws regulating the union activity of public employees.

SUGGESTED READINGS

Barbash, Jack. *American Unions: Structure, Government and Politics.* New York: Random House, Inc., 1967.

Bok, Derek C., and John T. Dunlop. *Labor and the American Community.* New York: Simon and Schuster, 1970.

Bureau of National Affairs. *Major Labor-Law Principles Established by the NLRB and the Courts* (December 1963–February 1968). New York: Bureau of National Affairs, 1968.

Chamot, Denis. "Professional Employees Turn to Unions." *Harvard Business Review,* Vol. 54 (May-June 1976): 119–127.

Commerce Clearing House. *1972 Guidebook to Labor Relations.* Labor Law Reports, 1972.

Constantino, G.E. "The Negotiation in Collective Bargaining." *Personnel Journal* (August 1975).

Coulson, R. *Labor Arbitration, What You Need to Know.* New York: American Arbitration Association, 1973.

Davey, Harold W. *Contemporary Collective Bargaining,* 3rd ed. Englewood Cliffs, N.J.: Prentice-Hall, Inc., 1972.

Dunlop, John T., and Neil W. Chamberlain, eds. *Frontiers of Collective Bargaining.* New York: Harper & Row, 1967.

Fleming, R.W. *The Labor Arbitration Process.* Urbana, Ill.: University of Illinois Press, 1965.

French, Wendell L. *The Personnel Management Process,* 4th ed. Boston: Houghton Mifflin, 1978, Chapters 22–25.

Healy, James J. *Creative Collective Bargaining.* Englewood Cliffs, N.J.: Prentice-Hall, Inc., 1965.

Jones, Dallas L., ed. *Arbitrator, the NLRB, and the Courts.* Proceedings of the Twentieth Annual Meeting, National Academy of Arbitrators. Washington, D.C.: Bureau of National Affairs, 1967.

Kassalow, Everett M. "What Happens When Everyone Organizes?" *Monthly Labor Review,* Vol. 95 (April 1972): 27–32.

Moskow, Michael H., J. Joseph Loewenberg, and Edward Clifford Koziaro. *Collective Bargaining in Public Employment.* New York: Random House, 1970.

National Industrial Conference Board. "White Collar Unionization." *Studies in Personnel Policy*, No. 220, 1970.

Prasow, Paul, and Edward Peters. *Arbitration and Collective Bargaining: Conflict Resolution in Labor Relations.* New York: McGraw-Hill Book Company, 1970.

Sloane, Arthur A., and Fred Whitney. *Labor Relations*, 2nd ed. Englewood Cliffs, N.J.: Prentice-Hall, Inc., 1972.

Stanton, Erwin S. "White Collar Unionization: New Challenge to Management." *Personnel Journal*, Vol. 51 (February 1972): 118–124.

Trotta, Maurice S. *Arbitration of Labor-Management Disputes.* New York: Amacom, 1974.

U.S. Department of Labor. *Exploring Alternatives to the Strike.* Reprints of 18 articles from *The Monthly Labor Review*, September 1973.

Walton, Richard E., and Robert B. McKersie. *A Behavioral Theory of Labor Negotiations.* New York: McGraw-Hill Book Company, 1965.

44
ATLANTA SANITATION STRIKE

WILLIAM VROMAN, JAMES HOWELL,
AND WALTER BOGUMIL

PART A

The fall 1969 election in Atlanta included four candidates for the mayor's office: Rodney Cook, Sam Massell, Everett Millican, and Horace Tate. These candidates represented widely divergent views. Cook was a wealthy, young Republican; Massell was a dynamic, young former vice-mayor under the outgoing mayor, Ivan Allen; Millican was a perennial candidate for the mayor's office; and Tate was a prominent and respected member of the black community.

The political positions of these candidates were evident from the press statements they made before the elections of October 7. Massell claimed that Cook should be considered the front-runner, since he had the backing of "the heads of larger business" behind his campaign. As for himself, he stressed the position that he could "deal with blacks and whites on their separate as well as common interest." (Atlanta had for the first time in her history an equal population of the white and the black races.)

As the campaign progressed, important individuals and groups began to align themselves with the candidates. The Atlanta Journal endorsed Rodney Cook, while Mrs. Martin Luther King, Jr., State Representative Julian Bond, and Ralph Abernathy of the Southern Christian Leadership Conference (SCLC) endorsed Horace Tate. Labor and prominent leaders of the black community endorsed Sam Massell.

The black leaders' rationale for supporting the white instead of the black candidate was, "We cannot elect a black man mayor. Hence, we have decided to endorse a man who can be elected mayor." The application of this reasoning generated great controversy that caused, by election eve, a split in the black community between the supporters of Horace Tate and Sam Massell.

The October election resulted in no candidate's receiving a majority of the popular vote for mayor. A young Negro, Maynard Jackson, garnered 58% of the vote and won the position of vice-mayor. Massell received 31% of the total vote and 45% of the black vote forcing a runoff with Cook (26% of the vote) on October 21.

The retiring mayor, Ivan Allen, entered the campaign for the first time on

Reprinted with permission from *Administrative Policy: Text and Cases in the Policy Sciences* by Hodgetts and Wortman (N.Y.: John Wiley & Sons, Inc., 1975 c.) pp. 629–638.

October 13, appearing on local television to endorse an "operation-vote" campaign. The Massell camp viewed this as a subtle push to increase votes for his adversary. On October 16, labor backers of Sam Massell specifically charged: "The Chamber of Commerce has converted the excellent idea of Mayor Allen into a partisan effort on behalf of their candidate, Rodney Cook."

The tempo of the campaign increased when Allen went on television to ask Massell to step out of the campaign because of "misuse of power." His brother had pressured nightclub owners to contribute to his campaign. Sam Massell subsequently admitted that his brother had used bad judgment in soliciting contributions from the nightclub owners; however, he stated that the accusation that his brother had put pressure on the owners was a fabrication and part of a smear campaign against him because he was a Jew.

Despite the frenzy of activity before the election and then before the runoff, the campaigns ended on a rather low key the night before the runoff when Cook and Massell met on television. Cook emphasized community togetherness and his experience, while Massell stressed human relations. It was a remarkably unemotional meeting.

Sam Massell won the runoff with a 54.97% plurality. The composition of the vote was very interesting. Analysis revealed that Massell had received 18,500 white votes (approximately 27%) and 43,000 black votes (93.5%), while Cook had received 47,000 white votes (68.5%) and 3000 black votes (6.5%). Clearly, when Massell took office on January 1, 1970, it was largely because of the black voters of Atlanta.

Even while the election and runoff were occurring, other events were taking shape in Atlanta that could greatly affect the course of the political lives of Massell and several others. In January of 1970, the Aldermanic Finance Committee had approved a pay increase for the city's employees. The employees were represented by the American Federation of State, County, and Municipal Employees on the basis of an informal agreement between the city and the union. The reason for this casual relationship was the state law that excluded formal recognition of governmental employees' unions. At any rate, the city had granted a $5 million raise to the city employees in January of the same year.

On October 23, 1969, the lame-duck chairman of the Aldermanic Finance Committee, Milton Farris, had publicly proposed that the new administration give all city employees an additional two- or three-step raise in pay at an estimated cost to the city of approximately $3 million. He based this proposal on an anticipated increase in revenues for the coming year.

The AFSCME (American Federation of State, County, and Municipal Employees), representing the black sanitation workers and headed locally by Morton Shapiro, was encouraged by the election of Massell. Based on his platform, the black vote, and his appointment of a black to chair the Finance Committee, they renewed the clamor for an additional increase; specifically demanding a one-step increase retroactive to January 19, 1970. As time progressed, the political inexperience of Finance Committee Chairman, Joel Stokes, began to show as: (1) legal constraints in the city's budget cycle threatened an immediate increase (March 31 deadline); (2) he evidently agreed with the union on the retroactive one-step increase on March 10, only to have the Finance Committee vote on March 16 to deny the union demand because the city lacked the funds and, in addition, denied giving a raise at the next legal opportunity, fall 1970. The reason was the same—lack of funds.

Enraged and disappointed at the decision, the members of the union voted to take a "holiday" on St. Patrick's Day, March 17, 1970, to protest it. Twenty-five hundred of 7200 city workers and most of the sanitation men remained home on March 17. Coming as it did directly after a legal three-day weekend, the uncollected garbage was already a problem.

PART B

Jesse Epps, assistant to Jerry Wurf, national president, AFSCME, started the verbal battle with, "There ain't no wheels gonna turn in this city, the villain is down at City Hall. Massell is a boy in a man's job. I hope he grows up." Massell's retort was, "I will not let the union run the city."

As could be expected, action on the problem came immediately. Sam Massell offered the workers an increase aggregating $400,000 if they returned to work immediately. If they stayed out they faced being fired. The union, however, rejected the increase as trifling and countered with the demand for the two to three-step increase mentioned by the former finance committee chairman, Milton Farris.

Evaluated, the demand and counteroffer looked like this:

o Union Demand: $2.5 million used to raise the salary of over 7200 employees.

o City Offer: $400,000 resulting in a raise in minimum pay from $1.67 to $2.13 per hour, plus $5000 in free life insurance for all employees.

That afternoon, Massell showed the public a copy of a letter which was part of the informal understanding between the city and the union. The city had agreed to submit to binding arbitration any issue over which an impasse was reached in return for a no-strike provision. The local AFSCME leader, Shapiro, countered that the letter was a summary of the provisions for negotiations after the employees received a one-step pay increase. He contended that had the agreement of the mayor's appointee, Stokes, stood, the letter would have too, but as the agreement fell through, the substance of the letter was void.

In final defense of the union's position, Shapiro alleged that the new administration was not taking the union's demands seriously—the union had worked hard to elect the present administration and deserved consideration for it. Specifically, Shapiro claimed that the union had gone out and personally registered 8000 blacks to vote.

All of the offers and counteroffers and threats did not ease the burden of the Atlanta community dwellers or the business districts. On March 18, it was estimated that garbage was piling up at the rate of 1000 tons per day.

The mayor took a hard-line stand Wednesday evening, March 18, and issued the following ultimatum: either those city employees out on strike return to work on Thursday or they would be fired. When Massell issued this ultimatum there were approximately 2500 city employees on strike. Of the 2500, approximately 1400 were from the Public Works Department of which more than 800 were from the Sanitation Division. Following this ultimatum, Jesse Epps, a national union representative, implored the city to make contracts with the striking workers, but with little positive response.

However, on Thursday morning, Mayor Massell did postpone sending out dismissal notices. Although approximately 1400 city employees stayed out, there were encouraging signs of a return to work and Massell agreed to allow a citizens' committee to try to bring the two parties together.

By the end of the third day, March 19, the major issues surrounding the city employees' strike seemed clear. The union and its members, led by Morton Shapiro, were disenchanted with the existing pay scales and had relied on the new administration to grant a one-step pay raise in addition to the pay raise the city employees received at the beginning of the year.

The city, led by Mayor Massell, felt the union had breached negotiations by condoning a strike that the union had supposedly agreed not to condone while negotiations were still in progress.

PART C

On Friday, March 20, 1970, after the citizens' committee had failed to bring the parties together, Mayor Massell sent special delivery dismissal letter to those workers still involved in the walkout.

In response to this action, Morton Shapiro issued the following statement: "National President Jerry Wurf has declared he will put the full resources of the union behind the striking Atlanta employees." Shapiro went on to charge the mayor with union-busting tactics, claiming the mayor was undermining the union and the city employees by allowing the supervisors throughout the Public Works Department to decide which employees could go back to work.

The union's main argument was still that the city had reneged on a promise of a one-step pay increase for all city employees. However, Shapiro found a new cudgel in the mayor's paradoxical action—while the mayor claimed to be a friend of labor he fired 1500 city labor workers, mostly blacks. The union official further pointed out that Massell admitted workers had the right to strike. In talking to his union, Shapiro put it like this: "The mayor says you've got the right to strike, but you're fired."

The mayor's defense to this argument was to refuse to recognize that a strike existed. Instead, he considered it a work stoppage as the city had no contract with the union; therefore, the city employees could not legally strike.

At this point the city versus the AFSCME controversy moved in a physical direction—that is, no longer was it just at the negotiation level. Saturday, March

21, Mayor Massell opened the city personnel office to take applications for the strikers' jobs. He also ran an advertisement in the newspapers calling for applicants. As applicants began arriving at the personnel office, a picket line began to form. Saturday's attempt at hiring new city workers culminated in a virtual jamming of the process by union members. They crowded the application lines, discouraged those who were genuinely applying, and falsified applications to make it as difficult as possible for the city.

Threats of violence began circulating, and when Shapiro was confronted with this possibility he claimed that any talk of violence was emanating from the mayor's office. He even accused Massell of carrying a gun, which the mayor subsequently denied.

The city issued a statement over the weekend saying that an estimated 1100 of 2500 original strikers had already returned to work.

Raleigh Bryans, an *Atlanta Journal* correspondent, took time to reflect on the events of the first week of the strike: "It is reasonable to deduce from all this that Massell may be treading on dangerous ground politically—that he stands in some danger of being accused of pleasing his enemies and critics while displeasing his friends and supporters." Bryans drew a comparison here between Massell's situation and a similar sanitation strike situation experienced by Ivan Allen in 1968, saying that at this early stage of Massell's strike the difference between the two was as follows:

1. In the current strike there was no massive civil rights involvement as there was in Allen's.

2. In sitting down at the negotiating table with the city officials, the union officials (mostly blacks) were confronted by a black man—Joel Stokes, Chairman of the Finance Committee.

The confrontation between the city and the union was not without its effect on the citizens of Atlanta. Atlanta's daily garbage pickup was in excess of 1000 tons, and at the beginning of the strike it was obvious that something had to be done quickly regardless of how fast a negotiation settlement might come about. Thus the mayor distributed approximately 750,000 heavy-duty plastic bags throughout the communities of Atlanta and implored the people to use these bags for their garbage and to place them out in front of their curbs where he had arranged for consolidated pick-ups. This makeshift setup appeared to run more smoothly than anyone had anticipated, and its successful implementation definitely seemed to hurt the union's bargaining power.

As the strike moved into its second week, Vice-Mayor Maynard Jackson publicly voiced his sympathy for the strikers and called for binding arbitration of the strike without Shapiro's taking part in any of the negotiations. However, the mayor, as part of his tough stance in failing to recognize the strike's existence, had already rejected such a possible solution. In addition, John Dougherty, assistant district attorney, stated that this would be impossible (binding arbitration) as it would be tantamount to delegating the power of the mayor and the aldermen, which the state law prohibited. Dougherty emphasized that only the mayor and the aldermanic committees could make city policy.

On March 25 the AFSCME rejected the city offer, which consisted of the following two conditions (not unlike the initial proposal):

1. Take back all strikers, but without pay for the time lost.

2. Grant an increase in minimum wage from $1.67 an hour to $2.13 an hour and a free $5000 life insurance policy.

Mayor Massell's reaction to the rejection was predictable: "It would be a terrible mistake for the poor employee if he is used as a tool by some out-of-town official who is just trying to build some power base." By "out-of-town official" the mayor was referring to Jerry Wurf, the national AFSCME leader, who had come to Atlanta to bolster the union's demands following the kidney ailment and the consequent hospitalization of the regional representative, Morton Shapiro, on March 25. The mayor charged that Wurf had packed the union meeting, which voted down the city's offer, with nonunion members to insure the continuation of the strike.

Massell asked for, and got, television time the evening of March 25 to state to the citizens of Atlanta his facts and the city's position on the strike. Essentially, the mayor emphasized the following:

1. City employees received a $5 million raise in January 1970.

2. The city did not have the additional $2.5 million requested; however, the city did honor the request by seeking additional revenue from the Legislature—but unsuccessfully.

3. The union promised not to strike and struck without a request for arbitration.

4. The union had no contract with the city, therefore, the strike was illegal.

5. The union signed an agreement with the city whereby the union was supposed to have recommended initial settlement negotiations to its members on March 17 when, in fact, at the meeting, the union refused to endorse the settlement to its members.

6. The city, a week after the strike had begun, was willing to hire back all the strikers (reportedly at the request of the union) with no lost benefits.

On Saturday, March 28, final checks were sent out to 925 striking city employees of which 660 were in the Sanitation Department.

In spite of Mr. Bryans' comparison earlier, this strike did take on civil rights overtones as it became clear that the workers were the group suffering. The meager strike fund with which the national AFSCME was supporting the workers was already nearly exhausted. Influential civil rights leaders, Ralph Abernathy (SCLC) and Jesse Hill (SCLC), echoed Vice-Mayor Jackson's sentiment, calling for immediate arbitration. Abernathy described the urgency of the situation in the following metaphor: "I realize the city is filthy now with uncollected garbage, and we all want Atlanta to be clean and beautiful, but filth is not only measured in terms of garbage. It is also measured in terms of man's exploitation of his brother and the destruction of human dignity."

Atlanta NAACP leader, Lonnie King, rapped the mayor by saying, "You don't kick people in the behind who put you in office. . . . The subtle issue here is, is there going to be a union? I believe that if Massell could find a way to give money and get rid of the union, he would do it."

A black coalition of Jesse Hill, Vice-Mayor Jackson, and State Senator Leroy Johnson continued to urge the mayor to submit the strike to arbitration, but they were still unable to get the mayor to admit there was a strike. Instead, he continued to refer to the work stoppage.

The relations between Massell and Wurf continued to deteriorate, with a televised meeting on March 31 ending in a shouting match. Typical of Wurf's comments were:

> You lie! You're a contemptible, irresponsible little man. You're playing games with human beings. How sick you must be. You're a little man who suddenly got power and can't handle it.

and

> You ugly, vicious rumor-monger! You contemptible strike-breaker. You are a sorry example of a human. You're not fit for the synagogue. You're the type that was a concentration guard for the Germans.

Mayor Massell accused Wurf of trying to destroy the city. After two meetings that degenerated into shouting matches, the mayor vowed to avoid Wurf. And he did so for the duration of the strike.

As the city and union continued to remain far apart on a settlement in the beginning of April, overtones and warnings of violence became more pronounced. Surprisingly, though, the strike in its entirety was marred very little by any major violence. The following is a brief, chronological account of the demonstrations and confrontations between the city and the union that occurred:

○ *March 21.* Strikers picketed the city personnel office in reaction to its opening on Saturday to accept applicants for the strikers' jobs.

○ *March 23.* Six strikers were arrested for not allowing employees to cross picket lines.

○ *March 28.* A large march was planned with Mrs. Ralph Abernathy to speak at its conclusion. The march was apparently ineffective—only 200 out of an expected 10,000 participated; it began two hours late; and Mrs. Abernathy never showed.

○ *April 4.* A mass rally/march was held this Saturday on the anniversary of the assassination of Martin Luther King, Jr., at his tomb. His father delivered an address urging nonviolent action in the strike. Ironically, the day was marred when a worker on a city garbage truck shot a sanitation striker in the leg after a fight broke out between members of the SCLC march and the crew of the truck (both the individuals involved, incidentally, were charged with battery).

○ *April 6.* Six strikers were arrested for blocking entrances used by garbage trucks.

○ *April 9.* Black strikers, headed by Hosea Williams, hurled abuse at the black leaders who were pleading with the strikers to return to work. Williams labeled Senator Johnson, Jesse Hill, Martin Luther King, Sr., Reverend Williams, and others as "egghead, handkerchief-head niggers." Irony lends itself here too as Hosea Williams was a member of the SCLC—an organization Martin Luther King, Sr.'s son founded.

○ *April 12.* One hundred twenty-five protesters, led by Hosea Williams, kicked off a boycott campaign by marching on some of Atlanta's bigger businesses and stores, exhibiting signs such as "things go bad with Coca-Cola until city workers get a raise," "Rich's starves garbage men," and "Stay out of Sears until we get a raise."

○ *April 13.* Thirty-six strikers were arrested during a mass picketing disturbance. Signs carried such epithets as "Sam, sleep in dread, until my children are fed" and "Think Massell, a hungry man is a dangerous man."

○ *April 20.* Picketing begins again as the truce during the garbage talks ended when negotiations once again broke down. That evening the relationship between the city and the union reached its most strained point. Strikers marched from the union hall to the city hall where an aldermanic committee meeting was in session. Mayor Massell called out the riot squad, some 120 policemen, to prevent the strikers from marching back to the union hall (the union had not obtained a license to legally march that evening), but the aldermen averted possible major violence by convincing the mayor to back down and allow them to march back.

Two days after this confrontation, the realization of the major violence posed by the mayor's hard-line stance caused those black leaders who were sympathetic to the strikers—for example, Vice-Mayor Jackson and Ralph Abernathy—to put added pressure on the union to accept the city's latest offer.

The following is an abbreviated listing and discussion of negotiations throughout the strike which had now lasted 37 days:

1. *March 18.* The union rejected an increase in minimum pay from $1.67 to $2.13 an hour and a free $5000 life insurance package.

2. *March 25.* The union rejected essentially the same proposal.

3. *March 31.* Since this was the legal deadline established by the city charter for granting city employees a pay raise, Mayor Massell called a special meeting of the aldermanic council to consider a last-minute offer to the union. The council considered two proposals:

    a. A $5 weekly bonus for the city's lowest paid employees (2300) for perfect attendance.

b. A 10 cent per-hour increase for the waste collectors.

The aldermanic council approved the former, but the union rejected this offer. One striker's reaction was that accepting the bonus would take away his pride.

Senator Leroy Johnson also found the bonus offer to be demeaning—that it implied that the lower echelon employees, mostly black, were lazy and would not show up for work.

4. *April 7.* Union proposed the following to the Finance Committee:

a. That the city agree to give a one-step pay raise to about 3600 of the lowest paid employees on January 1, 1971.

b. That the $5-a-week bonus be converted to a one-step pay raise effective January 19, 1970, with the union lending the money (estimated at $400,000 by Wurf) to make up the difference between available city funds and the cost of the raise.

c. That the city have only a "moral understanding" with the union to repay them for the borrowed money (this last proposal was worded this way because the city could not legally contract with the union to repay such an outlay).

The city rejected this offer of using funds to bankroll a city pay raise, and Chairman Stokes of the Finance Committee counteroffered:

a. To convert the $5 bonus to a one-step pay raise for the 2300 lowest paid employees.

b. To promise a one-step raise January 1, 1971.

c. To reinstate all fired workers.

d. To not prosecute any striker arrested during the strike.

The union did not agree to these terms either.

5. *April 20.* A new city proposal was offered:

a. To grant a one-step pay increase to those 2300 lowest paid employees on July 1, 1970.

b. To request a study to see if 550 employees could be reclassified, beginning July 1, 1970, thereby possibly increasing their pay.

As was becoming the habit, the union rejected this proposal as well. By April 22, 1970, the union and the city were still at a stalemate, after 36 days of fruitless negotiations.

PART D

On April 23, 1970, the city garbage workers were back on the job, ending a 37-day holdout. The union accepted the following city proposal:

1. Conversion of the $5 bonus proposal to a one-step pay raise for the 2300 lowest paid employees, effective May 1, 1970.

2. A reclassification study to be completed by May 9, 1970, to determine if approximately 550 city employees could be placed in a higher pay scale.

3. Reinstatement of all fired workers.

4. Amnesty for those arrested.

QUESTIONS AND REQUIREMENTS

1. What is the initial basic issue according to the city? According to the union?

2. What were the ultimate issues for both parties?

3. How, and at what point, could the principals have avoided the strike?

4. What advice would you have given the mayor for dealing with the strikers? With all city employees?

5. Could the city legally have agreed to arbitration? How?

6. Should strikes in the public sector be legal? Why or why not?

45
THE THREATENING LETTER

For a long time it had been the practice in a wire mill to let union stewards take time off without pay to attend union meetings and conventions. Such leaves of absence were granted on oral request, and the day of return was also stated orally. But late in 1961, management decided to place union leaves of absence on the same basis as all others. Stewards were asked to file their requests in writing, and they were told that the leave of absence would be granted in written form.

The first request for a leave under the new policy was granted, but when the steward read his letter of approval from the company, he found this statement: "You are due back on November 14. Failure to report on that day will result in termination of your employment."

At this the steward exploded. "Where do you get off threatening me with discharge?" he demanded. "Leaves of absence were always given for union business before with no strings attached."

"There's nothing in the contract that says we have to give leaves of absence for union business. It's discretionary with us," answered the industrial relations manager. "If we can grant leaves or deny them as we see fit, there is nothing to stop us from stating the conditions under which the leave is taken."

Eventually the case went to an arbitrator selected from the panels of the American Arbitration Association.

QUESTIONS AND REQUIREMENTS

1. If you were the arbitrator, what matters would you take into account in your decision? What would you probably decide? Why?

2. Could this policy be interpreted as harassment of the union? Under what circumstances might the two parties be carrying on a campaign of harassment against each other? To what degree might such a campaign further the goals of (a) the company, (b) the union?

From the files of the American Arbitration Association. Used by permission.

46
VANN ENGINEERING
UNIONIZATION

GERALDINE B. ELLERBROCK

Colin Vann founded Vann Engineering in 1940. He was a skilled mechanic at Prinz Pump Company. Three of his co-workers, Marvin Lawrence, Hank Jerome and Don Patrick joined the firm after he discussed his plans with them and said, "This will be the end of time clocks for you. You have always wanted a piece of the action. This is your opportunity. Remember that some of your ideas were used by Prinz and you never got a cent for them. Here is your chance to get in on the ground floor. As the company makes more money so will you. You know me. I have never let my friends down. They can always trust me."

The management system was informal and unsophisticated. Mr. Vann, Marvin, Hank and Don hired operatives and supervisory personnel from among their personal friends as the business grew. Mr. Vann paid whatever he wished to pay and promoted his friends regardless of merit and ability. He gave his friends a car for both company and personal use; the company also paid charges on the gasoline credit cards it issued to these employees. Everyone, from the newly hired maintenance employee to the Vice-President, called President Colin Vann by a shortened version of his name—Lin.

Mr. Vann understood hydraulic systems and could discuss them fluently. He was well thought of by his customers. The company became one of the main sources for hydraulic systems for the Armed Services. As technology advanced and the company became larger and more complex, it began to feel the pressures of growth. This was indicated by declining profitability, poorer quality of workmanship, turnover, absenteeism, loafing on the job and employee complaints.

Mr. Vann was troubled by the firm's financial statements, but he had other problems as well. Feamster Local 008 succeeded in unionizing the employees in 1969. When no contract was agreed upon, a strike occurred. The most highly skilled employees did not support the strike and crossed the picket lines after several days. This weakened the union's position as other employees soon followed suit. The union could not get the benefits and working conditions from Vann Engineering that they had promised the employees. It made little progress, so the union relinquished its right to represent the employees until at least August 31, 1970.

Some employees felt the work environment had not improved by September, 1970, and asked Local 008 to begin another unionization campaign. The union sent some of their representatives to talk to interested employees at a restaurant located a couple of blocks from the plant. The employees complained: "We don't get a fair deal at Vann's. We need someone to look out for us." "They play favorites around the company. I should have been promoted, not Sam." "Yeah, I got suspended for a week when Bill and I had that fight. He started it, but nothing happened to him." "It doesn't pay to do good work. No one notices." "I never know when the foreman is going to jump on me. There is no rhyme or reason for what he does." After hearing what the employees had to say, Local 008 agreed to try to get Vann Engineering employees a union.

CHANGE OF OWNERSHIP

Mr. Vann tried a variety of tactics to improve Vann Engineering's financial situation, but finally recognized that he could not cope with the problems and maintain a profitable company. The firm began to lose money and was sold to Milton Industries, a conglomerate in June, 1970.

Initially, Mr. Vann was retained as president. He made oral and written reports to Milton Industries each week. When he told them that unionization was being attempted, a vice-president, H. H. Cook, was sent to investigate and empowered to take any action he considered necessary.

Upon his arrival Mr. Cook informed Mr. Vann that no decisions were to be made without his approval. After being briefed about the unionization attempt, he said he would assume responsibility for the company's actions and would keep in contact with all managerial personnel.

SUPERVISORS—MANUFACTURING AND ENGINEERING

The company supervisors and managers had worked for the company at least ten to fifteen years. They worked in a relaxed environment, but sometimes one would grumble, "Lin filled that promotion in my department with Carl Sayman. I didn't recommend him, even though he was here before I came. I wish he would realize that it is not enough to be an old-timer. Carl is a nice guy, but he just doesn't have the expertise. I'll just have to find a sharp assistant for him." Another would say, "I know how you feel. We lost that sale to McDerrick because Patrick made some poor estimates off-the-top of his head without checking the figures. Patrick doesn't trust the computer and refuses to use it." Again they would hear, "You know how long I have been trying to change the inventory system, and still I have made no progress with Lin." Then came the retort, "Well, what can you expect? The majority of people who work here have never worked any place else. They don't have any idea how other companies operate." These gripe-sessions would always end with someone reiterating, "Lin is one swell guy. There isn't anything he wouldn't do for you. I guess we can put up with a few faults."

Manufacturing felt that they were the main objective for which the company existed, and that the organization should be geared to serve the product they were building. All members of the Manufacturing Department were friends of the president and felt no need to justify their actions. They did what they thought needed to be done, without consulting the engineering staff. This meant that sometimes the engineers had to analyze what Manufacturing had already done and then put it into blueprints. When this resulted in changes from the original specifications, customers were displeased. The Sales Department had to try to appease them. They were not given opportunities to interpret the customers' needs to either Engineering or Manufacturing. Manufacturing personnel made sure that engineers and salesmen overheard their remarks, "If it wasn't for Manufacturing, there wouldn't be a Vann Engineering Company. Our product sells itself." Engineering reacted to this by designing sophisticated models, even if more basic designs were acceptable and less costly to produce.

Preliminary drawings and estimates by Vann Engineering were done by the Engineering Department. The engineers considered themselves professionals and took pride in their work, but the manufacturing superintendent often made changes in the estimates and plans. Although the methods used by the Manufacturing Department were dated by as much as twenty years, the department resisted any changes by Engineering as a threat to their authority. In revising the estimates, Manufacturing customarily added many extra hours to avoid pressure in completing the job. These practices were feasible under cost plus conditions, but became detrimental when the firm had to take on a more competitive role. Sales were lost because of the inefficient methods and extra hours estimated, and profitability decreased.

SALES DEPARTMENT

The sales were consumated not by sales people, but by top-level people in the organization—technical, financial, or general management. After the Engineering and Manufacturing Departments had completed their work, it was sent to the Accounting Department to determine the cost, and lastly to the Sales Department for pricing. The Sales Department was anxious to sell, but the Manufacturing and Engineering Departments often forgot that they were in competition with other firms for sales. Many times the cost figures were unrealistic and the Sales Department had to say it would be impossible to price the product competitively. The Manufacturing Department took a negative attitude, preferring to lose business rather than cut costs.

PERSONNEL POLICIES AND PRACTICES

The relationship of department staff with upper level management and with other departments affected the employees. The unresolved conflicts created tensions which affected the treatment of subordinates. The favoritism shown by the president toward selected employees hurt morale and created personnel problems.

UNIONIZATION 1969

In 1969 Local 008 of the International Brotherhood of Feamsters was chosen by a majority of employees in a union election. After the election and a total of twenty-two meetings held over a period of three months, union and management officials were still unable to agree on a contract. Management would not consent to a union shop, which would have required that all present and future employees join the union as a condition of employment.

Failing to negotiate a contract, the Local called a strike and set up mass picketing. Vann Engineering obtained a temporary restraining order limiting the number of pickets and prohibiting interference with people entering the plant. However, those office and plant workers who crossed the picket lines were subjected to violence, both at the plant and at their homes. In order for Vann Engineering to keep its commitments to the U.S. Government for defense needs, new employees were hired to take the place of those workers who did not cross picket lines.

Production increased and more employees were hired. Some old employees returned to work across the picket lines. The 1969 production was approximately equal to that of 1968, with a work force of forty percent returned employees and sixty percent newly hired employees. By the end of 1969, some striking employees were requesting reinstatement to their previous jobs. Some were reinstated and others were advised that their positions had been filled by the new employees hired since the strike had commenced.

Four meetings were held under the auspices of the Federal Mediator. At the last meeting on November 21, 1969, the Union agreed to accept the Company's original proposed contract, if the Company would reinstate all striking employees. The Company would not reinstate the strikers in place of its new employees.

Production continued to improve and on February 6, 1970, the Union agreed to terminate the strike. "The Union hereby disclaims representation of all employees in the collective bargaining unit described above, effective immediately after the execution of this agreement, and further disclaims any interest in representing such employees of the Company in said unit and agrees not to claim to represent such employees in said unit until at least August 31, 1970."

There were one hundred forty-four employees in the bargaining unit on May

27, 1969, when the strike was called. On February 6, 1970, one hundred and sixty-five days later, fifty-two of these original one hundred and forty-four persons were still working at Vann Engineering. After February 6, 1970, twenty-three more returned to bring the total to eighty-one employees, who did not strike or who returned to work before the strike was terminated.

UNIONIZATION 1970

Because of the inequities and discontent within the Company, several employees contacted Feamster Local 008. On September 4, the Union began circulating literature, a flyer entitled "Why Go Union?" (Appendix I). The flyer explained the advantages to the employees of joining a Union. They were told that by signing authorization cards (Appendix II) they could have a Union represent them. The benefits from the representation were stressed in terms of wages, benefits, job security, and a grievance procedure.

On September 21, a registered letter from Brock and Eller, Attorneys representing Feamster Local 008, was received by the Company (Appendix III). Mr. Barnes advised the Company that his client, Feamster Local 008, had been designated by a majority of the Vann Engineering employees as their representative for collective bargaining. There was a request for an early meeting with representatives of the Company for the purpose of negotiating a written collective bargaining agreement covering wages, hours, and other terms and conditions of employment. The Attorneys agreed to a crosscheck of the authorization cards and the payroll records if there was any doubt about the Union's majority status.

In acknowledging the request of the Local to represent the employees, Mr. Vann said that he did not believe that a meeting should be held at this time. He did not believe that a majority of the employees wished Union representation. He thought the signatures had been obtained by misrepresentation of facts. The Company preferred to bargain only in a situation where the National Labor Relations Board had certified the Union as the collective bargaining representative, after Board-conducted elections.

Feamster Local 008 then petitioned the National Labor Relations Board for certification as representative of the employees of Vann Engineering for the purposes of collective bargaining. The regional office of the National Labor Relations Board sent a Notice of Filing of Petition (Appendix IV) to the Vann Engineering Company. The letter included a NLRB Commerce questionnaire to be filled out by the firm, and requested information about the employees' collective bargaining agreements in effect, labor organizations representing the employees, and the Company's position as to the appropriateness of the Union. In addition, the Company was told that if an election was agreed upon or directed, names and addresses of all employees would be required to be made available to the Union. The National Labor Relations Board also requested that

Vann Engineering post an enclosed Notice to Employees (Appendix V), apprising the employees of their rights and of the proper conduct of the employer.

Vann Engineering completed the NLRB Commerce Questionnaire Form (Appendix VI) and returned it. Then they began their in-plant strategy in preparation for the election. On September 29 a memorandum (Appendix VII) was sent to department managers and supervisors, stating in detail what they could say and do in regards to unionization. Additional information "Preventing Unionization" was discussed in a supervisory meeting on October 26 (Appendix IX).

The Company sent a letter (Appendix VIII) to employees stating that Feamster Local 008 had filed a petition with the National Labor Relations Board for an election to determine whether or not the production and maintenance employees should be represented by a Union. The Company said they did not feel that the Union would be for the employees' best interests and urged them not to sign a Union card indicating their desire to be represented by a Union.

The employees were reminded that this Union had previously represented the employees of Vann Engineering but had been unable to give the employees promised benefits. After a six-month-long unsuccessful strike, the Local had renounced its bargaining rights. Not only had employees lost wages, but they had also lost peace of mind because of violence and threats of violence against them.

The NLRB sent a statement to Vann Engineering notifying them of a hearing to be conducted before the hearing officer of the National Labor Relations Board. The objective of the hearing was to ascertain the respective positions of management and the Union in regard to the petition for an election filed by Feamster Local 008. After the meeting, a date for the election, December 9th, was agreed upon.

The Company then sent a letter to the employees informing them of the election date. Furthermore, an explanation was given of the meaning of this election to employees and of the effect of their voting for the Union. An additional piece of information consisted of a detailed list of benefits gained by employees since the strike in 1969.

A meeting of management and leadmen was held to discuss ways to tell the employees of the advantages of working for Vann Engineering and the economic and personal costs of unionization. The election procedures were discussed.

A letter was sent to all Vann Engineering employees on November 9th by the president. It was a letter of congratulations and thanks for making 1970 a successful year. Changes in location of the various departments were taking place and the letter explained that the changes were being made to facilitate communication and cooperation among departments. Other changes were being made to improve handling and shipping of material. Mr. Vann moved to the ground floor to be more accessible to the employees. The employees were told that the improvements were possible because of the employee productivity. The letter ended, "Let's all look forward to a team effort in 1971."

The National Labor Relations Board required that all Companies involved in an NLRB-conducted election provide the Board with a list of names and addresses of all employees who are eligible to vote in the election. Mr. Vann wrote a letter to each employee telling them of the requirement. He said that he felt it was an invasion of their privacy. Feamster Local 008 had had a six-month-long strike against the Company during the past year before they had decided to represent the employees. Remembering instances of property damage to some homes during the strike, the management had investigated the possibility of not providing the names and addresses of employees. It was found that the NLRB had obtained an order from the Federal District Court compelling an employer to provide such a list. If the list were not provided, the election of December 9th would be set aside and new election directed. Mr. Vann expressed the hope that the list would not be used by the Union to harass employees. The last paragraph stated, "Express *YOUR CHOICE!* The best protection against repetition of the Union's violence and destruction of personal property is to use the SECRET BALLOT and VOTE *NO!*"

The employees of Vann Engineering were sent a letter to wish them and their families a happy Thanksgiving. In the letter Mr. Vann said that the Friday following Thanksgiving would be a fully paid holiday. He expressed appreciation for the fine job they had done during 1970. He hoped that the extra time, the free flu shots, increased wages, and improved working conditions had helped to make the past year a more thankful one for the employees and their families. Free coffee and cake were served to the employees during the afternoon coffee break to express the gratitude of management for the performance during the fiscal year.

Copies of the "Feamsters International Constitution," "By-Law of Local 008," and the "1969 Financial Report for Local 008" were received by the firm. "Stipulation for Certification Upon Consent Election" (Appendix X) was sent to the Company. This explained the election procedures and told the time, place and appropriate collective bargaining unit. Notices of Election, which the employer was requested to post in conspicuous places, were received by the firms on November 24, and an "Affidavit of Posting" (Appendix XI) had to be returned to the Regional Office. Instructions were included to insure the proper selection of election observers (Appendix XII).

The employees were cautioned to consider all the facts seriously before voting in the election. It was suggested that, as a result of doing so, they would realize that a *No vote* would be in their best interest. A pamphlet, "The Strike-Out" was mailed to Vann employees on November 24th. This was a baseball story used to illustrate the adverse effects and the costs of unionization.

On November 30th a letter was delivered to employees at their homes. Mr. Vann told the employees of the difficulty of removing a Union once it has been voted in. He illustrated the fact that, although there was a procedure for decertification, it was not a simple one. The procedure cannot be started until almost a year after the NLRB has approved the vote for the Union. If the union obtains a contract, no vote can be taken to get rid of the Union during the life of the contract, up to three years. He referred to the Research Institute Publication to illustrate a case (Richard C. Price, an individual, 154 NLRB 54) in which an individual was fined $500 by the Union, suspended from membership, and barred from attending meetings for five years as a disciplinary measure, because he had filed a decertification petition.

On December 1st, Vann Engineering employees received another communication signed by Mr. Vann. He reminded the employees that only the Company can give raises and benefits, and that the wage rates at Vann compared favorably with similar industries. The president said that the Company would continue to give the best wages compatible with remaining competitive and attracting new business. Wages is one of the factors any Company must consider along with other costs, he stated, and in a tight economy little differential is allowed.

To keep Vann's position in the industry necessitates a cooperative effort from management and the employees, the letter continued. Questions were posed as to what a third party—a Union—could do for the employees. Could a Union gain higher wages under the circumstances? How could it force payment of higher wages—feasible or not? True, it could call a strike, but who would pay the costs of the strike? Would the employees ever recover the income lost during a strike? If during a strike the firm did not fulfill orders, what would happen? Who would fill the orders? Could this lost business be regained? Were the Teamsters interested in personal losses by the employees or was their real concern dues, assessment and fines?

Mr. Vann concluded the letter by saying that unreasonable demands would lead to a costly strike for the employees. The alternative, which would be decidedly more beneficial, would be for all to "Pull Together."

In order to give the employees information about Local 008 Vann Engineering sent a "Fact Sheet" to the employees. This told them that the Local had seven officers. In order to vote for an officer a member must have been in continuous good standing for at least two years and must have attended a minimum of two-thirds of the Local meetings. A quorum in Local 008 required only seven members be present, including the officers. The "Fact Sheet" raised the possibility that these seven members might sway Local policy through their control of special meetings called on short notice.

The Fact Sheet quoted one of Local 008's By-Laws, which said, "No assessments shall be levied by this Union." The employees were told that the By-Laws of the International Brotherhood of Feamsters provides for assessing all Feamsters Unions—and this would include Local 008. An example was given of such an assessment levied contrary to the wishes of the local Union members.

Employees were encouraged to vote on December 9th. In a letter to the employees Mr. Vann reminded them that the election would be decided by a simple majority of those votes cast. Failure to vote would be the same as voting "Yes" and indicating the Union is desired.

"If you agree that you don't need the Feamsters between you and your Company's management   VOTE X "NO"

They were reminded that the election would be by *Secret Ballot*. Even if they had previously signed a union authorization card they could still vote "NO." No one would know how they voted.

The Feamsters sent a letter to the employees on December 4th. They stressed the lack of economic power of a single employee against a "large and wealthy corporation" and the need for employees to organize in order to achieve bargaining power for higher wages.

Another "Fact Sheet" documenting possible benefits and the costs of unionization was sent to employees on December 3rd by Vann Engineering. The employees' costs of unionization were shown. These included initiation fees, monthly dues, fines and assessments. Employees were told that the number of International Feamster strikes over a one-year period was two-hundred and thirty-four, yet it would take three years and twenty-eight weeks to get back lost wages after a strike lasting four weeks. The Fact Sheet ended thus:

"Can You Afford This False Economy?"
VOTE "NO" On December 9th

Mr. Vann in a separate piece of correspondence responded to each statement in the Teamster letter of December 4th. By clarification and explanation of the situation he sought to dispel erroneous information and assumptions.

The next day, a "Fact Sheet" was sent to acquaint new and remind old employees of the past relationships with Local 008. The "Fact Sheet" reviewed the history of the acceptance of the Union by employees; the Union's demand for a closed Union Shop; the failure to agree on a contract; the ensuing strike; the violence associated with the strike which occurred when employees crossed picket lines to return to their jobs. Management asked the employees to consider what this return to work indicated about the employees' satisfaction with Union Local 008 as their representative, and what the strike meant to the employees economically. For employees with a wage rate of $2.85 per hour who stayed off the job for the duration of the strike, it meant lost wages of $2,522.00. The question was asked, "CAN THIS BE IN YOUR BEST INTEREST?"

A memorandum was sent telling who could vote in the election and stressing that it was a secret election. They were reminded that with a Union Shop *all* employees must join the Union whether they wished to do so or not. The necessity for voting was shown. Employees were urged to vote, and to VOTE X NO."

On December 8th, all non-supervisory employees of Vann Engineering were handed a letter (Appendix XIII) by representatives of Feamster Local 008 as they approached Vann Engineering to begin work. The letter described benefits the employees could obtain as Union members but not as individuals.

During the election representatives from Local 008, Vann Engineering, and the regional office of the National Labor Relations Board were present at the Company cafeteria where the voting took place. Mr. Donn Lea, the NLRB representative, made certain that the observers understood which employees were eligible to vote, and what to do if any ballots were challenged. The observers were also expected to assist Mr. Lea in counting the ballots following the election. After the votes were tallied the Regional Director of the National Labor Relations Board sent a certificate of Results of Election to Vann Engineering.

Appendix I

Feamsters Local 008
9390 Montcalm Avenue, San Jose, CA   95134   Phone 546-2219 or 905-548-7771

Why Go Union?

A group of your fellow employees has contacted this Union with the idea of joining together in a bargaining unit and negotiating a contract with the company.

We are ready, willing and able to represent you if this is what you want. But, before you make that decision, we feel you should know what Union representation means. Here are the facts:

ONLY YOU CAN DECIDE.   If a sufficient number of your fellow employees sign a card authorizing the Union to represent them, the National Labor Relations Board will conduct an election to determine if a majority of the employees in the bargaining unit wish to be represented by the Union. The Employer is never told, either by the Union or the NLRB, which of his employees has signed a card. The election will be held by secret ballot under Government supervision and the Employer will never learn who voted for the Union or who voted against it.

YOU ARE PROTECTED FROM REPRISALS.   The principle of Unionism is protected by the National Labor Relations Act, which gives you the right to join a Union and makes it unlawful for the Employer to fire or discriminate in any way against an employee for activity in behalf of the Union.

WHAT'S IN IT FOR YOU?   Many prospective members wish to know what benefits they will receive if they join the Union. The answer is up to you. You, yourselves, will determine our contract demands and you, yourselves, will decide whether and when to accept management's proposals. No strike will be called unless you, yourselves, vote to strike.

TEAMSTERS ARE PROUD of our contracts. Our pay rates are far above the average of non-Feamster workers in similar jobs. We believe our fringe benefits are without parallel. Here are some of the provisions we have negotiated in present contracts covering our members. We cannot promise to achieve them all at once for you, but we can—and do—promise you able, honest, faithful representation and progress toward a better life for you and your family.

A JUST GRIEVANCE PROCEDURE and job security based on seniority
COMPANY-PAID HEALTH AND WELFARE programs including:
   Hospital and medical coverage for the entire family.
   Dental care for the entire family.
   Prescription drug insurance.
   Vision care.
   Pensions of $200 a month (plus your Social Security) with full credit for up to 18½ years
   of prior service with your company.
VACATIONS, paid holidays and overtime pay.
BIDDING RIGHTS for promotions based on seniority.
ON-THE-JOB representation.

If you wish us to represent you, please sign the attached authorization card and mail it at once. If you wish further information, call 546-2219, or toll-free, 905-548-7771. Your inquiries will be held in strictest confidence.

FEAMSTERS LOCAL 008

Appendix **II**

The National Labor Relations Act of 1947 Reads as Follows:

"RIGHTS OF EMPLOYEES—Sec. 7. Employees shall have the right to self-organization, to form, join, or assist labor organizations, to bargain collectively through representatives of their own choosing, and to engage in other concerted activities for the purpose of collective bargaining or other mutual aid or protection . . . "

"UNFAIR LABOR PRACTICES—Sec. 8 (a) It shall be an unfair labor practice for an employer—

"(1) to interfere with, restrain, or coerce employees in the exercise of the rights guaranteed in Section 7;

"(2) to dominate or interfere with the formation or administration of any labor organization . . . "

THE FEDERAL LAW UPHOLDS YOUR RIGHT TO ORGANIZE

PLEASE SIGN NOW!

Postage Will Be Paid By Addressee

No Postage Stamp Necessary If Mailed in the U.S.

BUSINESS REPLY MAIL
First Class Permit 7013, Long Beach, CA

FEAMSTERS UNION No. 008
9390 Montcalm Avenue
San Jose, California 95134

(Appendix **II** continued)

THIS CARD IS STRICTLY CONFIDENTIAL

All information shall be kept in absolute confidence by the Union and the National Labor Relations Board.

PLEASE FILL IN THE LOWER HALF OF THIS CARD, SEAL, AND MAIL IMMEDIATELY. THE POSTAGE IS PREPAID.

AUTHORIZATION FOR REPRESENTATION

I, the undersigned employee of

Company _____

Address of Company _____
authorize Feamsters Local 008 to represent me in negotiations for better wages, hours and working conditions.

Print name_____   _____ Date _____

Home address _____
               NUMBER AND STREET   CITY AND ZIP CODE

Present wage rate _____ Home phone _____

Kind of work _____ Shift Day / / Swing / / Graveyard / /

            Signature_____
ALL CARDS ARE KEPT CONFIDENTIAL BY THE FEAMSTERS UNION AND THE U.S. GOVERNMENT.

Appendix III

LAW OFFICES
BROCK AND ELLER
1873 Conquistador Rd.
San Jose, California 95100

September 16, 1970

Vann Engineering
6063 Montezuma Rd.
San Jose, California 95100

Gentlemen:

This firm represents the above-named labor organization. In behalf of our client, this is to advise you that a majority of your employees within the following appropriate collective bargaining unit have designated the Union as their exclusive bargaining representative:

Included: All production, maintenance, shipping and receiving employees, laboratory and test technicians, expediters, inspectors, timekeepers, plant clerical employees, janitors, lead employees and truckdrivers at the employer's plant located at 6063 Montezuma Road, San Jose, California.

Excluded: Office clerical employees, guards, professional employees and supervisors as defined in the Act.

Accordingly, this is to request an early meeting with duly authorized representatives of your concern for the purpose of negotiating a written collective bargaining agreement covering the wages, hours, and other terms and conditions of employment of the employees in the above designated appropriate unit. For that purpose, we suggest a meeting in our offices (1873 Conquistador Rd., San Jose, California 95100, telephone 885-3078) on Wednesday, September 23, 1970 at 2:00 P.M. In the event that you have suggestions regarding a date, time and place of the meeting which would be more convenient to you, we would be pleased to receive them. We will appreciate an early reply.

Should you have any doubt regarding the Union's majority status, we would be pleased to permit a cross check by the State Conciliation Service or any other responsible disinterested third party of the authorization cards in our possession and your payroll records.

Very truly yours,

BROCK AND ELLER

Charles Morley

Charles Morley

cc: Feamster Local 008
      9390 Montcalm Rd.
      San Jose, California

Appendix **IV**

NATIONAL LABOR RELATIONS BOARD
REGION 17
888 Paula Street, San Francisco, California
Telephone: 333-5087

September 25, 1970

Vann Engineering
6063 Montezuma Road
San Jose, California 95134

      Re: VANN ENGINEERING
      Case No. 33-GE-666

      NOTICE OF FILING OF PETITION

Gentlemen:

Pursuant to the provisions of the National Labor Relations Act, a petition for the purpose indicated in Item 1 of the attached document has been filed with this office. The Board agent assigned is Lester C. Gibson, Attorney, who can be reached at 489-5821.

Attention is called to your right, and the right of any party, to be represented by counsel or other representative in any proceeding before the National Labor Relations Board. In the event you choose to have a representative appear on your behalf, please have your representative complete "Notice of Appearance" Form NLRB-4701 and forward it promptly to this office.

Please submit as soon as possible to this office the following information:

a. The attached commerce questionnaire filled out in the appropriate sections. (An extra copy is enclosed for your records).

b. Copies of any presently existing or recently expired collective bargaining contracts covering any of the employees in the unit described, as well as any correspondence bearing on the question raised herein.

c. The names of any labor organizations which have claimed to represent any of the employees concerned, or other parties who should be apprised of these proceedings.

d. An alphabetized list of employees described in the petition, together with their job classifications, for the payroll period immediately preceding the date of this letter.

e. Your position as to the appropriateness of the unit.

In the event an election is agreed to or directed in this case, the Board requires that a list of names and addresses of all the eligible voters be filed by the employer with the undersigned, who will in turn make it available to all the parties to the case. This list must be furnished to the undersigned within seven (7) days of the direction of or agreement to election. I am advising you now of this requirement so that you will have ample time to prepare for the eventuality that such a list may become necessary. (This list is in addition to the list of employees requested in the proposed unit by job classification in Item (d) above.)

It has been our experience that by the time a petition such as this one has been filed, employees may have questions about what is going on and what may happen. At this point in the handling of this case, we of course do not know what disposition will be made of the petition, but experience tells us that an explanation of rights, responsibilities, and Board procedures can be helpful to your employees.

The Board believes that employees should have readily available information about their rights and the proper conduct of employee representation election. At the same time employers and unions should be apprised of their responsibilities to refrain from conduct which could impede employees' freedom of choice. Accordingly, you are requested to post the enclosed Notice to Employees in conspicuous places in areas where employees such as those described in the enclosed petition work. Copies of this Notice are being made available to the labor organization(s) involved. In the event an election is not conducted pursuant to this petition you are requested to remove the posted Notice.

Your cooperation in this matter will be appreciated.

Very truly yours,

Chriss Jonassen

Chriss Jonassen
Regional Director

Enclosures

Appendix V

National Labor Relations Board

A Petition has been filed with this federal agency seeking an election to determine whether certain employees want to be represented by a union.

The case is being investigated and no determination has been made at this time by the National Labor Relations Board. If an election is held notices of election will be posted giving complete details for voting.

It was suggested that your employer post this notice so the National Labor Relations Board could inform you of your basic rights under the National Labor Relations Act.

You have the right under federal law	To self-organization
	To form, join, or assist labor organizations
	To bargain collectively through representatives of your own choosing
	To act together for the purposes of collective bargaining or other mutual aid or protection
	To refrain from any or all such activities

It is possible that some of you will be voting in an employee representation election as a result of the request for an election having been filed. While the National Labor Relations Board wants all eligible voters to be familiar with their rights under the law and wants both labor and management to know what is expected of them if it holds an election.

You are therefore advised that the board applies rules which are intended to keep its elections fair and honest, and which result in a free choice. If agents of either labor or management act in such a way as to interfere with your right to a free election, they will risk the possibility of having the election set aside by the board.

NOTE:
The following are
examples of conduct
which interfere with the
rights of employees and
may result in the setting
aside of the election.
Where appropriate the
board provides other
remedies, such as
reinstatement with
backpay for employees
fired for exercising their
rights.

Making threats of loss of jobs or loss of benefits by a party capable of carrying out such a threat

Firing employees or causing them to be fired in order to encourage or discourage union activity

Making promises of promotions, pay raises, or other benefits, to influence an employee vote, by a party capable of carrying out any such promise

Making threats of physical force or violence to employees to influence their vote in the election

Making misstatements of important facts where another party does not have a fair chance to reply

Making campaign speeches to assembled groups of employees of company time within the 24-hour period before the election

Inciting racial or religious prejudice by inflammatory appeals

Exerting repeated pressures by persons or groups not themselves involved in the election which tend to create fear of job loss, violence, or other troubles

Please be assured that if an election is held every effort will be made to protect your right to a free choice under the law. Improper conduct, a few examples of which appear above, will not be permitted. We expect all parties to board elections to cooperate fully with this agency in maintaining basic principles of a fair election as required by law.

National Labor Relations Board an agency of the United States government

Appendix VI

Case No. 33-GE-666   NATIONAL LABOR RELATIONS BOARD

Commerce Questionnaire Form

Please read carefully, fill in all blanks, and return promptly.

1. Exact legal title of your firm: Vann Engineering Company _____

Is it: A corporation? Yes (X)   No ( )
An individual doing business under a trade name?   Yes ( )   No ( )

If answer is "Yes," please give full name of individual _____

A partnership? Yes ( )   No (X)
If answer is "Yes," please give full names of partners

2. Indicate with an X the classification(s) which best describe(s) your business: Processing and/or manufacturing (x), Wholesaling ( ), Retail outlet ( ), Service organization ( ), Public utility or transit system ( ), Newspaper and/or broadcasting station ( ), Other

( ), describe _____

Describe briefly the nature of your business; also state whether it is one of a chain or one of several separate but related enterprises.

Manufacturing of Hydraulic Components and Test Equipment. Is one of several separate
but related enterprises.

3. Number of employees 159
4. During the past calendar or fiscal year:
    a. Did dollar volume of your sales or performance of services to customers outside the
    State equal or exceed $50,000? Yes (x) No ( ) _____
    b. Did dollar volume of your sales or performance of services equal or exceed $50,000 to
    firms which, in turn, made sales to customers outside the State? Yes (x) No ( ) ___
    c. Did dollar volume of your purchases of goods or services from outside the State
    equal or exceed $50,000? Yes (x) No ( )_____
    d. Did dollar volume of your purchases equal or exceed $50,000 from firms which, in
    turn, purchased those goods from outside the State? Yes (x) No ( ) _____
    e. Did dollar volume of all your sales or performance or services equal or exceed
    $500,000? Yes (x) No ( ) _____
    f. If answers to a. through e. are "No," please specify amounts in each category. (If
    additional space is needed, please use reverse side of this sheet or separate sheet.)
5. Are you a member of, or participant in, an association or group which engages in
collective bargaining? Yes ( ) No (x) (If answer is "Yes," please give title and address.)
6. If you performed national defense work during the past calendar or fiscal year, give
dollar volume of such work, names of government agencies or private firms for which such
work was performed.

Approximately $2,750,000 to U.S. Navy, N.A.S.A., U.S.A.F., U.S. Army, Boeing
McDonnell, Gen. Dynamics, Lockheed, Grumman, Ling-Temco, Vought, AMF., etc.

7. Name and title of your representative best qualified to give further information:

William Good, Personnel Manager

29 September 1970

Appendix VII

Interoffice Correspondence

To: Dept. Managers & Supervisors
Subject: Union Campaign Policy

THE FOLLOWING IS AN OUTLINE OF WHAT YOU ARE LEGALLY PERMITTED TO
DO AND SAY DURING A UNION ORGANIZING CAMPAIGN.

YOU CAN SAY

1. We are opposed to having a union in our plant. We think a union will lead to
inefficiency and be bad for the Company.

2. Your best interests will be served by voting against the union. (This must be unrelated to any unlawful conduct and must not imply reprisals or promises of benefits depending on union rejection.)

"If I were eligible to vote, I would vote against the union" for these reasons. . . .

Tell employees what unionization would mean—things they should think about and consider in making their choice.

Employees could be called on to:

a. Pay dues to union ($5.00 per month).

b. Possible strikes, picket duty and loss of pay in strikes or union disputes that may have nothing to do with you directly.

c. Participation in union meetings and other functions.

d. Union may attempt to involve you or influence your action on political matters.

e. Union will use your money for union officials or other matters in hands of International Union.

f. Your dues money may be used in other union organizing drives.

3. Answer any union attack on Company—and answer any employee questions or charges in this area, particularly Company policy, integrity, etc. But—do not dignify every union attack with reply.

4. Urge employees to vote in the NLRB election. If they are opposed to the union and do not vote they may forfeit their right to handle their affairs individually, by default. Those in favor of union will certainly vote.

Can urge employees to vote against the union so long as this is not done in coercive manner and does not imply threats or promises.

"Everyone should vote"—this is decision each employee should make for himself.

"Do not be mislead by union statements or promises" find out for yourself whether they are in position to produce on their promises.

5. Unionization may destroy our ability to deal with employees individually and to recognize individual merit.

Wage increases based on your relative performance in accord with our merit rating plan would be out.

If there is a union in the plant, Company will have to negotiate with third party rather than deal individually, about such things as:

a. Work hours, conditions.

b. Transfers, promotions and work assignments.

c. Seniority rules that may not recognize individual qualifications, ambitions and merit.

d. Personal privileges, vacations, sickness, time off for personal reasons, etc.

e. Wage adjustments—union may ask to eliminate *any* merit increases.

(Be sure you do not threaten that present benefits will be taken away by Company arbitrarily—the point is, we would have to negotiate about them and negotiating general rules for all necessarily means changes in benefits and loss of flexibility and end of individual handling.)

6. Hold meetings of employees in groups to discuss unionization. "Speeches" are permissible but of doubtful effectiveness unless they lead to some questions and discussion from employees.

(*Cannot* hold any such meetings within 24 hours of election.)

Such meetings may be good way to explain what union election means, how conducted and rights of employees generally.

7. Stress advantages of working for Vann Co. Explain benefits. Compare to others in industry.

(See *Cannots*—be careful not to indicate that benefits will end with unionization—the fact is we would have to negotiate about them—many obviously would be changed and flexibility and individual treatment would be out. We cannot say anything that will give employees the impression they will lose all benefits and have to start bargaining "from scratch.")

8. Stress opportunities for growth of Company and individuals if growth not interfered with.

9. Those who join, promote or choose union will never have any preferred treatment over those who do not.

Company policy is to treat employees on basis of individual merit and qualification to the extent we can. Unionization will frustrate this but will not mean any preferential treatment for those who favor the union.

10. Talk about the union—how it is governed, who the officials are, where decisions are made, what their policies and results have been, where the money goes, fact that individual desires will have to be submerged to the will of majority of larger group and to policies of the International Union.

11. Read from union publications, other publications of general circulation about this and other unions. Also can use financial reports of union to Washington as required by "Disclosure Act."

12. Can point out that unionization trend nationally is on decline. (1956 unions represented about 35% work force—now 30%)

13. Keep union organizers from talking to employees on Company property and working time.

Union organizers have no right to interfere with work.

General

You should repeatedly and consistently assure employees that the choice is theirs to make freely, without fear of reprisals or promise of reward from the Company or the union.

Weight any statement or approach in terms of whether the NLRB might find a hidden threat or promise in what you say. Since employees are apt to be sensitive to what you say, you should make it very plain that the ultimate choice is theirs, and they should not read into what you say any implied threat or promise.

It is best to let employees volunteer what information they want or what is interesting them in the union. Be alert to opportunities to discuss these matters at their initiation under any circumstances.

There are many things you can talk about, such as the Union strike record, the cost of strikes, and what the union may do to force employees to support union activities.

The law says that "The expressing of any views, argument or opinion, or the dissemination thereof . . . shall not constitute or be evidence of an unfair labor practice under any of the provisions of this Act, if such expression contains no threat of reprisal or force or promise of benefit."

YOU CANNOT SAY

(Item numbers conform to "Can Say" list.)

1. Warn, or even hint, to employees that we will take any action against them for choosing a union in spite of our views. Make any outright or hidden threat or promises. Promise, or even suggest, that employees will be rewarded for rejecting the union.

2. Hide a threat or promise behind a statement of opinion or prediction. Make any deliberate or substantial misrepresentation of fact.

3. Avoid trying to answer every union charge or claim.

4. Interrogation of employees:

The NLRB frowns on any questioning of employees about their feeling about the union or how they intend to vote.

Anything that appears to be "spying" should be avoided.

You should not ask specific questions about these things, but instead, state your own views and get employees to thinking for themselves. You can say how you would vote, that employees in similar situations have voted against the union and can ask employees what they think the union might do for them that the company would not without a union.

But, *do not* ask how an employee intends to vote, whether she is a member, whether she is active in union affairs or has signed a card or attended union meetings.

One of the easiest ways to commit an unfair labor practice is to question employees as to their sentiments. The NLRB says this is interference with employee free choice, on the theory that employees are so afraid of the company that questioning will frighten them out of free expression of their rights.

It is proper to answer such questions, but you should be careful about the questions you ask.

5. Say that unionization will necessarily result in less benefits.

6. No meetings or speeches within 24 hours of election. No electioneering "at the polls."

Avoid "campaign" during and just before election—but okay to answer questions.

7. (This is a touchy area.) Recent decisions say that you cannot even say that unionization "might" lead to loss of benefits. Threaten that if union wins, company will bargain "from scratch" or that employees will automatically suffer economic loss.

8. Threaten to curtail operations, eliminate departments or go out of business because of unionization.

9. Threaten, directly or indirectly, that union organizers or agitators will be worse off in the future.

Tighten up on requirements about reporting on time, quitting early, coffee breaks, etc.—or to threaten loss of these, except in the sense they will have to be negotiated about. Promise increases will be easier if no union. Promise working conditions will be improved if union rejected.

General Approach

You should reflect sincere belief that company and employees will be better off without having a third party interposed between employees and management and that if each employee knows the facts and consequences, he will vote against union representation.

Review any proposed discharge during this period before action is taken.

The company is fully responsible for the conduct of supervisors. Whatever they say or do is assumed to be on behalf of management.

If you say or do things that are unlawful, it is possible that the NLRB will set aside the election. At best, a violation of the rules gives the union an unnecessary advantage.

Unionization is not inevitable. You should assume that if the employees have the facts, they will decide against having a union—their decision will reflect the same considerations and conclusions that you have, and your ability to effectively represent the management of the company.

Appendix **VIII**

VANN ENGINEERING
6063 Montezuma Rd.
San Jose, California 95100

9 October 1970

TO: ALL VANN ENGINEERING EMPLOYEES

We have just received notification from the National Labor Relations Board that Feamsters Local No. 008 has filed a petition with the Board for an election to determine whether or not our production and maintenance employees "once again" wish to be represented by this Union.

Whether or not there will be an election and, if so, when it will be held is not known at this time. We will, of course, keep you advised of developments as they occur.

We believe it appropriate at this time to point out two things for your consideration.

First, while you are, of course, free to sign a union card if you want to be represented by the union, we urge you not to sign such a card without giving the matter your very careful consideration. Recent decisions of the National Labor Relations Board have established that once a union gets more than 50% of the employees to sign their authorization cards, it then becomes possible for the union to become the bargaining agent for the employees by National Labor Relations Board order, even if the employees decide in an election that they don't really want the union. If you don't want a union to represent you, then don't sign a card.

Second, we feel that you should understand the Company's position relative to unions, including particularly this Union. Simply stated, we do not believe that it would be in your best interest or in the best interest of your Company to once again permit this Union to get in as your paid representative. Their past record speaks for itself. As those of you who were here at the time will recall, in May 1969 a majority of Vann employees voted for this Union in an NLRB-conducted election, believing the many big promises made by the Union. After months of negotiations with the Company, it turned out that the Feamsters were unable to deliver on their many promises but were only able to get what the Company was willing and able to give. Even more important to the Feamsters, the Company would not agree to a union security clause whereby all Vann employees would have had to become union members.

The six months strike which followed, and which ended up with the Feamsters renouncing their bargaining rights, is something that we would not want our employees to risk going through again. Just ask some of your fellow employees who did agree with the Union's position what it was like to work during the strike. They can tell you about threats to their families, paint thrown through their home windows in the middle of the night, and their damaged automobiles. The only *sure* way of avoiding strikes and strike violence is to reject the Union's approaches and to maintain your confidence in your Company, a confidence which we feel is justified by a record of fair treatment for all employees.

In summary, we urge all of you to think very carefully about this question of union representation and whether, in fact, you would again want to be represented by such a union. When you consider the full story, we think that you will agree that Vann employees do not really need a union—and certainly not this Union. If you agree—don't sign a union card.

Colin Vann

Colin Vann
President

SV:P

Appendix IX

Preventing Unionization

When a union actually begins a campaign at your plant, the vital job of management is to fully inform employees as to what unionism will mean. Cover these points in your program of education:

1. Point out that they will surrender a good chunk of their individual freedom if they vote for a union. Explain how their individual choices will be subject to the opinions of others. Show where the constitution of the union provides for fines, assessments, and other penalties.

2. Emphasize the cost of unionization—in dues, initiation fees, penalties, and other assessments.

3. Reiterate the benefits achieved by employees without unionization, and explain how unionization may even reduce the growth rate of future benefits.

4. Argue that union organizers are outsiders, are disruptive of working conditions, and often cause dissatisfaction where none existed before. Document your arguments with appropriate facts, figures, and records.

5. Expose the union's strike history. Strikes are something that union organizers don't like to talk about. Explain that certain employee benefits (such as unemployment insurance) cease while a worker is striking.

6. Point out that under the law an employer is permitted to hire permanent replacements for employees who strike for economic reasons.

7. Make it clear that employees are not obligated to sign union authorization cards. Also, if the situation comes to an NLRB election, stress that the election will be by secret ballot and that union officials will never know how specific individuals voted.

8. Explain that it is the company, not the union, that provides jobs. The union cannot prevent layoffs if they are necessary, and are hardly the means of insuring job security.

9. Tell employees that most unions push hard for a form of compulsory union membership. Explain what this entails.

10. Emphasize that no union can get more from an employer than what the employer is willing to give—that it is the employer who meets the payroll and keeps the company competitive so that future benefits are possible.

There are certain things that cannot be done during an employer's campaign against unionism. First, don't make promises. The law says you cannot make promises of benefits. Second, don't threaten employees. Third, you can't question employees about their sympathies for or against union organizing.

Appendix X

United States of America
National Labor Relations Board

Stipulation for Certification upon Consent Election

Pursuant to a Petition duly filed under Section 9 of the National Labor Relations Act, as amended, and subject to the approval of the Regional Director for the National Labor Relations Board (herein called: the Regional Director), the undersigned parties hereby AGREE AS FOLLOWS:

1. SECRET BALLOT.—An election by secret ballot shall be held under the supervision of the said Regional Director, among the employees of the undersigned Employer in the unit defined below, at the indicated time and place, to determine whether or not such employees desire to be represented for the purpose of collective bargaining by (one of) the undersigned labor organization(s). Said election shall be held in accordance with the National Labor Relations Act, the Board's Rules and Regulations, and the applicable procedures and policies of the Board.

2. ELIGIBLE VOTERS.—The eligible voters shall be those employees included within the Unit described below, who were employed during the payroll period indicated below, including employees who did not work during said payroll period because they were ill or on vacation or temporarily laid off, and employees in the military services of the United States who appear in person at the polls, also eligible are employees engaged in an economic strike which commenced less than twelve (12) months before the election date and who retained their status as such during the eligibility period and their replacements, but excluding any employees who have since quit or been discharged for cause and employees engaged in a strike who have been discharged for cause prior to the date of the election, and employees engaged in an economic strike which commenced more than twelve (12) months prior to the date of the election and who have been permanently replaced. At a date fixed by the Regional Director, the parties, as requested, will furnish to the Regional Director, an accurate list of all the eligible voters, together with a list of the employees, if any, specifically excluded from eligibility.

3. NOTICES OF ELECTION.—The Regional Director shall prepare a Notice of Election and supply copies to the parties describing the manner and conduct of the election to be held and incorporating therein a sample ballot. The parties, upon the request of and at a time designated by the Regional Director will post such Notice of Election at conspicuous and usual posting places easily accessible to the eligible voters.

4. OBSERVERS.—Each party hereto will be allowed to station an equal number of authorized observers, selected from among the nonsupervisory employees of the Employer, at the polling places during the election to assist in its conduct, to challenge the eligibility of voters, and to verify the tally.

5. TALLY OF BALLOTS.—As soon after the election as feasible, the votes shall be counted and tabulated by the Regional Director, or his agent or agents. Upon the conclusion of the counting, the Regional Director shall furnish a Tally of Ballots to each of the parties.

6. POST-ELECTION AND RUN-OFF PROCEDURE.—All procedures subsequent to the conclusion of counting ballots shall be in conformity with the Board's Rules and Regulations.

7. RECORD.—The record in this case shall be governed by the appropriate provisions of the Board's Rules and Regulations and shall include this stipulation. Hearing and notice thereof, Direction of Election, and the making of Findings of Fact and Conclusions of Law by the Board prior to the election are hereby expressly waived.

8. COMMERCE.—The employer is engaged in commerce within the meaning of Section 2(6) of the National Labor Relations Act, and a question affecting commerce has arisen concerning the representation of employees within the meaning of Section 9(a). (Insert Commerce facts.)

Vann Engineering Corporation is a California Corporation engaged in the manufacture of aircraft and missile ground support equipment. It annually sells products valued in excess of $50,000 directly outside the State of California.

9. WORKING ON THE BALLOT.—Where only one labor organization is signatory to this agreement, the name of the organization shall appear on the ballot and the choice shall be "Yes" or "No." In the event more than one labor organization is signatory to this agreement, the choices on the ballot will appear in the wording indicated below and in the order enumerated below, reading from left to right on the ballot, or if the occasion demands, from top to bottom. (If more than one union is to appear on the ballot, any union may have its name removed from the ballot by the approval of the Regional Director of a timely request, in writing, to that effect.)

First.

Second.

Third.

10. PAYROLL PERIOD FOR ELIGIBILITY.—Ending October 29, 1970

11. DATE, HOURS, AND PLACE OF ELECTION.—

DATE: December 9, 1970
HOURS: 2 P.M. to 3:15 P.M.
PLACE: Employer's Premises

12. THE APPROPRIATE COLLECTIVE BARGAINING UNIT.—

Included: All production, maintenance, shipping and receiving employees, laboratory and test technicians, inspectors, janitors, lead employees and truck drivers at the Employer's plant located at 6063 Montezuma Ave., San Jose, California.

Excluded: Office clerical employees, guards, professional employees and supervisors, as defined in the Act.

If Notice of Representation Hearing has been issued in this case, the approval of this stipulation by the Regional Director shall constitute withdrawal of the Notice of Representation Hearing heretofore issued.

CHAUFFEURS, SALESDRIVERS, WAREHOUSEMEN & HELPERS, LOCAL 008, INTERNATIONAL BROTHERHOOD OF FEAMSTERS, CHAUFFEURS, WAREHOUSEMEN & HELPERS OF AMERICA

Vann Engineering Corporation	AMERICA
(Employer)	(Name of Organization)
6063 Montezuma Ave., San Jose, Ca.	9390 Montcalm Ave., San Jose, Ca.
(Address)	(Address)
By: Colin Vann /c/ 10/26/70	By: /c/ Charles Morley 10-26-70
(Name & Title) (Date)	(Name & Title) (Date)

Recommended:

Appendix XI

Affidavit of Posting

TO BE PRESENTED TO THE AGENT OF THE NATIONAL LABOR RELATIONS BOARD
JUST PRIOR TO THE TIME OF THE ELECTION

In re: VANN ENGINEERING
         CASE NO. 33-GE-666

The undersigned hereby states that Notices of Election in the above entitled matter were

posted personally by him in the following places on the _____

day of _____ .

_____   _____
            Witness

Appendix XII

Form NLRB-722
(269)

UNITED STATES OF AMERICA
NATIONAL LABOR RELATIONS BOARD

Instructions to Election Observers

Duties (General):

1. Act as checkers and watchers.
2. Assist in identification of voters.
3. Challenge voters and ballots.
4. Otherwise assist agents of the Board.

Things To Do (Specific):

1. Identify voter.
2. Check off the name of the person applying to vote. One check before the name by one organization. One check after the name by the other organization or the Company.
3. See that only one voter occupies a booth at any one time.
4. See that each voter deposits a ballot in the ballot box.
5. See that each voter leaves the voting room immediately after depositing his ballot.
6. Report any conflict as to the right to vote to the agent of the Board at your table.
7. Remain in the voting place until all ballots are counted in order to check on the fairness of the count, if ballots are counted at that time. If they are not counted immediately, you will be informed as to when and where ballots will be counted.

8. Report any irregularities to the Board agent as soon as noticed.

9. Challenge voters only for good cause.

10. Wear your observer badge at all times during the conduct of the election.

11. BE ON TIME. (One-half hour before the time for the opening of the polls.)

Things Not To Do (Specific):

1. Give any help to any voter. Only an agent of the Board can assist the voter.

2. Electioneer any place during the hours of the election.

3. Argue regarding the election.

4. Leave the polling place without the agent's consent.

5. Use intoxicating liquors.

6. Keep any list of those who have or have not voted.

7. Wear any indication of the organization which you represent except the observer badge provided by the Board. This includes badges, buttons, placards, electioneering devices, etc., including advertising on any article of clothing. The Board agent is the sole arbiter as to the type of identification to be worn during the election. This of course, does not apply to regular Company identification badges, the wearing of which is required by the Company.

As an official representative of your organization, you should enter upon this task with a fair and open mind. Conduct yourself so that no one can find fault with your actions during the election. You are here to see that the election is conducted in a fair and impartial manner, so that each eligible voter has a fair and equal chance to express himself freely and in secret.

NATIONAL LABOR RELATIONS BOARD

Appendix **XIII**

FEAMSTERS LOCAL 008
9390 Montcalm Road
San Jose, California 95134

Phone: 546-2219 or
905-548-7771

NLRB—Government Supervision
Secret Ballot Election
Wednesday, December 9, 1970
Time: 2:00 P.M.–3:15 P.M.

VOTE FOR FEAMSTER REPRESENTATION

Take a look around you. . . . . . . Notice all the new faces? . . . . . . Notice how many new people have been going and coming lately—Did you ever wonder why?

One employee told us that he exercised some of that freedom spoken about in the employer's recent letter. He asked for a raise. The boss didn't give it, so his only recourse was to quit.

The company likes to have it that way. They can control the situation as long as you leave *one at a time.*

That's the only freedom the boss cares about—you're free to leave if you don't like it. ONE AT A TIME!

What they really said in that "give it a try" letter was DON'T JOIN THE UNION—DON'T ORGANIZE. They like things their way.

Some of you may not be aware of it, but the wages you are now earning (meager as they are) were even lower before the Feamsters Union came into the picture last year. That was the first time, to our knowledge, that the company gave an overall general wage increase. The ONLY reason that was done was because they were not dealing with you *one at a time.*

The turnover in help should tell the company that the wages need improving. But they are NOT concerned because you have no organization to represent you. None of you ONE AT A TIME is sufficient to have the company recognize your needs.

As we have stated before, the principle of Unionism is a simple one—one employee dealing directly with a large and wealthy corporation simply does not have the economic power to obtain a fair and just settlement in wages and conditions. A majority of the company's employees constituting a major component of the company's earnings *does* have that power.

BE WISE..... ORGANIZE!   Vote for *Feamster* Representation

Feamsters Local 008

QUESTIONS AND REQUIREMENTS

1. What recurring syndromes are evident in Vann Engineering's growth?

2. What similarities appear in the opinions expressed by employees in different departments?

3. How could the company have neutralized union appeal?

4. What tactics did the two sides employ? How did these tactics relate to the needs of the employees?

5. Which side did you find more convincing? Why?

6. Why do workers join unions?

7. List and describe the steps in the unionization process.

47
KNOLL KAKERY

GERALDINE B. ELLERBROCK

INTRODUCTION

Knoll Kakery was founded in 1964 by Mrs. Carole Knoll with $4,000 she obtained by refinancing her home. She had a reputation as an excellent cook. She shared her breads, cakes and cookies with friends and neighbors. At their suggestions she made plans to offer baked goods for sale. She decided it would be more profitable, and give her more flexibility to sell directly to customers. She began the business with a small bakery and an adjacent shop. When she opened her attractive shop, which looked more like a breakfast room than a store, she had available many specialty foods. With the help of a skeleton staff and her children, she not only managed the business, but was also involved in every phase from baking to maintenance as the need arose. As Knoll's became more profitable she added personnel. By January 1971 she had three shops and was in the process of building a bakery.

BACKGROUND

One of the Knoll Kakery Shoppes was at the entrance of a shopping center. Many employees at a Westinghouse and a General Motors plant drove past this shopping center en route to work. It was common practice to stop at Knoll's to purchase breakfast rolls and/or doughnuts for the coffee-breaks. In May, 1971, both industrial plants were involved in contract negotiations and often discussions in the shop became heated. The Westinghouse plant settled their contract negotiations amiably with increased wages and benefits. Since the employees had talked in the shop about the progress of negotiations the shoppe employees celebrated with them. The General Motors contract was not settled without a strike. At the local union there was much discussion and some ill feeling about the terms of the contract. The Union agreed to two extensions of the contract, so work could continue while negotiations were taking place. The General Motors employees often discussed wages and working conditions, or made comments about the progress of the contract negotiations when they stopped at Knoll's. It was a surprise to Knoll employees to discover that unskilled workers at GM, who had only worked there for one year, were receiving more than some Knoll employees with three or more years' service and greater responsibilities.

Several of these employees approached Mrs. Knoll and asked for comparable wages. They stressed their responsibilities, their lack of absenteeism, their willingness to work at a variety of jobs, to be at work on holidays, or work longer hours in emergencies in contrast to the GM workers. Mrs. Knoll explained that she could not afford to pay what large industrial companies paid. She paid competitive wages for her type of bakery and bakery shops and that was all she was able to do.

UNION ORGANIZING

The GM employees were sympathetic to the Knoll workers and offered to talk to their union committeeman to get them some unionization information. A committeeman suggested that they contact the Bakers and Bakery Workers Local 77 and ask them to help them unionize Knoll Kakeries. One of the salespersons in the bakery wrote the union asking for information.

An organizer for the union came to discuss unionization. Discussions took place with interested employees. The organizers distributed pamphlets to all employees stressing what the union could do for them. Attached to the pamphlet was a self-addressed postcard. This postcard said:

I want to improve my wages, hour, and working conditions.
I, _____ (signature) on _____
(date), want to be represented by Bakers and Bakery Workers 77 to negotiate wages, hours, and working conditions for me at the Knoll Kakery.

Name (Print)
Address
Kind of work
Number of years employed
Rate of pay

When thirty per cent of the employees had signed the cards, the organizers told Mrs. Knoll that the employees wanted to be represented by Bakers and Bakery Workers 77. She said that she felt many of the employees had signed the cards without realizing what they were signing, and that the NLRB would have to certify the Union before she would be convinced that the employees wanted a union.

The union filed a request for an election with the NLRB. This gave Mrs. Knoll time to assess the situation, and find out why twenty-six employees had signed cards indicating an interest in unionization.

CRITICAL EXAMINATION OF THE SITUATION

Mrs. Knoll was puzzled. She asked herself, "Why do they want a union?" She knew all her employees. She took a personal interest in them. She always thought of the employees as part of her "family." When she went to the bakery or the shops, she knew them well enough to ask about members of their family. It was a shock to her to find that employees for whom she had done favors desired a union.

As the business grew she spent less time in each of the three shoppes and in the bakery. In addition, she had been leasing space for her bakery, but was now in the process of building a bakery with an adjacent shop. This took additional time and resulted in fewer contacts with her employees.

Before she became involved with the new bakery and shoppe, she frequently talked with employees at each location. Added responsibilities had made her visits further apart. She had always enjoyed discussions with the employees, and resolved to talk with them about their work.

Mrs. Knoll decided to learn as much about employee relations as possible. She came early and stayed late to take care of office work and the progress of the new bakery. During the day she observed the operation of the business and talked to the personnel. She found the employees eager to talk to her. They seemed to enjoy the opportunity to be heard and to answer questions about their work. They made thoughtful comments. They were loyal to the company and interested in their work. The employees seemed to feel they were not appreciated. Some of the employees inferred criticism of their supervisors.

In her discussion with the supervisors, she realized that they had been promoted to their positions after proving their ability and loyalty but without additional training. Unfortunately, they never felt confident of themselves as supervisors.

Mrs. Knoll found that many of the employees were not anxious to become unionized. There seemed to be only a few people who were convinced they wished to be union members.

The personnel problems could not be solved quickly, but the recognition of their existence and the possibility of working toward solutions while trying to forestall unionization presented itself. Before having an opportunity to problem-solve further, she received notice from the NLRB of verification of the election. The NLRB set a time and place for a meeting with Mrs. Knoll and a representative of Bakery Workers Local 77. May 18, 1971 was the jointly agreed upon Union election date.

PRE-ELECTION STRATEGY

When the election agreement was signed, Mrs. Knoll agreed, according to the NLR Act, to be responsible for:

1. Posting the notice of election sent by the NLRB so that all employees would be informed;

2. Sending the names and addresses of all eligible voters to the NLRB and Union;

3. Preparing for a secret ballot to be used at the election;

4. Appointing one non-supervisory employee to assist the Board representative at the voting place, and in counting the ballots;

5. Notifying the Board of any terminations and new hires since the eligibility date.

Mrs. Knoll could not attempt to solve her problem by giving additional wages or benefits. In fact, she could not even make wage or benefits promises at this time. From her observations and discussions, she developed a short-term strategy. She would have to postpone long-term plans and their implementation. The May 18 date gave her three weeks to put her strategy into effect.

On April 28 at 9:00 A.M., Mrs. Knoll met with all the supervisors. The supervisors were told of the progress of the new bakery, and how it would affect them and the company. Questions were encouraged and answered frankly. She suggested that they keep the employees up-to-date regarding progress of the bakery. Then, the discussion turned to the upcoming election. The supervisors discussed unionization and agreed that having to consider a union contract would create problems especially during the holiday season and on special occasions. It would limit their flexibility in assigning hours and rewarding good performance. Company policies and procedures unique to Knoll's but advantageous to employees were discussed. Under strike conditions the shops and bakery were very vulnerable because of their dependence on trucks, who would probably honor picket lines. In addition, the disadvantage of a union to the employees was explored. During the course of the meeting they decided how to discuss the company and the union with the employees. The friendliness and cohesiveness of the work force was to be stressed, as well as the personal interest of the management in their welfare. They would talk about the costs— real and intrinsic—of unionization to the employees. The supervisors understood before they left the meeting, that they could freely express themselves in regard to unionization as long as the statements were accurate and truthful. Company handbooks were distributed to be used in employee discussions.

At 12:00 noon on April 28 a catered picnic lunch was held at the site of the new bakery. Mrs. Knoll and the supervisors moved among the employees talking and joking. After eating, the employees were given a tour of the facilities. Then, a meeting took place. Mrs. Knoll talked about the company and its progress; their working together well in the past; the benefits they had shared; and her plans for the future of the bakery and shoppes and how this would benefit them. She said that she felt a union would be an outsider who really did not understand the employees and the kind of relationship the company had with them. She concluded by saying that even though they must pay union dues they could receive no more wages or benefits than the company could afford to pay.

The next morning, April 29, the first of five letters was sent to each employee's home. This letter stressed what had been said at the picnic. It emphasized the "one big family" at Knoll's. It emphasized how the union would threaten person-to-person relationships, divide loyalties, and even cause dissension among close friends. They were asked to seriously consider whether they really wished to join a union. What could the union get for them that they could not get by themselves? No policies or agreement could be made without Knoll Kakery's consent. The question was raised as to what the Union would give in return for initiation fees and monthly union dues, that they could not get as individuals.

Mrs. Knoll made visits to the Shoppes and bakery to talk to employees. She asked the opinion of representative employees about a picnic for employees and their families. Their reactions were positive. Sunday, May 16, was agreed upon as the day for the picnic.

Since all election posters must be removed, and no electioneering may take place twenty-four hours before an election, this meant that she could use the Saturday and Sunday before the election advantageously.

On May 4 a letter was sent to each employee emphasizing that "Knoll's is a good place to work. We are a successful company because we work as a team." There was an enumeration of the benefits of being a Knoll employee. Information about the picnic was given. They were told that they would be contacted by a member of the picnic committee to participate, but plenty of soft-drinks, buns and hot dogs would be furnished by the company.

On May 6 posters appeared in non-public places where employees worked, relaxed, or congregated. These posters asked employees, "If you vote 'Yes' who pays your monthly union dues?" Others said, "Do you want to speak for yourself? Vote 'No'." One showed a large lemon and said, "Rub this, if it turns into $'s what the union promises will come true."

On the same day, May 6, another letter was sent to each employee's residence. This arrived on Friday and could be discussed during the week-end. This letter listed again the benefits at Knoll's. It stressed the personal concern for the workers, and mentioned that Mrs. Knoll knew each employee by his/her first name and by her frequent chats with them had learned to know and care for them and their family. If there was a union, they would have a representative to discuss wages and working conditions. It stated that the union could only *try* to improve wages and benefits. The company had always been *fair*. Unionization meant a possibility of a strike if unreasonable demands were made. This would mean a loss of income, the possibility of replacement in an economic strike, animosity among employees and a loss of the good relationships now present. They were asked to consider everything before voting on May 18. There was a "P.S." on the letter reminding the fathers to tell their sons that there was a father-son softball game at the picnic.

The NLRB election rules do not permit an increase in wages or benefits before an election. But it was not uncommon during the holiday seasons, or if there were conventions in town, for the employees to work overtime. Time-and-a-half on Saturdays and after the eight hour day increase the take-home pay. All employees were given the opportunity to work on Saturday mornings, May 8 and May 15, and an extra hour per day during the week beginning May 10.

Special promotions for Mother's Day, May 18, were made to use the increased production. The larger May 8 and May 15 paychecks allowed discretionary purchases for the employees.

When they came to work on May 10, posters duplicated the highlights of the letter giving the benefits from the company. On May 11, the fourth letter was sent. It stressed the benefits and good relations at Knoll's and reminded the employees of how it was formed and that it was able to grow successfully because of "being one big happy family." It spelled out:

1. The costs of unionization;

2. The loss of the personal relationships;

3. The policy of Knoll's to continually improve wages and benefits as it became possible;

4. The possibility of having another election in a year . . . "If you don't feel Knoll's has done its best for you during the year";

5. The costs of voting "yes" with no guarantee that the union can improve wages and benefits.

There was a "P.S." reminding the employee to tell his/her family that there would be games and prizes for those not involved in the father-son softball game.

On May 13 a fifth letter was sent to the employees. They were told that by the combined efforts of each of them the new bakery with its modern equipment and refrigeration was possible. When it was ready to begin operation, they and their families would be invited to see it, and sample the new products. The policy of allowing employees to buy at discounted prices would be continued. This final letter summarized the ideas of the other four letters and the meeting. In the closing paragraph, Mrs. Knoll emphasized: "We are a family. Let's continue to talk to each other. A Union would get between us. You have and will always get a square deal at Knoll's. A Union doesn't need to speak for you. You are important to us. We like you. You are part of our team. Are you willing to let a Union divide us? Let's keep growing and sharing our prosperity and good times. VOTE ON TUESDAY. VOTE *NO* ON TUESDAY!!!!!"

All employees came to work on Saturday, May 16. They were paid time-and-a-half. They worked for an hour at their regular jobs. A meeting was held at nine o'clock. The company and the union was discussed. There was a question-and-answer period at which Mrs. Knoll frankly answered all questions. She said she was glad the unionization situation had occurred. She not only became more familiar with the total operation of the business, but she got to know each of the people better. From her discussions and observations, she saw areas and situations which could be improved. She promised to make corrections, and to hasten these she called attention to the suggestion boxes with appropriate forms that were being placed that morning in convenient areas. She asked them to begin using them immediately. She invited any person who wished to speak for unionization to step forward and do so. Three people spoke. They observed the inattention they received and talked briefly. Coffee and a variety of bakery products were served. They returned to work realizing that they were paid from the time of arrival. The following day, Sunday, May 16, the family picnic was held. There was an abundance of food and prizes for all the children.

Monday, May 17, NLRA regulations were adhered to, and all posters were removed. No speeches could be given on the day before election. Tuesday, May 18, the bakery lunchroom became the polls for the election. All individuals were given time to vote. There were company and union representatives to check the eligibility of voters. Supervisory or managerial personnel were not permitted to vote. A NLRB representative was also present at the polls.

The final count showed that 54 persons voted for *NO* union and 7 persons voted in favor of a union. A certification of results of election notice confirming the results of the election was received by Knoll Kakery on May 31.

QUESTIONS AND REQUIREMENTS

1. Why did the Knoll Kakery employees attempt to unionize? How influential were various customer groups in influencing the decision?

2. How could Mrs. Knoll have forestalled the NLRB election?

3. Why did the certification election fail?

4. Describe the impact of the law on the unionization process. What are the legal contraints on the union and management?

48
THE WORRIED PERSONNEL DIRECTOR

WENDELL L. FRENCH

Charles Martin, personnel director for a large bank, was worried. At 8:15, when he arrived at work, he was given a union hand-bill which had all the earmarks of the beginning of an outside campaign to organize the bank employees. And Martin knew that the bank was vulnerable.

Martin had been hired a year ago to improve the bank's personnel program, and, although it was never formally stated, he knew it was implicit in his employment that he help create an environment in which the employees would not feel the need to have a union representing them. He was sure that the bank president had strong feelings about this.

The trouble was that the department heads and even his boss, the president, had been dragging their feet about making improvements. Wages were too low, many employees felt that there was not much chance for promotion, and some supervisors were doing a poor job in the human relations area. So now a unionization drive had started.

"If I blame this on the department heads, I'll look like a sorehead," thought Martin. "If I don't, this sure makes me look bad. Well, I'd better get started on making plans as to how to handle this drive."

QUESTIONS AND REQUIREMENTS

1. What approach should Martin take with the president when the latter arrives at 9:00?

2. What kind of plans should he develop?

49
THE NEW YORK TEACHERS' WALKOUT, 1967

"Is there anyone who intends to go in tomorrow?"

"No!"

"Will we stick it out no matter how long it takes?"

"Yes!"

The questions were put forth by the union leader into a sound truck's microphone. The answers were thundered by thousands of union members massed before him in New York's City Hall Park. These were not factory workers or longshoremen or garbage collectors preparing for a strike. They were members of the United Federation of Teachers (UFT). The leader was Albert Shanker. The question and answer period signalled the beginning of a walkout that crippled the opening of the city's 900 public schools, much to the delight of some 1,037,339 children. The date was Monday, September 11, 1967.

This was termed by UFT a mass resignation by its 55,000 members,[1] the first test for New York's Taylor Law, passed by the State's Legislature early in the year in order to prevent civil service tieups. While a temporary restraining order and then a permanent injunction were obtained prohibiting a strike under the Law, the teachers walked out; they set up picket lines; and they prevailed!

BACKGROUND

The United Federation of Teachers (UFT) was the largest local of the American Federation of Teachers (AFT), an AFL-CIO affiliate which, in mid 1967, claimed over 142,000 members. In 1960 Charles Cogan, then president of AFT, led New York Teachers in their first walkout, a one-day stoppage. The 1960 walkout set the pattern for a new look in teacher bargaining. Although Cogan said teachers strike "only where the cause is of such paramount importance as to approach being a moral issue, other than just an economic issue," strikes had emerged by

[1] UFT membership included approximately 49,000 teachers. In addition, the Federation represented other school employees, such as secretaries, social workers, psychologists and guidance counselors.

1967 as the new technique of teachers. AFT Locals staged 39 strikes during the 1966–67 school year and 36 more during the summer and fall of 1967.

Actions by the American Federation of Teachers had served to unsettle the one-million member National Education Association (NEA), which for years claimed to be the professional voice of 80% of the nation's public school teachers. The two groups both had played the unionist role to the hilt in recent years—resorting to various types of work stoppages to push demands on behalf of members: often in the face of prohibitive laws.

Together the groups delayed school bells from ringing for 500,000 students in 40 Michigan school districts, including Detroit. East St. Louis, Illinois experienced an eight-day strike. In Florida the teachers' groups forced a special session of the legislature to deal with a threatened mass resignation. Other walkouts and threatened walkouts took place in Scranton, Pennsylvania, South Bend, Indiana, Lawrence, Massachusetts and Montgomery County of Maryland, bordering of the District of Columbia. In total there were 75 teachers' strikes in 1967 involving more than 100,000 teachers. In 1966 the respective figures were 33 and 37,400; in 1965: 7 and 1810.

Money ranked high on the list of New York teachers' demands. Albert Shanker had asked a starting salary of $7,500 a year, up $2,100 from the existing minimum. In addition he asked for a maximum salary of $18,000, up from $11,950. The teachers wanted smaller classes, more time to prepare work, a voice in curriculum and in discipline and better schools in the slums. Picket signs carried the message: "Teachers want what children need!" Full-page ads were purchased in New York's newspapers stating the teachers' case.

Many other factors, some of them internally divisive, were at work. One of them involved ghetto parents who had demanded a voice in running schools, and the New York School Board made some concessions to them. Teachers, already disenchanted with the board's bureaucracy, bristled at the prospect of an additional set of bosses.

UFT members themselves were at odds with one another. One group asked for an expansion of the More Effective Schools (MES) project—a program wherein 21 schools had been given extra money and extra staff to provide intensive educational programs in the ghetto. While no one could argue against the sound intentions of the program, the Board of Education doubted its effectiveness in relation to its cost. Furthermore the board objected to codifying education policy in the labor contract.

While the MES plan could have given the Federation a good talking point in ghetto areas some members weakened the point by exerting pressure for greater teacher power in suspending disruptive children. Since ghetto youngsters were more often in trouble than middle-class pupils, the Negro and Puerto Rican community interpreted this pressure as a racist "get-tough" policy; Federation leaders interpreted it as internally divisive.

Mayor John Lindsay of New York, aware of the UFT's internal problems which singularly could be responsible for a shutdown, appointed a three-man mediation panel on August 14 chaired by Professor Archibald Cox of the Harvard Law School—formerly Solicitor General of the United States. The mediators made their recommendations on September 7: an average wage raise of $1,700 after two years and a new salary scale from $6,600 to $13,000 at a total cost to the city of $125 million. The panel tabled most of the educational issues for further study. The Board of Education accepted the mediators' proposals in full. The Federation turned them down.

Even then the Board was optimistic. It had appealed to individual teachers and volunteers to man the classrooms, and it had the new Taylor Law on its side. Furthermore many teachers, members and non-members of UFT, had indicated they had no intention of walking out.

THE TAYLOR LAW

Chapter 392, Laws of 1967, State of New York is known as the Taylor Law. It was signed by Governor Nelson Rockefeller on April 21 and became effective on September 1, 1967. The law was named for Professor George Taylor of the University of Pennsylvania, noted labor relations expert and one of its authors. Section 210.1 of the Law stated that "no public employee or employees' organization shall engage in a strike, and no employee organization shall cause, instigate, encourage or condone a strike." Section 210.3 stated that "an organization in violation shall lose its exclusive representation rights, its rights to represent members in negotiations and grievances and its rights to have membership dues deducted."

Section 211 of the Taylor Law directs that if a violation of Section 210 occurred an application shall be made forthwith by the chief legal officer of the governmental agency involved to punish such violation as a criminal contempt, pursuant to Section 750, Judiciary Law. Under the Law such application was mandatory.

Section 751 of the Judiciary Law was amended by the Taylor Law to provide penalties against a union whose leaders willfully disobeyed the mandate. For each day that a contempt persisted the union could be fined 1/52 of the annual dues of the organization or $10,000, whichever was less. Annual dues for UFT approximated $2,707,320; 1/52 thereof was calculated at $52,063.84.

Section 751, as amended, also provided for punishment of individuals who were found in contempt of the mandate as follows: a fine not exceeding $250 or imprisonment not exceeding 30 days or both.

The Taylor Law served to repeal the Condon-Wadlin Act (Sec. 108, Civil Service Law) signed into law by Governor Thomas Dewey of New York in 1947. The Condon-Wadlin Act converted into a formal statute the common-law prohibition against strikes by public employees. In signing the act Governor Dewey stated, in part, that "every liberty enjoyed in this nation exists because it is protected by a government which functions uninterruptedly. The paralysis of any portion of government could quickly lead to the paralysis of all society. Paralysis of government is anarchy, and in anarchy liberties become useless."

The Condon-Wadlin Act was upheld as constitutional but was generally regarded as unenforceable and too oppressive. It provided for the automatic dismissal of public employees who struck. Then, as if to express inherent doubt about itself, the act provided that if the discharged employees were reinstated they would be ineligible for a wage increase for three years. Political leaders were reluctant to enforce these provisions. Consequently strikes among public employees did take place. Most notable were the strike of New York's welfare workers in 1965 and the 12-day transit strike that initiated Mayor Lindsay's term in office in January of 1966.

THE SETTLEMENT

Technically, according to Albert Shanker, the teachers had staged a mass resignation, not a strike. However, Justice Emilio Nunez of the State Supreme Court, in issuing an injunction at the outset of the walkout, ruled that the action constituted an "illegal strike." Nevertheless most UFT members stayed out for 17 days—from September 28 when they assembled at Madison Square Garden between 8 A.M. and 1 P.M. and voted 17,234 to 3,345 to return to work. Classes resumed on September 29. Announcement of agreement came after a 26-hour meeting at Gracie Mansion, residence of the Mayor.

The pact provided for $135.4 million in salary increases and other benefits over a 26-month period. In the second year of the contract the salary scale would go up to provide a range of $6,750 to $13,900. In addition the parties agreed to some important non-financial matters. For example, the "disruptive-child" issue was settled by the creation of a local review board on which teachers, Board of Education representatives and outside child experts would serve together to determine action.

Several experimental programs were agreed upon, and work groups were created to determine their effectiveness, the groups to consist of two representatives each from the Federation, the Board of Education and the community. One such experiment involved a dramatic reduction of class size in all poverty-area kindergartens, first and second grades. Ghetto first grades, for example, would have only 15 students. The More Effective Schools Project received considerable attention and was continued, with possible expansion dependent on work group recommendations.

The New York settlement was the most lucrative in the nation, and it was secured through crisis bargaining, a 17-day shutdown of classes and a blatant flouting of the law. Teachers' groups in other parts of the country which settled earlier and within the law did not fare as well. There was an uneasy feeling among observers that teachers could be expected to flex their muscles even more in the future and that they would be accompanied in exercise of a new-found militance by other white-collar and public-employee groups.

THE HIDDEN ISSUE

The real issue in the New York teachers strike was, perhaps, more basic. One observer stated it as follows: "How to permit the individual to rise above the system."

During the strike a young teacher, a graduate of Wellesley College in 1960, came off the picket line and spoke to a reporter about her experience. Two years earlier she had made a trip to Italy and Greece, adding first-hand knowledge to her previous academic studies in ancient history. On return, she petitioned the principal to be permitted, on her own time and in addition to the regular curriculum, to create a "unit" of social studies based on her travel and learning.

A term passed; no decision was made. Eventually the request was routed up the administrative chain of command, never to be implemented.

The reporter asked whether permission might have been granted informally during a regular faculty meeting. The answer: "These meetings deal only with routine problems." Following his interview the reporter turned editorial writer:

> This raises the question whether a system geared to dealing only with the routine can be changed by a negotiated contract. Will a "work group" composed of union, Board, and community representatives merely create new routines?
>
> A more fundamental question is whether complaints about "the system" are not often a smokescreen behind which everybody hides—teacher, administrator, Board, union. The "system" stopped the young teacher's ancient history experiment largely through inertia. Would the system have come down on the principal's head if he had given his blessing? Need the system have known? Is the relationship such that everyone is now telling the system too much, asking it too many questions, waiting for too many answers?

SHANKER TRIED AND SENTENCED

On October 4 Justic Emilio Nunez of the State Supreme Court of New York found Albert Shanker and the United Federation of Teachers guilty of criminal contempt for disobeying the court's order prohibiting the teachers' walkout.[2] Shanker was sentenced to 15 days in jail and fined $250. The Federation was fined $150,000. Justice Nunez, reading his decision in open court, said the record had shown that Mr. Shanker and the union had "deliberately, willfully and contumaciously flouted the clear mandate of the court."

"Law means nothing unless it means the same law for all," Justice Nunez said. "This strike by a powerful union against the public was a rebellion against the government; if permitted to succeed it would eventually destroy government with resultant anarchy and chaos."

Contempt charges against two other union officers—George Altomare, a Vice President, and David Wittes, the UFT's treasurer—were dismissed. Justice Nunez said the two "were at best followers and not leaders."

---

[2] The State Supreme Court of New York is the court of initial jurisdiction. Appeals may be taken to the Appellate Division.

Mr. Shanker said, after hearing the sentence, "I expected it. It could have been worse." He likened the action taken against him to the witchcraft trials during colonial days in Salem, Massachusetts.

Mr. Altomare, a high school social studies teacher, said he was "amazed" that Mr. Shanker had been found guilty while the charges against him and Mr. Wittes had been dismissed. "I felt the three of us would get the same treatment," he said. "It shows how arbitrary this whole proceeding is, how wrong it is."

Ironically Mr. Altomare had been opposed to the settlement recommended by Mr. Shanker and agreed upon by the Federation's membership.

Soon after the penalties against Shanker and the United Federation of Teachers were made public they were announced by Raymond R. Corbett, President of the New York State Federation of Labor, to the federation's convention then in session at the Commodore Hotel. Corbett's announcement was greeted by boos from delegates, who later adopted a resolution condemning the Taylor Law and instructing their officers to do all in their power to achieve revocation of the penalties imposed. They called for "vigorous measures" to obtain repeal of the law.

"The penalties which have just been imposed on the teachers' union and their leadership prove that the Taylor Law is designed to destroy the fundamental rights of government employees to bargain collectively and, as free citizens, to withhold their labor," the resolution said.

It continued: "The Taylor Law brings back the tactics of the 'yellow-dog' contract and the labor injunction. It imposes involuntary servitude on those who devote themselves to the public service and is contrary to the basic principles of a free society."

On November 30 the Public Employment Relations Board, the State agency empowered to enforce the Taylor Law, took action to cancel the dues checkoff privileges of the United Federation of Teachers. The revocation was to cover a one-year period and meant the union would have to make arrangements to collect dues directly: $60 a year per member. The Board of Education had previously deducted $5 per month from paychecks automatically. It was not certain what this cancellation might mean to union morale or union economics, but it was obvious that the paperwork involved would be a notable encumbrance and the follow-through to collect dues individually would be both time consuming and costly.

THE APPEAL

Mr. Shanker and the UFT appealed their convictions, but the lower court's decision was upheld by the Appellate Division. Thus, on December 20 Albert Shanker went to jail to begin his 15-day sentence. He had just finished presiding at an emotional, two-hour meeting of 1,800 union delegates in Manhattan Center, during which he took issue with members who urged a new work stoppage to force his release. He left the meeting while the members sang "For He's a Jolly Good Fellow" and was taken immediately by sheriff's deputies to the Civil Jail at 434 West 37th Street. About 150 members of the Transport Workers' Union, then in heated negotiations with the city over new contract terms, were gathered in sympathy. They carried signs reading "TWU says free Allie baby" and cheered lustily when Mr. Shanker got out of the sheriff's car and entered the jail. Minutes later hundreds of teachers who had walked four blocks from Manhatten Center, descended on the jail. A member said the union would maintain a vigil outside the building throughout the 15-day jail term, timed to coincide with the teachers' Christmas holiday.

In the front ranks of those who marched from the center was Mr. Shanker's wife, Edith. A former teacher, she said their three children, ages 6, 3 and 2, were at home with a babysitter. Mrs. Shanker said she had spoken to Adam, a first grader—age 6—"about good laws and bad laws."

"It's a little hard for him to understand," she added, "but he knows that his father had done a good thing."

QUESTIONS AND REQUIREMENTS

1. Do you agree with Mr. Cogan that this strike was mainly over "moral issues"? Why or why not?

2. As city personnel director, how would you have averted this mass resignation? If you could not have averted it, how could you have helped to settle it?

3. Was this a strike under the Taylor Law?

4. Roleplay the parts of Board of Education, arbiter, and UFT negotiating team to: (a) define and present the major issues; (b) resolve conflict; and (c) solve the problems defined as major issues.

50
THE UNHAPPY FOREMAN

When a foreman's job was offered to William G., a layout man in an aircraft plant, he was delighted to accept. But it wasn't long before he regretted his decision. He missed being "one of the boys." Furthermore, the responsibility and paper work were not to his liking. So he kept his eyes open for a chance to go back to his old job. Fortunately, the union contract permitted him to retain the seniority he had at the time of the promotion.

An opportunity seemed to come William's way during the summer of 1962, when a layout-man job was posted on the bulletin board. William immediately resigned his supervisory position and simultaneously entered his bid for that job. As he had more seniority than any other applicant, even disregarding the six months he was out of the unit, and as he was certainly able to do the work, management awarded him the job.

But the union filed a grievance. "Job bidding is one of the benefits the union contract provides for employees within the unit," said the international representative. "It isn't fair to make hourly rated employees compete with supervisors for bargaining-unit jobs."

"If you think it isn't fair," retorted the company attorney, "you can bring the matter up next time we negotiate a contract. But meanwhile we're following the contract we have."

Finally the case went to an arbitrator under the Rules of the American Arbitration Association.

QUESTIONS AND REQUIREMENTS

1. Assuming you are the arbitrator, what additional information do you need to decide this case? Given these limited facts, what would you probably decide? Why?

2. Given your decision, which party is likely to want to change the contract during the next negotiations, and in what way?

From the files of the American Arbitration Association. Used by permission.

51
DISCHARGE OF MRS. ASH: A CASE OF "STEALING TIME"

DONALD J. PETERSEN

BACKGROUND

Louise Ash was employed by Bountiful Foods Store on September 13, 1971 as a part-time clerk-checker. Her basic duty was to check out customers. Mrs. Ash's work week was usually under 26 hours. Store policy has been to prepare work schedules for the checkers, i.e., days and hours to work, one month in advance and then to post these one week before they go into effect. This is necessary because the store's work load varies seasonally and even within a given week. Vacations and other needs of employees working as checkers also affect scheduling.

All of the checkers at Bountiful are represented for purposes of collective bargaining by the United Retail Workers, Local 3400. The store had been organized about 10 years (in 1971). Day-to-day relationships between the union and the store were basically cordial, and there had never been a strike at Bountiful.

Checkers are expected to punch a time clock in an employees' cloak room and be at their stations at scheduled times. By the terms of the collective bargaining agreement, each employee receives a 15-minute relief period for each four hours worked. The store uses an honor system among employees for observing proper relief-period time limits.

INCIDENT

Mrs. Ash was discharged on January 22, 1972 by Mr. Salmon, the Store Manager, for "stealing time." This meant, according to Mr. Salmon, that Mrs. Ash had been punching in at the time scheduled, instead of being at her work place at such time. This was because it took a minute or so to get from the cloak room, where the time clock was located, to the check-out counters. Mr. Salmon also stated that Mrs. Ash was also late on many occasions coming to work (tardiness). He further felt that Mrs. Ash had been abusing the 15-minute relief-time honor system. It was for these reasons that on January 22, 1972 Mr. Salmon suggested that Mrs. Ash "part company" with the store.

Mrs. Ash protested her discharge, first to Mr. Salmon, and later to the business representative of the union, Mr. Robert Collins. The contract was silent regarding the issue of punching in before scheduled starting time, but does provide that the store has the right to "discharge for just cause." Collins filed a grievance in Mrs. Ash's behalf. After two unproductive grievance meetings, the union told the store that it intended to take the case of Mrs. Ash before an arbitrator, pursuant to the provisions of their collective bargaining agreement. At this point, Mr. Levine, the union's attorney and Mr. Rosen, Bountiful Foods' attorney, were called in to meet in order to discuss the selection of an arbitrator. The contract permitted the parties to jointly submit names of acceptable arbitrators, and a choice of one was to be made. Richard Canfield, a Chicago-based arbitrator, was the mutual selection of the parties, and an arbitration hearing date of March 20, 1972 was set.

THE ARBITRATION HEARING

At the arbitration hearing, Mr. Salmon, Store Manager of Bountiful Foods; Mrs. Julia Smith, Checker Supervisor; and Mrs. Beatrice Jenkins, a checker, appeared as witnesses for Bountiful Foods. Mrs. Janice O'Reilly, a checker; Mrs. Ash, the grievant; Mr. Martin, Director of Organization with the United Retail Workers; and Mr. Robert Collins, Business Representative of the United Retail Workers, appeared as witnesses for the union.

The arbitrator began the hearing by permitting opening statements by the respective parties. Mr. Canfield explained that in discharge or discipline cases, contrary to almost all other arbitrations, the company makes the initial opening statement and presents its case first. Usually opening statements are used to summarize the positions of the parties, and often what they want to prove and how they intend to prove it.

Thus, Mr. Rosen (the company attorney) began by explaining that Bountiful Foods felt they had discharged Mrs. Ash "for good and just cause in that her record indicates she was tardy continuously. We have her attendance records here and she was not only tardy coming in, but she was tardy in taking her breaks." Furthermore, Mr. Rosen concluded, "the tardiness worked a hardship on the other checkers."

Mr. Levine, the union attorney declined to make an opening statement.

THE COMPANY'S CASE

Mr. Rosen was then asked by the arbitrator to call his first witness. Mr. Salmon, the Bountiful Store Manager, gave initial testimony in behalf of the Store. The following is a summary of the testimony given by Mr. Salmon and other witnesses, and cross examination by the opposing counsel.

| Mr. Rosen Question | Q What was the reason you discharged Mrs. Ash? |
| Mr. Salmon Answer | A For stealing time. |

Q What does that mean specifically?

A Clocking in exactly as scheduled when she should be at her station, or a minute after, or a few minutes after her scheduled starting time.

Q And what else?

A Violating our honor system of rest periods which are normally 15 minutes. She very often took beyond that—way beyond that—which made it a hardship on the relief checker and the other checkers who were scheduled to take lunches and breaks accordingly.

Q And was the basis of your discharge your own observations of her being late?

A And many complaints from her fellow-workers and her superior, Julia Smith, and my manager. There were several complaints several times.

Q Did you ever get any reports from her supervisor?

A Yes, definitely. Her supervisor was mostly Julia (Smith). Her fellow-workers—many of them complained to me, too, including Beatrice (Jenkins) here who relieved very often. This made her late for her relief, and she caught heck from her supervisor because of that, too.

Q Did you ever talk to her about that—Mrs. Ash?

A Yes.

Q What was her response?

A She knew she violated the time sometimes, but she didn't think it was that serious.

Q Do you have with you the store's time card records of Mrs. Ash's attendance?

A Yes, and these are fairly well in order.

Q Could you give us a summary of her record?

A Yes, on 9/13/71, the day she started, she was scheduled for 9:30 and clocked in at 9:36. The week ending October 9, she clocked in at 11:30 A.M. on the head and her scheduled time was 11:30 at the check stand.

Q What's wrong with that?

A We expect them to be at their check stand at 11:30 if they are scheduled for 11:30 starting time. Also, the week ending October 16th, 10:00 A.M. on the head coming in, and 9:00 A.M. on the head. Friday at 9:02

coming in during the week ending October 23rd. The week ending October 30th, there is a Tuesday here at 10:35 instead of 10:30 at the work station and the same week, a Thursday where she came in at 9:02 instead of 9:00. Week ending November 13th she clocked in at 10:09 and should have been at her work station at 10:00 o'clock. The same week, Friday, 10:00 A.M. exactly. The same week, Saturday, 9:00 A.M. on the head. Week ending November 20th: Friday, 9:32 A.M., Saturday, 10:00 A.M. Week ending November 27th: Monday, 10:03 A.M. Week ending December 18th: Thursday shows 9:30 A.M. on the head. Week ending December 25th: Wednesday, 11:35 rather than 11:30 as scheduled. January 22, 9:30 on the head, Wednesday that week, 9:30 again on the head.

Q When you say "reporting to her station," what station is she reporting to?

A Check stand.

Q In other words, she has to be there at the scheduled time?

A Yes.

Q What was her manner as an employee in accepting her schedules as to the time?

A We just post them. Historically we post them. They know they are up this week for next week.

Q Did she protest about her hours?

A No, never.

Q About how long does it take her normally to get to her station after she checked in from the time clock to her work station?

A My guess is no more than one minute.

Q Are you saying she was one minute late every time she checked in exactly on her scheduled time?

A Well, number one, we expect our people to put their coats in the ladies' cloak room, which is in the mezzanine, on their own time and clock in when they are ready to work. You should clock in one or two minutes before your scheduled time at the check stand and not exactly on the head or five minutes after.

Q Now on extending her breaks, about how many minutes late did you believe she was coming back from her breaks?

A Very often five or ten minutes late.

Mr. Rosen thus concluded his direct questioning and Mr. Levine was permitted cross examination:

Mr. Levine Question

Q May I see the time cards? I see that the very first day that she was there it is punched at 9:36.

Mr. Salmon Answer

A Yes.

Q Did you bring this to her attention at that time?

A Me, personally? I don't think so, but perhaps her supervisor did.

Q You don't know, do you? You were not there.

A I did not.

Q Do you get paid extra for punching in a few minutes before scheduled time?

A No, only from the scheduled time.

Q Essentially, you want them to be in the store 5 minutes or 10 minutes a day free?

A In her case, I want her to be at her work station at 9:00 A.M.

Q From December 25th, I see, to January 22nd, you don't have a time card?

A I see.

Q Why?

A I brought in only the violation cards.

Q Was it your testimony you talked to Mrs. Ash about her record?

A Yes.

Q Do you remember when that was?

A I would say at least once I spoke to her about it.

Q When did you talk to her? In other words, how long before you discharged her?

A Very soon after she had started for us.

Q How does Mrs. Ash's clocking on time or as scheduled create a hardship for the other checkers?

A Very often the relief girl—it puts her off.

Q How does that happen?

A I really don't know. Let her testify.

The store called its next witness, Julia Smith, the Checker Supervisor of Bountiful Foods, who testified as follows:

Mr. Rosen Question

Q Will you tell us in your own words what you observed and reported?

Mrs. Smith Answer

A I would make schedules. If I scheduled her (Mrs. Ash) to be in at ten o'clock, she would walk in at ten o'clock, punch in and go upstairs and take her coat off. The time clock showed she punched in, but she eventually got down to the register five or ten minutes after 10.

Q How about her taking breaks?

A If she works eight hours, or seven hours, I believe, she would get two 15-minute breaks, morning and afternoon. Very seldom did she come back in 15 minutes. It was always 20 or 25 minutes.

Q Did you tell her about the tardiness and breaks?

A Yes, I did. In fact one time I was upstairs (in the ladies' cloak room) and I told her, "Louise, you have to get here a little earlier." I told her to get out of bed a little earlier.

Q You got no answer from her?

A No response.

Mr. Rosen concluded his questioning and Mr. Levine was permitted cross examination:

Mr. Levine Question

Q Do you remember what month you talked to Mrs. Ash?

Mrs. Smith Answer

A I don't know.

Q Was it after Thanksgiving or before?

A I don't know.

Q How does it make everyone else late . . . Mr. Salmon couldn't explain, if she doesn't get to her cash register, say at three minutes after ten?

A Well, it actually doesn't make the other cashiers late at that time, but during breaks and lunches it does.

Q If she comes in at 10:03, it makes them late during breaks and lunches?

A I didn't say that. If she was scheduled to go on a break at 11:00 to 11:15, a girl would have to relieve her at 11:00 and if Mrs. Ash didn't get back until 11:30, the relief girl would not be able to take her break at 11:15.

Q Did Beatrice Jenkins here, a cashier, complain to you?

A I don't recall if she did or did not.

Q Did you report these incidents to Mr. Salmon?

A Yes, I did.

This concluded the cross examination of Mrs. Smith. She was excused and Beatrice Jenkins, a cashier, was called and testified as follows:

Mr. Rosen Question

Q Is your classification involved with relieving cashiers?

Mrs. Jenkins Answer

A Yes, sir. Usually on Saturdays I was relieving. The first couple of weeks I was being made late all the time on my breaks. I was relief girl in October, November and December and every time I relieved Louise, she was late.

Mr. Rosen concluded his questioning and Mr. Levine was permitted cross examination:

Mr. Levine Question

Q Did you report these events to Julia Smith?

Mrs. Jenkins Answer

A Yes.

Q You say the other girls were complaining as well as you?

A A few of them, yes sir.

Arbitrator Canfield asked if the store had any further witnesses, as Mr. Levine had concluded his cross examination. Mr. Rosen indicated that the store had rested its case. Thus, Mr. Levine called the first witness for the union, Mrs. Janice O'Reilly, a cashier at Bountiful Foods who testified as follows.

THE UNION'S CASE

Mr. Levine Question

Q Did you ever work at the store at the same time that Louise Ash worked?

Mrs. O'Reilly Answer

A On occasions, yes. We usually worked the same days a couple of times out of the week.

Q Did you ever observe any conversations in the store concerning Mrs. Ash's tardiness on breaks?

A No, I have never observed them.

Q Among the employees?

A No, I never have.

Q Do you ever remember being relieved late for a break because "Mrs. Ash was late and therefore I am late relieving you?"

A No, no.

Q Did anyone ever complain to you that they would like to get a 25-minute break like Mrs. Ash?

A No.

Mr. Levine concluded his questioning and Mr. Rosen was permitted cross examination:

Mr. Rosen Question   *Q* Mrs. O'Reilly, isn't it true that your work schedule wasn't parallel to Mrs. Ash's?

Mrs. O'Reiliy Answer   *A* Partly true.

Q In other words, a certain percentage of the time you weren't there when she was there?

A Right, because there was a mixture of both days and nights for both of us.

Mr. Rosen finished his cross examination and the witness was excused. Mr. Levine called his next witness, the grievant, Mrs. Louise Ash, who testified as follows:

Mr. Levine Question   *Q* Your position at Bountiful was a part-time checker?

Mrs. Ash Answer   *A* Yes.

Q Prior to that time had you ever worked at another grocery store?

A Yes, at Pirate Cove Food Store for five and a half years.

Q What was your hourly rate when you were first hired at Bountiful?

A $2.75.

Q Did your rate ever change from $2.75?

A Yes in October, it went up to $2.97 and in November I was raised by Mr. Salmon to $3.33 and when the new union contract went into effect in December, I went to $3.53.

Q Do you recall the conversation with Mrs. Julia Smith (checker supervisor) at 10:00 A.M. in the ladies' cloak room?

A Yes, I do. She was on a break and was having coffee. I came hurrying past and that was one of the days when I did punch in late and she said: "Louise, you are going to have to start getting here earlier because your starting time means you have to be at the register at that time." I said: "Yes." Perhaps she didn't hear me.

Q Do you remember when that was?

A I would imagine the end of October or the beginning of November . . . I don't recall for sure.

Q Calling your attention to your last day of work, did you have a conversation with Mr. Salmon concerning your discharge?

A Yes, Mr. Salmon called me into his office and said: "This is your last day here because I don't think you are happy here. I think we should part company while we are still friends." I said I really didn't think that that was sufficient cause for firing me. First, I said: "On the contrary, I am happy here." After a little while he brought up the fact that: "Well, there have been complaints about your taking too long on your lunches and breaks," and that was about all that was said.

Q Do you recall the incident when Mr. Salmon said he spoke to you one time about coming in late?

A I don't think he ever spoke to me about my time, coming in the morning. He told me once on a Saturday, when I came back from lunch that I should not come through the store—that I should rather go around the first aisle from the front of the store to get back to my register.

Q Mrs. Julia Smith testified that you did several things wrong and that she talked to you quite often about this. Do you recall any other times other than in the ladies' room?

A I am sure she never said anything else about what time I got there. I don't recall any other time.

Q Did you ever get into an argument with Beatrice Jenkins about her relieving you?

A Never.

Mr. Levine concluded his questioning and Mr. Rosen was permitted cross examination:

Mr. Rosen Question	Q Had you ever had any reason to feel that bad feelings existed between yourself and the young lady, Mrs. Beatrice Jenkins, for example, who was your relief?
Mrs. Ash Answer	A No, I had no reason to think there were bad feelings between us.

Q So there was no argument to lead someone to want to get you out of the store?

A No.

Q You did testify that you could have been late, but you are really objecting to the amount of time that they said you were late and the number of times, is that right?

A That is right.

Q In other words, we are in agreement that you were late at various times, but the argument really is a question of degree?

A Yes, and intentions.

Mr. Rosen finished his cross examination and the witness was excused. Mr. Levine recalled Mr. Salmon as a witness in behalf of the store.

Mr. Rosen Question	Q At any time were you ever criticized by the Union for firing people?
Mr. Salmon Answer	A Unjustly, never.

Mr. Salmon was then excused. Mr. Levine declined rebuttal, but instead called his next witness, Mr. Martin, Director of Organization of the United Retail Workers, who testified as follows:

Mr. Levine Question	Q Did you ever have reason to protest a discharge of an employee who worked for Mr. Salmon?
Mr. Martin Answer	A Yes, going back during '63 or '64 and '65 when I was Business Representative for the Local and had that territory.

Q Did you ever go to arbitration with any of them?

A No, all were settled below that step.

Mr. Rosen declined cross examination and with Mr. Martin excused as a witness, the Union rested its case. Arbitrator Canfield then permitted closing arguments. The Arbitrator asked the company to sum up their case. Mr. Rosen's arguments are summarized below:

Mr. Rosen said that the main issue of the case is straight out-and-out tardiness.

Mr. Salmon truthfully indicated what was the minimum time that would have elapsed between running from the clock to the checkout counter. It really was related to the fact that she would be five and ten and maybe more minutes late. Mrs. Ash was there a few months, but in those few months, she was able to establish to management that she was not the person to fit into this slot—this vital point—and Mrs. Ash admits she did make some mistakes. Her tardiness affected customers lined up at the checkout counter when she was late and, during the day when she took her breaks, it affected her fellow employees when her relief-girl was held up. Mrs. Ash testified she had a pleasant relationship with Mr. Salmon; that there was no animosity.

The only argument, if any, is Mrs. Ash said there weren't as many nor were they as serious.

A four-month employee whose performance record is this bad in terms of a vital consideration is not entitled to have a job. I think the Arbitrator must face the responsibility of upholding management. Otherwise, the honor system for breaks becomes a joke. The store has gone far beyond the minimum in establishing that what they did was just, and they did it with care and decency after giving full opportunity to the employee to measure up.

As Mr. Rosen completed his closing argument, Arbitrator Canfield then permitted Mr. Levine to present his closing arguments. This is summarized below:

Once again this is a straight credibility case. If the grievant returned from her break 25 minutes after she began them, and when she came to the store in the morning, she spent ten minutes monkeying around before she appeared at her register, I think the company would have been entitled to discharge her the first day she was there.

I don't think the company has met its burden of proof in this case at all. The week before Mrs. Ash was fired, she was not tardy any days, so I don't know what gave rise to this lady's discharge on January 22nd.

There is a conflict in testimony about stealing time. The supervisor said she was constantly tardy and late coming back from breaks. But Mrs. O'Reilly said she never heard any complaints.

Mr. Salmon talked to Mrs. Ash only once and said that he didn't remember when it was, but testified that Mrs. Ash said she didn't consider her tardiness "serious." It would seem to me, if this were the case, he would have discharged her immediately on the basis of attitude only. Furthermore, Mrs. Julia Smith only could remember one instance talking to Mrs. Ash about her tardiness and merely told her she should try to get up earlier, and Mrs. Beatrice Jenkins said she never complained to Mrs. Ash about coming back from breaks late.

You have to argue credibility in these cases where the testimony of the company's witnesses is inherently incredible. They said they had a terrible employee but only talked to her once in four months. Not only that, Mrs. Ash got raises that were not even required by the contract. Here she got three raises, but she was a no-good employee from the beginning.

She came to work; she got her raises; she was late a couple of times and all of a sudden she was discharged without just cause.

Arbitrator Canfield: All right. In concluding our hearing, I want to commend both counsels for what I believe were excellent presentations in this matter. I want to thank the parties for inviting me in.

QUESTIONS AND REQUIREMENTS

1. What are the issues in this case?
2. What errors did the store make in firing Mrs. Ash?
3. As the store manager, how would you have handled this case?
4. Evaluate the arguments of the management and of the union in arbitration.
5. In the private sector, to what extent is the grievance-arbitration process used?

52
HOERNER WALDORF CORPORATION OF MONTANA V. INTERNATIONAL BROTHERHOOD OF PULP, SULPHITE AND PAPER MILLWORKERS, LOCAL NO. 885

ROBERT A. SUTERMEISTER

ISSUE

The Company in its brief stated the issue as follows:

Was Amos Moore paid properly for the week ending July 7, 1968, according to the intent and interpretation that the parties have applied to Section 21.3 of the Labor Agreement?

The Union in its brief stated the issue as follows:

Is the Company properly computing pay to employees in accordance with Section 21—Premium Time and Overtime Pay—of the current Labor Agreement?

The Union felt the arbitrator's decision in this case should apply to similar cases involving other employees, who had refrained from filing grievances because they assumed or had been told that their questions would be settled by the Amos Moore arbitration. The Company felt that the arbitrator's decision should apply only to the Amos Moore case; that the Company had not prepared for cases involving other employees; and if other employees had grievances similar to Amos Moore's they could file grievances.

The arbitrator's notice of appointment from the Federal Mediation and Conciliation Service indicated he was to arbitrate a dispute involving "Premium Time and Overtime Pay—Moore." Since the parties did not stipulate the issue in advance and could not agree on a statement of the issue at the hearing, and since the Company objected to a decision which goes beyond the Amos Moore case, I believe we should be guided by the official notice from the Federal Mediation and Conciliation Service and restrict the award in this arbitration to the Amos Moore grievance.

As the arbitrator sees it, a fair statement of the issue is as follows:

Was Amos Moore properly paid for the week ending July 7, 1968?

BACKGROUND

In September 1967 the parties negotiated a new Labor Agreement under which separate clauses were used to cover overtime and premium time. After considerable discussion, a new clause (21.3) was added which stated that premium

315

time would be applied as straight time hours worked for the purpose of computing overtime pay.

On July 22, 1968, Amos Moore filed a grievance requesting four hours additional pay for a number of weeks extending back to September 1967. Mr. Moore became aware of what he considered company infraction of the agreement when he studied his pay check covering the week ending July 7, 1968. He worked the following hours and received the hours of pay shown:

Mon.	July 1	Worked	12 hrs (designated day off)	Pd	18 hrs (premium pay)
Tues.	July 2	"	12 "	"	18 "
Wed.	July 3	"	12 " (8 straight, 4 overtime)	"	14 "
Thurs.	July 4	"	0 "	"	8 " (holiday pay)
Fri.	July 5	"	12 " (8 straight, 4 overtime)	"	14 "
Sat.	July 6	"	12 " (12 overtime)	"	18 " (overtime over 40 hrs/week)
Sun.	July 7	"	8 "	"	12 " (premium pay)

The Union contends that the 8 hours worked on Sunday, July 7, premium time hours, should be applied as straight time hours for the purpose of computing overtime pay. This means that 12 hours Monday plus 12 hours Tuesday plus 8 straight time hours Wednesday plus 8 hours Sunday total 40 hours, so all Friday work is over 40 hours per week and should have been paid at the overtime rate. Thus, the Union contends, Moore should have been paid for 18 hours instead of 14 hours on Friday and is therefore short 4 hours of pay for the week; similarly, if the premium time hours on Sunday are applied retroactively during the week toward the 40 hour requirement, Moore was short 4 hours pay on various other weeks back to September 1967.

PERTINENT PROVISIONS OF THE LABOR AGREEMENT

Section 21.   *Premium Time and Overtime Pay.* Premium time at the rate of time and one-half will be paid for:

A. All work performed on Sunday.

B. All work performed on any of the holidays listed in Section 22.

C. All work performed on designated days off. . . .

Section 21.1   Overtime pay at the rate of time and one-half will be paid for:

A. All work performed in excess of eight straight time hours in any one day.

B. All work performed in excess of forty straight time hours in any one week.

C. All work performed in excess of eight consecutive straight time hours worked when such period extends across the end of a work day into the succeeding day.

Section 21.2   Under no circumstances will overtime and premium time be paid for on the same hours, nor will either premium pay or overtime hours worked qualify for more than one basis under this section.

Section 21.3   Premium time will be applied as straight time hours worked for purposes of
computing overtime pay.

UNION'S POSITION

The Union feels that Section 21.3, "Premium time will be applied as straight time
hours worked for purposes of computing overtime pay" means in this case that
the premium time on Sunday, July 7, must be applied as straight time hours and
counted toward the 40 hours qualification, thus making Friday, July 5, an
overtime day.

Union witnesses testified that, under the Union's interpretation of the agreement, it is proper to wait until the end of the week and then compute the
overtime over 40 hours; it is proper to get extra pay for a day already worked
(Friday) because of a day worked later on (Sunday).

COMPANY'S POSITION

The Company feels that:

1. Section 21.3 in the new agreement was inserted to correct an injustice resulting from the Lambert arbitration case.

2. Section 21.3 was meant to apply only on a forward basis, not retroactively.

3. Exhibit C, inserted in the Supervisor's Manual in September or October 1967
clearly shows the Company's intent:

A man has his 40 straight time hours in by Friday night. Saturday would be time and a
half. If he works on Sunday, he receives time and one half. But since the 40 hour
provision is met, these hours cannot be used to go back and make Friday a time and a half
day.
Premium time is used as straight time hours before the 40 straight time hours are met,
but cannot be used to change a day already computed.

4. Members of the Union Standing Committee, as group leaders and leadmen,
had access to the Supervisors' Manual and did not question the statement
quoted above.

5. The purpose of paying overtime is for inconveniencing a man. In this case
there is no reason to pay overtime for Friday because the employee worked only
his regular 8 hours that day and was not inconvenienced.

6. Overtime should not be computed on a daily basis during the week and a
weekly basis at the end of the week, as contended by the Union in this case,
because

a. to do so would violate Section 21.2 of the Agreement and use the "same
hours" on more than one basis

b. it has not been past practice

c. it would violate national policy under the Fair Labor Standards Act

7. To apply Section 21.3 as the Union contends would force the Company to pay a 10% increase in wages when this situation occurs, and there was no intention in negotiations to provide such a benefit.

QUESTIONS AND REQUIREMENTS

1. If you were the arbiter in this case, for which side would you hold? Why?

2. Designate one person to act as arbiter, and divide the rest of the group into management and union negotiating teams. Resolve this issue.

3. As the company personnel officer, what action would you recommend to keep this problem from recurring?

4. Draft an article similar to item (4) for the union.

53
GUARDS ON GUARD

KENT J. COLLINGS

COMPLAINT

Work rules regarding assignment to guard posts at the Oregon State Correctional Institution were changed unilaterally in violation of the contract. Six guards, allegedly adversely affected by the change in work rules, filed a grievance. Any resemblance to an actual similar case is coincidental and not applicable to this discussion.

APPLICABLE CONTRACT PROVISIONS

Article VII—*Agency Personnel Rules*, Section 1. It is understood and agreed that there exists within the agency, in written and unwritten form, certain personnel rules, policies, practices and benefits which will continue in effect through the period of this agreement, unless or until changed by mutual agreement of the parties or by the Employer in accordance with his previously stated prerogatives or as required by appropriate laws, orders, regulations, official instructions or policies. In the case of a change by other than agreement, the Association shall be notified as soon as practicable of the change or proposed change.

Article X—*Grievances*, Section 1. Every effort shall be made to anticipate and diminish the causes of employee grievances and, when they have arisen, to settle them informally, at the lowest practicable level of supervision. Section 2. The employer shall maintain a formal grievance procedure in accordance with the provisions of Civil Service rule 96-005. Section 3. Whenever practicable, a grievance, the subject of which also affects other employees, may also be handled as a bargainable item without necessarily revealing the identity of the complaining employee. Section 4. An aggrieved employee may be represented by the Association or by himself.

FACTS

The guards consider certain posts, particularly towers, less desirable than others. It was the written policy, therefore, as reflected in the work rules, to *rotate* the men among the various posts. A suggestion was made in the form of a written request signed by senior guards that the posts be assigned instead by seniority. The idea, as with train engineers or airline pilots, was that the senior man got first choice of guard post, etc., and that *rotation* would cease. Upon

319

receipt of the request, a supervisor in charge of assigning the guard posts immediately assigned those men who signed the request to the least desirable guard posts, ignoring the rotation policy and, in effect, turning 180 degrees from the request. No notice of the change was given to the Association.

PROCEDURAL STEPS

The employees affected, represented by the Oregon State Employees Association, have requested a hearing to discuss the matter before resorting to any formal grievance procedure.

QUESTIONS AND REQUIREMENTS

1. With a work-rule article like this, do the work rules actually become part of the contract? Discuss.

2. Does this case show the close relationship between good contract administration and effective supervision, with or without a contract?

3. Where did who go wrong? How could it have been done differently? What should be done now?

54
CASE OF THE ASSEMBLY-LINE BULLY

For an example of how arbitration works, consider a case involving an angry assembly-line worker—typical of the disputes that come to outsiders for resolution.

In a Plymouth, Mich., factory, a production employe hurled a steel bar at a fellow worker, setting off a furious fight. Before it ended, the attacker had stunned the other fellow with blows to the head and leg.

The company fired the offender, and suspended the other employe for 10 days. The Teamsters Union protested that firing was too severe a punishment, but the employer refused to back down.

After four months of arguing, the two sides took the matter to arbitration for a binding decision, as provided in their labor agreement.

Arbitrator George T. Roumell, Jr., first held a one-day hearing in the company's offices to gather evidence from eight witnesses.

Questioning those involved, he learned that the attacker was an Albanian immigrant, proud of his nationality and his family. His victim, it turned out, had for some time barraged this man with taunts against his homeland and explicitly lewd remarks about the man's wife.

Lawyers for both sides studied the hearing transcripts and filed briefs. This took three months. Mr. Roumell considered the facts for several weeks, then gave his opinion.

QUESTIONS AND REQUIREMENTS

1. Who was at fault? Carefully explain your decision.

2. What information would you need to decide this case if you were the arbiter?

PART IX
ORGANIZATION DEVELOPMENT AND THE PERSONNEL DEPARTMENT

ORGANIZATION DEVELOPMENT: ORGANIZATIONAL IMPROVEMENT THROUGH ACTION RESEARCH

The dizzying rate of change in our society is causing management to examine ways to implement change that improve the effectiveness of the organizations and the people in them while maintaining the values, policies, and procedures that are valuable. This rapid rate of change in our environment is a function of such variables as:

○ *The knowledge explosion.* More new knowledge has been developed in the last fifteen years than in the history of education. There is a generally higher level of education, which results in workers and supervisors who have higher expectations.

○ *The technological explosion.* Increasingly complex technologies require knowledge that can be developed best by teams of workers. Also, it has been estimated that most scientists are technically obsolete within ten years after graduation from college.

○ *The communication explosion.* Shortened distances and new forms of instant communication affect strategy and policy in large organizations. The effective media coverage of the Vietnam conflict obviously shaped public opinion in this country. Managers now can be linked to other managers anywhere in the world on a moment's notice.

○ *The economic explosion.* The changing nature of the work force and the increasing emphasis placed on quality of work life (QWL) are affecting employer-employee relationships. Employees have more choice about their work, and they can ask for greater shares of the rewards.

○ *The freedom explosion.* Since the 1960s, there has been a trend toward greater individual freedom and initiative. This trend has encouraged organizations to be less autocratic.[1]

To cope with these forces for change, personnel managers have developed strategies that emphasize management-initiated change, e.g., a series of special courses, taught by local university professors, which are designed to introduce management skills to new supervisors. Normally, the enterprise would require new supervisors to attend the courses as part of their career progression. The courses are usually held during working hours, and are often taught at the work place. Another example of management-initiated change, in a collaborative mode, is organization development (OD). More will be said about OD; however, first we will examine the role of the personnel manager in change efforts.

The conditions that are necessary to facilitate the change efforts of an organization include: "(1) maintenance of communication among subordinates, (2) top-level support and reassurance, (3) encouragement of legitimate and relevant participation, (4) reorganization of the reward and appraisal systems, and (5) development of appropriate personnel policies for such matters as layoff and separation."[2] Although the personnel department typically plays a major role in conditions (4) and (5), the progressive personnel department also functions as an internal change agent for the first three conditions by advising all organization members on their roles in the management of change. Further, if the organization is receiving guidance from an outside consultant, the personnel department typically is the primary contact point between the organization and the consultant.

Organization development (OD) is one of the fastest growing and most popular change strategies.[3] Although its boundaries are not entirely clear, OD is rapidly evolving into a definable field of the behavioral sciences. *Organization development* is defined as

". . . a long-range effort to improve an organization's problem-solving and renewal processes, particularly through a more effective and collaborative management of organization culture—with special emphasis on the culture of formal work teams—with the assistance of a change agent, or catalyst, and the use of the theory and technology of applied behavioral science, including action research.[4]

Two significant focal points of OD are the management of change organizationwide and the direction of human energy toward specific goals. Im-

---

[1] Robert A. Zawacki and D.D. Warrick, *Organization Development: Managing Change in the Public Sector* (Chicago: International Personnel Management Association, 1976), p. 2. This is a modification from Rensis Likert, *New Patterns of Management* (New York: McGraw-Hill, 1967), pp. 1–3, and Richard Beckhard, *Organization Development: Strategies and Models* (Reading, Mass.: Addison-Wesley, 1969), pp. 3–4.

[2] Wendell French, *The Personnel Management Process: Human Resources Administration,* 3rd ed. (Boston: Houghton Mifflin Co., 1973), p. 659.

[3] "EDP Leads Most Popular Management Techniques," *Administrative Management* (June 1973): pp. 26–29.

[4] Wendell French and Cecil H. Bell, Jr., *Organization Development: Behavioral Science Interventions for Organization Improvement* (Englewood Cliffs, N.J.: Prentice-Hall, 1973), p. 15.

plicit in the definition of OD is the primary value of human and nonexploitative treatment of people in organizations. Other values that relate to this include:

1. *Trust and openness.* An open and nonmanipulative sharing of data is required for effective problem solving.

2. *Leveling.* All team members should "tell it like it is!"

3. *Feedback.* Feedback is a communication skill for checking the accuracy of assumptions and data. Feedback must be shared in a helpful and nonaccusatory manner.

4. *Confronting conflict.* Conflict is a natural occurrence between people on work teams, and it should not be "swept under the rug."

5. *Risk taking.* The ability to take an unpopular stand on an important issue is important.[5]

The four cases in Part IX were chosen to emphasize both management-initiated change and change implemented organizationwide or teamwide through OD processes. The case "A Visit to a Power Laboratory" requires a few words of explanation about power laboratories.

Power laboratories are conducted at locations away from the company under the guidance of a qualified behavioral scientist. They normally last about one week and the participants are strangers; however, they have similar management experiences and normally occupy like positions of responsibility in various organizations. For example, a laboratory may be designed for presidents of large corporations. The objective of the laboratory is to create an environment where executives can experiment with the uses and results of power given various situations. Executives are encouraged to try different management styles; they receive feedback from the other laboratory participants. The feedback is descriptive of how they are doing and of the effects they are having—not threatening and judgmental about what they are as people. The feedback is specific with good and clear examples from the laboratory.

Thus, the incidents and cases in Part IX must be analyzed very carefully because of the turbulent environment in which personnel managers function. Further, personnel managers must also be sensitive to the need for and commitment to change in the organization. The best OD technology available is doomed to failure if it is implemented based on an improper diagnosis of the organization.

Continuing research regarding the effectiveness of the various personnel management processes is the mark of a progressive personnel department. Personnel research is concerned with the efficacy of past personnel practices, because this information is needed to make decisions on present and future personnel systems. Bernthal has suggested that "the extent to which an organi-

[5] Lyman K. Randall, "Common Questions and Tentative Answers Regarding Organization Development," *California Management Review*, Vol. 12 (Spring 1969): pp. 47–48.

zation can tolerate such impartial scrutiny and learn from it, may itself be a measure of the degree of professionalism of management in that organization."[6]

One survey of forty-four corporations indicated that the following topics were being researched by personnel departments: (1) 98 percent were investigating the joining-up process, (2) 75 percent were using attitude surveys, (3) 30 percent were researching management training and development programs, and (4) 16 percent were investigating organizational effectiveness.[7] The study merely indicates where personnel research dollars are being spent; it says nothing about the quality of the research.

Although personnel departments may not have the resources to conduct good research, periodicals and journals are excellent sources of personnel research results. We recognize that personnel managers cannot read all the journals; however, we recommend that they review two or three of the following journals each month and read the articles of interest. Some research-oriented journals are:

○ *Academy of Management Journal*

○ *Academy of Management Review*

○ *Administrative Science Quarterly*

○ *Human Organization*

○ *Human Relations*

○ *Industrial & Labor Relations Review*

○ *Industrial Relations*

○ *Journal of Applied Behavioral Science*

○ *Journal of Applied Psychology*

○ *Journal of Business Communications*

○ *Journal of Industrial Relations*

○ *Journal of Management Studies*

○ *Journal of Social Psychology*

○ *Journal of Social Issues*

○ *Management Science*

○ *Organizational Behavior & Human Performance*

○ *Personnel Psychology*

○ *Research Management*

○ *Sloan Management Review*

○ *Social Science Research*

---

[6] Wilmar F. Bernthal, "New Challenges Demand that 'WE' Change Roles," *Personnel Administration* (November-December 1968): p. 33

[7] William C. Byham, *The Uses of Personnel Research* (New York: AMA Research Study 91, 1968), p. 14.

Articles in applied journals normally are aimed at the practitioner and are written to discuss and summarize past, present, and future research and administrative applications:

- *Administrative Management*
- *Advanced Management Journal*
- *Business Horizons*
- *California Management Review*
- *Colorado Business Review*
- *Conference Board Record*
- *Fortune*
- *Harvard Business Review*
- *Human Behavior*
- *Human Resource Management*
- *Labor Law Journal*
- *Management Review*
- *Michigan Business Review*
- *Michigan State University Business Topics*
- *Monthly Labor Review*
- *Organizational Dynamics*
- *Personnel*
- *Personnel Administration*
- *The Personnel Administrator*
- *Personnel Journal*
- *Personnel Management*
- *Public Personnel Management*
- *Psychology Today*
- *Supervisory Management*
- *Training and Development Journal*

Previously we discussed the variables that contribute to the dynamic and uncertain environment in which the organization exists. This turbulent environment is further disturbed by such forces as legislative, union, and employee trends.

During the late 1960s and the early 1970s there has been a proliferation of federal laws and regulations that restrict personnel managers' options. Three of the most significant pieces of legislation are the Civil Rights Act of 1964 (EEOC), the Occupational Safety and Health Act of 1970 (OSHA), and the Employee Retirement Income Security Act of 1974 (ERISA).

There is evidence that there will be an increase in federal and state legislation through the 1970s and 1980s that will further constrain and restrict the options of personnel managers. For example, a noted behavioral scientist recently called for increased government intervention to change the quality of work life.[8] He proposed that government tax or fine organizations for such negative social outputs as high turnover, alcoholism, and drug addiction. Whether you agree or disagree with this proposal, the point is that we have seen a proliferation of federal and state legislation that apparently will be a trend through the 1980s.

Unions are making inroads into the public sector of our economy. By 1980, the public and services sectors are expected to employ over 35 percent of our labor force. As the number of unionized workers increases in the public sector, personnel managers will be less concerned with personnel cutbacks and more concerned with the total compensation package, the four-day workweek, and variable working hours. As compensation packages continue to grow erratically, personnel managers will assume an increasing advisory role to boards of directors and will make recommendations for change that are supportive of the organization's goals.

An increasing number of employees of American corporations refuse to transfer. One study[9] of 617 firms in 1975 indicated that in 42 percent of the companies surveyed some employees refused to move. This is an alarming increase over 1974. The primary reason is that, overall, employees are beginning to place quality of work life above considerations such as career progression. This pattern indicates that personnel managers must consider the West and Southwest when they advise top management on site locations.

A second employee trend is that while the population increased by a rate of 19 percent from 1966 to 1976, the labor force increased by a rate of 26 percent.[10] Furthermore, from 1966 through 1976 the male labor force increased 16.8 percent while the female labor force went up a drastic 42.3 percent.[11] The number of female job holders and job seekers increased by just about two million between 1975 and 1976. The reasons for this drastic shift in the composition of the labor force are: (1) government legislation and women's liberation efforts have resulted in more jobs for women, (2) most jobs today can be done by women as well as by men, (3) women are increasing their freedom from housework through labor-saving devices, and (4) the cost of living requires two or more workers in many households.[12] Personnel managers of the future will have difficulty in finding a "payroll spot" for everyone who wants to work. Furthermore, preventing conflict between the sexes will become increasingly important as the female percentage of the labor force continues to grow. If organizations

[8] Edward E. Lawler III, "Should the Quality of Work Life Be Legislated?" *The Personnel Administrator* (January 1976): 17–21.
[9] *The Wall Street Journal*, August 3, 1976, p. 1.
[10] *The Wall Street Journal*, September 20, 1976, p. 1.
[11] Ibid.
[12] Ibid.

and personnel managers cannot respond to this need, further federal legislation may be forthcoming.

Present trends indicate that the most important personnel functions of the future will be organization development, human resources planning (including retirement), organizational planning, and the total compensation package. One director of personnel even predicts that the title of the position in the 1980s will be "Director of Human Resource Planning."[13] Clearly, personnel management has gone through a period of transition in the 1960s and early 1970s. Although the personnel officer is now recognized as a top advisor to management, some tentative new roles for the 1980s will be internal consultant and change agent. One noted author[14] recently suggested that personnel directors are the new corporate heroes, because corporations have discovered that an alert personnel director is in a unique position to make a major contribution to the corporation's productivity and profits through effective human resource planning. The progressive personnel manager must continue to diagnose the environment; to develop roles to meet the needs of the organization, the organization's members, and society; and to reflect changes in managerial philosophies and styles.

SUGGESTED READINGS

American Society for Personnel Administration. "Some Questions and Answers about the ASPA Accreditation Programs." Berea, Ohio: ASPA Accreditation Institute.

Beckhard, Richard. *Organization Development: Strategies and Models.* Reading, Mass.: Addison-Wesley Publishing Company, 1969.

Bennis, Warren G. *Organization Development: Its Nature, Origins, and Prospects.* Reading, Mass.: Addison-Wesley Publishing Company, 1969.

Blake, Robert R., and Jane S. Mouton. *Consultation.* Reading, Mass.: Addison-Wesley Publishing Company, 1976.

Boyer, Robert K., and Campbell Crockett. "Organizational Development in Higher Education: Introduction." *Journal of Higher Education,* Vol. 44 (1973): 339–351.

Evans, Martin G. "Failures in OD Programs—What Went Wrong." *Business Horizons,* Vol. 17 (April 1974): 18–22.

Famularo, Joseph J., ed. *Handbook of Modern Personnel Administration.* New York: McGraw-Hill Book Company, 1972.

Fordyce, Jack K., and Raymond Weil. *Managing with People.* Reading, Mass.: Addison-Wesley Publishing Company, 1971.

---

[13] Gary C. Foss, "Perspective on Changing Profession," *IPMA News* (September 1976): 5.
[14] Herbert E. Meyer, "Personnel Directors Are the New Corporate Heroes," *Fortune* (February 1976): 84–88, 140.

French, Wendell L. "Organization Development Objectives, Assumptions and Strategies." *California Management Review*, Vol. 12 (Winter 1969): 23–24.

———, and Cecil H. Bell, Jr. *Organization Development: Behavioral Science Interventions for Organization Improvement*. Englewood Cliffs, N.J.: Prentice-Hall, Inc., 1973.

———, ———, and Robert A. Zawacki. *Organization Development: Theory, Practice and Research*. Dallas: Business Publications, Inc., in press.

Friedlander, Frank. "Organization Development." *Annual Review of Psychology*, Vol. 25 (1974): 313–341.

Giblin, Edward J. "Organization Development: Public Sector Theory and Practice." *Public Personnel Management*, Vol. 5 (1976): 108–119.

Journal of Contemporary Business, Vol. 1 (Summer 1972): 1–73.

Lawler, Edward E., III. "Should the Quality of Work Life Be Legislated?" *The Personnel Administrator* (January 1976): 17–21.

Lundberg, Craig C. "Organization Change in the Third Sector." *Public Administration Review*, Vol. 35 (September 1975): 472–477.

Margulies, Newton. "Organization Development in a University Setting: Some Problems of Initiating Change." *Educational Technology*, Vol. 12 (1972): 48–52.

Meyer, Herbert E. "Personnel Directors Are the New Corporate Heroes." *Fortune* (February 1976): 84–88, 140.

Somers, Gerald G., ed. *The Next Twenty-Five Years of Industrial Relations*. Madison, Wis.: Industrial Relations Research Association, 1973.

Walton, Richard E., and Donald P. Warwick. "The Ethics of Organization Development." *Journal of Applied Behavioral Science*, Vol. 9 (1973): 681–698.

Warrick, D.D. "Applying OD to the Public Sector." *Public Personnel Management*, Vol. 5 (1976): 186–190.

———, and Robert A. Zawacki. "The State of the Art of Organization Development Courses in Schools of Business Curriculums." *Training and Development Journal*, Vol. 31 (August 1977): 31–35.

White, Sam E., and Terence R. Mitchell. "Organization Development: A Review of Research Content and Research Design." *The Academy of Management Review*, Vol. 1 (1976): 57–73.

Yoder, Dale, and Herbert G. Heneman, Jr. *Planning and Auditing PAIR*. Handbook of Personnel and Industrial Relations, Vol. IV. Washington, D.C.: The Bureau of National Affairs, 1976.

Zawacki, Robert A., and D.D. Warrick. *Organization Development: Managing Change in the Public Sector*. Chicago: IPMA, 1976.

55
A VISIT TO A POWER
LABORATORY

ROBERT A. ZAWACKI AND D.D. WARRICK

Dr. Mildred A. Barter, head of the psychology department at a leading western university, attended an NTL Institute for Applied Behavioral Sciences (power laboratory) during the summer of 1974. Before attending the conference, Dr. Barter was known at the university as a politically aware person who was a hard driver, used coercive power, and almost always obtained her goal. She exhibited an autocratic leadership style, although she was known to be flexible if it would help her obtain an objective. Through the years, she had developed a power base that was feared and respected by other full professors and department heads.

Although behavioral science courses such as organizational development and organizational behavior were taught by faculty in her department, she did not subscribe to the value systems of those disciplines. Further, she openly told the other professors that her department was teaching the courses because it permitted her to have authorization and funding for more full-time faculty.

One of the professors within the department occasionally functioned as an external OD change agent to various private business organizations. That professor had received a national grant to accomplish research on an ongoing OD project and at the end of the fiscal year had monies remaining that could be used for education of selected OD practitioners.

The change agent, concerned about the climate of the psychology department, suggested to Dr. Barter that she attend a power laboratory in Aspen, Colorado. The change agent gave as his overt reason the fact that OD courses were within her academic department and that it might help her power position in faculty meetings if she were more familiar with OD values, objectives, and strategies. He also stressed that Aspen was a nice location to spend an expenses-paid summer. The change agent's hidden agenda was to expose Dr. Barter to the values of OD and, hopefully, to lead her to re-examine her use of power.

The idea appealed to Dr. Barter. She told the change agent to complete the necessary registration forms and brief her on the details of the workshop. As the date for the workshop drew near, she appeared to be slightly threatened by the workshop, uncertain as to the objectives of the workshop, but still committed to

Reprinted by permission of the International Personnel Management Association, 1313 East 60th Street, Chicago, Illinois 60637.

attending. During June, she departed for Aspen with almost everyone in the department calculating just what her leadership style would be like when she returned.

After attending the workshop and taking a short vacation, Dr. Barter returned during August and immediately called a meeting of all full and associate professors. She explained that she had learned at the workshop that power relationships can be "win-win" and don't always have to be "win-lose" as she assumed previously. Although she viewed her past style as effective, she now recognized that she had needlessly hurt other department heads with her power tactics and was committed to changing her leadership style. She asked for comments from the professors present; however, they appeared uncertain as to her real motivation and very guarded in their responses.

She excused the professors from the meeting; but, as they were leaving, she asked the change agent who recommended the workshop to remain behind for a few minutes. She thanked him for arranging for her to attend the power laboratory. Further, she told him she was convinced that a change in climate was long overdue in the department. She instructed the change agent to gather data on the organization and be prepared to discuss the organization's profile with her in about one week. When the change agent asked for clarification on the use of the data, Dr. Barter replied, "You gather the data and then I will function as my own internal change agent—I know what I want in the way of change!"

QUESTIONS AND REQUIREMENTS

1. Assuming that you are the change agent, how would you respond to Dr. Barter's ending statement?

2. What are some of the advantages and disadvantages of internal change agents?

3. How do you assess Dr. Barter's new value system?

4. Assume that Dr. Barter came to you as an external change agent and asked for help. How would you handle the interview and what would you recommend?

5. What meaning would you attach to the fact that the other professors were guarded in their responses to Dr. Barter's new style?

6. Analyze the faculty change agent's behavior of sending Dr. Barter to an NTL laboratory with a hidden agenda.

7. What do you think the future holds for Dr. Barter and the psychology department?

56
CONFLICT MANAGEMENT

JAMES C. CONANT

Area Manager John H. was surprised and astounded by the conversation he had just heard—if you could call it a conversation! He could hardly believe that two of his key managers could be involved in such a bitter feud. One accused the other of trying to undermine his department by stealing his best people and the other accused in rebuttal that the other manager was simply finding excuses for his bad management. There had been accusation and counteraccusation followed by hot denials and bitter recrimination. He finally decided there was nothing to be gained by further outbursts and sent both men back to their departments. This, he hoped, would give them a cooling off period and himself a chance to try and sort it all out.

It wasn't unusual for Technical Development and Product Engineering to have these differences, but they rarely took on such a heated aspect. John's thoughts turned to Ralph, Manager of Technical Development. He had come highly recommended by the President of another Division. He had been very successful in development work and seemed well suited to this assignment. In his six months on the job he had reorganized several sections and initiated new projects. It wasn't spectacular but it appeared competent from all John could see. There had been a few gripes that he was too aloof and reserved, but that was natural in view of the man he had replaced. It always took a little time for these management transitions to settle down. It appeared Ralph was aware of his problem since he had inserted a new manager under him (Frank) who was effective in personal relationships. It was too early to tell how that was working out but it seemed a wise move.

John knew there were problems, however. He had talked with Personnel after the recent Opinion Survey and learned the morale in Ralph's group was down from its usual mark. There seemed to be more employee apathy, more lateness and absences, and more transfer requests. This latter was the most surprising since there were few such requests usually. It was odd to find morale at such a low ebb since the group was well knit and had strong group identity. Personnel had talked informally with a few of the people and their view was (1) the work load was too low and they didn't feel meaningfully utilized and (2) they felt their present management was too distant and reserved.

It was difficult to put these in perspective. From Ralph's viewpoint the low work load was directly traceable to the "game" George was playing. He contended one of George's people would request a "sizing" for a particular job. His people would carefully give cost, technology and schedule estimates, but then nothing happened. One of his people would call over to find out where the work requisition was and would be told the job had been cancelled by George. His manager would be offered a much smaller job—provided they transferred the people key to the former job request—"to help keep your people busy." When this finally came to Ralph's attention he "hit the roof" and this is what led to the recent confrontation. George's views varied greatly, hence the hot argument.

George had been in the department longer than Ralph. He was known as an effective, "hard-nosed" manager who got the job done. He was ambitious and had grown rather rapidly over the last two years. He was adaptable as shown by the fact that he had made the transition from Chemistry to Product Engineering. The Product Engineering Department had a poor reputation prior to George's moving over and he had been instrumental in changing its image to a very positive one. As a result the Department had grown considerably under George. All in all it was a good record.

George contended Ralph was an inefficient manager, with too much fat in his organization, who was unwilling to cut back to a reasonable level. As a result Ralph was pricing himself out of the business. He had to cancel jobs because the costs were prohibitive. George laid some of the blame on the previous manager, Henry, claiming it was Henry's doing that caused the Lab to reach the present ridiculous size. George felt Ralph should reevaluate his situation and curtail the department size and become competitive again. If the cost problem had merit as an argument it could go back to Henry. There was nothing to indicate Ralph's costs were out of line with past history.

George freely admitted to wanting several of Ralph's people. He felt they would be better placed and better utilized in his area, but he hotly denied he had "played any games" to get them. The pressure of the new releases had caused a backlog in his department and he could use expert help.

John wondered why George steadfastly refused to use the Technology group. He was slipping schedules and the overtime costs would eventually overtake the claimed excessive costs of Ralph's group. He wasn't in any serious trouble as yet and might be gambling he could pull his chestnuts out by the transfer of a few key people. If this was his gamble he might be trying to force Ralph's hand.

John decided he had better talk to Henry in order to clarify this matter further. After that was concluded he sorted out the following impressions. Henry had no love for Ralph. He felt it was still his "shop" and Ralph was doing a poor job of taking over. On the other hand Henry supported Ralph's contentions about George. He indicated he had similar problems in the past and had called him on it a number of times. He flatly denied that the group was too large and indicated it would function well if George didn't feel he had to have the managership of all operations necessary to his function. The conversation left John more puzzled than edified.

Well, there it was. All made good points. If George is correct an overhaul is in order and Ralph should get his costs in line. If Ralph is right George must be stopped from disrupting the department and risking full project success for the sake of his own gain. In all probability both have valid points and the problem will be how to respond appropriately to both managers.

RALPH'S VIEWPOINT

Ralph was transferred into this division after several successful projects in Engineering Development. He came highly recommended by the President of another Division, under whom he had worked, and was deemed a candidate for higher management in the near future.

There was little doubt about his technical competence. He was informed and innovative. He preferred small groups to large, complex ones, and this was a partial reason for giving him this assignment. Higher growth would depend on his ability to handle larger groups. For this reason the job had been enlarged to encompass additional functions. This meant Ralph had a substantially larger group to manage than his precedessor.

Although Ralph never commented on his reaction to this change in operations for him, he appeared a little overwhelmed by it. He spent considerable time in his office planning and integrating the various functions. He only rarely met with the Lab people and had staff meetings on an irregular basis. It must be emphasized he had only been in the job about six months and still was getting his feet on the ground.

He had never been much of a delegator. Some of this was by temperament and some from the nature of the reward structure. He had been heard to comment: "I do my business in the halls. When I run into the Division President and he asks about my project I can get away with maybe one 'I don't know' and after that I'm known as an 'I don't know guy.'" The result was a tendency to know details that usually are reserved for subordinates. The new job stretched him to the point that he had greater difficulty doing this, but it may account for the inordinate amount of time he spent in his office.

In his approach to others he was direct and confronting. People knew where they stood, and in general their comments indicated they liked this style of managing. He was aware he interacted somewhat stiffly with others and this had occasioned the insertion of Frank at the Lab level. In addition he was planning to change some of the procedures Henry had instituted, and he felt Henry would be an obstacle to these plans. Frank would be a major factor in assuring that the new procedures went as smoothly as possible.

His relationship to Henry was cordial but distant. He had no particular dislike for Henry, but felt the group could be more effectively organized. He was in the process of developing these plans when the problem broke.

His relationship with John, the Director, was essentially ok as far as one could tell. On the whole his "clout" with John was undeveloped, as was his impact on his peers. He seemed to be regarded as an unknown quantity—perhaps something of a threat in view of his reputation.

He was disappointed with the way the meeting turned out. He didn't like shouting matches but he wasn't going to stand by and have George put him or his Lab group down. He was sure they were effective and as soon as he completed some of the new project planning he knew their work load would be more than adequate. He was familiar with people trying the kind of thing George was doing and the only way to avert it was through direct confrontation. He only wished he could better predict John's reaction.

HENRY'S VIEWPOINT

Henry was an "old timer" and had been the Lab's Manager for many years. He was affable and outgoing, walking the shop regularly and virtually on a first name basis with everyone in the Lab. It had been his assignment to create and staff the Lab, and over the several years he managed it he exercised care in the selection and placement of the staff. It had been generally conceded the Lab was staffed with topnotch people.

The Lab group had strong ties with one another. There were a few who had turned down promotions in order to remain with the group. That it was not all one big happy family was indicated by a few dissidents who felt they had been passed over for promotion. On the whole, however, they worked well together and enjoyed a favorable reputation by all concerned.

As Henry had indicated George had tried to lure some of his better talent away during the recent past. Henry learned of these rather quickly because of his close relationships to the group and effectively aborted each of these. George had finally given up on this and had gone to outside recruiting for the talent he wanted. This meant a slower indoctrination process for him and slowed down his growth potential. It was Henry who first became aware that George was up to his "old tricks."

He probably should have gone to Ralph with the information about George but he felt at odds with Ralph's methods. He resented the Staff role into which he had been put, even though medical advice was the basis for the move. He sensed that Ralph was planning changes and he had not been consulted. When Frank was brought in he felt even more resentful. He regarded his assignment as a "make work" one and did not feel meaningfully utilized. He still felt a strong proprietary interest in the Lab group and would take whatever measures he could to prevent its disruption.

Given a choice of choosing between Ralph or George he would choose Ralph, and eventually this choice had to be made. In his meeting with John he had been fully candid regarding George's tactics and hoped this once John would put a stop to them. He did it more to insure the Lab remaining intact than because of Ralph. He certainly didn't want to see the Lab destroyed after all the years he'd spent building it to its present state.

GEORGE'S VIEWPOINT

George was dynamic, energetic and technically proficient. He had taken over the Product Engineering group when it was regarded with disfavor and had steadily built it into its present respectable state. He had ambition and sought to enlarge his sphere of influence whenever possible. He viewed the situation in this way. "I like this environment. It is highly fluid and I have a lot of freedom to do things the way I believe they should be done. I get reprimanded when I make a mistake—and that's only fair as far as I'm concerned. My attitude is to take over and operate any group I can. If I'm successful it will soon come under my jurisdiction. I keep pushing until I'm told to stop by someone who can make it stick."

This had been George's method of operation as long as he had been a manager. It had paid off handsomely for him, and from the Company's standpoint they had benefited too. His group was well managed, competently staffed, and morale was at least as good as one could find in the Division. His people were loyal to him and respected his ability. He had considerable "clout" because of his past success and had more than the usual influence with the Director.

He had no personal antipathy for Ralph. He was anxious to secure some of the key Lab people and honestly believed they would be more effective in his organization. He felt this would be better for the Company and would provide the people with greater opportunities for growth. There was some accuracy to the latter, but the former was a matter of opinion.

As he regarded the Lab group he felt they were overstaffed and underutilized. He didn't think Ralph was effective in moving to reorganize the department and felt the people were fair game for his managerial approach.

(It was interesting to this observer that direct methods were never utilized. The ground rules permitted making offers to people in other departments, through promotions, raises, etc. Why George never did was unclear.)

George felt he was an effective manager, better than his peers (possibly including the Director). He felt Ralph was running a country club and that it needed effective management. If possible he wanted to absorb the Lab into his operation, but that would require a restructuring of the organization. Since the Lab served many groups in addition to his, his functions would have to be broadened, an unlikely move at this time.

He was taking a calculated risk in not using the Lab for some of his immediate jobs because he might well get into a last minute "crunch" and, failing to meet schedule, lose some of the ground he had gained. On the other hand if he could secure some key people, he could come in on schedule and be in a position to take over other Lab functions that would arise later. In the meantime it would appear as if the Lab was not as necessary because of the low work load. He, at this time, was the major user of the Lab—although this was not always the case. This depended on the development cycle, which was at a low ebb for other groups, but would probably pick up fairly soon.

All in all George was satisfied with his progress and felt he had a good chance at the Director's job when John was promoted. He wasn't happy about this current situation with Ralph, but felt he could weather it and perhaps make Ralph appear foolish or somewhat less competent. It would be a good time for a put down, his being new and all. The last meeting with John left him uncertain as to where each stood. He was sure he had not heard the last of the situation.

QUESTIONS AND REQUIREMENTS

1. If you were in John's role, how would you proceed?

2. Assume that you are the company's personnel director and Ralph came to you to discuss George's "head hunting." How would you advise him?

3. What inferences can you draw about the organization's climate? About management styles?

57
PLASTICS INTERNATIONAL LTD. (A)

WENDELL L. FRENCH

THE ATTITUDE SURVEY CONCEPT IS INTRODUCED

PERSONS CENTRAL TO THE CASE

- Alton Barrow—Personnel Director, P.I.L.
- William (Bill) Bauer—E.C.L. Labor Relations Director
- Alan (Al) Brooke—Central Labor Relations
- Dr. Harold (Hal) Gibson—American behavioral science consultant
- Dr. Dietrich Hallbach—Deputy Chairman of P.I.L.
- Dr. Oliver Hammond—P.I.L. Training Officer
- Leland Jackson—Central Labor Relations
- Dr. Charles (Chuck) Morris—American behavioral science consultant
- Dr. Wolfgang Mueller—Production Director, P.I.L.
- Eric Olson—Central Labor Relations
- Dr. Paul Shelley—Chairman, P.I.L.
- Dr. Scott Starbrock—Director of R & D, P.I.L.
- Wayne St. George—Central Labor Relations
- Dr. Morton Wiesler—Manager of Textile Development, P.I.L. (Cologne)
- Dr. Larry Wilson—Manager of Research, P.I.L. (Cologne)

Euro-Chemicals Ltd. (E.C.L.) employs some 120,000 employees in ten major divisions marketing throughout Europe. In addition there are subsidiaries in all major foreign countries. Headquarters are in Bonn, Germany. There is a good deal of mobility within the company among the management group, and significant numbers of executives are from Sweden, England, France, and Switzerland, as well as from Germany.

Plastics International Ltd. (P.I.L.) is a wholly owned division of E.C.L. The division took its present form approximately six years ago when E.C.L. decided to integrate their existing first-stage conversion plant vertically by acquiring a large company that was operating in the plastics market. As a result of the merger the research and development activities were located at two sites, Bonn and Cologne.

There were the normal problems associated with any merger. These had been coped with well—the division was expanding and, in spite of the vagaries of the plastics market, was very profitable.

Dr. Dietrich Hallbach, Deputy Chairman of P.I.L., had worked for some time with a partially owned subsidiary in the United States and had been impressed with the apparent usefulness of an attitude survey which had been used there. He talked over the idea with Alton Barrow, Personnel Director, on his return and suggested that P.I.L. might get good value from such an initiative. Alton Barrow was impressed with the report, but was aware that a number of attitudes surveys had already been "carried out in various parts of E.C.L." and, as he said, "were fascinating documents that always ended up in the bottom right-hand drawer." He wanted to be sure that the next survey would be of practical use and would form a useful pattern for the future.

Nevertheless, he talked the problem over with William (Bill) Bauer, Labor Relations Director of E.C.L. He discovered that Bauer was himself interested in the possibilities of a new form of attitude survey which an outside consultant had tried in another company. The basis of this survey was to use the questionnaire only for the purpose of focusing attention on problems and to give all the emphasis to the group meetings that would follow in order to solve the problems.

Alton Barrow saw the theoretical value of such an approach but was cautious at the prospect of "letting a whole crowd of long-haired fancy boys stop all work while they tested their latest gimmick at our expense." However, after a good deal of discussion about who would pay for the consultant, Barrow felt that it was in the division's interest to proceed, and Bauer agreed to divert all possible resources from the center to assist.

The American consultant and behavioral scientist Dr. Harold (Hal) Gibson was visiting the head office during the month of March. Although time was short Bill Bauer felt that it should be possible to achieve success, at least with a limited pilot scheme, provided adequate back-up resources were made available to Hal Gibson. He therefore wrote briefly to Hal explaining the problem and stating in broad terms what he expected from him on his arrival in Bonn.

Dr. Gibson arrived from the States knowing little about what P.I.L. might want. During a meeting at P.I.L. headquarters with Alton Barrow, it was decided to explore the possible use of the attitude questionnaire brought over from the United States by Dr. Hallbach, but to modify it based on divisional needs. (Dr. Gibson had had extensive experience in the design and use of attitude surveys, but this seemed to be reasonably well designed and had already had some acceptance in the division.)

At a subsequent meeting attended by fourteen people, including Dietrich Hallbach, Alton Barrow, two department managers and several assistant managers, possible use of the questionnaire was discussed. It developed that the assistant managers of the Textile Development Departments and the Research Departments were interested in participating in the project (the managers of those departments could not attend the meeting), but the P.I.L. Production

Director, Wolfgang Mueller, withdrew from this meeting, leaving his assistant who commented "This is hard to oppose. It sounds like we are being unfashionable."

Much of the time and emphasis during those early meetings was inevitably spent on the form the questionnaire should take. Subsequently, Hal Gibson was emphatic that the necessity for workshops where action would be planned had twice been stressed. However, as will be seen, events suggested that the long process of turning replies to a questionnaire into a practical change program with action as the main criterion was not fully appreciated.

PLASTICS INTERNATIONAL LTD.
(B)

THE QUESTIONNAIRE IS ADMINISTERED

A week later, after checking out computer capability, Dr. Gibson took copies of the questionnaire, with items categorized under major subject headings, to a meeting of the original group. This group, which by now did not include representatives from Production, but continued to include the assistant managers of the two Research Departments and the two Textile Development Departments, made some revisions and additions. A small subcommittee met further that evening to finalize the revision.

Very shortly thereafter, all nine hundred employees of the four departments were assembled, approximately one hundred at a time, and requested to fill out the questionnaire. All employees participated, up to and including section heads. There were four such sessions at Cologne and five at Bonn. The employees were informed of the nature and purpose of the project, and told, "This is voluntary; you may hand it in blank, if you wish." Two questionnaires were used. The "white" version was filled out by everyone, including section heads, and was to be used for total departmental analysis. The "blue" version, much shorter, was filled out by everyone except section heads and was aimed at section analysis. (See Figure 1 for the questionnaire items and total sample responses pertaining to "Organizational Climate." Other parts of the questionnaire were "Pay and Benefits," "Relations with Other Units," "Communications," "Supervisor/Employee Relations," "Performance Counseling," "My Job," "Pressure of Work," "Management by Objectives," "Opportunities for Personnel Growth and Advancement," and "Training.")

As a next step, in a memorandum to the Central Labor Relations, Dr. Gibson outlined suggested steps in utilizing the data. (See Figure 2.)

Figure 2   P.I.L. Research and Textile Development Departments

Feedback and Use of Opinion Survey Results

The usefulness of the opinion survey within the Research and Textile Development Departments of P.I.L. hinges entirely on the feedback process in which results are discussed, their implications explored, and needed actions agreed upon and later carried out. The survey is justified only as it provides an intervention for change and improvement.

Figure 1 Questionnaire items and sample responses on organizational climate

| Question no. | | Organizational climate | * | Overall mean | Overall distribution % | | | | |
Blue	White				SA (1)	A (2)	U (3)	D (4)	SD (5)**
39	99.	There is good cooperation and teamwork in my work group.	F	2.3	20	55	9	12	4
	90.	Employee safety is adequate in my department.	F	2.5	8	61	12	16	4
25	30.	Management side-steps or evades things which bother people on the job.	U	2.7	13	32	27	24	4
	71.	I think some practical steps for improvement may come out of filling in this questionnaire.	F	2.5	15	42	28	11	4
	40.	An excessive number of senior staff leave our department.	U	3.2	8	22	23	37	10
	86.	Staff transfers in my department are excessive.	U	3.4	5	13	23	49	10
5	8.	P.I.L. is a friendly place to work.	F	1.9	22	68	6	4	0
	58.	P.I.L. management are more concerned with productivity than people.	U	2.7	16	32	24	25	3
34	92.	The achievements of our group are not recognized at senior levels of management.	U	3.0	9	23	30	34	4
	91.	If I "stick my neck out," I am usually unpopular with management.	U	2.8	10	31	29	28	2
	9.	You "know where you stand" in P.I.L.	F	3.0	5	32	30	25	8
6	17.	We do not get the kind of backing we need from higher levels of management.	U	2.8	9	32	30	27	2
	31.	I feel I am considered to be a part of management.		3.7	2	17	17	39	25
	41.	Supervisors do not get the help they need to solve day-to-day problems.	U	3.2	4	16	40	34	5
	7.	The quality of food in the canteen is satisfactory.	F	2.8	5	48	14	26	7
	18.	P.I.L. is not yet working satisfactorily as a single company.	U	2.8	14	29	27	26	4
	19.	The external social events arranged for our department are not adequate.	U	3.0	11	27	20	35	7

* F is used to indicate that agreement is a favorable response. U is used to indicate that agreement is an unfavorable response.

** Scores of 1, 2, 3, 4, and 5 were assigned to the responses SA, A, U, D, and SD, respectively.

Now that the results of the survey questionnaires have been tabulated and made available, it is clear that there are important problems to be discussed at several levels throughout the two departments at Bonn and Cologne, and with top management. A plan for the feedback process which will make best use of the survey results is needed and this memorandum outlines my thoughts in chronological sequence.

1. 27th March   *First Feedback and Planning Meeting.* This meeting at Bonn attended by Directors, Department Managers and Assistant Managers from the two departments has as its purposes:
i) to examine a small sample of survey results and the problems they reveal.

ii) to discuss and agree upon plans and ground rules for subsequent feedback sessions of various kinds, and resources needed.

2. mid-April–May   *Preparation of Feedback Sessions.*
i) Further study, preparation, and organization of survey data for subsequent feedback sessions (Hammond, Jackson).

ii) Establish planning work-group for four feedback sessions (workshops) within Research and T.D.D. at Bonn and Cologne, and design these meetings (combined P.I.L., Central Labor Relations exercise).

3. mid-May   *Summary Booklets.* Publication and distribution of summary booklets on survey results by Research and Textile Development Departments.

4. mid-May–June   *Departmental Feedback Workshops.* Four working conferences, or workshops, are proposed for Assistant Managers and Section Heads (leaders) of the two departments at Bonn and Cologne (about 15 at each workshop). These meetings should be a minimum of three days each and should be conducted with the help of internal P.I.L. consultants and trainers (e.g., Training Section, Central Office Liaison Officers, etc.). The purpose of these workshops would be:
i) to review the survey results and select priority problems which could be dealt with at departmental, group, or section level;

ii) to begin to develop tentative action plans for solution of several problems at department level;

iii) to prepare Section Heads for conducting their own feedback sessions and to develop action plans with their section staff.

5. June–July   *Sectional Feedback Sessions.* Each of the 50 plus Section Heads or leaders should work through with his section the Blue Questionnaire material for his section on his own schedule during this period. He should have help available if desired. The purposes of these sessions are:
i) to discuss the section's views, to select problems for working through;

ii) to prepare a sectional plan-of-action steps which can be reported upward to Assistant Managers and senior management, and which represent reasonable commitment by Section Head and his section.

6. July–August   *Group and Departmental Follow-up Discussion.* There should be several follow-up meetings of Assistant Managers and Section Heads.
i) To review the action proposals by Section Heads and to integrate them where they involve group or departmental actions.

ii) To review the feedback process and determine what further steps might be needed to use the survey data fully as an intervention for improvement.

iii) To learn what training or other needs have arisen from the development of sectional action plans.

iv) To prepare departmental/location reports to top management on actions initiated and progress made.

General Comments

1. As shown on the previous page, I am proposing a feedback sequence starting at the top of the organization and filtering down with some preparation of Assistant Managers and Section Heads in the process, then up again with departmental plans for action made up of the Sectional Action Plan. I do not believe there are shortcuts to this sequence if participants at each level are to be personally involved and committed to their own actions for improvement.

2. A good deal of time and careful planning of these feedback sessions is required, and I stress the importance of using all available resources from within P.I.L. and the Bonn office to ensure that these sessions are learning experiences, to demonstrate problem-solving techniques and to assist in developing action plans at several levels. The Section Head, in particular, often will be "on the spot," and need both the training during the first workshops and a supportive environment by top management.

3. Because of the interest of top management in having improvements, there will be pressure on lower levels to act. This is not unreasonable. However, top management itself may have to take some action, and at all costs a punitive attitude by superiors to subordinates must be avoided.

4. Since this kind of survey with feedback is relatively new in P.I.L. and in the company generally, it represents a pilot effort for the whole organization. P.I.L. has the opportunity to show how survey data can be used as an intervention strategy for improvements in operations and productivity. I advise making every effort to ensure that this is successful, or subsequent surveys will not be very effective.

5. I am writing a separate memorandum on the additional analysis of the survey data to help explore more fully the uses to which it can be put.

Prof. Harold Gibson
School of Management
State University

PLASTICS INTERNATIONAL
LTD. (C)

SOME CRUNCHES

After some preliminary computer runs were available, Dr. Gibson developed a partial report (see Figure 3) in order to give some brief feedback to the original planning group. In addition, certain other management personnel met with the group, including Dr. Larry Wilson, Manager of Research at Bonn. Also attending was Leland Jackson, who had been involved from the beginning and had been appointed by Bill Bauer to coordinate the project and to act as liaison between the consultants and the various departments of P.I.L. who were using the questionnaire. Jackson also had been assigned the task of coordinating any workshops which might grow out of the questionnaire project.

Meanwhile, Dr. Hal Gibson, Bill Bauer, and Eric Johnson, the Assistant Labor Relations Director, conferred about who might handle any feedback sessions or workshops which might develop. Dr. Gibson had commitments in Asia and the U.S., and needed to leave after his one-month stay. At this time the name of Dr. Charles ("Chuck") Morris was mentioned and agreed upon. Dr. Morris already had been doing some work as a behavioral science consultant for the Central Labor Relations Department, was currently traveling in Europe and the Middle East, and was about to return.

Simultaneously, Leland Jackson had written a letter to Dietrich Hallbach, partially in an attempt to clarify the issue of the three-day workshops, but the letter was never answered. The matter then implicitly rested with the department heads at P.I.L. (Leland Jackson's letter is shown in Figure 4.)

As the next step, Leland Jackson, Dr. Morris, who had just returned from the Middle East, and Wayne St. George met to review the history of the project and to discuss the feasibility of meeting with each of the four department managers involved. (Dr. Gibson had left Germany just prior to Dr. Morris' return.) It became quite clear that Bill Bauer was very committed to the notion of three-day workshops, and the three-man team all felt a strong urgency to successfully "sell" the department managers on such meetings. Some of the details of the potential workshops were then discussed, including the distribution and format of the questionnaire data. For example, Dr. Morris felt strongly that section head answers to the questions be passed out in each department and be made available to the appropriate departments in the form of "% Strongly Agree," etc.

Figure 3   P.I.L. summary of my job (white questionnaire) for Research Department ($n = 549$)

		Agree (%)	U (%)	Disagree (%)	
70. Overall, I am well satisfied with my present job.	(F)	57	18	25	(U)
52. My present job is one in which I can continually learn.	(F)	81	3	16	(U)
47. My work is interesting.	(F)	89	5	6	(U)
53. Too many people give me instructions.	(U)	13	6	81	(F)
25. I usually know whether I am doing well or badly on my job.	(F)	77	9	14	(U)
14. I feel I am often unable to use my full capabilities in the performance of my job.	(U)	59	10	31	(F)
67. I often feel that I have achieved something really worthwhile in my job.	(F)	62	14	24	(U)
68. I would put more effort into my work if other things were put right.	(U)	44	17	39	(F)
73. My work is often held up by the customs and practices of the company.	(U)	42	19	39	(F)
96. My job provides sufficient opportunities for my efforts to be recognized by others.	(F)	53	16	31	(U)
46. I do not have enough say in deciding how my job is to be carried out.	(U)	29	8	63	(F)
37. It is quite possible for me to introduce new (untried) ideas on my job.	(F)	68	10	22	(U)
63. Within my department I do not get sufficient facilities and equipment to perform my job adequately.	(U)	30	10	60	(F)
95. I am frequently expected to perform tasks in my job which I consider unimportant or unnecessary.	(U)	33	10	57	(F)
15. If I had a chance to get a different job outside my department that paid as well as my present one, I would take it.	(U)	22	30	48	(F)
36. I often feel that my job is one that can be dropped.	(U)	19	9	72	(F)

The matter was resolved at a later planning meeting with the support of Alan Brooke who formed the consulting team.

Leland Jackson then arranged for half-day meetings with the managers and assistant managers of the four departments to discuss the proposed sessions, with one day to be spent at Bonn and one at Cologne. The first meeting took place in Dr. Larry Wilson's office at Bonn. In attendance were Dr. Wilson, his four assistant managers (each in charge of several section heads), Leland

Figure 4   Letter clarifying the three-day workshops

From: Leland Jackson
        Central Labor Relations Department
To: Dr. Dietrich Hallbach
        P.I.L.
        Bonn

Our Ref. LJ/RHM
31st March, 1969.

Following the meeting last Thursday and a further discussion I have had with Dr. Harold Gibson before he left the country, I thought it would be helpful for you to have a revised programme in addition to his paper on the Feedback and Use of the Opinion Survey Results which you already have.

1. *Performance Ranking and Rating of Sections by Assistant Managers and Above.*
During the week after Easter I shall be sending to Dr. Oliver Hammond for distribution to the departments concerned their Ranking and Rating of Sections and a synopsis of the factors taken into consideration when Assistant Managers and above were rating their sections' performance of High and Low.

2. *Results of Opinion Survey.*
   a. Towards the end of the week after Easter a condensed summary of the results of this opinion survey will be available to Assistant Managers and above. Dr. Hammond and I will be discussing the layout of this summary here tomorrow. Our objective will be to display the information in such a way that Managers can focus down on problem areas as quickly and easily as possible.
   b. Dr. Hammond and I also will be discussing the layout of Department Results for the leaflet which will be distributed to those who filled in the questionnaire. We shall be aiming to have this available for the printers during the week after Easter.

3. *Feedback Workshops.*
We shall be asking Dr. Hammond to arrange during the week beginning the 14th April with the Department Managers at Bonn and Cologne a meeting of about two hours (i.e., a morning with Research Department Bonn and an afternoon with T.D.D. Bonn or vice versa with a similar programme at Cologne) in order to discuss the design of the four three-day workshops. At the same time we would be wanting to fix dates for the workshops to take place as soon as possible. At last Thursday's meeting it was agreed that Managers, Assistant Managers, and Section Heads should attend the workshops. There will therefore be between 15–20 people attending each of them. For this exercise we shall be using the resources we have available here to act in a consultancy role.

Jackson, Wayne St. George, and Dr. Morris. In addition, Dr. Oliver Hammond, Training Officer for P.I.L., attended. Hammond had been working with Leland Jackson on processing the data and developing the format of the various reports that might emerge.

At the beginning of the meeting in Dr. Wilson's office, Jackson briefly described the history of the project as he saw it. He then turned to Dr. Morris and asked him to describe what typically happens in meetings involving questionnaire results. Before Dr. Morris had said more than a few words about "feedback sessions" and "workshops," Dr. Wilson interrupted and stated with some heat: "I'm tired of all of the American behavioral science jargon," and then expressed his annoyance with the "jargon" he had heard at the meeting with Dr. Gibson. Dr. Wilson then asked Morris to continue. Dr. Morris, who by this time was upset and angry, stated: "This discussion makes me feel quite uncomfortable, Larry. I have the feeling that no matter what I say, you are going to attack it as American behavioral science jargon." Morris then lapsed into silence. Leland Jackson then talked for a minute about problems of semantics and terminology, and suggested to Larry Wilson that Morris should be given a chance to answer questions. Dr. Wilson appeared to be somewhat more willing to listen at this point, and Dr. Morris continued.

Later during the meeting, Larry Wilson expressed the strong opinion that his section heads absolutely could not be gone from their jobs for a period of three days. Another concern which he expressed was as follows: "We have been managing well and successfully in the past. Now we are told all of a sudden that we are not doing things properly, that we have to have an attitude survey, and then we have to go spend three days talking about it."

PLASTICS INTERNATIONAL
LTD. (D)

AGREEMENT ON THE WORKSHOPS

The meeting with Dr. Wilson and his assistant managers ended with an agreement to start the session on a Thursday noon and work on through Saturday afternoon, and through Saturday evening, if necessary. The meeting ended on a reasonably friendly basis.

The luncheon which followed involved Dr. Wilson, one of his assistant managers, the consulting team, Dr. Morton Wiesler, Manager of Textile Development (Cologne), and one of his assistant managers. This luncheon partially served the purpose of briefing Dr. Wiesler on what had transpired in the morning, and as an introduction to discussions with him in the afternoon. The tone of the luncheon was friendly and jovial, and Dr. Morris and Dr. Wilson appeared to have resolved any differences between them.

The afternoon with Dr. Wiesler and one of his assistants proceeded smoothly. Dr. Wiesler agreed to a meeting involving himself, his assistant managers and the section leaders, beginning with lunch at 1:30 P.M. on a Thursday and finishing late Saturday afternoon, or early evening. During this meeting, Dr. Wiesler suggested that each section head be prepared to report about one segment of questionnaire results. This was agreed to, and section heads were to be asked to interpret the data and to discuss possible underlying causes for the questionnaire responses.

Two days later the consulting team met with the managers at the Bonn site to discuss the possibility of three-day discussions sessions. In the first meeting the two assistant managers of the T.D.D. Department were favorably predisposed toward the workshops (a manager of the group had not yet been appointed), but the meeting with the manager of the Research Department ran into some difficulties. There were concerns about what actually would happen at the meetings, what was to be the role of the outside "experts"; why was a meeting necessary, and why couldn't people from headquarters simply develop a report with recommendations? Although people seemed to be talking past each other, partly due to time pressures, a meeting with the manager, his assistant managers, and section heads was agreed upon with the stipulation that the consultants develop some kind of analysis of the data to submit to the group prior to the sessions.

As a result of these "negotiations," the following meetings were agreed upon:

a. T.D.D., Cologne
Thursday, 15 May, starting with lunch at 1:30 P.M. and finishing about 10 P.M. on Saturday, 17 May, at the Peterman Hotel. Consultants: Morris, St. George, Brooke, Jackson, Hammond.

b. T.D.D., Bonn
Sunday, 18 May, starting with coffee at 11 A.M. and finishing after lunch on Tuesday, 20 May, at the Alpen Hotel. Consultants: Brooke, Jackson.

c. Research, Cologne
Thursday, 5 June, starting with lunch at 1:30 P.M. and finishing about 10 P.M. on Saturday, 7 June, at the Greater Rhine Hotel. Consultants: Morris, Olson, St. George, Jackson.

d. Research, Bonn
Monday, 9 June, starting with lunch at 1:30 P.M. and finishing about 10 P.M. on Wednesday, 11 June, at the Schoeffle Hotel. Consultants: Morris, Brooke, St. George, Hammond.

One short, additional preparation session was held with each manager a few days before the workshop during which a number of important details were clarified. For example, in such a meeting with Dr. Wiesler, it was agreed that Wiesler would chair the meeting with the consultants acting as resource persons and facilitators and being concerned about the evolving design.

PLASTICS INTERNATIONAL
LTD. (E)

THE WORKSHOPS AND SOME OUTCOMES

When the T.D.D., Cologne group assembled for their three-day session, Dr. Wiesler made some opening comments in which he welcomed the group and mentioned some hoped-for outcomes. Following this, Alan Brooke made some statements on behalf of the consulting team concerning the objective which he mentioned, which the staff had agreed upon earlier, which could change the climate surrounding the attitude survey and the discussion sessions from one of a "pressure" situation to a more collaborative one. Dr. Morris then started to make a very brief overview of the survey results, but was quickly interrupted by the section heads who felt Dr. Morris was beginning to report on the areas they had been asked to analyze and report on. Although somewhat taken aback, Dr. Morris acknowledged that that would indeed be a much better procedure. He later confided to his consultant colleagues that "that was the best thing that could have happened." Subsequent planning for the meetings with the three remaining groups built that feature into the sequence as follows: (1) an introduction by the manager of the department involved, (2) a brief statement by one of the consultants as to objectives, and (3) section heads reporting on the data.

Some aspects of the questionnaire and survey were criticized by several of the section heads. The mean scores, for example, were criticized as misleading because a high percentage of "Strongly agree" plus a high percentage of "Strongly disagree" responses would result in an average score. The consultants agree that the means were much less useful than the percentages. The "Undecided" category also was attacked. When questioned as to what he thought this category means, Dr. Morris stated, "It can mean: (1) I don't have strong feelings one way or the other, (2) I'm indifferent, (3) I don't know, (4) It might be the case, or I'm not sure, or (5) The particular practice varies so much I can't say." This answer seemed to satisfy the critics, who seemed to be content, after a period of attacking the questionnaire, to move on to learn what they could from the answers.

Although the three-day workshops with each group had many different features, a number of common problems such as the above emerged, and the sequence tended to be approximately the same. The sequence and some of the content of the third workshop involving Dr. Wilson and his group were as follows:

1. Introduction.

2. Objectives, Sequence, Time Blocks, and Administrative Matters.
   A. Objectives
       a. Identify problem areas by examining the data.

       b. Get behind the data to specific causes.

       c. Agree on action plans to deal with causes.

       d. Familiarize section leaders with data in preparation for feedback and planning sessions with sections.

       e. Move the climate of the exercise from a pressure operation to one of collaboration.
   B. Sequence
   C. Time Blocks and Administration

3:00 P.M.   3. Reports from each section head based on question data and discussion.

12:00 Noon   4. "A Task-Reward-Satisfaction Model," and other behavioral science inputs.

Friday
12:30 P.M.   5. Development of priorities—Total group discussion.

1:00–4:00 P.M.   6. Lunch, followed by a staff meeting to categorize problem areas seen by participants as being the most important.

4:00 P.M.   7. Team assignments (Section Heads were assigned to make teams as heterogeneous as possible).
   Group A—"Job Factors"
   a. More responsibility and say about how work is carried out, and objectives.

   b. Remove customs and practices that are getting in the way.

   c. Deal with the "artificial crisis" problem.

   d. Long-term versus short-term projects.

   Group B—"Personal Development and Rewards"
   a. Counseling (both the system and factors).

   b. Career planning (both pertaining to promotion and development on the job).

   c. Training (on and off the job and keeping up to date).

d. Pay (information, personnel department role, the relationship between reward and performance and the role of the section heads).

Group C—"Communications—Delegation"

a. What is appropriate to communicate?

b. Why do people "feel in the dark?"

c. Communication with Bonn and other departments.

d. The role and authority of section head (including the problem of their being perceived as side-stepping problems).

Group D—(The Manager and the Assistant Managers)—"Boss-Subordinate Relationships"

a. Access (opportunities for contact across more than one level of management, and the problem of management approachability).

b. Not enough support, encouragement, praise, recognition.

c. Risks of "sticking one's neck out" and the problem of receptiveness to ideas.

d. Delegation to section heads.

4:30–6:30 P.M.   **8.** General discussion of each assigned topic. (The entire group spend one-half hour on each topic exploring underlying causes.)

6:30–8:30 P.M.   **9.** Cocktails and Dinner.

8:30–Midnight   **10.** Teams meet separately.

a. Depth discussion of causes.

b. Tentative action recommendations.

9:00 A.M.   **11.** Four teams report back to the total group.

Saturday
12:30–2:00 P.M.   **12.** Lunch.

2:00–4:30 P.M.   **13.** Finalization of Action Plans.

During the three days the group was together, the external staff performed several functions as follows:

1. Continuous planning in response to developments and to the expressed needs and concerns of the group. Dr. Wilson was consulted several times about next steps.

2. Raising questions about some of the questionnaire data when the staff felt the group was ignoring or trying to explain away problems.

3. Serving as "process" observers, i.e., commenting on the dynamics of how the group was working together.

4. Supporting or challenging some of the assumptions underlying statements that people would make about managerial style, leadership, etc.

5. Giving brief "lecturettes" from the behavioral sciences or decision theory when appropriate.

When the session broke up late Saturday afternoon, the participants, including the consultants, expressed sentiments that the meetings had been very successful. All seemed generally very pleased at the outcome. In a few days the following resulting "Action Plan" was distributed. (See Figure 5.)

At various times during the planning sessions and workshops, the consulting staff discussed the dynamics of what was going on. One conclusion was that constantly there tended to be some common high and low points. For example, the meetings tended to start with some feeling of uncertainty, anxiety, and reluctance, but very quickly people began to feel fairly positive as the section leaders reported on their blocks of data and as discussions began to emerge. By late the second day, people tended to be somewhat discouraged, confused, and frustrated and wondering where it was all heading. However, as action planning began to emerge, the feelings again became more positive and reached a high point as consensus was obtained on action plans. Roughly, the cycle appeared to be as diagrammed in Figure 6. Illustrative of this cycle is a comment from one manager: "The first day and one-half I didn't know what was happening and wished I hadn't come. But it turned out very well and I think it was a successful exercise."

Another observation made by Dr. Morris was that all the workshops tended to take on many of the characteristics of "team-building" sessions. While the questionnaire data was based on responses from section heads and all employees below that level, probably half of the discussion and action planning focused on relationships between section heads, assistant managers, and the manager. (See Figure 5 for the Action Plans emerging from the third workshop.)

During the many planning sessions of the consulting staff prior to and during the workshop, the performance of the consulting team itself and relationships within the team were topics for regular review. This was due largely to the insistence of Dr. Morris who felt that the effectiveness of the consultants, both short- and long-range, would be a function of their own ability to model the behavior they were implicitly "selling." For example, the way the questionnaire was being used suggested norms of support, helping, openness to feedback, facing up to issues, and the expression of feelings.

During the period of time in which the workshops were being held, Leland Jackson reported to the consulting group that Dietrich Hallbach had agreed to meet for a day or two with the four managers and their superior, Dr. Starbrock, later in the year to discuss the results of the workshops and the need for any further action planning required relative to the total division. Dr. Morris was to

Figure 5 Research Department Cardiff action plan resulting from three-day seminar at the Greater Rhine Hotel, June 5–7, 1969

Problem	Cause	Action
My job		
1.1 *More responsibility and say in objectives* Delegation of objectives downwards is lacking. Appreciation of overall departmental objectives is lacking.	S.H.s have not ensured sufficient involvement at all levels. Technical dominance of juniors by seniors.	S.H.s to examine the work of junior levels in relation to work of their seniors and their objectives; they must reach agreed objectives with junior levels and give scope for increased responsibility and contribution. Junior levels to make a written contribution within their section towards the next issue of quarterly project sheets.
1.2 *Customs and practices in Research Dept., Cologne* Customs and practices "getting in the way."	Stores delays in Cologne Works.	A.R.M.s to re-examine immediately the system of receiving equipment through Main Plant Stores.
	Restraint of monetary sanctions.	R.M. and A.R.M.s where appropriate to anticipate sanctions in agreement with senior management.
	Paper work that "must go through Bonn."	Try and anticipate paper work by verbal agreement with Purchasing Dept. Bonn.
	Limited authorized signature list.	R.M. to make an immediate review of the authorized signature list.
1.3 *Artificial crises* Artificial crises exist in Research Dept., Cologne.	Delaying requesting reports and briefs until the last moment.	R.M. and A.R.M.s to give longest feasible notification time of requirements for reports and briefs. R.M. and A.R.M.s to issue an advance list of such reports where practicable.
	Bad planning for visitors and interviewers.	A.R.M.s to minimize delays in communication.
	Unfounded optimism in setting target conclusion date for projects and in underestimating costs.	S.H.s to investigate methods of improved estimating of project timing (possible use of network planning). Review quarterly report of objectives at end of quarter.

Problem	Cause	Action
		Timing of projects, when agreed, will be adhered to by R.M. and A.R.M.s.
	Unreal emergencies from other departments.	No solution to this problem found.
1.4 *Long-term v. short-term projects* The reconciliation of long-term projects with short-term projects.	Lack of involvement of other departmental resources (e.g., especially T.D.D.).	R.M./Textile Manager to agree on long-term objectives. S.H. to make specific recommendations to R.M. for specific allocation of T.D.D. evaluation effort for long-term research.
	No clear Company policy on the effective implementation of long-term work.	R.M. to discuss with Director of Research and Development.
Supervisor/Subordinate climate		
2.1 *Recognition of personal achievement* Insufficient opportunities for "contact up."	Lack of personal contact.	S.H. to assist the R.M. in making personal contact by recommending discussions with personnel on specific projects so that achievements are recognized.
		All supervision to make a conscious effort to involve people at least "next but one below" in discussions.
		The R.M. to give an annual departmental review.
		A.R.M.s to give a 6-monthly group review.
		All staff in the department to attend these reviews.
		R.M. and A.R.M.s to tell secretaries not to turn people away, unless specifically instructed to do so.
		One S.H. from each group to monitor that there is improved "contact up."
		The R.M. and A.R.M.s would reconsider the departmental organization.

Figure 5   Research Department Cardiff action plan (*cont.*)

Problem	Cause	Action
2.2 *Receptiveness of new ideas* People are reluctant to "stick their necks out." Ideas not readily accepted.	Managers chop ideas.	R.M. and A.R.M.s to make a conscious effort not to diminish people. Other members of the group could and should support an individual and his presentation of his new ideas. S.H.s to take more risks.
2.3 *Delegation to Section Heads* Managers are short of time.	Managers do things they could delegate.	R.M. to review the authorized signature list and consult with other departments where appropriate. In particular signing for teas, cars, and advances to be done by S.H.s/Secretary as appropriate. Representation on meetings and committees to be reviewed by R.M. (e.g., S.H. might attend N.P.T.C. and New Nylons) and delegation at his discretion. A.R.M.s to authorize attendance at conference.
Communication and delegation		
3.1 *Communications within R.D., Bonn* People feel they are "kept in the dark."	Not clear.	S.H.s must attempt to discover reasons and what people feel they are "kept in the dark" about.
	The necessary graduation of information that may be released.	S.H.s to inform staff that there is a necessary graduation of information that may be released.
	Insufficiency of personal contact.	S.H.s to hold section meetings to include technical and personnel discusses.
Communication lines cluttered within the department.	Petty chit signing.	R.M. to review authorized signature list.
Information to communicate is unclear.	Lack of directives.	R.M. to discuss with Research Director.

Problem	Cause	Action
	Poor use of line management.	R.M. and A.R.M.s to divulge more information when given appropriate authority.
		R.M. to request Personnel Dept. to ensure simultaneous site announcements.
	Poor use of the English language.	
3.2 *Communications with other departments* Communications with Bonn.	Delays in the telephone system.	R.M. to investigate means of improving the telephone system.
		Use telex where appropriate.
Waste of resources.	Unhealthy competition.	S.H.s to have access to and be able to put items on the agenda for R.M.s meeting when necessary.
		Bonn 3-monthly project sheets to be more widely circulated.
		Visits from Bonn Research Dept. to Cologne to be encouraged.
Numerous contacts on a single project.	Unsatisfactory re-organization in T.D.D. Bonn.	R.M. to discuss with T.D.D. Manager.
Part of pioneering effort is neglected in T.D.D. Bonn.	Pressure of other work. Failure of communications in T.D.D.	R.M. to discuss with T.D.D. Manager (Cologne) the introduction of corresponding pioneering effort in T.D.D.
3.3 *Role of authority of Section Head* Evasion and side-stepping of decisions by management.	Lack of clear knowledge on the role and extent of authority of S.H. and A.R.M.	R.M. and A.R.M.s to clear doubts in the area of S.H. responsibility as they arise.

Figure 5 Research Department Cardiff action plan (*cont.*)

Problem	Cause	Action
Personal matters		
4.1 Career planning		
Ignorance of the existence and mechanism of career planning.	Lack of direct information.	R.M. and A.R.M.s to inform S.H.s of all permissible available information immediately. This information to be communicated as appropriate to lower levels before September, 1969.
4.2 Counseling		
Insufficient appreciation of staff assessment factors.	Inadequate knowledge of procedure. The existence of undisclosed factors suspected.	S.H.s to explain assessment and salary adjustment procedures at next counseling interview, including the showing of the appropriate blank specimen assessment form.
	Inadequacies of counseling due to the time delay between assessment, counseling and reward.	R.M. to discuss with Personnel Dept. the telescoping of the three stages.
		R.M. to arrange training for counselors.
4.3 Pay		
Lack of knowledge of salary structure.	Secretive policy. Failure to pass sufficient information via line management.	R.M. and Personnel Dept. to make appropriate arrangements before Sept. 1969 to provide information explaining the Haslam system and disclosing as appropriate Haslam levels.
Lack of confidence in justice of the salary review.	Insufficient correlation in the relationship between merit and reward.	A.R.M.s to discuss proposed final salary adjustments with S.H.s.
	Undue influence of Personnel Dept. in deciding merit raises suspected.	R.M. or A.R.M.s to sign salary letters.

Abbreviations: S.H. = Section Head
A.R.M. = Assistant Research Manager
R.M. = Research Manager

Copies: All participants
Dr. Dietrich Hallbach
Dr. Scott Starbrock

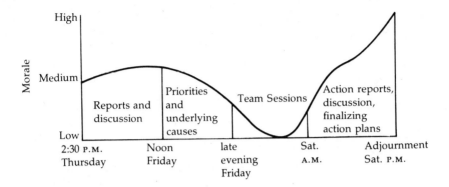

Figure 6 Cycle of response in workshop planning sessions

return to the United States shortly after the four workshops, but Dr. Gibson was due back in Germany in the fall and could participate. Additional consulting help to P.I.L. section heads was to be presented through the Central Labor Relations Department.

QUESTIONS AND REQUIREMENTS

1. Discuss the diagnosis. Did it achieve its purpose?

2. What are the alternatives to using a questionnaire to diagnose an organization?

3. How could the company's personnel department benefit from this survey and the results?

4. Should the personnel department have played a larger role in designing the survey and evaluating the results? If so, how? If not, why?

5. How would you characterize the health of Plastics International in personnel terms? Would you like to be the personnel director in this organization?

58
A CRISIS CHANGE PROGRAM

D.D. WARRICK

BACKGROUND

The Park and Recreation Department in a major city was well known for its lack of progressive accomplishment. The director was an easygoing man who had worked for the city for 30 years. He got along well with people and had many close friends in his department and in the city government. However, he did little to improve his department. When the director retired, the City Manager and the City Council decided that it was time to bring in a dynamic new director who could turn the department around and produce visible results that the public would recognize.

A new director was found who seemed to fit the needs of the City Manager and City Council perfectly. He was a large man (about 6'4" and stocky) who seemed to have an unlimited supply of energy and innovative ideas. He was quite knowledgeable in the field of parks and recreation, and he was dedicated to making a name for himself (he was in his mid-30's) by making his Parks and Recreation Department a model for other cities.

CHANGES UNDER THE NEW DIRECTOR

The changes made by the new director came fast and furious. New parks, new equipment, and new recreation programs began to appear. Even though many of the changes were not budgeted, the director became known as a wheeler-dealer who could bargain and make special deals to get whatever was needed. However, the rapid changes and the new director's style also began to result in a number of serious problems. Shortly after he arrived, the new director had fired several key people in the organization and replaced them with younger, more dynamic persons. The firings, along with the autocratic style that he used to get things done, quickly resulted in considerable internal turmoil. He was also beginning to get a lot of negative reactions from other department heads because of what they began to label as his "wheeler-dealer style of crisis management." This was particularly true of the purchasing department because the new director was continuously short changing the system to get changes funded and implemented more rapidly.

CRISIS SITUATION

After about a year and a half under the new director, the situation reached a crisis stage. In addition to the internal problems, a local newspaper began a series on the Parks and Recreation Department with the obvious goal of getting the director fired. Trust began to break down in the department because the information for the newspaper stories was being supplied by department members as well as by the employees who got fired. This resulted in a state of near paranoia in the department. Rumors became rampant and genuine communication and problem-solving deteriorated because no one knew for sure who was involved in supplying the newspaper with material. Employees became divided on the issues—some agreeing that the director should be fired and others supporting the director because he had accomplished many improvements in the Parks and Recreation programs and facilities.

CHOOSING AN INTERVENTION STRATEGY

The City Manager had been aware of the problems in the Parks and Recreation Department for some time and had tried to work with the director in solving them. However, little progress was made. The City Manager was now faced with the dilemma of deciding what to do about the situation. He believed that the Parks and Recreation Director had tremendous potential if he could develop a more appropriate management style and resolve some of the pressing organizational problems, so he decided to hire a consultant to work with the director and give the director one more chance to turn the situation around.

The City Manager, consultant, and director met, and the City Manager made it clear that he believed the problems could be resolved but that it should also be clear that this was a last chance approach for the director. Because of the limited time and funds available to improve the situation, a short-range strategy was worked out that included the following:

1. Phase I (3 weeks) The consultant would spend time building rapport with the director and Parks and Recreation division heads.

2. Phase II (2 weeks)—An analysis would be made of the internal operations of the department. The consultant used an approach he called an "Organizational Physical." An Organizational Physical consists of a computer-based questionnaire given to all employees and a sampling of personal interviews from all levels of an organization. The questionnaire and interviews provide a profile of the whole organization, each division, and each supervisor's workgroup.

3. Phase III (2 weeks)—A comprehensive report was prepared showing the findings from the Organizational Physical. The consultant then reviewed the findings first with the director, then with the director and City Manager, and finally with the director and his five division heads. The consultant also met with each division head to review the results for his division. In addition, the

consultant met with the supervisors in groups to give them their profiles and discuss what to do with the information.

4. Phase IV—A decision would be made on the most appropriate action to take next.

5. Phase V—Six weeks after Phase IV, the consultant was to conduct a sampling of interviews to determine what progress had been made.

WHAT ACTUALLY HAPPENED

The director reluctantly agreed to the program and expressed strong feelings that he was fed up with having to work under such adverse conditions where other department heads, the press, some citizens (he and his family were sometimes harassed by citizens calling his home) and now the City Manager were all out to get him. The City Manager tried to explain that he hired the consultant because he believed in the director, but the director wasn't convinced of the City Manager's intentions.

The consultant spent considerable time with the director listening to problems and talking about different management approaches and their consequences. He gradually gained the director's confidence until the results came back from the Organizational Physical. The results confirmed the suspicions about the internal problems and the negative reaction to the director's management style. When the consultant reviewed the results with the director, the director became very angry and denied the results. After a three hour discussion, the consultant finally said that the prospects for change really boiled down to one thing: the director's willingness to accept responsibility for his part of the problems.

THE DIRECTOR BEGAN TO CHANGE

The consultant continued the feedback part of Phase III which resulted in several of the division heads and supervisors making significant changes in response to the findings. However, the major issue was whether the director would change. After several weeks, the director began to mellow, and he gradually accepted responsibility for his part of the problems. He and the consultant then began to explore ways to rebuild the department and to change the director's management style.

CHOOSING A ONE-SHOT STRATEGY TO TURN THE SITUATION AROUND

Unfortunately, the funding for the consultant was almost depleted, and the consultant and director were faced with the dilemma of having to choose one strategy that would have the greatest potential for turning the situation around. It was decided that the best strategy would be to work with the top management team (the director and the five division heads) and try to build them into an effective team in hopes that unity and organization at the top would begin to bring unity in the rest of the departments. The choice was a high-risk one because the funding allowed for only one more day of consulting time to accomplish such a difficult objective. However, the director felt that without a team effort at the top, his chances for turning the situation around were next to zero, so he decided to go with the strategy.

THE TEAM BUILDING WORKSHOP

The consultant decided that because of the open hostility and lack of trust among the top management team, the best approach would be to spend one half day talking to each of the five managers individually and then use the other half day for a team building workshop. During the personal interviews, the consultant primarily explained what would happen at the workshop, asked for commitment to accomplishing the workshop objectives, discussed potential problems that might occur in the workshop, and expressed a strong belief in the director's commitment to making constructive changes in the organization and in his management style. The interviews alleviated many of the concerns of the division heads that the workshop would be a disastrous, head-rolling fiasco.

TEAM BUILDING DESIGN

An off-site location was selected for the workshop. The workshop began at 12:00 P.M. with a catered lunch and was to end by 5:00 P.M. The agenda for the workshop was:

○ Lunch

○ Introduction by the Department Head

○ Overview of the agenda, workshop objectives and ground rules by the consultant

○ Review of the major strengths and problems in the top management team by the consultant

○ Additions to the strengths and problems made by the team members

○ Prioritizing the problems and selecting the most important ones to resolve

○ Solving the problems and assigning responsibilities for follow-up

○ Workshop wrap-up

WHAT HAPPENED AT THE TEAM BUILDING WORKSHOP

As the workshop began, the tension was very high, and most of the division heads were visibly nervous. The director broke the ice by admitting to many of the problems he had caused and by expressing a desire to use more of a team approach to managing the department. The consultant then introduced some ideas on healthy and unhealthy ways for teams to work together. He then asked the team members to agree on some ground rules for how they wanted to work together during the workshop and for what they would do if any of the members became unconstructive. This exercise began to open the group up, and one of the managers said that while they had some constructive ground rules to work from, he would like to get some things out in the open. This led to each manager expressing concerns about the director and the other managers. The openness by all members, including the director, made it possible to clear the air about a number of apprehensions and differences the managers had. Many difficult issues were brought out, but the gist of the process was to produce a marked change in caring, trust, and a willingness to work together among the team members.

The remainder of the meeting went smoothly, and all of the agenda items were accomplished. The group also agreed to a plan for how they would restructure their staff meetings so they would operate as an executive team. They also agreed to confront each other when any of them, including the director, began to do anything to hamper their ability to work as a team. At this point the director was so elated with the results that he suggested that they have another similar session at which the group would, as a team, establish the objectives for the department so that they would all be working towards the same goals. There was unanimous agreement to the recommendation, and the meeting ended on a high note.

PROGRESS SINCE THE CRISIS WORKSHOP

The consultant did a follow-up report six weeks after the workshop. The report showed that considerable progress had been made. For example, the management team completed their objectives and began to work very effectively as a decision-making team. Also, the director made a conscientious effort to improve his management style; and most employees were aware of the changes, although a few employees felt that he either had mellowed too much or that he was still just as overpowering as before. Two serious problems remained, however. First, the newspaper campaign continued. This caused some internal morale and communications problems and undermined external relations with the public and the City Council. The other problem was that while the director began to change, many of the other department heads in the city would not change their attitudes towards him because of past encounters. Therefore, even though the criticism of the Parks and Recreation director diminished considerably, the City Manager was still getting pressure from some of the other department heads to look for a new Parks and Recreation Director.

QUESTIONS AND REQUIREMENTS

1. Evaluate the strengths and weaknesses of the five-phase change program.

2. Do you think the changes resulting from the change program are likely to last? Why or why not?

3. Should the Parks and Recreation director fight the newspaper campaign? If not, why? If so, how?

4. What could the Parks and Recreation director do to overcome the resistance from the other department heads?

5. What would you advise if you were the personnel manager, and the city manager asked you for your recommendation?